ANATOMY OF A MELTDOWN:
A DUAL FINANCIAL BIOGRAPHY
OF THE SUBPRIME MORTGAGE
CRISIS

ASPEN PUBLISHERS

ANATOMY OF A MELTDOWN: A DUAL FINANCIAL BIOGRAPHY OF THE SUBPRIME MORTGAGE CRISIS

Michael P. Malloy
Distinguished Professor and Scholar
University of the Pacific McGeorge School of Law

 Wolters Kluwer
Law & Business

AUSTIN   BOSTON   CHICAGO   NEW YORK   THE NETHERLANDS

Printed in the United States of America.

1 2 3 4 5 6 7 8 9 0

ISBN 978-0-7355-9458-6

Library of Congress Cataloging-in-Publication Data

Malloy, Michael P., 1951-
  Anatomy of a Meltdown: A Dual Financial Biography of the Subprime Mortgage Crisis / Michael P. Malloy
    p. cm.
  Includes bibliographical references and index.
  ISBN-978-0-7355-9458-6 (pbk. : alk. paper) 1. Banking—Law and legislation—United States. 2. Banking regulation—Law and legislation—United States. 3. Mortgage banking—Law and legislation. 4. Securities—Law and regulation. I. Malloy, Michael P. II. Title.

KF

About Wolters Kluwer Law & Business

Wolters Kluwer Law & Business is a leading provider of research information and workflow solutions in key specialty areas. The strengths of the individual brands of Aspen Publishers, CCH, Kluwer Law International and Loislaw are aligned within Wolters Kluwer Law & Business to provide comprehensive, in-depth solutions and expert-authored content for the legal, professional and education markets.

CCH was founded in 1913 and has served more than four generations of business professionals and their clients. The CCH products in the Wolters Kluwer Law & Business group are highly regarded electronic and print resources for legal, securities, antitrust and trade regulation, government contracting, banking, pension, payroll, employment and labor, and healthcare reimbursement and compliance professionals.

Aspen Publishers is a leading information provider for attorneys, business professionals and law students. Written by preeminent authorities, Aspen products offer analytical and practical information in a range of specialty practice areas from securities law and intellectual property to mergers and acquisitions and pension/benefits. Aspen's trusted legal education resources provide professors and students with high-quality, up-to-date and effective resources for successful instruction and study in all areas of the law.

Kluwer Law International supplies the global business community with comprehensive English-language international legal information. Legal practitioners, corporate counsel and business executives around the world rely on the Kluwer Law International journals, loose-leafs, books and electronic products for authoritative information in many areas of international legal practice.

Loislaw is a premier provider of digitized legal content to small law firm practitioners of various specializations. Loislaw provides attorneys with the ability to quickly and efficiently find the necessary legal information they need, when and where they need it, by facilitating access to primary law as well as state-specific law, records, forms and treatises.

Wolters Kluwer Law & Business, a unit of Wolters Kluwer, is headquartered in New York and Riverwoods, Illinois. Wolters Kluwer is a leading multinational publisher and information services company.

"I've had all the fun I can stand in the investment banking business. To get bigger in it is not something I want to do."

– Kenneth D. Lewis, CEO, Bank of America
  quoted in FT.com, 19 October 2007

DEDICATION

Αυτό το βιβλίο αφιερώνεται, με τη βαθύτερους αγάπη και το σεβασμό, στη θεία Roula και θείος Jerry, πάντα στις καρδιές μας ακόμα και όταν είμαστε χώρια.

SUMMARY OF CONTENTS

CONTENTS

PREFACE

Big disasters demand dramatic metaphors. A financial disaster like the collapse of the U.S. mortgage market, leading to a world-wide credit crisis, invites full-throated imagery. Is it an airborne plague? A financial tsunami? Surely it must be more than a housing bubble – the abrupt and violent displacement of households, savings, and captains of industry seems poorly represented by the ephemeral "pop" of a bubble bursting. But perhaps that is the sad lesson to be learned from all this economic melodrama: the dignity of high finance is so thin-skinned that it bursts into low comedy when touched by the lightest breath of reality.

The metaphor that seems most apt for the chain of events discussed in this book is the financial crisis as meltdown. The image carries with it all the connotations we could hope for – the lethal, insidious threat of uncontrolled radioactivity, as once-prized businesses became dangerous to be near, let alone to touch, but also the absurdity of a Dali landscape, with the hard-edged reality of the financial services sector revealed to be fluid, sticky, oozing, and ridiculous. Our way through this nightmare vision is to trace the last year in the life of two contributors to – and, ironically, victims of – the meltdown, the iconic Wall Street firm Lehman Brothers, which became the largest bankruptcy in U.S. history, and Washington Mutual Bank, once the premiere U.S. savings bank, which was seized by its regulator and placed in FDIC receivership within weeks of the collapse of Lehman Brothers.

The respective fates of these two firms – one operating in the investment sector, the other in the consumer financial services sector – illuminate the nature and severity of the subprime mortgage crisis still roiling markets worldwide. Both firms stumbled largely as a result of their connections with the subprime mortgage market, though from opposite ends: WaMu in origination of mortgages and Lehman in the investment in and distribution of derivative products based on mortgages. Together, the story of their involvement in the market and its eventual collapse illustrates in clear and understandable terms the causes and course of the current financial crisis. This book tells that story and draws conclusions about the steps necessary to pull the financial system out of the current crisis.

Telling that story was possible for me because of the efforts and encouragement of many people. My wife, Susie A. Malloy, despite her own demanding responsibilities, intercepted the children, read drafts, and kept me honest. My research assistants, Ms. Rebecca Whitfield, of the McGeorge Law School Class of 2011, and Mr. Jimmy Chong Pak, McGeorge Law School Class of 2012, contributed significantly to the collection of the raw data and the quality of the end product. My editors at Aspen, Ms. Lynn Churchill, Senior Acquisitions Editor, and Mr. John Devins, Assistant Managing Editor, were very supportive and incredibly patient with me as unfolding events continued to outpace my efforts to finish the manuscript. I also appreciate the unerring eye of Ms. Sarah Hains, Editorial Project Coordinator, who knows where every comma and curly is in this book. Finally, I heartily thank Mr. Steve Errick, Managing Director of Aspen Publishers Legal Education Division, for coming up with the idea for this book and prodding me in the right direction.

Michael P. Malloy
London
Spring 2010

ACKNOWLEDGMENTS

I would like to thank the publishers and copyright holders listed here for their permission to reprint the various excerpts indicated.

Bar-Gill, Oren, The Law, Economics and Psychology of Subprime Mortgage Contracts, 94 Cornell L. Rev. 1073 (2009). Copyright © 2009 Cornell University; Oren Bar-Gill. Reprinted by permission.

Dash, Eric, Federal Mortgage Success Stories, N.Y. Times, Sept. 10, 2008, at C4, *available at* 2008 WLNR 17148626. Copyright © 2008 New York Times Company. Reprinted with permission.

Dash, Eric, So Many Ways to Almost Say 'I'm Sorry,' N.Y. Times, Apr. 18, 2010, at WK4, *available at* 2010 WLNR 8014905.

Gapper, John, Cost of a Wrong Turn: The Big Freeze Part 2 – The Future of Banking, FT.com, Aug. 5, 2008. Copyright © 2008 Financial Times. Reprinted by permission.

Joyce, Stephen, One Year After Lehman Failure, Need for Financial Reform Seen as Still Urgent, BNA Banking Daily (Sept. 14, 2009), available at http://pubs.bna.com . Copyright © BNA. Excerpted with permission from Banking Daily, 175 [BBD-BUL] Sep. 14, 2009. Copyright 2009 by The Bureau of National Affairs, Inc. (800-372-1033) <http://www.bna.com>

Malloy, Michael P., Banking Law and Regulation (3 vols., Aspen Publishers 2004 & Cum. Supps.). Copyright © 2010, 2009–1994 Michael P. Malloy. Reprinted with permission of the author.

Malloy, Michael P., The Subprime Mortgage Crisis: An International and Regional Threat in Need of a Solution, in David A. Frenkel & Carsten Gerner-Beuerle (eds.), Challenges of the Law in a Permeable World 9

CHAPTER 1

INTRODUCTION: TWO WINDOWS INTO A CRISIS

The meltdown of the financial services markets in 2008 is a mosaic of large and small pieces of economic activity that reveals a picture of panic and loss on a worldwide scale. Like archaeologists puzzling over an ancient ruin, we can identify important clues to the meaning of the larger picture by examining individual tesserae from the mosaic. Unlike the bits and pieces in most mosaics, however, the little shards in this one often display pictures of their own. We shall study two such pieces in this book – the collapse of a major U.S. investment bank, Lehman Brothers, and of a large U.S. thrift institution, Washington Mutual. Each of these pieces offers us a window into the crisis, a chance to observe the meltdown as it affected specific participants in the capital markets and in consumer finance.

A. THE MELTDOWN IN PERSPECTIVE

For now let us step back and take a look at the mosaic as a whole. The big picture is a complex one, and it is only with all the pieces in place that it seems to reveal a coherent story. Even then the story raises more questions for which policy makers are still seeking answers. How did events build to the point where a meltdown of the markets could occur on such a devastating scale? Why did the pervasive system of financial services regulation fail to detect the crisis, let alone prevent it? What can be done to avoid a repetition of this crisis in the future? We begin with a brief overview of the crisis. We then examine the structure of the residential real estate market in more detail.[1] Finally, we take a more critical look at the crisis itself that originated in that market.[2]

U.S. GOVERNMENT ACCOUNTABILITY OFFICE, *HOME MORTGAGES: PROVISIONS IN A 2007 MORTGAGE REFORM BILL (H.R. 3915) WOULD STRENGTHEN BORROWER PROTECTIONS, BUT VIEWS ON THEIR LONG-TERM IMPACT DIFFER*

GAO-09-741 (Washington, D.C.: July 31, 2009), *available at* 2009 WL 2358594

The U.S. housing and mortgage markets are experiencing severe stress, with over 3.2 million home mortgages 90 or more days delinquent or in the foreclosure process in the first quarter of 2009. The rise in delinquencies and foreclosures has been particularly acute in the nonprime segment of the mortgage market. Nonprime mortgages, which include subprime and Alt-A loans, grew dramatically in terms of dollar volume and share of the mortgage market from 2001 through 2006.[3] In 2001, lenders originated $215 billion in nonprime loans, but by 2006, had increased originations to $1 trillion. Likewise, the share of the nonprime market as a percentage of the total mortgage market increased from around 10 percent in 2001 to almost 34 percent in 2006. Further, investment banks increased the volume of nonprime loans they bundled into private label mortgage-backed securities (MBS) over this period.[4] In 2001, they bundled 46 percent of nonprime loans into private label MBS, but by 2006, were bundling 81 percent of these loans. The market for nonprime mortgages contracted sharply in mid-2007, as the nation entered

---

1. *See* § B, *infra.*

2. *See* § C, *infra*

3. The conventional mortgage market (i.e., mortgages not insured or guaranteed by the federal government) comprises prime loans for the most creditworthy borrowers and nonprime loans (i.e., subprime and Alt-A loans). The subprime market generally serves borrowers with blemished credit and features higher interest rates and fees than the prime market. The Alt-A market generally serves borrowers whose credit histories are close to prime, but the loans often have one or more higher-risk features, such as limited documentation of income or assets.

4. Securitization allows lenders to sell loans from their portfolios, transferring credit risk to investors, and use the proceeds to make more loans. Private label MBS, which are bought and sold on the secondary market, are backed by mortgages that do not conform to government-sponsored enterprise (GSE) purchase requirements because they are too large or do not meet GSE underwriting criteria.

a credit crisis and has not rebounded.

As we reported in October 2007, an easing of underwriting standards for nonprime mortgages and wider use of certain loan features associated with poorer loan performance contributed to increases in mortgage delinquencies and foreclosures.[5] These features included mortgages with higher loan-to-value ratios (the amount of the loan divided by the value of the home), adjustable interest rates, limited or no documentation of borrower income or assets, and deferred payment of principal or interest. In some cases, lenders engaged in predatory practices that resulted in loans with onerous terms and conditions.[6] Often, borrowers could not repay these loans and found themselves facing foreclosure or bankruptcy. Some of these predatory practices included providing the borrower with misleading information, manipulating the borrower through aggressive sales tactics, or taking unfair advantage of the borrower's lack of information about the loan terms and their consequences.

B. THE RESIDENTIAL REAL ESTATE MARKET

The residential mortgage market can be divided into a prime segment and a nonprime segment, with the latter further divided into Alt-A (lower risk) and subprime (higher risk). The line between Alt-A and subprime is blurry at the edges. In the traditional market (*Figure 1*), prime mortgages tend to dominate. What distinguishes the segments is the relative creditworthiness of the mortgagor/borrower, and hence the contractual protections that the mortgagee-lender builds into the loan agreement. In terms of relative degree of risk of counterparty failure (*Figure 2*), subprime mortgages present the most significant risk to a lender, and much of the story of the growth of the subprime mortgage market segment reflects efforts by mortgagees to manage or offset that risk.

---

5. GAO, *Information on Recent Default and Foreclosure Trends for Home Mortgages and Associated Economic and Market Developments*, GAO-08-78R (Washington, D.C.: Oct. 16, 2007).

6. While there is no uniformly accepted definition of predatory lending, a number of practices are widely acknowledged to be predatory. These include, among other things, charging excessive fees and interest rates, lending without regard to borrowers' ability to repay, refinancing borrowers' loans repeatedly over a short period of time without any economic gain for the borrower, and committing outright fraud or deception, for example, falsifying documents or intentionally misinforming borrowers about the terms of a loan.

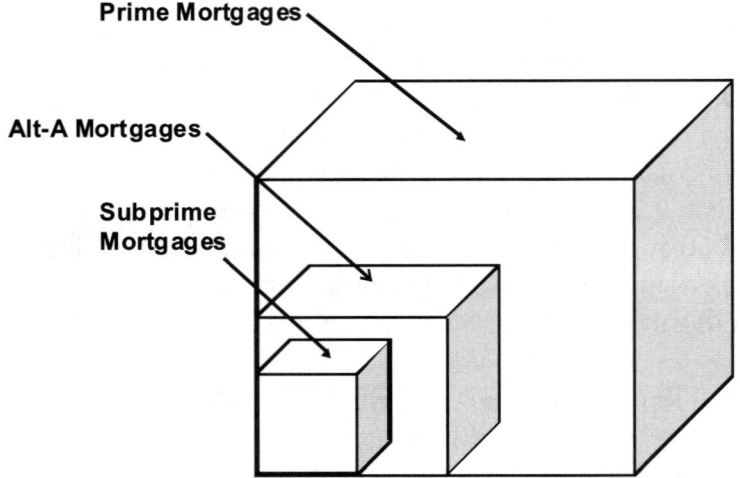

Figure 1. Structure of Mortgage Market

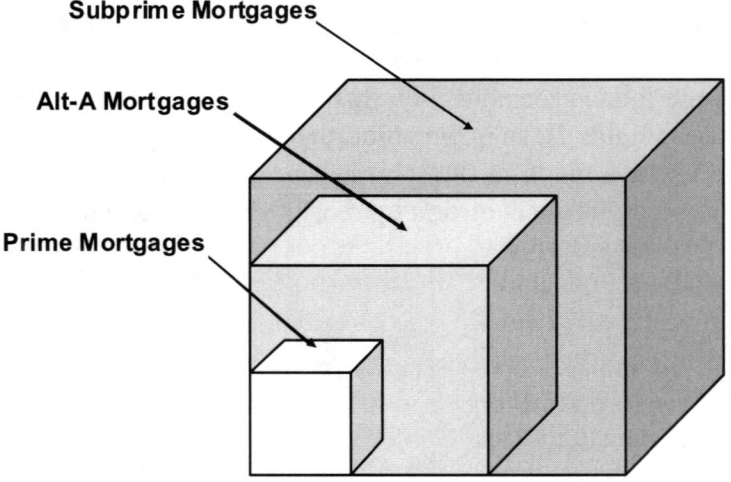

Figure 2. Mortgages in Terms of Risk

QUESTION

The following excerpt offers a detailed look at the structures and risk profiles of these various market segments. In examining the nature of the residential real estate market, what are the implications for the structure of the regulatory system that supervises participants within that market?

OREN BAR-GILL, *THE LAW, ECONOMICS AND PSYCHOLOGY OF SUBPRIME MORTGAGE CONTRACTS*

94 CORNELL L. REV. 1073 (2009)

Introduction

Almost three million subprime loans were originated in 2006, bringing the total value of outstanding subprime loans over a trillion dollars.[1] A few months later the subprime crisis began, with soaring foreclosure rates and hundreds of billions, perhaps trillions, of dollars in losses to borrowers, lenders, neighborhoods, and cities, not to mention broader effects on the U.S. and world economies.[2] . . . I argue that [the] contractual design features [of subprime mortgages] can be explained as a rational market response to the

---

1. *See* Yuliya Demyanyk & Otto Van Hemert, *Understanding the Subprime Mortgage Crisis*, 22 REV. FIN. STUD. (forthcoming 2009) (manuscript at 6 & n.6, 7 tbl.1, on file with authors) (analyzing data covering approximately 85 percent of securitized subprime loans. In 2006, 75 percent of subprime loans were securitized, and the authors' data set included 1,772,000 subprime loans originated in 2006, implying a total of 1,772,000 / (0.85 * 0.75) = 2,779,608); *see also State of the U.S. Economy and Implications for the Federal Budget: Hearing Before the H. Comm. on the Budget*, 110th Cong. 10 (2007) [hereinafter Hearing] (prepared statement of Peter Orszag, Director, Congressional Budget Office) ("By the end of 2006, the outstanding value of subprime mortgages totaled more than $1 trillion and accounted for about 13 percent of all home mortgages."). The Center for Responsible Lending estimates that as of November 27, 2007, there were 7.2 million outstanding subprime loans with an estimated total value of $1.3 trillion. *A Snapshot of the Subprime Market*, Center for Responsible Lending, http://www.responsiblelending.org/issues/mortgage/quick-references/a-snapshot-of-the-subprime.html (last visited Mar. 1, 2009) [hereinafter CRL Snapshot].

2. See Cong. Budget Office, *The Budget and Economic Outlook: Fiscal Years 2008 to 2018* 23 (2008) [hereinafter CBO Outlook], *available at* http://www.cbo.gov/ftpdoc.cfm?index= 8917&type=1 (noting estimates of between $200 billion and $500 billion for total subprime-related losses and noting the additional – and potentially substantial – indirect adverse effects of the subprime crisis on the economy); *see also* Henry M. Paulson, Jr., U.S. Sec'y of the Treasury, *Remarks on Current Housing and Mortgage Market Developments at the Georgetown University Law Center* (Oct. 16, 2007), *available at* http://www.treasury.gov/ press/releases/hp-612.htm (noting that foreclosures on subprime loans increased more than 200 percent between 2000 and 2006 and discussing the broad impact of these foreclosures on the economy).

imperfect rationality of borrowers. Accordingly, for many subprime borrowers, loan contracts were not welfare maximizing. And to the extent that the design of subprime mortgage contracts contributed to the subprime crisis, the welfare loss to borrowers – substantial in itself – is compounded by much broader social costs. Finally, I argue that a better understanding of the market failure that produced these inefficient contracts should inform the ongoing efforts to reform the regulations governing the subprime market.

During the five years preceding the crisis, the subprime market experienced staggering growth as riskier loans were made to riskier borrowers.[3] Not surprisingly, these riskier loans came at the price of higher interest rates that compensated lenders for the increased risk that they undertook.[4] But high prices themselves are not the central problem; the problem is that lenders hid these high prices and borrowers underappreciated them. In the prime market, the traditional loan is a standardized thirty-year fixed-rate mortgage (FRM). Lenders could have accounted for the increased risk of subprime loans by simply raising the interest rate on the traditional FRM. Yet the typical subprime loan is a far cry from an FRM. The subprime market boasted a broad variety of complex loans with multidimensional pricing structures. Hybrid loans, combining fixed and variable rates, interest-only loans, and op-tion-payment adjustable-rate mortgages (ARMs) – each product type with its own multidimensional design – were all common in the expanding subprime market. Many of these contractual designs were not new; they were known in the prime market since the early 1980s. But it was in the subprime market where they first took center stage.

Common subprime mortgage contracts share two suspect features. The first is cost deferral. (Of course, any loan contract involves deferred costs; I am referring to deferral of costs beyond that which is necessarily implied by the very nature of a loan.) The traditional prime mortgage required a 20 percent down payment, which implies a loan-to-value (LTV) ratio of no more than 80 percent. In the subprime market, in 2006, over 40 percent of loans had LTVs exceeding 90 percent. Focusing on purchase-money loans in 2005, 2006, and the first half of 2007, the median subprime borrower put no money down, borrowing 100 percent of the purchase price of the house. The schedule of payments on the loan itself exhibits the same deferred-cost characteristic.

---

3. *See* Demyanyk & Van Hemert, supra note 1 (manuscript at 5, 7 tbl.1); Center for Responsible Lending, *Mortgage Lending Overview*, http://www.responsiblelending.org/issues/mortgage/ (last visited Mar. 1, 2009).

4. *See* Lauren E. Willis, *Decisionmaking and the Limits of Disclosure: The Problem of Predatory Lending: Price*, 65 MD. L. REV. 707, 720-21 (2006) (describing the development of risk-based pricing in the mortgage market).

Under the standard prime FRM, the borrower pays the same dollar amount each month – a flat payment schedule. Under a conventional ARM, where the monthly payment is calculated by adding a fixed number of percentage points to a fluctuating index, the dollar amount paid varies from month to month but without any systemic trajectory. The majority of subprime loans, on the other hand, exhibited an increasing payment schedule: they set a low interest rate for an introductory period – commonly two years – and a higher interest rate for the remaining term of the loan. Other subprime loans exhibited an even steeper payment schedule. Interest-only loans and payment-option ARMs allowed for zero or negative amortization during the introductory period, further increasing the step-up in the monthly payment after the introductory period ended. A direct implication of an escalating-payments contract is the "payment shock," which occurs when a rate reset leads to a significant, up to 100 percent, increase in the monthly payment.

The second suspect feature of subprime contracts is their level of complexity. While the traditional FRM sets a single, constant interest rate, the typical subprime mortgage includes multiple interest rates, some of which are implicitly defined by nontrivial formulas that adjust rates from one period to the next. The typical subprime loan also features a host of fees – some applicable at different time periods during the loan term, some contingent on various exogenous changes or on borrower behavior. The numerous fees associated with a subprime loan fall under two categories: (1) origination fees, including a credit check fee, an appraisal fee, a flood certification fee, a tax certification fee, an escrow analysis fee, an underwriting analysis fee, a document preparation fee, and separate fees for sending emails, faxes, and courier mail; and (2) post-origination fees, including late fees, foreclosure fees, prepayment penalties, and dispute-resolution or arbitration fees. These fees can add up to thousands of dollars, or up to 20 percent of the loan amount. The prepayment option, of special importance in the subprime market, further complicates the valuation of these contracts. So does the (implicit) default option. Finally, since a borrower must choose among many different, complex products, each with a different set of multidimensional prices and features, the complexity of the borrower's decision is exponentially greater than the already high level of complexity of a single contract.[6]

What explains these contractual design features? I begin by exploring possible rational-choice explanations. Consider the cost-deferral feature. A common explanation for deferred-cost contracts is based on the affordability

---

6. *Truth in Lending*, 73 Fed. Reg. 44,522, 44,524-25 (July 30, 2008) (to be codified at 12 C.F.R. pt. 226) ("[P]roducts in the subprime market tend to be complex, both relative to the prime market and in absolute terms....").

argument. Many subprime borrowers, at the time they took out their loans, were liquidity constrained: they could afford only a small down payment and a small monthly payment. The catch, of course, is that a small down payment and a small initial monthly payment imply higher monthly payments in the future, after the initial rate resets to the post-introductory level. Accordingly, the rationality of the affordability argument depends on the ability of the borrower to either make the high future payment or to avoid it. And so the argument splits into two sub-arguments: the "make" argument and the "avoid" argument. The "make" argument is that the borrower will anticipate being able to make the higher payment if she expects her income to increase substantially by the end of the introductory period. Some subprime borrowers rationally expected such a substantial increase in income; many others did not.

Next, the "avoid" argument: the borrower will be able to avoid the higher payment if she expects to prepay the mortgage before the introductory period ends. The prepayment option depends on the expected ability to sell the house, on the expected availability of refinance loans with attractive terms, and on the expected ability to sell the house at an attractive price. Attractive refinancing and sale options will be available if (1) the borrower's credit score improves; (2) market interest rates fall; or (3) house prices increase. Some borrowers rationally expected that such positive realizations would enable them to refinance their deferred-cost mortgage and avoid the high long-term costs. For many other borrowers, these expectations were overly optimistic.

An alternative, rational-choice explanation portrays the deferred-cost mortgage as an investment vehicle designed to facilitate speculation on real estate prices. If house prices rise, the speculator will sell the house (or refinance) and pocket the difference between the lower buy price and the higher sell price, without ever paying the high long-term cost of the deferred-cost loan. If house prices fall, the speculator will default on the mortgage, again avoiding the high long-term cost. Of course, default is not a cost-free proposition, but as long as the probability of a price increase is high enough, the upside benefit will offset the downside risk. Some subprime borrowers were surely speculators. Many others, however, were not.

I now turn to the second identified design feature: complexity and multi-dimensionality. First consider the multiple, indirectly defined interest rates. The index-driven rate adjustments of an ARM – further complicated by maximum adjustment caps – can be explained as a means to efficiently allocate the risk of fluctuating interest rates between lenders and borrowers. This explanation, however, was more powerful when interest-rate risk was shared by the lender and borrower. During the subprime expansion, when securitization was prevalent, this risk could have been – and sometimes was – passed on to diversified investors. Next consider the proliferation of fees common in subprime mortgage contracts. A rational-choice model can explain at least some of these fees. Charging separate fees for separate services allows each borrower to pick and choose between the offered services according to her individual preferences. But this efficiency story applies only to optional services; it does not apply to the numerous non-optional, yet separately priced, services such as the credit check and document preparation. Another explanation views the proliferation of fees as reflecting efficient risk-based pricing. For example, delinquency imposes a cost on lenders. Late fees and foreclosure fees allocate this cost to the delinquent borrowers. Absent such fees, nondelinquent borrowers would bear a large share of the costs imposed by delinquent borrowers, as lenders would raise interest rates to compensate for the forgone fees. Again, this explanation is plausible for certain fees but not for others.

The rational-choice theories explain some of the observed contractual designs in some contexts. They do not, however, provide a complete account: a rational-choice model does not fully explain the prevalence of cost deferral and the exceedingly high level of complexity. To fill this explanatory gap, I develop a behavioral-economics theory of the subprime mortgage contract. I argue that the design of these contracts can be explained as a rational market response to the imperfect rationality of borrowers. Myopic borrowers unduly focus on the short-term dimensions of the loan contract and pay insufficient attention to the long-term dimensions. Optimistic borrowers underestimate the future cost of the deferred-cost contract. They overestimate their future income. They expect to have unrealistically attractive refinance options. Or, they overestimate the expected value of a bet placed on the real estate market, perhaps because they irrationally expect that a 10 percent price increase last year will be replicated next year.[9] If myopic and optimistic borrowers focus on the short term and discount the long term, then lenders will offer deferred-cost contracts with low short-term prices and high long-term prices.

A similar argument explains the complexity of subprime mortgage contracts. Imperfectly rational borrowers will not be able to effectively aggregate multiple price and nonprice dimensions and discern from them the true total cost of the mortgage product. Inevitably, these borrowers will focus on a few salient dimensions. If borrowers cannot process complex, multidi-

---

9. *See* Ben S. Bernanke, Chairman, Bd. of Governors of the Fed. Reserve Sys., *Speech at the Women in Housing and Finance and Exchequer Club Joint Luncheon*, Washington, D.C.: Financial Markets, the Economic Outlook, and Monetary Policy (Jan. 10, 2008), available at http://www.federalreserve.gov/newsevents/speech/bernanke20080110a.htm [hereinafter Bernanke January 2008 Speech] (suggesting that the ARM design responds to optimism about house prices).

mensional contracts and thus ignore less salient price dimensions, then lenders will offer complex, multidimensional contracts, shifting much of the loan's cost to the less salient dimensions.[10]

While focusing on only one part of the subprime picture – the design of subprime loan contracts – this Article develops an alternative account of the dynamics that led to the subprime crisis. One common account focuses on unscrupulous lenders who pushed risky credit onto borrowers who were incapable of repaying.[11] Another common account focuses on irresponsible borrowers who took out loans they could not repay.[12] Both accounts capture some of what was going on during the subprime boom, but both accounts are incomplete. In many cases borrowers were not reckless; they were imperfectly rational. And in many cases lenders were not evil; they were simply respond-ing to a demand for financing that was driven by borrowers' imperfect rationality.

This Article highlights a demand-side market failure: imperfectly rational borrowers "demanded" complex deferred-cost loan contracts and lenders met

---

10. *See* Edmund L. Andrews, *Fed and Regulators Shrugged as the Subprime Crisis Spread: Analysis Finds Trail of Warnings on Loans*, N.Y. Times, Dec. 18, 2007, at A1 (quoting Edward M. Gramlich, the former Federal Reserve governor, asking "Why are the most risky loan products sold to the least sophisticated borrowers? ... The question answers itself – the least sophisticated borrowers are probably duped into taking these products.").

11. There are numerous accounts of abusive practices falling under the general heading of predatory lending, many of them predating the recent subprime crisis. *See* U.S. Dep't of Hous. & Urban Dev., *Unequal Burden: Income & Racial Disparities in Subprime Lending in America* 1 (2000), available at http://www.huduser.org/Publications/pdf/unequal_full.pdf (documenting "the rapid growth of subprime lending during the 1990's" and calling for increased scrutiny of subprime loans due to "growing evidence of widespread predatory practices in the subprime market"). While there is surely some overlap between the contractual design features studied in this Article and the problem of predatory lending, the extent of the overlap is unclear, largely because there is no agreed-upon definition of predatory lending. *See* U.S. Dep't of Hous. & Urban Dev. & U.S. Dep't of the Treasury, *Curbing Predatory Home Mortgage Lending* 17 (2000), available at http://www.huduser. org/publications/hsgfin/curbing.html [hereinafter HUD-Treasury Report]. Yet, two observations can be made: First, the more severe instances of predatory lending go far beyond manipulation of contractual design. Second, the identified contractual design features are more ubiquitous than at least the more severe manifestations of predatory lending. *Cf.* Todd J. Zywicki & Joseph D. Adamson, *The Law & Economics of Subprime Lending*, 80 U. Colo. L. Rev. 1, 11-20 (2009) (discussing the relationship between predatory lending and subprime lending).

12. In some cases, borrowers engaged in outright fraud. See Jennifer E. Bethel, Allen Ferrell & Gang Hu, *Legal and Economic Issues in Litigation Arising from the 2007-2008 Credit Crisis* 17 (Harvard Law & Econ. Discussion Paper No. 212; Harvard Law Sch. Program on Risk Regulation Research Paper No. 08-5, 2008), available at http://ssrn.com/abstract=1096582 (citing evidence of widespread fraud in the application and appraisal processes among early payment default loans).

this demand. But the failures in the subprime mortgage market were not limited to the demand side. In fact, a supply-side market failure explains why lenders willingly catered to borrowers' imperfectly rational demand even when the demanded product designs increased the default risk borne by lenders.[13] The main is securitization – the process of issuing securities backed by large pools of mortgage obligations. Securitization created a host of agency problems, as a series of agents – intermediaries tasked with originating loans, pooling and packaging them into mortgage-backed securities, and assessing the risk associated with the different securities – stood between the principals, the investors who ultimately funded the mortgage loans, and the borrowers. The compensation of these agents-intermediaries was not designed to align their interests with those of the principals-investors: their fees were based on the quantity, not quality, of processed loans. As a result, the agents-intermediaries had strong incentives to increase the volume of originations, even at the expense of originating low-quality, high-risk loans, by promoting mortgage products that, with high levels of complexity and cost deferral, created the appearance of affordability.[14] Moreover, it is likely that even

---

13. An immediate response is that lenders priced the increased risk. And there is some evidence of such pricing. *See* Demyanyk & Van Hemert, *supra* note 1 (manuscript at 5). But this response is misleading. The evidence shows that subprime risks were not accurately priced. *See* U.S. Sec. & Exch. Comm'n, *Summary Report of Issues Identified in the Commission Staff's Examinations of Select Credit Rating Agencies* 34-35 (2008), available at http://www.sec.gov/news/studies/2008/craexamination070808.pdf [hereinafter SEC Rating Agencies Report] (finding that rating agencies underestimated risks associated with subprime mortgage-backed securities); Bethel *et al.*, *supra* note 12. Bethel, Ferrell, and Hu argue that even sophisticated market participants had limited experience with and understanding of the assets (subprime residential mortgages) underlying the securities (RMBSs and CDOs), and what risks these assets generate when pooled and securitized. In addition, credit-rating models underestimate the correlation of defaults and thus understate risk. Moreover, major investment banks are under investigation by the SEC, the FBI, and state attorneys general with respect to pricing of RMBSs and CDOs, suggesting that mispricing may be the result of malice, not only incompetence. *See* Bethel *et al.*, *supra* note 12, at 2; *see also SEC Rating Agencies Report, supra*, at 12 (citing an analyst from one rating agency who wrote in an e-mail that "her firm's model did not capture 'half' of the deal's risk"); Carrick Mollenkamp *et al.*, *Behind AIG's Fall, Risk Models Failed to Pass Real-World Test*, Wall St. J., Nov. 3, 2008, at A1 (discussing the failure of AIG's risk models and quoting Warren Buffett: "All I can say is, beware of geeks... bearing formulas.").

14. *See* Scott Woll, *The Buildup to a Fall*, MORTGAGE BANKING, Nov. 2007, at 50, 53-54 (describing how lenders and securitizers profiting from increased loan volume "started looking at new ideas [to increase loan volume]. . . . What followed was the largest introduction of new products to the mortgage market in decades."); *see also* Zywicki & Adamson, *supra* note 11, at 51-53 (discussing agency costs in the subprime market); Frederic S. Mishkin, Governor, Bd. of Governors of the Fed. Reserve Sys., *Speech at the U.S. Monetary Policy Forum*, New York, New York: Leveraged Losses: Lessons from the Mortgage Meltdown (Feb. 29, 2008), available at http://www.federalreserve.gov/newsevents/speech/mishkin20080229a.htm (arguing that

sophisticated investors and financial intermediaries were caught up in the frenzy of the real estate boom and underestimated the risks associated with the mortgage products that they were peddling.[15] The multibillion dollar losses

---

rating agencies, underwriters, and CDO mangers were driven by fees). *But see* Gary B. Gorton, *The Subprime Panic* 27-31 (Nat'l Bureau of Econ. Research, Working Paper No. 14398, 2008), available at http://www.nber.org/papers/w14398 (arguing that agency costs were not that large, as many agents along the securitization chain retained substantial risks on their balance sheets). On the compensation structure and incentives of loan originators, see Ben S. Bernanke, Chairman, Bd. of Governors of the Fed. Reserve Sys., *Testimony Before the Committee on Financial Services, U.S. House of Representatives: Subprime Mortgage Lending and Mitigating Foreclosures* (Sept. 20, 2007), available at http://www.federalreserve.gov/newsevents/estimony/bernanke20070920a.htm (noting that since originators profited from fees and yield-spread premiums, they were more interested in increasing loan volume than in increasing loan quality). On the compensation structure and incentives of the rating agencies charged with assessing the risk associated with mortgage-backed securities, see *SEC Rating Agencies Report, supra* note 13 (finding inadequate rating procedures and conflicts of interest, which led to underestimation of risk, which in turn contributed to the failure of investors and investment banks to press originators for safer loans); Jan A. Kregel, *Changes in the U.S. Financial System and the Subprime Crisis* 16 (Levy Econ. Inst. of Bard Coll., Working Paper No. 530, 2008), available at http://ssrn.com/abstract=1123937 (noting how rating agencies that provided more lax assessment of subprime risks got more business – and more fees – from securitizers). These interinstitutional agency costs come on top of the intrainstitutional agency costs stemming from the imperfect alignment of incentives between each one of the financial intermediaries and its employees. *See, e.g.*, Martin Wolf, *Why Regulators Should Intervene in Bankers' Pay*, Fin. Times, Jan. 16, 2008, at 13 (discussing the conflicts of interest that exist within lending institutions). Beyond these more subtle – albeit financially substantial – agency costs, there is evidence that some agents-intermediaries withheld information from principals-investors. *See Bethel et al., supra* note 12, at 2 (noting that investment banks are under investigation by the SEC, the FBI, and state attorneys general for withholding information affecting credit risk from rating agencies and investors).

15. *See* Bethel *et al., supra* note 12, at 27 ("The market appears to have not fully anticipated the probability or effect of correlated market events or the very small probability of an extremely negative outcome."); Martin S. Feldstein, Housing, *Credit Markets and the Business Cycle* 3-4 (Nat'l Bureau of Econ. Research, Working Paper No. 13471, 2007), available at http:// www.nber.org/papers/w13471 (arguing that investors underestimated and mispriced risks); Gorton, *supra* note 14, at 26 (arguing that the complexity of the securitization process led to a loss of information along the securitization chain); Joseph R. Mason & Joshua Rosner, *Where Did The Risk Go? How Misapplied Bond Ratings Cause Mortgage Backed Securities and Collateralized Debt Obligation Market Disruptions* 35-36 (SSRN Working Paper, 2007), available at http://ssrn.com/abstract=1027475 (arguing that investors and investment banks falsely believed that pooling mortgages diversifies risk). Much of this underestimation of risk harkens back to optimism about house prices. *See, e.g.*, Thomas L. Friedman, *Op-Ed., All Fall Down*, N.Y. Times, Nov. 26, 2008, at A33 (citing Michael Lewis, The End of Wall Street's Boom, Portfolio.com, Dec. 2008, http://www.portfolio.com/news-markets/national-news/portfolio/2008/11/11/The-End-of-Wall-Streets-Boom (reporting, based on a telephone conversation between hedge fund investor Steve Eisman and a Standard & Poor's employee, that

incurred by these sophisticated players provide (at least suggestive) evidence that imperfect rationality was not confined to the demand side of the subprime market.[16]

The proposed behavioral-economics theory offers a more complete account of the dynamics in the subprime market and of how these dynamics shaped the design of subprime loan contracts. These contractual design features have substantial welfare implications, especially when understood as a market response to the imperfect rationality of borrowers. First, excessive complexity prevents effective comparison shopping and thus hinders competition in the subprime mortgage market. Second, deferred-cost features are correlated with increased levels of delinquency and foreclosure, which impose significant costs not only on borrowers but also on surrounding communities, lenders, loan purchasers, and the economy at large. Third, excessively complex deferred-cost contracts have adverse distributive consequences, disproportionally burdening financially weaker – often minority – borrowers. Finally, concentrating a loan's cost in less salient or underappreciated price dimensions artificially inflates the demand for mortgage financing and, indirectly, for residential real estate. The proposed theory thus establishes a causal link between contractual design, on the one hand, and the subprime expansion and the real estate boom, on the other. Accordingly, the subprime meltdown that followed this expansion can also be attributed, at least in part, to the identified

---

S&P's models assumed that home prices would keep going up)); Kristopher S. Gerardi *et al.*, *Making Sense of the Subprime Crisis* 1 (Fed. Reserve Bank of Boston, Public Policy Discussion Paper No. 09-1, 2008), available at http://www.bos.frb.org/economic/ppdp/2009/ppdp0901.htm (finding that analysts in 2005 understood the risks of a steep decline in house prices but believed that the probability of such a decline was very low); *see also, e.g.*, JULIO ROTEMBERG, SUBPRIME MELTDOWN: AMERICAN HOUSING AND GLOBAL FINANCIAL TURMOIL 1 (2008) (quoting a letter that Fannie Mae CEO Franklin Raines sent to shareholders in 2001: "Housing is a safe, leveraged investment – the only leveraged investment available to most families – and it is one of the best returning investments to make.... Homes will continue to appreciate in value. Home values are expected to rise even faster in this decade than in the 1990's.").

16. *See* Bethel *et al., supra* note 12, at 21, 81 tbl.2 (summarizing the tens of billions of dollars worth of subprime-related write-offs by banks; citing an estimate of $150 billion in writedowns as of February 2008 and a forecast that this amount will more than double); Press Release, Standard & Poor's, Subprime Write-Downs Could Reach $285 Billion, But Are Likely Past The Halfway Mark (Mar. 13, 2008), available at http://www2.standardandpoors.com/portal/site/sp/ en/us/page.article/4,5,5,1,1204834027864.html (discussing Standard & Poor's increased estimate of writedowns at $285 billion, up from $265 billion earlier in the year). These losses do not provide conclusive evidence that sophisticated players made mistakes; they could be the realization of the large (!) down-side risk in an (ex ante) rational bet.

contractual design features.[17]

Importantly, the identified contractual design features and the welfare costs associated with them are not the result of the less-than-vigorous competition in the subprime market. In fact, enhanced competition would likely make these design features even more pervasive. If borrowers focus on the short term and discount the long term, then competition will force lenders to offer deferred-cost contracts. And if borrowers faced with complex, multidimensional contracts ignore less salient price dimensions, then competition will force lenders to offer complex, multidimensional contracts and to shift much of the loan's cost to the less salient price dimensions. Thus, ensuring robust competition in the subprime mortgage market would not solve the problem.

The subprime crisis has spurred a plethora of reform proposals. One of these proposals has recently matured into law, as the Federal Reserve Board (FRB), in July 2008, issued a new set of regulations governing mortgage lending.[20] . . . [T]he centerpiece of the current disclosure regime, the Annual

---

17. *See* Andrey Pavlov & Susan Wachter, *Subprime Lending and House Price Volatility* 2 (Univ. of Pa. Law Sch. Inst. for Law & Econ., Research Paper No. 08-33, 2008), available at http://ssrn.com/abstract=1316891 (establishing a link between the use of aggressive mortgage lending instruments and house price volatility). While contractual design contributed to the subprime expansion, there are other factors that likely played a more central role in generating the subprime expansion. One such factor is the advent of new technology that enabled efficient risk-based pricing. *See* U.S. Gen. Accounting Office, *Report to the Chairman and Ranking Minority Member, Special Committee on Aging*, U.S. Senate, GAO-04-280, Consumer Protection: Federal and State Agencies Face Challenges in Combating Predatory Lending 21 (2004) [hereinafter GAO Consumer Protection Report], available at www.gao.gov/new.items/d04280.pdf. Another factor is the increase in the supply (or availability) of funds brought about by securitization and the global saving glut. *See generally* Atif Mian & Amir Sufi, *The Consequences of Mortgage Credit Expansion: Evidence from the U.S. Mortgage Default Crisis* (Nat'l Bureau of Econ. Research, Working Paper No. 13936, 2008), available at http://ssrn.com/abstract=1072304 (arguing that the expansion in mortgage credit to subprime zip codes and its dissociation from income growth is closely correlated with the increase in securitization of subprime mortgages); Ben S. Bernanke, Governor, Bd. of Governors of the Fed. Reserve Sys., *Remarks at the Sandridge Lecture*, Virginia Association of Economics, Richmond, Virginia: The Global Saving Glut and the U.S. Current Account Deficit (Mar. 10, 2005), available at http://www.federalreserve.gov/boarddocs/speeches/2005/200503102/ (discussing how the global saving glut reversed the flow of credit to developing and emerging-market economies). A third factor is the increase in supply of funds for risky investments caused by investors' underestimation of risk. *See* Feldstein, *supra* note 15. It is important to emphasize that the main purpose of this Article is to explain the contractual design features common in subprime mortgages – not the subprime expansion itself – although, as argued above, contractual design did contribute to the subprime expansion.

20. *See Truth in Lending*, 73 Fed. Reg. 44,522, 44,524-25 (July 30, 2008) (to be codified at 12 C.F.R. pt. 226); *see also* Housing and Economic Recovery Act of 2008, Pub. L. No. 110-289, § 2502(a), 122 Stat. 2654, 2855-57 (to be codified at 15 U.S.C. § 1638(b)(2)).

Percentage Rate (APR) disclosure, has the potential to undo the adverse effects of imperfect rationality, including the identified contractual design features and the welfare costs they impose.

The APR disclosure was the most important innovation of the Truth in Lending Act (TILA) of 1968.[21] A normalized total-cost-of-credit measure, the APR was designed to assist borrowers in comparing among different loan products. In theory, the APR should solve – or at least mitigate – both the complexity problem and the cost-deferral problem. Complexity and multi-dimensionality pose a problem if they hide the true cost of the loan. The APR responds to this concern by folding the multiple price dimensions into a single measure. The APR should similarly help short-sighted borrowers grasp the full cost of deferred-cost loans, as the APR calculation assigns proper weight to the long-term price dimensions. Moreover, since the APR – in theory – strips away any competitive advantage of excessive complexity and cost deferral, lenders will have no reason to offer loan contracts with these design features.
. . .

I

The Subprime Mortgage Market

A. Defining Subprime

What is a subprime mortgage? In theory, subprime loans are sold to riskier borrowers. While low-risk borrowers get low price – specifically, low-interest-rate prime loans – high-risk borrowers get high price – specifically, high-interest-rate subprime loans. But this definition establishes a misleading dichotomy. The risk associated with different borrowers varies along a continuum, and, accordingly, loan prices vary along a continuum. Still, it is helpful to focus on a subset of high-risk, high-price loans, even if the line that divides this category of loans from the neighboring, lower-risk, lower-price category is both arbitrary and blurry. The mortgage industry itself follows this rough categorization. And so do policymakers. The recent credit crisis is dubbed the subprime mortgage crisis, and legislators and regulators are working to fix the problems in the subprime market.

While the boundaries of the subprime segment are arbitrary and blurry, the industry, researchers, and regulators have been using more- or less-common definitions of subprime. According to one rough division, borrowers with

---

21. Truth in Lending Act, Pub. L. No. 90-321, § 107, 82 Stat. 146, 149(1968) (codified as amended at 15 U.S.C. § 1606 (2006)) (defining the APR); Truth in Lending Act, Pub. L. No. 90-321, §§ 121-31, 82 Stat. 146, 152-57(1968) (codified as amended at 15 U.S.C. §§ 1631-49 (2006)) (requiring disclosure of the APR).

FICO scores[a] – a common measure of creditworthiness – below 620 are considered subprime borrowers. Of course, a borrower's FICO score is only one of several factors determining risk level. Thus, industry participants consider additional risk factors, such as the loan-to-value ratio, when classifying a loan as subprime. Moving from risk factors to price, a common subprime threshold is a loan APR that is three points (or more) above the treasury rate for a security of the same maturity; the three-point threshold defines "higher-priced loans" under the Home Mortgage Disclosure Act (HMDA). In its new subprime mortgage regulations the FRB adopted a slightly different definition of "higher-priced mortgage loans," setting the threshold APR at 1.5 points above the "average prime offer rate."

B. Subprime Mortgage Loans: The Numbers

The subprime mortgage market has grown substantially over the past few years (an increase ending in 2006). In 2001, about 985,000 first-lien subprime loans were originated, while in 2006 that number was approximately 2,780,000 and represented over 20 percent of total loan-origination volume. According to the Congressional Budget Office (CBO), subprime mortgages "accounted for about 13 percent of all home mortgages at the end of [2006]." The Alt-A market – covering "medium risk" loans between subprime and prime – also experienced significant growth, expanding from 2 percent of total originations in 2003 to 13 percent of originations in 2006.

The average size of a subprime loan has also increased. In 2006, the average size of a first-lien subprime loan was $212,000, up from $126,000 in 2001. In terms of loan purpose, in 2006, 42.4 percent of first-lien subprime loans were purchase loans, and 57.6 percent were refinance loans. The average subprime borrower had a debt-to-income ratio of approximately 40 percent and a FICO score of 618.1. The median subprime borrower had a FICO score of 620. The median Alt-A borrower had a FICO score of 705.

---

a. FICO credit scores are generated by credit reporting agencies using software licensed by FICO – a publicly-traded corporation that created the widely used credit score model in the United States. The FICO credit score, ranging between 300 and 850 with a median score of 723, is calculated statistically, with information from a consumer's credit files. – *Ed.*

C. Market Structure

1. Participants

Traditionally, a single entity, commonly the neighborhood bank, was the only party, other than the borrower, in the mortgage transaction. This bank would originate the loan, provide the funds for the loan, and service the loan. In the modern mortgage market, the different roles – origination, financing, and servicing – are often by different entities. . . .

In the subprime (and Alt-A) market, mortgages were originated mainly by depository institutions – that is, banks or bank subsidiaries and affiliates – and by mortgage companies,[43] with the bulk of loan volume originated by mortgage companies.[44] Another important group of participants in the mortgage origination process is the brokers: "Mortgage brokers act as intermediaries between lenders and borrowers, and for a fee, help connect borrowers with various lenders that may provide a wider selection of mortgage products." In 2006, brokerages accounted for 58 percent of total origination activity.

Traditionally, depository institutions originated loans and funded them with the deposits they held. During the subprime expansion, origination volume shifted to mortgage companies with no independent means to fund the originated loans. These mortgage companies, and increasingly also depository institutions, sold the loans that they originated to Wall Street investment banks that pooled the loans, carved up the expected cash flows, and converted these

---

43. U.S. Gov't Accountability Office, *Report to the Chairman, Subcommittee on Housing and Transportation, Committee on Banking, Housing, and Urban Affairs, U.S. Senate*, GAO-06-10-21, Alternative Mortgage Products: Impact on Defaults Remains Unclear, but Disclosure of Risks to Borrowers Could Be Improved 7 (2006) [hereinafter GAO AMP Report] ("Borrowers arrange residential mortgages through either mortgage lenders or brokers. The funding for mortgages can come from federally or state-chartered banks, mortgage lending subsidiaries of these banks or financial holding companies, or independent mortgage lenders, which are neither banks nor affiliates of banks."). Indirect originations also played an important role. *See* [Michael LaCour-Little, *Economic Factors Affecting Home Mortgage Disclosure Act Reporting*, 29 J. REAL EST. RES. 479, 498 (2007)] ("A little less than one-third of all loans were originated through indirect, wholesale channels, which include mortgage brokers, certain correspondent lending relationships, builder programs and the like.").

44. Robert B. Avery, Kenneth P. Brevoort & Glenn B. Canner, *Opportunities and Issues in Using HMDA Data*, 29 J. REAL EST. RES. 351, 353 (2007) ("Depository institutions account for the bulk of the reporting institutions, but mortgage companies report the majority of the applications and loans. In 2005, for example, nearly 80% of the 8,850 reporting institutions were depository institutions but together they reported only 37% of all the lending-related activity. Mortgage companies accounted for 63% of all the reported lending; 70% of these institutions were independent and not related in any way to a depository institution.").

cash flows into bonds that were secured by the mortgages.[45] At the peak of the subprime expansion, most mortgages were financed through this process of securitization. As a result, the "owners" of the loans are the investors who purchased shares in these Mortgage (or Asset) Backed Securities (MBSs or ABSs).

The loan originators have direct control over the design of the mortgage contract. The investment banks and their clients also influence the design of mortgage contracts, as the demand for MBSs – and thus the price that the investment banks are willing to pay the originators for the loans – depends on the contractual design. . . .

D. Regulatory Scheme

The regulatory authority over mortgage lending is divided between the federal and state levels and among several regulators at the federal level. Federal banking agencies [*see* Figure 3, *infra*] – the Federal Reserve Board (FRB), the Office of the Comptroller of the Currency (OCC), the Office of Thrift Supervision (OTS), the Federal Deposit Insurance Corporation (FDIC), and the National Credit Union Administration (NCUA) – regulate depository institutions. The Federal Trade Commission Improvements Act of 1980 authorized the Federal Reserve to identify unfair or deceptive acts or practices by banks and to issue regulations prohibiting them.[61] Moreover, the federal banking agencies can use § 8 of the Federal Deposit Insurance Act to prevent unfair or deceptive acts or practices under § 5 of the Federal Trade Commission Act, whether or not there is an FRB regulation defining the particular act or practice as unfair or deceptive.[62] Focusing on high-priced mortgage loans – that is, loans with an APR that is three points (or more) above the treasury rate for a security of the same maturity – the Home Ownership and Equity Protection Act (HOEPA) grants the FRB broad powers to police unfair or deceptive lending practices.[63] The FRB also promulgates disclosure regulations

---

45. *See, e.g.*, Kathleen C. Engel & Patricia A. McCoy, *Turning a Blind Eye: Wall Street Finance of Predatory Lending*, 75 FORDHAM L. REV. 2039, 2045 (2007).

61. [15 U.S.C. §§ 57b-1 - 57b-4].

62. *See* Comptroller of the Currency, Administrator of National Banks, Guidance on Unfair or Deceptive Acts or Practices, Advisory Letter No. AL 2002-3 (Mar. 22, 2002), available at http://www.occ.treas.gov/ftp/advisory/2002-3.doc; see also Julie L. Williams & Michael S. Bylsma, *On the Same Page: Federal Banking Agency Enforcement of the FTC Act to Address Unfair and Deceptive Practices by Banks*, 58 BUS. LAW. 1243, 1244 (2003).

63. *See Truth in Lending*, 73 Fed. Reg. 44,522, 44,527 (July 30, 2008) (to be codified at 12 C.F.R. pt. 226); Raphael W. Bostic *et al.*, *State and Local Anti-Predatory Lending Laws: The Effect of Legal Enforcement Mechanisms*, 60 J. ECON. & BUS. 47, 49 (2008); Willis, *supra* note 4, at 744-54.

under TILA. Additional disclosure regulations are promulgated by HUD under RESPA, which governs the loan-closing process.[65]

Nondepository institutions – that is, nonbanks, including mortgage companies, brokers, and advertisers – fall under the jurisdiction of the FTC. . . .

At the state level, mini-FTC statutes prohibit unfair and deceptive acts and practices. Likewise, mini-HOEPA statutes, as well as other statutes, ban or restrict specific practices, such as prepayment penalties and balloon clauses. There is substantial variation in the scope and enforcement of state-level laws.[69] Because some states clearly go further than federal regulators in their attempts to protect borrowers, there have been heated preemption battles, especially with the OCC and other federal banking agencies. State law is being increasingly preempted by federal law.[70]

---

65. *See Real Estate Settlement Procedures Act (RESPA): Rule to Simplify and Improve the Process of Obtaining Mortgages and Reduce Consumer Settlement Costs*, 73 Fed. Reg. 68,204 (Nov. 17, 2008) (to be codified at 24 C.F.R. pts. 203, 3500). RESPA applies to all "federally related mortgage loans," a somewhat broader category than loans originated by depository institutions. 24 C.F.R. § 3500.5(a) (2008).

69. *See* . . . Anthony Pennington-Cross & Giang Ho, *The Termination of Subprime Hybrid and Fixed Rate Mortgages* 8-9 (Fed. Reserve Bank of St. Louis, Research Div., Working Paper No. 2006-042A, 2006), available at http://research.stlouisfed.org/wp/2006/ 2006-042.pdf; Ctr. for Responsible Lending, CRL State Legislative Scorecard: Predatory Mortgage Lending, http:// www.responsiblelending.org/issues/mortgage/statelaws.html (last visited Mar. 12, 2009).

70. *See* Julia Patterson Forrester, *Still Mortgaging the American Dream: Predatory Lending, Preemption, and Federally Supported Lenders*, 74 U. CIN. L. REV. 1303 (2006); Christopher L. Peterson, *Preemption, Agency Cost Theory, and Predatory Lending by Banking Agents: Are Federal Regulators Biting Off More Than They Can Chew?*, 56 AM. U. L. REV. 515 (2007); *see also* [Oren Bar-Gill & Elizabeth Warren, *Making Credit Safer*, 157 U. PA. L. REV. 1, 79-83 (2008)] Despite the increasing federal preemption on the substantive law dimension, state agencies enforce the state or federal law on lenders and brokers that fall outside the jurisdiction of the federal banking agencies. See GAO AMP Report, *supra* note 43, at 9-10.

> State regulators oversee independent lenders and mortgage brokers and do so by generally requiring business licenses that mandate meeting net worth, funding, and liquidity thresholds. They may also mandate certain experience, education, and operational requirements to engage in mortgage activities. Other common requirements for licensees may include maintaining records for certain periods, individual prelicensure testing, posting surety bonds, and participating in continuing education activities. States may also examine independent lenders and mortgage brokers to ensure compliance with licensing requirements, review their lending and brokerage functions for state-specific and federal regulatory compliance, and look for unfair or unethical business practices. When such practices arise, or are brought to states' attention through consumer complaints, regulators and State Attorneys General may pursue actions that include licensure suspension or revocation, monetary fines, and lawsuits.

Id.

NOTES AND QUESTIONS

1. *Regulatory Structure.* As the excerpt explains, the structure of regulatory authority over participants in the mortgage market is extremely complex, divided among six federal regulators and the individual state levels and among several regulators at the federal level. *See* Figure 3, *infra.* The five federal regulators responsible for depository institutions – the Office of the Comptroller of the Currency, the Federal Reserve Board (FRB), the Federal Deposit Insurance Corporation (FDIC), the Office of Thrift Supervision (OTS), and the National Credit Union Administration (NCUA) – each have "prudential" authority over the safe and sound operation of their respective segments of the depository sector, and in addition the FRB has extensive overlapping authority system-wide over deceptive lending practices, pursuant to the Truth in Lending Act (TILA). The Federal Trade Commission (FTC) has similar authority over nondepository institutions – "nonbanks," including mortgage companies, mortgage brokers, and advertisers. In addition, the states replicate much of this oversight authority as to state-chartered banks, savings associations, credit unions, and nonbanks. As should be obvious from the figure itself, this is a confusing and duplicative structure. Is there any rational justification for this complexity? The situation is further complicated by the effect of federal preemption on various features of state regulation, particularly in consumer protection. The preemption problem will be explored in Chapter 5.

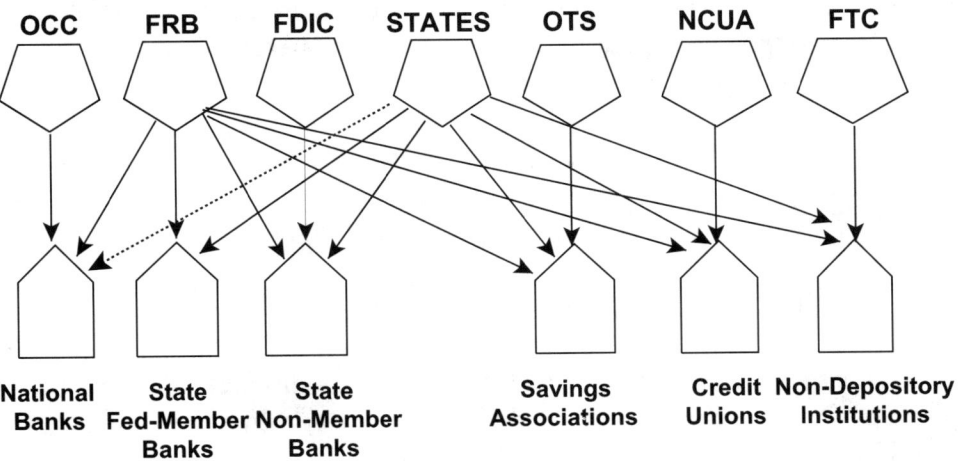

Figure 3. Regulatory Structure
(*excluding SEC with respect to securitized interests*)

2. *Battle of the Forms*? Regulatory overlap can often create artificial inefficiencies in the home mortgage process. For example, as of January 1, 2010, the Department of Housing and Urban Development (HUD) requires real estate lenders and brokers to provide borrowers with a new "Good Faith Estimate" form pursuant to the Real Estate Settlement Procedures Act (RESPA), to provide borrowers with detailed information on loan conditions and closing costs (*e.g.*, current interest rate and potential changes; pre-payment penalties; potential balloon payments; and total closing costs) early in the home purchasing process. Apparently, mortgage originators and settlement companies have been upgrading their computer systems and training personnel to comply with the new RESPA requirement.[3] However, now lenders are concerned that they might have to rework their systems and training *again* because new TILA disclosure forms covering finance charges and the annual percentage rate are under development at the FRB. Doubling the paperwork requirements and increasing compliance costs could obviously result from this situation. How would you resolve this problem? One approach being explored by the FRB is to develop a single cost disclosure form, in cooperation with HUD, that could be provided to borrowers under both TILA and RESPA.[4]

---

3. *See* Mike Ferullo, *Fed Seeks to Harmonize TILA Disclosure With HUD Rule on Good Faith Estimates*, BNA BANKING DAILY (Dec. 7, 2009), *available at* http://bna.com.

4. *Id.*

3. *Form and Substance.* The required disclosures under RESPA are not simply a concern because of compliance costs. There may also be litigation risks. What happens, for example, if the lender's estimate of closing costs are significantly below the actual costs? Consider the following case.

DOBROSHI V. BANK OF AMERICA, N.A.

— N.Y.S.2d —, 2009 WL 2852063 (App. Div. 2009)

ANDRIAS, J.P., MOSKOWITZ, DEGRASSE, RICHTER, JJ.

[A home buyer who financed her purchase through Bank of America complained of a significant increase in the settlement costs after the issuance of the Good Faith Estimate of Settlement Services (GFE) and the required HUD-1 statement, and she also complained that she had been informed of this increase only one day before the closing. The buyer sued the bank, alleging, *inter alia,* fraud, negligent misrepresentation, breach of duty to disclose, conversion, unjust enrichment, and negligent training and supervision. The borrower also made class action allegations. The trial court granted in part and denied in part the bank's motion for partial summary judgment and denied the bank's motion to strike class action allegations. On cross appeals by both parties, the Appellate Division affirmed as modified, holding that: (*i*) the buyer stated a claim for fraud and pleaded the fraud with sufficient particularity; (*ii*) the claimed damages due to the bank's alleged fraud were not speculative; (*iii*) the bank's alleged superior knowledge of matters such as legal fees typically charged by its counsel did not support the negligent misrepresentation claim; (*iv*) the buyer could not establish a claim for breach of a duty to disclose; (*v*) the buyer could not establish an unjust enrichment claim; and, (*vi*) striking the class action allegations was warranted. The excerpted portions of the court's opinion deal with the fraud and misrepresentation claims.]

Contrary to defendant's claim, the second cause of action pleads fraud with sufficient particularity to satisfy CPLR 3016(b). . . . . It informs defendant that plaintiff complains of the significant increase in settlement costs between the [GFE] and the HUD-1 statement, and of the fact that she was informed about this increase only one day before the closing.

Plaintiff's allegation that defendant deliberately underestimated settlement costs to induce her to obtain a loan from it, rather than from a competing lender states a claim for fraud. . . . The GFE was not a mere statement of future intent, and the issue of material misrepresentation is not subject to summary disposition. . . .

The motion court also noted that plaintiff went forward with the closing despite the increased costs. However, under the circumstances, that was the only sensible thing for plaintiff to do. . . . Contrary to defendant's contention, plaintiff's damages are not speculative. She alleges that she was forced to pay $4,000 for defendant's attorney's services, that this amount was excessive, that the GFE estimated that the attorney's fees would be $450, and that the prevailing customary charge in New York City for the lending bank's attorney's fees ranges from $450 to $800. Furthermore, because the fraud claim is reinstated, plaintiff's demand for punitive damages is also reinstated, since "[i]t is for the jury to decide whether [defendant's actions] were so reprehensible as to warrant punitive damages" (*Swersky v. Dreyer & Traub,* 219 A.D.2d 321, 328 [1996]).

The third cause of action (negligent misrepresentation) was correctly dismissed. "[L]iability for negligent misrepresentation has been imposed only on those persons who possess unique or specialized expertise, or who are in a special position of confidence and trust with the injured party such that reliance on the negligent misrepresentation is justified." . . . This court has repeatedly held that an arm's length borrower-lender relationship is not of a confidential or fiduciary nature and therefore does not support a cause of action for negligent misrepresentation. . . . Defendant's alleged superior knowledge of, among other things, the legal fees typically charged by its counsel does not constitute the "unique or special expertise" required to depart from this rule.

For similar reasons, the fourth cause of action (breach of the duty to disclose) was correctly dismissed. Plaintiff has not established that defendant's superior knowledge of essential facts renders the transaction without disclosure inherently unfair (*see generally Swersky v. Dreyer & Traub,* 219 A.D.2d at 327-328, 643 N.Y.S.2d 33) and plaintiff's claim of excessive fees fails to overcome the rule that the legal relationship between a borrower and a bank is a contractual one and does not give rise to a fiduciary relationship. . . .

NOTES AND QUESTIONS

1. *Meltdown Part II?* Elsewhere in his article, Bar-Gill points out that the subprime meltdown may only be part of the story. "While the crisis began with subprime, it did not end there. Defaults and foreclosures are also already

appearing in substantial numbers in the Alt-A and even prime markets."[5] Hence, in considering legislative and regulatory reforms in response to the subprime mortgage crisis, we need to keep in mind that it is not *only* a subprime crisis. The need for broader structural reform is discussed in Chapter 5.

     2. *Assuming a Rationale.* If it is true that disclosure requirements like the APR blunt the competitive advantage of excessive complexity and cost-deferral, does that mean that "lenders will have no reason to offer loan contracts with these design features"? The hidden assumption here is that potential consumers of the loan products will read the disclosure (or secondary reports about the disclosure), understand its implications, and modify their behavior accordingly. Is that what is likely to happen, in real world terms? We assume that curative disclosure about *securities* can be effective in protecting *investors*, but can we assume that curative disclosure would work the same way in the retail mortgage market?[6] To some extent, the debate over the effectiveness of disclosure as a device of consumer protection in the mortgage market parallels a broader tension between securities and bank regulators over disclosure-oriented approaches to market regulation *versus* "prudential" regulation approaches. *See generally* Michael P. Malloy, *Public Disclosure as a Tool of Federal Bank Regulation*, 9 ANN. REV. BANKING L. 229 (1990) (offering comparative critique of two approaches).

C. DYNAMICS OF THE CRISIS

Out of the market structure and practices described in the last section, a crisis emerged that would eventually overwhelm the financial markets. How did we get from point A to point B – from a complex, regulated residential market to a world-wide financial disaster? Consider the following excerpt.

---

    5. Bar-Gill, 94 CORNELL L. REV. at 1086, *citing* Stan J. Liebowitz, *Anatomy of a Train Wreck: Causes of the Mortgage Meltdown*, in Indep. Inst., Housing America: Building Out of a Crisis (Randall G. Holcombe & Benjamin Powell eds., forthcoming July 2009), available at http://ssrn.com/abstract=1211822 (explaining that ARM defaults and foreclosures are as prevalent in the prime market as in the subprime market); Gary B. Gorton, *The Subprime Panic* 21 (Nat'l Bureau of Econ. Research, Working Paper No. 14398, 2008), available at http://www.nber.org/papers/w14398 ("Problems in the Alt-A market are still mostly in the future, and it is likely that this market will also shut down.").

    6. Recall, for example, the *Dobroshi* court's practical insight, *supra*, concerning the behavior of the home buyer faced with higher-than-expected costs: Going forward with the closing on a personal residence "under the circumstances, . . . was the only sensible thing for plaintiff to do."

MICHAEL P. MALLOY, THE SUBPRIME MORTGAGE CRISIS: AN INTERNATIONAL AND REGIONAL THREAT IN NEED OF A SOLUTION

DAVID A. FRENKEL & CARSTEN GERNER-BEUERLE (eds.),
CHALLENGES OF THE LAW IN A PERMEABLE WORLD 9
(Athens Institute for Education and Research: 2009)

The financial crisis that has erupted around the growing failures in the U.S. subprime mortgage market[1] has profoundly undermined economic conditions in the United States. However, despite the fact that the crisis was precipitated by an asset-quality failure involving a particularly "localized" type of asset – collateralized loans for the purchase of personal residences – the crisis itself is international in its impact and dimensions. . . .

At the heart of the problem of dealing with the crisis is a problem of perspective. It is tempting to think about the crisis in terms of specific manifestations – the wave of foreclosures affecting individual homeowners, the effects on lenders and the mortgage market as well as credit markets generally, the meltdown of securitized mortgage portfolios held by institutional investors – and to treat those manifestations separately. Yet the subprime mortgage crisis is systemic, and understanding it requires an appreciation of the system that developed around the subprime mortgage business to sustain its funding and dramatic expansion. This system may be illustrated in simple terms by Figure 4, *infra*.

This market involves an "origination-to-distribution" model of debt securitization, a mark-to-market system, believed to be a more robust way of spreading risk than the more conservative investment analysis of the 1960s. While the subprime mortgage market emerged as a result of aggressive marketing by non-bank lenders such as "lightly regulated" mortgage finance companies (MFCs)[2] to less credit-worthy borrowers, larger depository institutions responded to the increased MFC market share by easing credit standards, often through state-chartered MFC subsidiaries. Lenders of all types vigorously sold these loan products to subprime mortgagors, and then

---

1. For background on the subprime mortgage crisis and a discussion of the initial congressional reaction to the Administration's proposed responses, see Richard Cowden, *Banking Panel Members Show Impatience With White House's Mortgage Rescue Moves*, BNA BANKING DAILY (Feb. 1, 2008), *available at* http://pubs.bna.com/ip/bna/bbd.nsf/eh/ A0B5U2B5B8.
2. Thecla Fabian, *Regulatory Lapses Spurred Crisis, Bair Says; Reform Effort Should Restore Common Sense*, BNA BANKING DAILY (Feb. 25, 2008), *available at* http://pubs.bna.com/ip/ bna/bbd.nsf/eh/A0B6B5J7X3 (quoting FDIC Chairman Sheila Bair).

packaged the portfolios of mortgages into such securitized products as collateralized debt obligations (CDOs) that were analyzed and rated by credit rating agencies and marketed to institutional investors by investments banks. Securitization of these portfolios ameliorated lending risk, and the net proceeds of CDO placements provided lenders with funding to expand the subprime mortgage market itself. The cycle continued to operate, expanding as it drew more investors into the system and encouraged ever-increasing competition for subprime products and programs. When the cycle eventually wobbled – as the inherent counterparty risk manifested itself in the inability of the mortgagors to sustain markedly increasing levels of indebtedness – the system began to break down as the value of the CDO portfolios dramatically contracted.

The results of this systemic breakdown have been dramatic. CDOs have been the source of significant losses across the U.S. banking sector. In November 2008, for example, Citibank announced losses of $8 billion to $11 billion on its sub-prime investments.[3] The recent losses have been so striking that the Chair of the Basel Committee on Banking Supervision at the Bank for International Settlements[4] has suggested that the newly revised capital adequacy rules[5] may have to be reevaluated in light of the risk from CDO

---

3. *See, e.g.*, Daniel Pruzin, *Subprime Crisis Signals Need for More Work On Capital Accord, Basel Panel Head Says*, BNA BANKING DAILY (Mar. 6, 2008), *available at* http://pubs. bna.com/ip/bna/bbd.nsf/eh/A0B6D7Y0T7 (reporting on Citibank experience).

4. On the role of the Basel Committee, particularly in the establishment of international capital adequacy standards, see 3 MICHAEL P. MALLOY, BANKING LAW AND REGULATION § 12.2.3.1 (Aspen Publishers, 1994 & Cum. Supp.).

5. For the revised rules, see Committee on Banking Supervision, Bank for International Settlements, *International Convergence of Capital Measurement and Capital Standards: A Revised Framework* (June 26, 2004), *available at* http://www.bis.org/publ/bcbs107.htm. In December 2007 the Office of the Comptroller of the Currency, the Federal Reserve, the FDIC, and the Office of Thrift Supervision jointly published final rules implementing the revised Basel rules for the largest, internationally active U.S. banks. 72 Fed. Reg. 69,288 (2007) (codified at 12 C.F.R. pts. 3 (OCC rules), 208, 225 (Fed rules), 325 (FDIC rules), 559-560, 563, 567 (OTS rules)). For simplicity, the final rule uses the term "bank" to include banks, savings associations, and bank holding companies (BHCs). 72 Fed. Reg. at 69,288 n.1. The terms "bank holding company" and "BHC" do not include savings and loan holding companies regulated by the OTS. *Id.* The final rules were effective April 1, 2008. 72 Fed. Reg. at 69,288. While U.S. banking institutions are expected to begin a preliminary phase of implementation early in 2008, compliance with the revised Basel rules is not required until January 1, 2009, when the new standards will begin to be phased in over a three-year period. R. Christian Bruce, *Fed's Governors, Eyeing Credit Turmoil, Welcome New Capital Rules Under Basel II*, BNA BANKING DAILY (Nov. 5, 2007), *available at* http://pubs.bna.com/ip/bna/bbd.nsf/eh/-A0B5H8M7E8. However, the overwhelming majority of U.S. banking institutions will be required either to continue to apply the original 1988 Basel standards, or a new and more risk-sensitive version of the 1988 standards expected to be promulgated by the regulators within the

Figure 4: The Subprime Mortgage Market

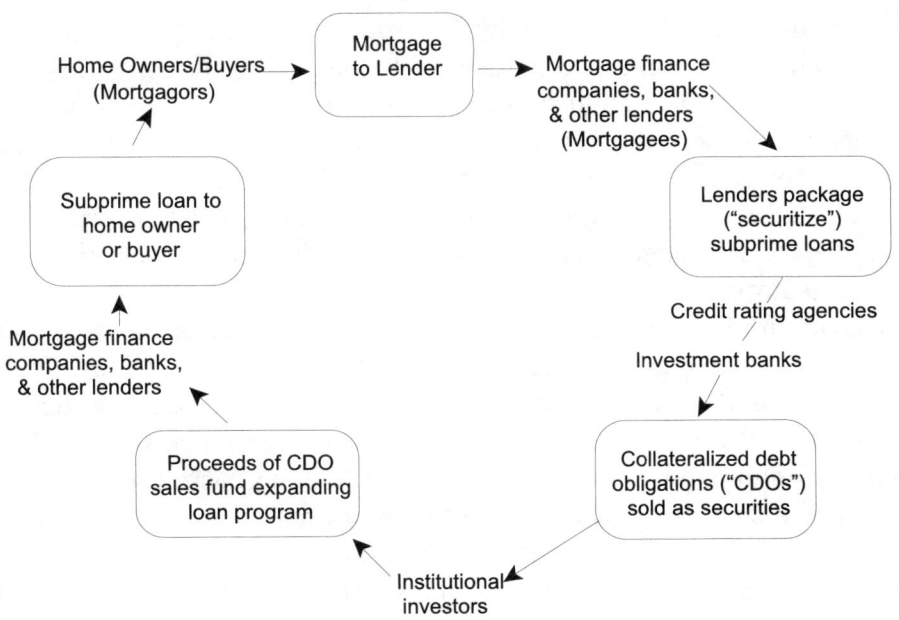

downgrading.[6] There is serious question "whether the capital charges for these types of exposures are calibrated appropriately in relation to their risks and complexity."[7] Quite simply, the crisis precipitated by the contraction of CDO values was unanticipated. As the Basel Chair observed, "when [CDO portfolios] start experiencing losses, these can build very rapidly, producing a real cliff effect. . . . This explains the unprecedented downgrades we have seen on triple-A super senior tranches, which exceed anything we have seen in traditional corporate bonds."[8]

Faced with the downturn in the housing market, the view of the Administration and the regulators was to deny that this was a crisis. Rather, it was a temporary pause, or a slowdown. Indeed, as late as April 2008, Federal Reserve chairman Ben Bernanke was still touting the joys of the CDO market. At worst, he acknowledged that the risk management capacity of debt

---

next few months. *Id.*

6. *See, e.g.,* Daniel Pruzin, *Subprime Crisis, supra* (discussing public remarks by Basel Committee Chair Nout Wellink).

7. *Id.*

8. *Id.* (quoting public remarks of Wellink).

securitization "proved to be much less extensive than many believed."[9] Although the subprime mortgage market had emphatically broken down at virtually every stage – mortgage lending, underwriting, credit rating, investor due diligence – the Chairman blithely proclaimed that, "[t]hese problems notwithstanding, the originate-to-distribute model has proven effective in the past and with adequate repairs, could be so in the future."[10] In March 2008 hearings, members of the Senate Banking Committee excoriated the federal regulators for failing to anticipate the risks involved in the burgeoning CDO market.[11] Yet, even after the crisis had begun to unfold, the Administration and the regulators had seemed reluctant to acknowledge that the subprime crisis was a regulatory issue.

Instead, an administration-backed "HOPE NOW Alliance," formed in October 2007 by a wide group of lenders, loan servicing firms, and institutional investors focused on aiding subprime borrowers through loan modifications or repayment plans. By late January 2008, however, members of the Senate Banking Committee were criticizing this private approach to the crisis and were demanding new public initiatives to respond to the rising home mortgage foreclosures.[12] The apparent response from the Administration was to increase proposed Fiscal 2009 Budget resources for mortgagor counseling and education.[13]

Regulatory responses on the subprime crisis [were at first] inconsequential. In July 2007, for example, the OCC, the Fed, the FDIC, the OTS, and the NCUA issued an interagency Statement on Subprime Mortgage Lending[14] providing "guidance" developed to clarify how depository institutions could offer certain adjustable rate mortgage (ARM) products in a safe and sound manner, and in a way that clearly discloses the risks that borrowers may

---

9. Jeff Day, *Bernanke Touts Fed's Action in Credit Crunch, Contrasts It With 1929's Passive Central Bank*, BNA BANKING DAILY (Apr. 11, 2008), *available at* http://pubs.bna.com/ip/bna/bbd.nsf/eh/A0B6H3F9T2.

10. *Id.*

11. Richard Cowden, *Senators Grill Financial Regulators on Failure To Supervise Banks During Mortgage Crisis*, BNA BANKING DAILY (Mar. 5, 2008), *available at* http://pubs.bna.com/ip/bna/bbd.nsf/eh/A0B6D6Q7U1

12. Richard Cowden, *Banking Panel Members Show Impatience With White House's Mortgage Rescue Moves*, BNA BANKING DAILY (Feb. 1, 2008), *available at* http://pubs.bna.com/ip/ bna/bbd.nsf/eh/A0B5U2B5B8.

13. *See* Richard Cowden, *Several Federal Agencies Slated to Get Boost In FY 2009 Budget Related to Housing Issues*, BNA BANKING DAILY (Feb. 5, 2008), *available at* http://pubs.bna.com/ip/bna/bbd.nsf/eh/A0B5X4F4F7 (discussing proposed budget increases).

14. 72 Fed. Reg. 37,569 (2007).

assume. The statement was effective July 10, 2007.[15] The guidance is thin at best; among other shortcomings, it steadfastly refuses to define the term "subprime mortgage," which is the supposed focus of the statement, beyond general characteristics that might lead to "payment shock."[16] It tends to focus on adjustable rate mortgage (ARM) products, as typifying subprime mortgages, but also considers ARM products as offered to non-subprime borrowers.

Significantly, it was not the mortgage crisis itself, as it affected borrowers, that prodded the regulators into action, but rather the near-failure of investment firms involved in the CDO market that focused the attention of policy makers. This focus reached its most intense moment on March 13, 2008, when Bear Stearns & Cos. Inc. saw its liquidity fall from approximately $12.4 billion to $2 billion, as a result of the dissipation of the market's confidence in the firm and the refusal of its counterparties to act. Bear Stearns informed the Federal Reserve Bank of New York and the [Securities and Exchange] Commission that it was on the brink of bankruptcy. Swiftly the Federal Reserve and the Treasury Department facilitated a loan to Bear Stearns through bank holding company JPMorgan Chase & Co., followed by a loan to JPMorgan to support its outright acquisition of Bear Stearns at a price of $2.00 per share (later raised to $10.00).[17]

Attention to the dire circumstances threatening home mortgage borrowers did not receive such swift attention. It was not until the very end of March 2008 that negotiations over H.R. 3221, a bipartisan housing stimulus package, reached the stage where a final Senate floor vote could be scheduled for April 8.[18] Even so, the Senate Banking Committee Chair emphasized that the bill would be only the first step in addressing the housing finance crisis and the wave of foreclosures looming on the financial horizon.[19] In the interim, the House Ways and Means Committee endorsed a different approach to the crisis in the housing market, emphasizing home-buyer tax credits,[20] while the House

---

15. *Id.* at 37,569.

16. *Id.* at 37,571.

17. Aaron Lorenzo, *Regulators Defend Bear Stearns Decision; Senators Ask If Fed Needs Additional Powers*, BNA BANKING DAILY (Apr. 4, 2008), *available at* http://pubs.bna.com/ip/bna/bbd.nsf/eh/A0B6G6Y8J1

18. Thecla Fabian, *Senate Starts Housing Stimulus Debate; Bankruptcy Amendment on Indefinite Hold*, BNA BANKING DAILY (Apr. 7, 2008), *available at* http://pubs.bna.com/ip/bna/bbd.nsf/eh/A0B6G7Z5T7.

19. *Id.*

20. Heather M. Rothman, *Ways and Means Set to Consider $11 Billion Housing Tax Measure*, BNA BANKING DAILY (Apr. 9, 2008), *available at* http://pubs.bna.com/ip/bna/bbd.nsf/eh/A0B6H0V4J3.

Financial Services Committee considered a foreclosure prevention bill, H.R. 3221, that included authorization for wholesale refinancing of mortgages in danger of default, a provision much maligned by White House policy advisers.[21]

Of course, the subprime mortgage crisis is not just about the personal financial tragedies triggered by improvident mortgage lending. Fueling the dramatic expansion of this sector was the facility of the investment markets in securitizing these mortgages into CDOs sold to a wide range of institutional investors. The existence of the CDO market had the apparent effect of moderating the risk of lenders and feeding their liquidity levels, with the result that the subprime mortgage market experienced growth at significant rates. The poor quality of the underlying mortgage obligations has now had serious adverse effects on the value of CDO portfolios, to the great distress of many institutional investors. The Chairman of the Securities and Exchange Commission made it clear during remarks at the annual *SEC Speaks* conference in February 2008[22] that the Commission was investigating possible securities fraud and breaches of fiduciary duty in the marketing of CDOs.[23] In its investigation, the Commission may be expected to consider whether the banking enterprises that packaged the mortgages and the securities firms that marketed the CDOs made appropriate public disclosures concerning the valuation of CDOs and the risks involved.[24]

Nevertheless, it was not until a March 2008 Senate Banking Committee hearing that the regulators grudgingly admitted that they had not "fully appreciated all [the] risks out there"[25] and acknowledged the gravity of the dramatic reductions in bank earnings, the mounting foreclosures, and the difficulties still to be faced in restoring liquidity in the credit markets.[26] At that point, capitulation to the need for regulatory responses to the crisis was

---

21. Richard Cowden, *Frank, White House Advisers Exchange Barbs Over Features of Foreclosure Prevention Bill*, BNA BANKING DAILY (Apr. 11, 2008), *available at* http://pubs. bna.com/ip/bna/bbd.nsf/eh/A0B6H3F9X6.

22. For the text of the speech by Commission Chairman Christopher Cox, see http://www. sec.gov/news/speech/2008/spch020808cc.htm.

23. Rachel McTague, *Cox Outlines SEC Agenda for 2008, Including Initiatives Related to Subprime*, BNA BANKING DAILY (Feb. 11, 2008), *available at* http://pubs.bna.com/ip/bna/ bbd.nsf/eh/A0B5X8X3F5.

24. *Id.* In addition, one can expect the Commission to consider whether broker-dealers complied with suitability requirements in selling CDOs and other debt-related derivatives to their customers. *Id.*

25. Richard Cowden, *Senators Grill Financial Regulators, supra* (quoting Federal Reserve Governor Donald Kohn).

26. *Id.*

becoming complete.

The broadened responses of the Administration and the regulators still tend[ed] to be somewhat unfocused. With much fanfare, the Administration announced in mid-March 2008 proposed measures intended to prevent future financial crisis, rather than to respond to the present one.[27] These measures represent a call to states and market participants to tighten market supervision. Thus, states are urged to establish nationwide licensing standards for MFCs, while lenders would be required to improve the quality of the disclosure that they provide to borrowers about payment terms, and stronger conflict of interest rules would apply to credit rating agencies that assess the risk of CDO offerings. The proposals were widely dismissed as ineffective and limited, though they were praised by industry representatives.[28]

Also in March, the President's Working Group on Financial Markets (PWG), chaired by the Treasury Secretary, offered a broader and more detailed set of proposals.[29] In its report the PWG identified short-term recommendations, designed to be implemented immediately;[30] intermediate-term recommendations, designed to be implemented in the intermediate term, to increase the efficiency of financial regulation;[31] and, a long-term "Optimal Regulatory Structure," intended to reform and strengthen the regulation of U.S. financial institutions.[32] The basic features of these three sets of recommendations are illustrated in Figures 5-7, *infra*.

---

27. *See* Stephen Labaton, *White House Offers Plan To Ward Off Credit Crisis*, N.Y. TIMES, Mar. 14, 2008, at A1, col.5 (reporting on prospective plan).

28. *Id.* at A17, col. 2.

29. U.S. Department of the Treasury, *Blueprint for a Modernized Financial Regulatory Structure* (Mar. 2008), *available at* http://www.treas.gov/press/releases/reports/Blueprint.pdf.

30. *Id.* at 75-86.

31. *Id.* at 89-133.

32. *Id.* at 137-179.

Figure 5: Treasury Short-Term Recommendations

Modernize current PWG Executive Order to enhance PWG effectiveness as coordinator of financial regulatory policy.
New Mortgage Origination Commission to develop uniform minimum licensing qualification standards for state mortgage market participants.
Federal Reserve to retain sole authority to write regulations implementing TILA as applied to mortgage lending.
Mortgage lending compliance and enforcement authority over mortgage originators that are affiliates of depository institutions within a federally regulated holding company, must be clarified.
Enhance current temporary liquidity provisioning to ensure process is calibrated and transparent; appropriate conditions attached to lending; and, adequate information flows to Federal Reserve by on-site examination or other means

Figure 6: Treasury Intermediate-Term Recommendations

Phasing out and transitioning federal thrift charter into national bank charter.
Direct federal supervision of insured state-chartered banks to be placed with one federal agency (Federal Reserve or FDIC).
Federal charter for systemically important payment and settlement systems to be created, with preemptive effect over competing state systems.
Establishing optional federal charter (OFC) for insurers within the current structure.

Establishing Office of National Insurance (ONI) and Commissioner of National Insurance within Treasury, with specified regulatory, supervisory, enforcement, and rehabilitative powers to oversee organization, incorporation, operation, regulation, and supervision of national insurers and national agencies engaged in the business of insurance pursuant to an OFC.

Establishing Office of Insurance Oversight (OIO) within Treasury to exercise newly granted statutory authority to address international regulatory issues (e.g., reinsurance collateral) and to advise Treasury Secretary on major domestic and international policy issues.

Merging CFTC and SEC to provide unified oversight and regulation of futures and securities industries.

Mandating SEC to use its exemptive authority to adopt core principles to apply to securities clearing agencies and exchanges, modeled on core principles adopted for futures exchanges and clearing organizations under Commodity Futures Modernization Act.

Mandating SEC to update and streamline self-regulatory organization rulemaking process to recognize market and product innovations.

Mandating SEC to undertake general exemptive rulemaking under Investment Company Act of 1940 (ICA), consistent with investor protection, to permit trading of products already actively trading in U.S. or foreign jurisdictions.

Mandating SEC to propose to Congress legislation to expand ICA to permit registration of new "global" investment company.

Permitting by statute that all clearing agency and market self-regulatory organization (SROs) to self-certify all rulemakings (except those involving corporate listing and market conduct standards), effective upon filing; SEC to retain right to abrogate rulemakings.

Harmonizing, pursuant to joint CFTC-SEC staff task force, futures regulation and federal securities regulation concerning, e.g., margin, segregation, insider trading, insurance coverage for broker-dealer insolvency, customer suitability, short sales, SRO mergers, implied private rights of action, the SRO rulemaking approval process, and agency's funding mechanism.

Figure 7: Long-Term Optimal Regulatory Structure

Adopt objectives-based regulatory approach in establishing future optimal regulatory structure, consolidated and focused on market stability regulation (by Federal Reserve), prudential financial regulation, and business conduct and consumer protection regulation.

Reconstitute FDIC as Federal Insurance Guarantee Corporation to administer deposit insurance and proposed Federal Insurance Guarantee Fund.

Establish corporate finance regulator with responsibility for general issues related to corporate oversight in public securities markets, including current SEC responsibilities over corporate disclosures, corporate governance, accounting oversight, and other similar issues.

The Treasury recommendations [were] ambitious and complex, but they ultimately feed into the recommended long-term "optimal regulatory structure." This structure is itself a model of simplicity, based upon fundamental principles of functional regulation.[33] In contrast to the current thicket of institutional regulators that now supervise financial services in the United States,[34] the recommended structure would include a relatively small core group of spe-

---

33. On functional regulation, which establishes regulatory structures relating to functions and activities to be regulated rather than the nature of the particular institution being regulated, see *Report of the Task Group on Financial Services* 39-40 (1984). *See generally* 1 MICHAEL P. MALLOY, BANKING LAW AND REGULATION §§ 1.4.1 - 1.4.2 (Aspen Publishers, 1994 & Cum. Supp.) (discussing and contrasting institutional and functional regulation).

34. For a description and critique of the current regulatory system, see 1 MICHAEL P. MALLOY, BANKING LAW AND REGULATION §§ 1.3, 1.4 (Aspen Publishers, 1994 & Cum. Supp.).

cialized regulators, as is illustrated in Figure 8, *infra*.

Figure 8: Objectives-Based Regulatory Structure

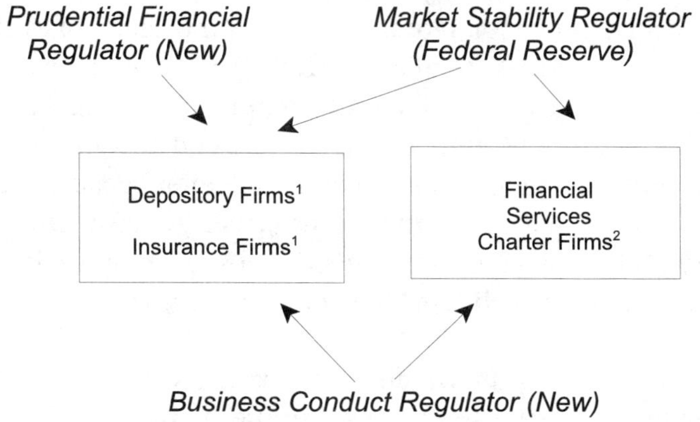

¹Includes depository firms with access to federal deposit insurance and insurance firms with access to an insurance guaranty fund.
²Includes securities firms, futures firms, exchanges, investment advisors, privates pools of capital, and surplus lines insurers.

Unfortunately, the Treasury Blueprint follows in a long tradition of over-arching studies of financial services regulatory structure that have never come to fruition.[35] Particularly for a study that emerges in the last months of a presidential term, the prospects for adoption of its recommendations seem rather limited. What we are left with are the current responses to the subprime

---

35. *See, e.g., Blueprint for Reform: The Report of the Task Group on Regulation of Financial Services* (1984) (recommending fundamental changes to U.S. regulatory structure); *Modernizing the Financial System: Recommendations for Safer, More Competitive Banks* (1991) (same). *See also* 1 MICHAEL P. MALLOY, BANKING LAW AND REGULATION §§ 1.4.1, 1.4.4 (Aspen Publishers, 1994 & Cum. Supp.) (discussing *Task Group* and *Modernizing*, respectively). The Treasury *Blueprint* itself notes:

> Over the past forty years, a number of Administrations have presented important recommendations for financial services regulatory reforms. Most previous studies have focused almost exclusively on the regulation of depository institutions as opposed to a broader scope of financial institutions. These studies served important functions, helping shape the legislative landscape in the wake of their release.

Blueprint for a Modernized Financial Regulatory Structure, supra at 3 (footnote omitted). For background on the prior Administration studies referred to in the quotation, see *Id.*, Appendix B, at 197-206.

mortgage crisis as they now exist, responses that to date have done little to assuage the markets or bring significant relief to borrowers.

One implication of the Treasury Blueprint is quite striking, however. The burgeoning subprime mortgage crisis is linked to issues of regulatory realignment. There is no single regulator accountable for the U.S. banking system, let alone a phenomenon like the subprime mortgage market, and this allows for a certain amount of "regulatory arbitrage," in which participants in the market can exploit the gaps in the multi-regulator system. As I argued in a December 2007 interview with Reuters, "A trend toward something as questionable as subprime mortgages can easily develop because there are too many cooks, too many supervisors, and no one is really coordinating."[36] By the end of February 2008, this view was echoed in a speech by FDIC Chairman Bair,[37] who argued that for the future "the home mortgage market needs strong rules."[38]

One unresolved issue with which policy makers are still struggling is whether the regulatory response to the subprime mortgage crisis should be distinct and independent of generally applicable supervisory requirements.[39] Comments from many financial institutions and industry groups on the interagency Statement on Subprime Mortgage Lending[40] urged that responsive consumer protection goals could be accomplished more effectively through amendments to generally applicable regulations, such as Regulation Z, concerning the Truth in Lending Act,[41] or Regulation X, mandating real estate settlement procedures).[42] Other comments questioned the efficacy of additional required disclosures and expressed concern that the Statement would contribute to "consumer information overload."[43] The agencies essentially split the

---

36. John Poirier, *Mortgage woes spotlight U.S. bank regulation*, GUARDIAN UNLIMITED (Dec. 7, 2007), *available at*, http://www.guardian.co.uk/ feedarticle?id=7135495 (quoting Malloy). *Cf.* U.S. Government Accountability Office, *Industry Trends Continue to Challenge the Federal Regulatory Structure* (GAO-08-32, Oct. 12, 2007), *reprinted at* 2007 WL 3015229 (identifying need to modernize financial regulatory system; criticizing difficulties of multiple specialized regulators in identifying and responding to risks that traditional cross industry lines).

37. *See* Thecla Fabian, *Regulatory Lapses Spurred Crisis, Bair Says; Reform Effort Should Restore Common Sense*, BNA BANKING DAILY (Feb. 25, 2008), *available at*, http://pubs. bna.com/ip/bna/bbd.nsf/eh/A0B6B5J7X3 (quoting Bair as saying "Weaknesses and holes in our bank regulatory structure lie at the heart of our current housing predicament").

38. *Id.*

39. *See Statement on Subprime Mortgage Lending*, 72 Fed. Reg. 37,569, 37,573 (2007) (discussing controversy over regulatory responses).

40. *Id.*

41. 12 C.F.R. pt. 226.

42. 24 C.F.R. pt. 3500.

43. *Id.* at 37,573.

difference, determining that "given the growth in the market for the products covered by the Statement and the heightened legal, compliance, and reputation risks associated with these products, guidelines are needed now to ensure that consumers will receive the information they need about the material features of these loans."[44] Unfortunately, there is little that is new and nothing that is binding in the Statement.

The fact remains that perennial attempts at structural reform – often prompted by disasters like the collapse of the savings associations sector in the 1980's or the subprime mortgage crisis of the late 2000's – are always vulnerable to political attack by interested constituencies. In June 2007, for example, the Treasury Department announced a major "capital markets competitiveness plan" that would, inter alia, modernize the regulatory structure of U.S. financial institutions.[45] This might include merging operations of the OCC and the OTS,[46] a recommendation included in the Treasury Blueprint approach along with the elimination of thrift charters. In response, the American Bankers Association and America's Community Bankers wrote Treasury Secretary Henry Paulson in July 2007, urging him not to merge the operations.[47]

The sad irony is that the Administration's March 13 plan to prevent future credit crises relies upon two basic elements that are simply no longer reliable. One is the notion of market discipline and voluntary restraint as a protection against disaster,[48] features that have obviously not been very efficacious in the present crisis. The other is the assumption that state regulation of MFCs and the mortgage markets can be harnessed to "tighten their oversight of financial markets."[49] In the wake of the sweeping preemption of state consumer protection-based supervision of mortgage bankers resulting from longstanding

---

44. *Id.*

45. Richard Cowden, *ABA, ACB Urge Treasury Not to Merge Thrift, National Bank Regulatory Agencies*, BNA BANKING DAILY (July 10, 2007), *available at* http://pubs.bna.com/ip/bna/bbd.nsf/eh/A0B4W3E4B3.

46. *Id.*

47. *Id.*

48. The Treasury *Blueprint* itself looks favorably on market discipline as a complement to supervisory policy. At one point, it notes that the "PWG, the Federal Reserve Bank of New York, and the OCC have previously stated that market discipline is the most effective tool to limit systemic risk." *Blueprint for a Modernized Financial Regulatory Structure, supra* at 15 n.2, *citing Agreement among PWG and U.S. Agency Principals on Principles and Guidelines Regarding Private Pools of Capital* (Feb. 2007). *See also* PWG, HEDGE FUNDS, LEVERAGE, AND THE LESSONS OF LONG-TERM CAPITAL MANAGEMENT 24-25, 30 (Apr. 1999); PWG, OVER-THE-COUNTER DERIVATIVES MARKETS AND THE COMMODITY EXCHANGE ACT 34-35 (Nov. 1999).

49. Labaton, *White House Offers Plan, supra* at A1, col. 5.

preemption initiatives of the Office of the Comptroller of the Currency[50] and the decision of the Supreme Court in *Watters v. Wachovia Bank, N.A.*[51] broadly confirming the Comptroller's policy, it would be foolish to expect state-based supervision of MFCs and mortgage banking to be effective in the current legal environment. We may agree with the Treasury Blueprint that vigorous change is needed, but the roots of the subprime mortgage crisis are to be found in the aggressively preemptive, market-oriented policies of the [Bush] Administration.

---

50. *See, e.g.*, 69 Fed. Reg. 1895 (2004) (codified at 12 C.F.R. § 7.4000(a)(3), (b)) (adopting regulations asserting broad preemptive authority).

51. — U.S. —, 127 S.Ct. 1559 (2007). For discussion of *Watters* and its implications for state regulation of financial services, see [Chapter 5, *infra*].

2

LEHMAN LOSES BIG

Lehman Brothers began as a dry goods store in Montgomery, Alabama, in 1850.[1] Gradually transforming into a cotton dealer, by 1855 it had become a commodities trading and brokerage operation. In 1858, the firm established a branch in Manhattan, and by 1870 it had moved its headquarters to New York where it was involved in the founding of the New York Cotton Exchange. It became a member of the Coffee Exchange in 1883, and a New York Stock Exchange member in 1887. By 1906, it had begun to act as an underwriter, often partnering with Goldman, Sachs & Co.

As the name might suggest, Lehman Brothers was a family-owned partnership until the mid-1920s, but by 1928 – when it moved to its iconic One William Street headquarters – the partnership had expanded well beyond those family roots. With the death of the last Lehman partner in 1969, the firm began a period of fifteen years of metamorphosis and acquisition, in which it gradually took on the characteristics of a typical large-scale investment banking house. By 1977 it had become the fourth-largest investment bank in the United States, a position it retained until its demise. After several years of internal rivalries over the direction of the firm, Lehman was acquired by American Express in 1984, and the resulting conglomeration continued primarily as a broker-dealer until 1994, when it was spun off by American Express in an initial public offering. Thus, Lehman Brothers Holdings, Inc. was born.

---

1. This historical summary is based largely upon the following texts: STEPHEN BIRMINGHAM, OUR CROWD – THE GREAT JEWISH FAMILIES OF NEW YORK (1967); CHARLES R. GEISST, THE LAST PARTNERSHIPS (1997); LAWRENCE G. MCDONALD, A COLOSSAL FAILURE OF COMMON SENSE: THE INSIDE STORY OF THE COLLAPSE OF LEHMAN BROTHERS (2009).

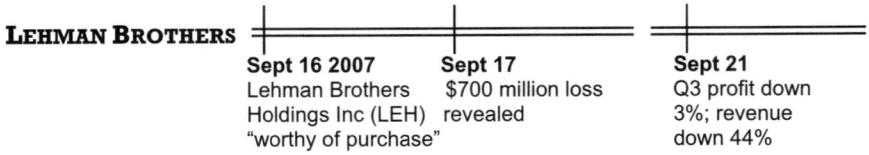

LEHMAN BROTHERS

Sept 16 2007
Lehman Brothers
Holdings Inc (LEH)
"worthy of purchase"

Sept 17
$700 million loss
revealed

Sept 21
Q3 profit down
3%; revenue
down 44%

A. YEAR IN THE LIFE OF LEHMAN

The last year in the life of Lehman Brothers began auspiciously enough with reports that shares of Lehman Brothers Holdings Inc. (LEH) were "worthy of purchase."[2] That was not a recommendation with a very long shelf-life, however. The following day, Lehman revealed that it had suffered a $700 million loss in residential mortgages.[3] By the end of the same week, bad news was tumbling out all over the business press. Lehman's 2007 third quarter profit was expected to decline 3 percent, with revenue declining 44 percent.[4] Ten percent of its trading assets were now reported to be difficult to value, hardly encouraging news in the worsening market environment.[5] By the weekend, the press reported the ominous news that the NAACP had brought suit accusing eleven major mortgage lenders, including Lehman's now-defunct subsidiary BNC Mortgage, of targeting African-Americans for costly subprime loans.[6]

At this point, you might expect the market to begin to react to these developments – that market that policymakers had been depending upon to supervise economic activity without heavy-handed regulation. You would be surprised. This was, after all, merely a "credit correction," and according to

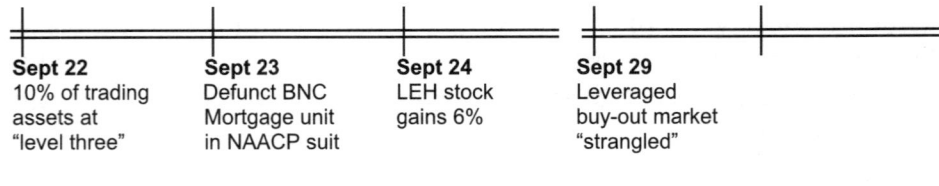

Sept 22
10% of trading
assets at
"level three"

Sept 23
Defunct BNC
Mortgage unit
in NAACP suit

Sept 24
LEH stock
gains 6%

Sept 29
Leveraged
buy-out market
"strangled"

---

2. Andrew Leckey, *Finding Gem in Financial Rubble*, CHI. TRIB.,Sept. 16, 2007, at 7, *available at* 2007 WLNR 18117529.

3. *Looking Ahead*, N.Y. TIMES, Sept. 17, 2007, at C3, *available at* 2007 WLNR 18155337.

4. Eric Dash & Landon Thomas Jr., *Credit Turmoil Bruised Most on Wall Street, but Pain Was Not Shared Equally*, N.Y. TIMES, Sept. 21, 2007, at C6, *available at* 2007 WLNR 18520651.

5. *Investment banks: Books of revelation*, THE ECONOMIST, Sept. 22, 2007, at 34, *available at* 2007 WLNR 18454251.

6. Bob Tedeschi, *The N.A.A.C.P. vs. 11 Lenders*, N.Y. Times ,Sept. 23, 2007, at 12, *available at* 2007 WLNR 18641665.

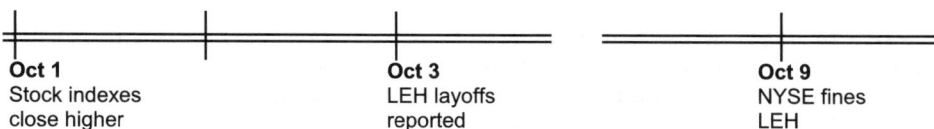

Oct 1
Stock indexes
close higher

Oct 3
LEH layoffs
reported

Oct 9
NYSE fines
LEH

Lehman's CFO, the worst of it was over.[7] On the Monday following this string of events, Lehman stock rose six percent.[8] In the subtle logic of the Street, disclosure of bank write-downs in the billions of dollars apparently was a sign that the worst might be over for the financial services sector, and that any losses could be contained.[9] By October 1, 2007, stock indexes were closing higher.[10]

1. Pile Up

Negative news accounts began to pile up again throughout October 2007. Reports surfaced that Lehman had dismissed some 2,500 employees in its residential mortgage operations over the previous summer.[11] On October 9, there were reports that the New York Stock Exchange had imposed fines on 15 brokerage firms, including Lehman Brothers, for supervisory and operational violations.[12] By late October, Lehman was said to be contemplating further cuts to its mortgage-related staff.[13] Two days later came the news that American Home Mortgage Investment Corp., a mortgage company in bankruptcy, had sued Lehman, on the grounds that the latter had made unjustified margin calls on American and had seized $84.1 million in securities as collateral when

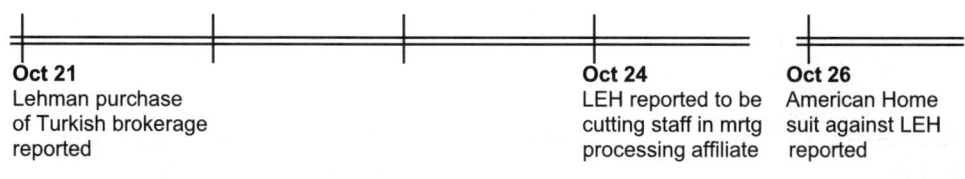

Oct 21
Lehman purchase
of Turkish brokerage
reported

Oct 24
LEH reported to be
cutting staff in mrtg
processing affiliate

Oct 26
American Home
suit against LEH
reported

---

7. *Some Say the Credit Crisis Still Not Over*, CHI. TRIB., Sept. 24, 2007, at 7, *available at* 2007 WLNR 18704155.

8. *Id.*

9. *See, e.g.*, Eric Dash, *Banks Admit Loan Losses; Stocks Rally*, N.Y. TIMES, Oct. 2, 2007, at A1, *available at* 2007 WLNR 19243426 (reporting on "cleanup quarter" and comparing current crisis to earlier technology bubble, 1990s commercial real estate down-turn, and 1980s third world debt crisis).

10. *Id.*

11. Jed Horowitz, *Job Cuts on Wall Street Spread*, WALL ST. J., Oct. 3, 2007, at A13.

12. *NYSE Censures 15 Firms*, WALL ST. J., Oct. 9, 2007, *available at* 2007 WLNR 19780967.

13. Jane Croft, *Mortgage Industry's Champagne Goes Flat*, FT.com, Oct. 24, 2007.

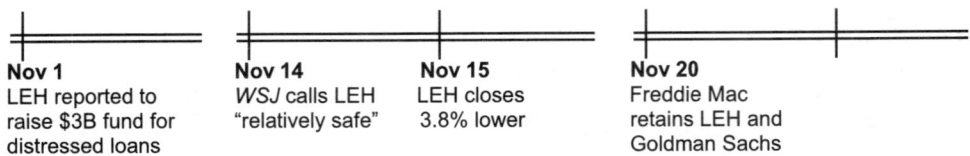

Nov 1
LEH reported to
raise $3B fund for
distressed loans

Nov 14
WSJ calls LEH
"relatively safe"

Nov 15
LEH closes
3.8% lower

Nov 20
Freddie Mac
retains LEH and
Goldman Sachs

American failed to pay.[14]

2. Bargains in a Falling Market

Wisps of optimism still occasionally floated over the market. On November 1, 2007, the NEW YORK TIMES reported that Lehman had raised $3 billion to invest in distressed leveraged loans,[15] on the theory that there were bargains to be had in the midst of a falling market. By mid-month, the WALL STREET JOURNAL was calling Lehman "relatively safe" and commenting on its "robust risk-management structure to head off bad bets."[16] Still, amidst concerns about weakness in consumer spending and the economy overall, Lehman stock closed the following day 3.8 percent lower.[17]

Some of the softness in the economy was undoubtedly reflected in the sorry condition of the government-sponsored enterprises operating in the mortgage market, the Federal National Mortgage Association (Fannie Mae) and the Federal Home Loan Mortgage Corporation (Freddie Mac). On November 20, 2007, Freddie Mac disclosed third quarter losses of $2 billion, and expected further losses from mortgage operations to reach $10 billion through 2009 before any upturn.[18] Freddie retained Lehman and Goldman Sachs to help

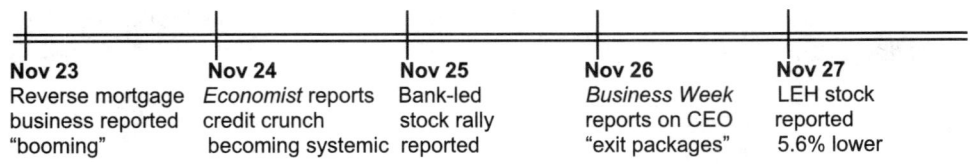

Nov 23
Reverse mortgage
business reported
"booming"

Nov 24
Economist reports
credit crunch
becoming systemic

Nov 25
Bank-led
stock rally
reported

Nov 26
Business Week
reports on CEO
"exit packages"

Nov 27
LEH stock
reported
5.6% lower

14. Daniel Wagner, *Troubled Mortgage Firm Sues Lehman*, L.A. TIMES, Oct. 26, 2007, *available at* 2007 WLNR 21039197.

15. Vikas Bajaj, *Investors Divided on the Fed's Rate Cut*, N.Y. TIMES, Nov. 1, 2007, at C4, *available at* 2007 WLNR 21511363.

16. Kate Kelly, Gregory Zuckerman & Carrick Mollenkamp, *Ducking the Subprime Hit*, WALL ST. J., Nov. 14, 2007, at C1.

17. *Persistent Worries Cool Investor Activity*, N.Y. Times, Nov. 16, 2007, at C9, *available at* 2007 WLNR 22697600.

18. Thomas Heath, *Freddie Mac Loses $2B; Expects More Losses from Mortgages*, WASH. POST, Nov. 20, 2007, *available at* 2007 WLNR 22983695.

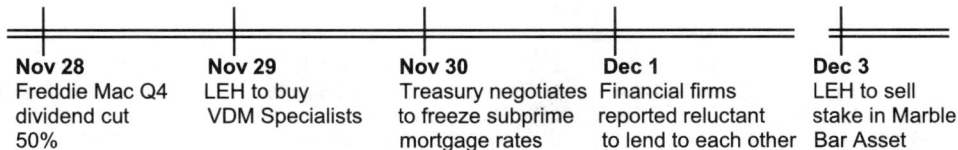

Nov 28	Nov 29	Nov 30	Dec 1	Dec 3
Freddie Mac Q4 dividend cut 50%	LEH to buy VDM Specialists	Treasury negotiates to freeze subprime mortgage rates	Financial firms reported reluctant to lend to each other	LEH to sell stake in Marble Bar Asset

it raise funds.[19] Some segments of the mortgage securities market continued to produce, however. Three days after Freddie's announcement, there were reports that the reverse mortgage business – structures that permit homeowners to sell a significant portion of their home equity back to a lender in exchange for a lump sum, monthly payments, or a line of credit – was heating up.[20] Tapping into this last source of liquidity, investment banks, including units of Lehman and Bank of America, were reported to have expanded their reverse mortgage portfolios, with the expectation that they would package, securitize, and sell them into the market.[21]

The week of Thanksgiving 2007 ended with a weak rally, prompted by financial stocks,[22] but the last week in November saw dark events beginning to overshadow the nervous optimism that had been driving the market. On Saturday, THE ECONOMIST reported that the credit crunch was becoming systemic.[23] By Monday, the journalistic drumbeat was drawing public attention to the fantastical exit compensation packages that financial firms – led by Lehman – had promised their chief executives.[24] The following day Lehman stock closed 5.6 percent lower,[25] and on Wednesday Freddie Mac cut its fourth

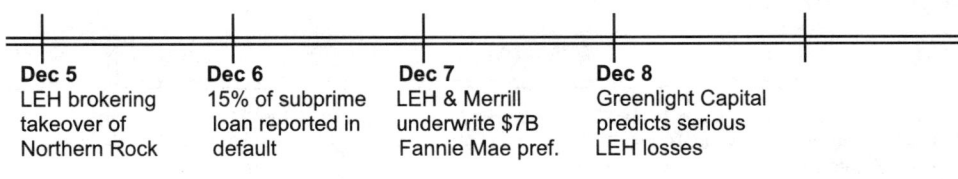

Dec 5	Dec 6	Dec 7	Dec 8
LEH brokering takeover of Northern Rock	15% of subprime loan reported in default	LEH & Merrill underwrite $7B Fannie Mae pref.	Greenlight Capital predicts serious LEH losses

19. *Id.*

20. Kelly Greene & Valerie Bauerlein, *Choices Expand for Those Seeking Reverse Mortgages,* CHI. TRIB., Nov. 23, 2007, at 2, *available at* 2007 WLNR 23186665.

21. *Id.*

22. Michael M. Grynbaum, *Banks Lead Stock Rally; Week Still Shows Loss*, N.Y. TIMES, Nov. 25, 2007, at C1, *available at* 2007 WLNR 23274924.

23. *Buttonwood: Serial Crunching*, THE ECONOMIST, Nov. 24, 2007, at 39, *available at* 2007 WLNR 23370682.

24. *See, e.g.*, Lauren Young, Paula Lehman, Jena McGregor & David Polek, *How Golden Are Their Parachutes*, BUS. WEEK, Nov. 26, 2007, at 34, *available at* 2007 WLNR 23053048 (noting that Lehman CEO Richard Fuld was entitled to approximately $299.2 million).

25. Tim Paradis, *Wall Street Sees Another Sharp Drop*, PITTS. POST-GAZETTE., Nov. 27, 2007, at A7, *available at* 2007 WLNR 23418835.

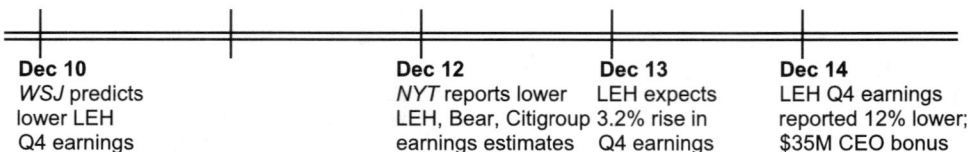

Dec 10		Dec 12	Dec 13	Dec 14
WSJ predicts lower LEH Q4 earnings		*NYT* reports lower LEH, Bear, Citigroup earnings estimates	LEH expects 3.2% rise in Q4 earnings	LEH Q4 earnings reported 12% lower; $35M CEO bonus

quarter dividend in half.[26]

3. Frantic Activity

What followed was a great deal of apparently frantic activity on Lehman's part. On Thursday, November 29, 2007, it was reported that Lehman had agreed in principle to buy Van Der Moolen Specialists USA.[27] This would enable Lehman to take up a position once again on the floor of the New York Stock Exchange with the low-cost staff and technology of the relatively small market maker.[28] Four days later came the news that Lehman was selling its 20 percent stake in the London hedge fund firm Marble Bar Asset Management Lehman for $117 million, almost twice what it paid for its interest over a two year period.[29] By December 5, it was reported that Lehman was brokering a rescue acquisition of the failing Newcastle, UK-based consumer bank Northern Rock by the British investment bank Olivant.[30] Two days later came the report that an underwriting group led by Lehman and Merrill Lynch had completed the sale of $7 billion of Fannie Mae noncumulative, nonconvertible, perpetual preferred stock at a dividend rate of 8.2 percent, believed to be the largest known placement.[31]

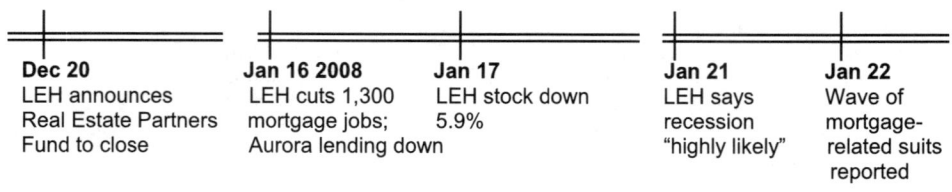

Dec 20	Jan 16 2008	Jan 17	Jan 21	Jan 22
LEH announces Real Estate Partners Fund to close	LEH cuts 1,300 mortgage jobs; Aurora lending down	LEH stock down 5.9%	LEH says recession "highly likely"	Wave of mortgage-related suits reported

---

26. *Freddie Mac Cuts Dividend in Half,* N.Y. TIMES, Nov. 28, 2007, at C4, *available at* 2007 WLNR 23464128.

27. Roddy Boyd, *Lehman Buying VDM Specialists*, N.Y. POST, Nov. 29, 2007, at 40, *available at* 2007 WLNR 23569156.

28. *Id.*

29. James Mackintosh & Haig Simonian, *Marble Bar's $400m Bonanza for Managers*, FT.com, Dec. 3, 2007.

30. Jane Croft, James Mackintosh, George Parker & Nikki Tait, *Ovlivant Puts Its Market on Rock*, FT.com, Dec. 5, 2007.

31. Deborah Lynn Blumberg & Anusha Shrivstava, *Treasurys Fall with Job Report in Wings*, WALL ST. J., Dec. 7, 2007, at C2.

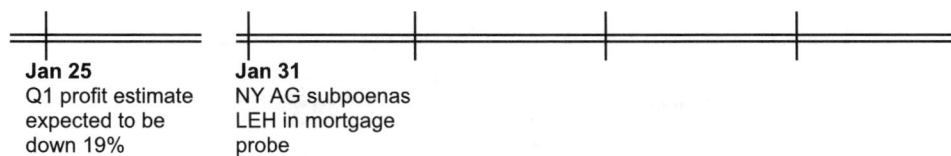

Jan 25
Q1 profit estimate
expected to be
down 19%

Jan 31
NY AG subpoenas
LEH in mortgage
probe

What all this activity did not reflect was the worsening condition of the markets in general and Lehman in particular. While the Bush Administration, led by Treasury and the bank regulators, was negotiating with major banking firms for a plan to freeze interest rates on troubled subprime loans temporarily,[32] major financial firms were becoming increasingly reluctant to lend to one another, occluding the credit market.[33] By December 6, it was reported that 15 percent of the mortgage loans backing $16.5 billion worth of securities sold by Lehman in the first nine months of 2007 were in default.[34] Two days later, hedge fund Greenlight Capital predicted serious losses at Lehman "far beyond what the market [was] expecting."[35] On December 14, 2007, it was reported that Lehman fourth quarter earnings were down twelve percent, while its CEO was awarded a $35 million annual bonus in restricted stock.[36] With 2007 ending and the mortgage market continuing to contract, Lehman announced that it was closing its Real Estate Partners Fund,[37] its largest property fund.

4. A Series of Unfortunate Events

The new year brought a series of unfortunate events. By mid-January 2010,

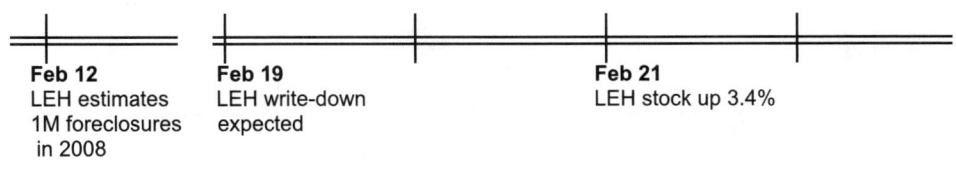

Feb 12
LEH estimates
1M foreclosures
in 2008

Feb 19
LEH write-down
expected

Feb 21
LEH stock up 3.4%

32. Deborah Solomon & Michael M. Phillips, *U.S. Banks Near a Plan to Freeze Subprime Rates*, WALL ST. J., Nov. 30, 2007, at A1.

33. Justin Lahart, *Central Banks Get Creative – Some Unusual Remedies Are Considered to Fix Liquidity Problems*, WALL ST. J., Dec. 1, 2007, at B1.

34. Jenny Anderson & Vikas Bajaj, *Wary of Risk, Bankers Sold Shaky Debt*, N.Y. TIMES, Dec. 6, 2007, at A1, *available at* 2007 WLNR 24050678.

35. Whitney Tilson, *Look Beyond Generalizations*, FT.com, Dec. 8, 2007.

36. Jenny Anderson, *Lehman Earnings Fall 12% in a Season That Could Have Been Worse*, N.Y. TIMES, Dec. 14, 2007, at C10, *available at* 2007 WLNR 24656637.

37. *Lehman to Close Property Fun*, WALL ST. J., Dec. 20, 2007, *available at* 2007 WLNR 25196978.

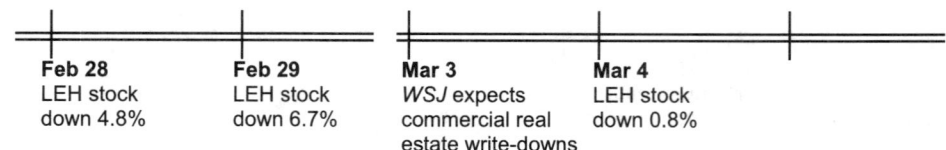

Feb 28
LEH stock
down 4.8%

Feb 29
LEH stock
down 6.7%

Mar 3
WSJ expects
commercial real
estate write-downs

Mar 4
LEH stock
down 0.8%

Lehman had eliminated some 1,300 jobs in its mortgage-related operations.[38] It also disclosed that it had also reduced lending activities by its Aurora Loan Services subsidiary, which makes loans to prime borrowers.[39] Following these disclosures, Lehman stock closed down 5.9 percent on January 17, 2008.[40] By the following Monday, Lehman was reported as expressing the view that a recession was "highly likely."[41] Coincidentally, on Tuesday, January 22, 2008, the NEW YORK TIMES reported on the wave of litigation that was beginning to wash over the troubled mortgage market, including potential multi-billion dollar litigation risks for Lehman in suits emerging around the world.[42] In addition, first quarter profits were expected to decline 19 percent at Lehman. The month closed with reports that the New York Attorney General was investigating whether Wall Street firms had improperly packaged and sold mortgage securities in violation of fraud rules and had issued subpoenas to Bear Stearns Cos., Deutsche Bank AG, Morgan Stanley, Merrill Lynch & Co., and Lehman, among others.[43]

5. A Turning Point

By mid-February, Lehman was estimating that U.S. mortgage foreclosures would rise to one million in 2008 and 2009, approximately four times the

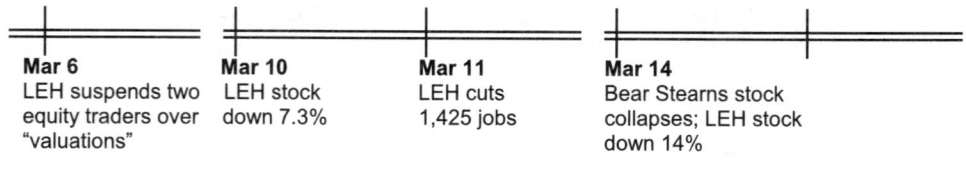

Mar 6
LEH suspends two
equity traders over
"valuations"

Mar 10
LEH stock
down 7.3%

Mar 11
LEH cuts
1,425 jobs

Mar 14
Bear Stearns stock
collapses; LEH stock
down 14%

---

38. Ben White, *Lehman to Axe 1,300 Mortgage Jobs*, FT.com, Jan. 17, 2008.

39. *Id.*

40. *Lehman Cuts Back in Mortgages*, N.Y. TIMES, Jan. 18, 2008, at C6, *available at* 2008 WLNR 1016911.

41. Gillian Tett, *Sentiment Shifts as Credit Woes Sink In*, FT.com, Jan. 21, 2008.

42. Vikas Bajaj, *If Everyone's Finger-Pointing, Who's to Blame?*, N.Y. TIMES, Jan. 22, 2008, at C1, *available at* 2008 WLNR 1206485.

43. Kate Kelly, Amir Efrati & Ruth Simon, *State Subprime Probe Takes a New Tack*, WALL ST. J., Jan. 31, 2008, at A3.

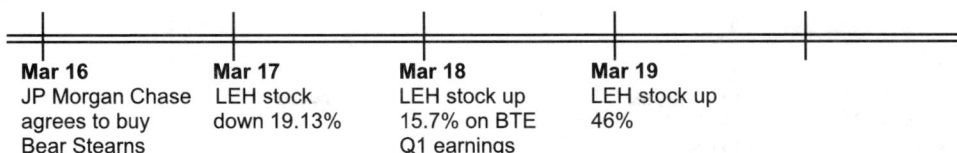

Mar 16	Mar 17	Mar 18	Mar 19
JP Morgan Chase agrees to buy Bear Stearns	LEH stock down 19.13%	LEH stock up 15.7% on BTE Q1 earnings	LEH stock up 46%

annual rate in 2007.[44] Still, Lehman had managed to avoid some of the worst of the fallout from the growing mortgage market failure, until something of a turning point came on February 19, 2008. On that date the press reported that Lehman anticipated an asset write-down of approximately $1.3 billion.[45] Indications of continuing Federal Reserve support for the economy buoyed the market, however, and the following day Lehman stock rose 3.4 percent.[46] By the end of the month, however, the market was taking a harsher look at Lehman. It finished the last two trading days of the month down 4.8 percent and 6.7 percent.[47]

6. Spreading Crisis

Already the crisis was spreading to commercial real estate. The first week in March 2008 began with a WALL STREET JOURNAL report anticipating commercial real estate write-downs, the negative effects of which could persist longer than the initial subprime mortgage crisis.[48] The next day Lehman stock closed down 0.8 percent.[49] The following week, Lehman stock was down 7.3 percent,[50] and Lehman cut another 1,425 jobs in anticipation of significant first

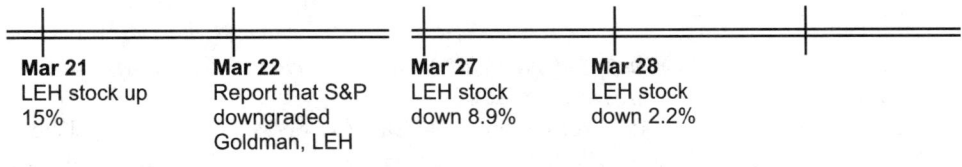

Mar 21	Mar 22	Mar 27	Mar 28
LEH stock up 15%	Report that S&P downgraded Goldman, LEH	LEH stock down 8.9%	LEH stock down 2.2%

---

44. Damian Paletta & James R. Hagerty, *Banks Boost Their Efforts to Head Off Foreclosures*, WALL ST. J., Feb. 12, 2008, at A3.

45. Peter Eavis & Susanne Craig, *Now, Lehman Gets Pelted – Firm Seemed to Outrun Fallout of Credit Crisis, Until One Market Slid*, WALL ST. J., Feb. 19, 2008, at C1.

46. *Looking to the Fed, Investors Decide to Buy*, N.Y. TIMES, Feb. 21, 2008, at C8, *available at* 2008 WLNR 3356493.

47. Stacy-Marie Ishmael, *Bernake Comments Drive Wall St. Lower*, FT.com, Feb. 28, 2008; Walter Hamilton, *Stocks Sink on Finance Worries*, L.A. Times, Mar. 1, 2008, at 1, *available at* 2008 WLNR 4101197.

48. Lingling Wei & Randall Smith, *Wall Street Gears for Its New Pain – Commercial Real Estate to Yield Write-Downs; Defaults Slim So Far*, WALL ST. J., Mar. 3, 2008, at C1.

49. Stacy-Marie Ishmael, *Wall Street Rally Tampers Off*, FT.com, Mar. 5, 2008.

50. Chris Bryant, *US Stocks Slump Amid Risk Aversion*, FT.com, Mar. 10, 2008.

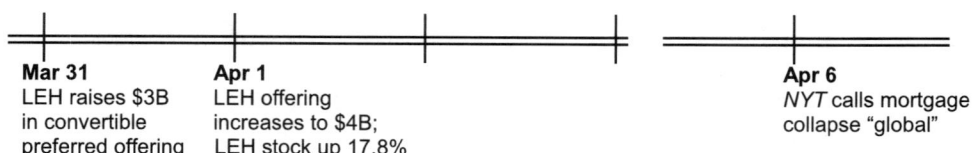

quarter write-downs of home mortgage, commercial real estate, and loan assets.[51] The game-changer occurred in mid-March, when Bear Stearns collapsed and JP Morgan Chase agreed to acquire its assets.[52] On the day that the Bear Stearns collapse was announced, Lehman stock lost 14 percent in market value.[53] Three days later, it was down more than 19 percent.[54] Neverthe less, on disclosure of better than expected first quarter earnings, Lehman stock rose steadily over the next four days, until Friday, March 21, when Standard & Poor's lowered its "stable" outlook on both Goldman Sachs and Lehman to a "negative" outlook.[55] Deterioration in the market value of Lehman stock followed, until Lehman closed the month with successive sales to institutional investors of convertible preferred shares, eventually reaching a reported $4 billion, to reconstitute Lehman's capitalization and rebuild market confidence in the firm.[56] Lehman stock rose 17.8 percent on the news.[57]

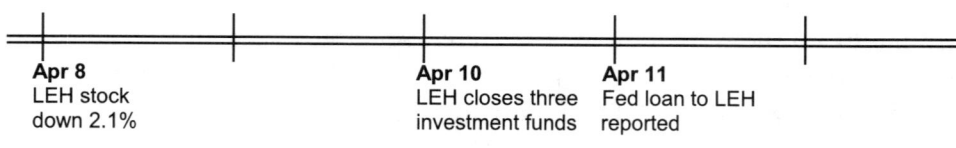

---

51. Jed Horowitz, *Credit Crunch: Lehman Cuts Its Work Force by 5% as Mortgage Crisis Erodes Assets*, WALL ST. J., Mar. 11, 2008, at C2.

52. *See* Chapter 1, *supra* at 34=35 (discussing Bear Stearns). *See also* Stacy-Marie Ishmael & Aline Van Duyn, *Wall Street Plunges on Bear Sterns News*, FT.com, Mar. 14, 2008 (reporting on collapse of Bear Stearns); Andrew Ross Sorkin, Jenny Anderson & Eric Dash, *In Sweeping Move, Fed Backs Buyout and Wall St. Loans*, N.Y. Times, Mar. 17, 2008, at A1, *available at* 2008 WLNR 5189440 (reporting on JP Morgan Chase acquisition).

53. Ishmael & Van Duyn, *supra.*

54. Jeremy Lemer & Stacy-Marie Ishmael, *Goldman and Lehman Boost Mood on Wall St.*, FT.com, Mar. 18, 2008.

55. Jed Horowitz, *Credit Crisis: S&P Flags Goldman, Lehman*, WALL ST. J., Mar. 22, 2008, at A15. However, S&P did not change the credit ratings on the senior-debt ratings of Goldman (AA-minus) or Lehman (A-plus). *Id.*

56. *See, e.g.*, Jenny Anderson, *Lehman Tries to Quash Talk by Raising $3 Billion*, N.Y. TIMES, Apr. 1, 2008, at C8, *available at* 2008 WLNR 6115203 (reporting $3 billion Lehman offering); *Demand Is Strong for Lehman's Offering*, N.Y. Times, Apr. 2, 2008, at C5, *available at* 2008 WLNR 6177055 (reporting on additional sales of $1 billion in oversubscribed offering).

57. *Demand is Strong, supra.*

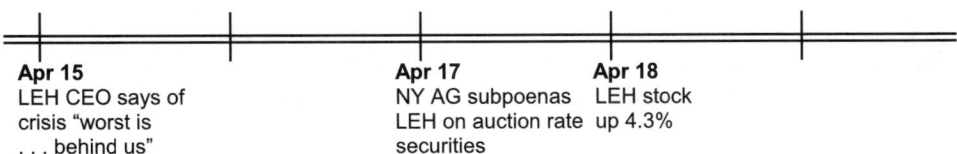

Apr 15
LEH CEO says of
crisis "worst is
. . . behind us"

Apr 17
NY AG subpoenas
LEH on auction rate
securities

Apr 18
LEH stock
up 4.3%

7. The Crisis Goes Global

By April 6, 2008, the NEW YORK TIMES would report that the mortgage crisis had gone global.[58] Banks worldwide had "taken at least $232 [billion] in writedowns and losses because of the subprime and credit crises."[59] The TIMES reported that total losses from the global crisis could reach $945 billion, and Lehman itself had already written off $3.93 billion of credit and loans since third quarter 2007 – $1.8 billion in first quarter 2008 alone.[60] By April 8, Lehman stock was down 2.1 percent.[61] By April 10, Lehman had liquidated three investment funds with a total asset value of approximately $1 billion.[62] The following day the press reported that the Federal Reserve had extended Lehman a low-interest, short-term cash loan to finance its operations.[63]

At least short term, this appeared to be a turning point for Lehman. By April 15, Lehman CEO Richard Fuld was encouraged that "The worst of the impact on the financial-services industry is behind us."[64] By April 18, Lehman stock closed up 4.3 percent,[65] and two days later Lehman's U.S. Aggregate Bond Index was up 2.3 percent.[66] By April 24, Lehman stock closed up 6

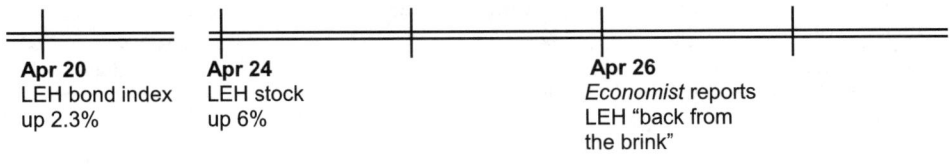

Apr 20
LEH bond index
up 2.3%

Apr 24
LEH stock
up 6%

Apr 26
Economist reports
LEH "back from
the brink"

---

58. Nelson D. Schwartz, *The Mortgage Bust Goes Global*, N.Y. TIMES, Apr. 6, 2008, at 1, *available at* 2008 WLNR 6456763.

59. Dan Pimlott, *Lehman Closes $1bn Funds*, FT.com, Apr. 10, 2008.

60. *Id.*

61. Jeremy Lemer, *Wall St Falls as Results Season Starts*, FT.com, Apr. 8, 2008.

62. Pimlott, *supra.*

63. Serena Ng & Susanne Craig, *How Lehman Opened the Fed's Spigot – Deal Takes Advantage of New Lending Facility*, WALL ST. J., Apr. 11, 2008, at C1.

64. Jed Horowitz, *Credit Crisis: Lehman's Chief Provides Tempered Hope on Markets*, WALL ST. J., Apr. 16, 2008, at C2.

65. Rob Curran, *Citigroup Rises on Earnings Results – Google Rallies 20% Its Best Day on Record; Lehman Brothers Gains*, WALL ST. J., Apr. 19, 2008, at B3.

66. Shefali Anand, *Many Bond Funds Proving Not to be Such Safe Havens*, SEATTLE TIMES, Apr. 20, 2008, at C4, *available at* 2008 WLNR 7387191.

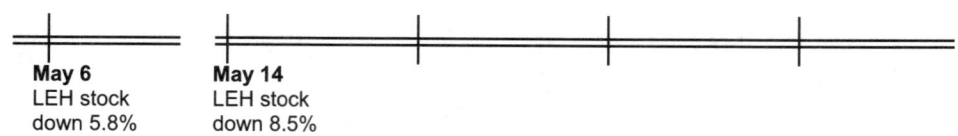

May 6
LEH stock
down 5.8%

May 14
LEH stock
down 8.5%

percent.[67] Two days later, THE ECONOMIST would report that Lehman was "back from the brink."[68] And yet dangers were gathering nonetheless – in mid-April the New York Attorney General had issued subpoenas to eighteen banks, including Lehman, with respect to auction rate securities business.[69] Far worse was on the horizon.

8. A Likely Takeover Target

Ironically, the slide in Lehman market value may have been nudged forward by speculation that new regulatory efforts might force financial firms to disclose further losses.[70] On May 6, the stock value was down 5.8 percent.[71] By May 14, it was down 8.5 percent, at a time when the S&P Index was down only 1 percent.[72] Four days later, *Financial Times* identified Lehman as a likely takeover target.[73] At that point, the stock began a steady decline in market value, with relatively few upticks.[74]

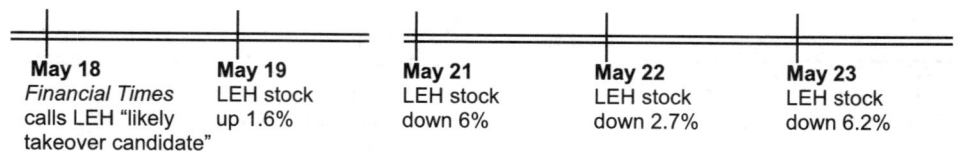

May 18
Financial Times
calls LEH "likely
takeover candidate"

May 19
LEH stock
up 1.6%

May 21
LEH stock
down 6%

May 22
LEH stock
down 2.7%

May 23
LEH stock
down 6.2%

---

67. Peter Eavis & David Reilly, *Lehman Brothers Seen as Cheap Recovery Bet*, WALL ST. J., Apr. 25, 2008, at C2.

68. *Face Value: Fuld of Experience*, THE ECONOMIST, Apr. 26, 2008, at 91, *available at* 2008 WLNR 7732642.

69. Joanna Chung, Aline Van Duyn, & Ben White, *NY Investigates Auction Securities Market*, FT.com, Apr. 17, 2008.

70. Jeremy Lemer, *Wall Street Drop Sharpest in a Month*, FT.com, May 7, 2008.

71. *Id.*

72. *Investors Heartened as Price Index Rises More Slowly*, N.Y. TIMES, May 15, 2008, at C9, *available at* 2008 WLNR 9132072.

73. Francesco Guerrera & Ben White, *Shrunken Street: Financials Groups Eye Potential Predators and Prey*, FT.com, May 18, 2008.

74. *See, e.g.,* Mark Gonloff, *Ahead of the Tape*, WALL ST. J., May 29, 2008, at C1 (noting Lehman market value decrease of 19 percent since April 2008).

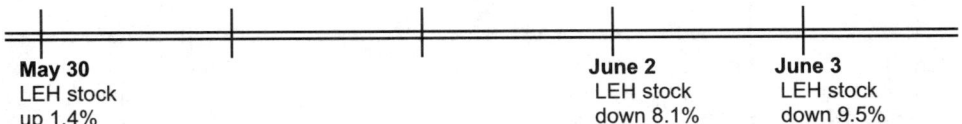

May 30 LEH stock up 1.4%			**June 2** LEH stock down 8.1%	**June 3** LEH stock down 9.5%

9. A Vulnerable Investment Bank

This trend continued in June. By June 7 THE ECONOMIST was calling Lehman the most vulnerable investment bank on Wall Street.[75] Two days later came the news of Lehman's second quarter loss of $2.8 billion, which it planned to address by selling $6 billion in common stock.[76] Over the next two days, Lehman stock dropped over 30 percent of market value.[77] Lehman's immediate response on Thursday, June 12, was to replace Lehman president Joe Gregory, and to demote finance chief Erin Callan.[78] Fifteen days later, CEO Richard Fuld and newly-appointed president Bart McDade announced that they would forgo their bonuses for 2008.[79] The market was apparently unimpressed. On June 30, on the strength of rumors that Barclays would buy Lehman at $15 per share – well below book value – Lehman market value sank 11 percent.[80]

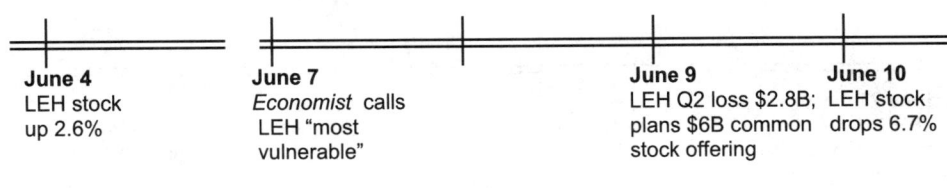

June 4 LEH stock up 2.6%	**June 7** *Economist* calls LEH "most vulnerable"	**June 9** LEH Q2 loss $2.8B; plans $6B common stock offering	**June 10** LEH stock drops 6.7%

---

75. *Investment Banks: Out of the Frying Pan*, THE ECONOMIST, June 7, 2008, at 39, *available at* 2008 WLNR 11427116.

76. Jeremy Lemer, *Lehman Losses Hit US Financial Stocks*, FT.com, June 9, 2008. This $2.8 billion loss was Lehman's first deficiency since going public in 1994. Jenny Anderson & Louise Story, *As Losses Mount, the Fed and the White House Step Up Fortunes Reverse for a Bank and Its Leader*, N.Y. TIMES, June 10, 2008, at C1, *available at* 2008 WLNR 10909021.

77. *See* Rob Curran, *Coke, Citi, AIG Rise; Lehman Falls 6.7% – Ford Drops on Rush to Sell to Kerkorian; Energy Shares Slide*, WALL ST. J., June 11, 2008, at C6 (reporting three-day 19 percent loss in Lehman market value); Ben White, *Lehman Shakes Up Management After $3bn Loss*, FT.com, June 12, 2008 (reporting additional 13 percent loss).

78. White, *Lehman Shakes Up Management, supra*. The management shake-up continued twelve days later with the rehiring of two Lehman alumni and the promotion of two current executives into key management positions for capital markets, equities, principal investing, and strategy. Saskia Scholtes, *Lehman Veterans Brought Back in Shake-up*, FT.com, June 24, 2008.

79. Francesco Guerrera, *Lehman Chief to Forgo Annual Bonus*, FT.com, June 27, 2008.

80. Ben White, *Lehman Issues Shares to All Its Employees*, FT.com, July 2, 2008.

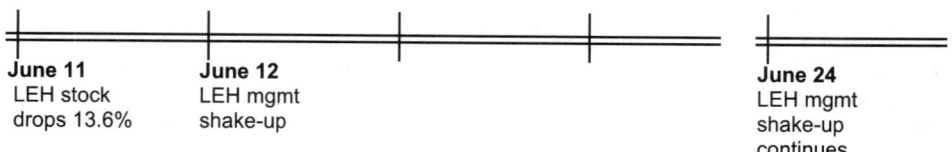

June 11
LEH stock
drops 13.6%

June 12
LEH mgmt
shake-up

June 24
LEH mgmt
shake-up
continues

10. Short-Selling Victim

Lehman stock, a major target of short-sellers,[81] was down 66 per cent through mid-year 2008.[82] However, after analysts discredited the Barclays rumor, the stock closed up 6.7 per cent on July 2.[83] As the month proceeded, Lehman stock returned to a rising trend of daily losses. On Monday, July 7, the rout in the financial sector broadened, triggering a widespread sell-off, with Lehman stock dropping 8.2 percent.[84] The following day it was back up 6.9 percent on favorable macroeconomic news.[85] On Wednesday, however, the stock declined 11 percent,[86] and it lost another 12 percent on Thursday.[87] This trend continued the following week. On Monday, July 14, Lehman stock closed down 14 percent.[88] However, favorable macroeconomic news on Wednesday pumped Lehman stock value up 26 percent.[89]

On Friday, July 18, pursuant to section 12(k)(2) of the Securities Exchange

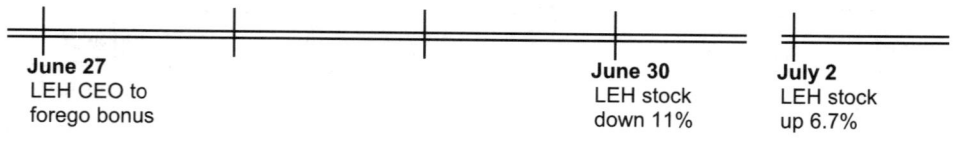

June 27
LEH CEO to
forego bonus

June 30
LEH stock
down 11%

July 2
LEH stock
up 6.7%

---

81. In a short sale, a trader borrows stock and sells it, expecting to repay the loan later with new shares bought at a subsequent lower price. *See* Andrew Ross Sorkin, *Psst! Hear the Rumor of the Day?*, N.Y. Times, July 8, 2008, at C1, *available at* 2008 WLNR 12755396 (discussing effects of short selling and rumor mongering on Lehman stock values).

82. White, *Lehman Issues Shares, supra.*

83. *Id.*

84. Jeremy Lemer, *Wall St Plunges as Financials Sell Off*, FT.com, July 7, 2008.

85. Tom Petruno, *Stocks Get a Boost as Oil Declines*, L.A. Times, July 9, 2008, at 5, *available at* 2008 WLNR 12837105.

86. Rob Curran, *Large Stock Focus: Fannie, Freddie Lead Financials' Tough Day – Merrill Sinks 9.3%; U.S. Steel, Nucor Recover Strength*, Wall St. J., July 10, 2008, at C5.

87. Jenny Anderson, *Shares of Lehman Take a Beating as Anxiety Builds in the Mortgage Market*, N.Y. Times, July 11, 2008, at C6, *available at* 2008 WLNR 12997809.

88. Susanne Craig, *Lehman Is Rehiring Executive*, Wall St. J., July 15, 2008, at C3.

89. Rob Curran, *Large Stock Focus: Fannie, Freddie Surge After Weeks of Losses – Lehman, Goldman, GM, Intel Also Rise; Seagate Slides 15%*, Wall St. J., July 17, 2008, at C5.

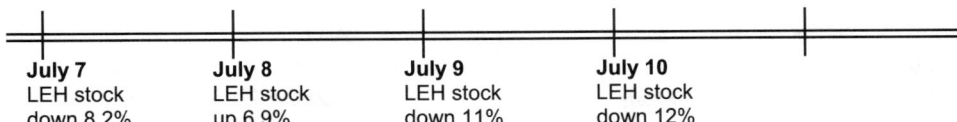

Act of 1934,[90] the Securities and Exchange Commission (SEC) approved an emergency order prohibiting "naked short selling"[91] by requiring that

> in connection with transactions in the publicly traded securities of substantial financial firms [identified in the Figure reproduced *infra*] no person may effect a short sale in these securities using the means or instrumentalities of interstate commerce unless such person or its agent has borrowed or arranged to borrow the security or otherwise has the security available to borrow in its inventory prior to effecting such short sale and delivers the security on settlement date.[92]

The order was effective at 12:01 a.m. EDT on Monday, July 21, 2008, and was to terminate at 11:59 p.m. EDT on Tuesday, July 29, 2008 unless further extended by the SEC.[93] On July 29, the SEC approved an extension of the emergency order until August 12, 2008.[94] The order was intended to protect investors, to maintain fair and orderly securities markets, and to prevent substantial disruption in the securities markets by suspected market manipulation resulting from the dissemination of false rumors. The SEC believed that this manipulation was effected by naked short selling of the target stocks as their market value was debilitated by rumors. The emergency order would "eliminate any possibility that naked short selling may contribute to the disruption of markets in these securities."[95]

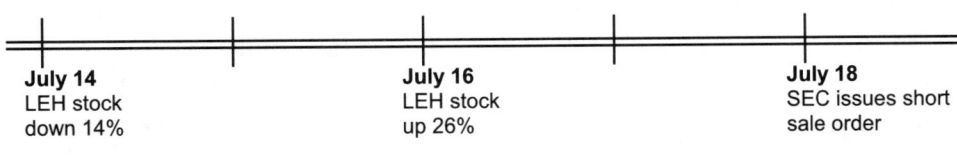

---

90. 15 U.S.C. § 78*l*(k)(2) (authorizing Securities and Exchange Commission summarily to issue order to alter, supplement, suspend, or impose requirements or restrictions with respect to matters or actions subject to regulation by Commission in appropriate circumstances).

91. Naked short selling involves a stock sale in which the subject stock is not borrowed or purchased prior to the contract to sell, but is purchased at a declining market price post-sale in order to fulfill the transaction. *Cf.* Note 80, *supra* (discussing traditional short selling).

92. 73 Fed. Reg. 42,379, 42,379 (2008) (footnotes omitted).

93. *Id.*

94. 73 Fed. Reg. 45,257, 45,257 (2008).

95. *Id.*

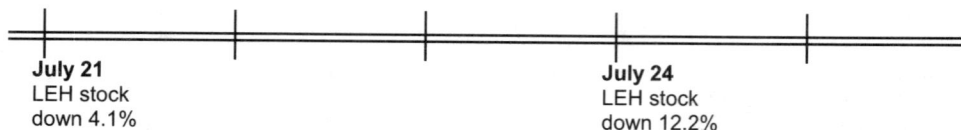

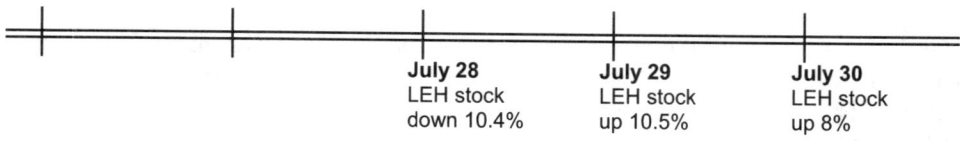

Source: Securities and Exchange Commission, *Emergency Order Pursuant to Section 12(k)(2) of the Securities Exchange Act of 1934 Taking Temporary Action To Respond to Market Developments*, Appendix A, 73 Fed. Reg. 42,379 (2008).

An amendment to the order clarified that it did not apply to any person effecting a short sale in a restricted security,[96] which would not generally be traded in a public market.[97] The order also did not apply to short sales by underwriters, or members of a syndicate or group participating in distributions of the identified financial stocks in connection with an over-allotment of securities, or any lay-off sale by such person in connection with a distribution

---

96. On restricted securities, see 17 C.F.R. § 230.144.

97. *Amendment to Emergency Order Pursuant to Section 12(k)(2) of the Securities Exchange Act of 1934 Taking Temporary Action to Respond to Market Developments*, 73 Fed. Reg. 42,837, 42,838 (2008).

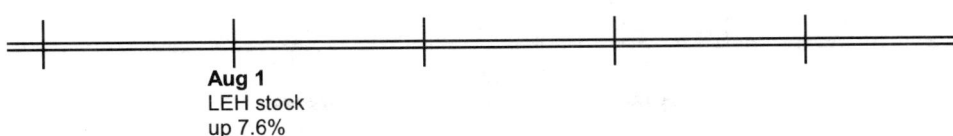

Aug 1
LEH stock
up 7.6%

of the securities through a rights or a standby underwriting commitment.[98]

While Lehman's CEO had insisted that speculative short selling had been the primary reason for the precipitous decline in Lehman market value,[99] the SEC order had little immediate effect on Lehman market value.[100] On Monday, July 21, the effective date of the emergency order, Lehman stock declined 4.1 percent.[101] By mid-week, it lost an additional 12.2 percent,[102] and the following Monday it lost 10.4 percent.[103]

11. Slipping in Unison

Market value of Lehman stock regained some ground at the end of July,[104]

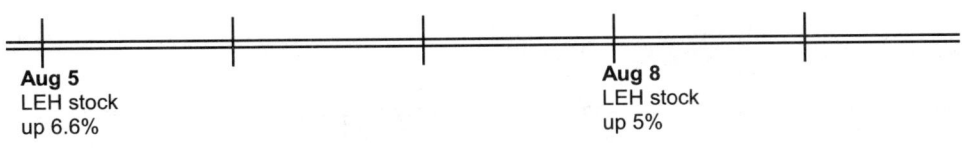

Aug 5
LEH stock
up 6.6%

Aug 8
LEH stock
up 5%

---

98. *Id.* Coverage by the emergency order was unnecessary because short selling of securities in a public offering were already covered by the anti-manipulation rules of the SEC Regulation M, 17 C.F.R. §§ 242.100 *et seq.*, and "does not raise the same concerns as 'naked' short selling in secondary markets." 73 Fed. Reg. at 42,838.

99. *See* Andrew Ross Sorkin, *Psst! Hear the Rumor of the Day?*, N.Y. TIMES, July 8, 2008, at C1, *available at* 2008 WLNR 12755396 (reporting that CEO Fuld blamed short sellers for spreading rumors about Lehman).

100. The SEC quickly commenced formal investigations into market manipulation involving short selling of Lehman stock. *See* Kara Scannell & Susanne Craig, *SEC Intensifies Efforts to Rein in Short Selling – Agency Subpoenas Focus on 4 Rumors That Hit Lehman*, WALL ST. J., July 28, 2008, at C1 (reporting on SEC subpoenas issued to twelve hedge funds seeking records of phone calls and messages, focusing on rumors that sent Lehman shares down in preceding month).

101. Rob Curran, *Large Stock Focus: Financial Stocks See Rally Fade Late – Morgan Stanley, Lehman Decline; Genentech Gains*, WALL ST. J., July 22, 2008, at C5.

102. Jeremy Lemer, *Fear of More Bank Losses Hurt Wall Street*, FT.com, July 24, 2008.

103. *Market Movers*, CHI. TRIB., July 29, 2008, at 6, *available at* 2008 WLNR 14103754.

104. *See, e.g.*, Paul Tharp, *Bank Rally Ignites Rest of Market*, N.Y. POST, July 30, 2008, at 35, *available at* 2008 WLNR 14190967 (reporting Lehman stock up 10.5 percent); *Dow Rally Continues, Fed by Energy Sector*, L.A. TIMES, July 31, 2008, at 5, *available at* 2008 WLNR 14230840 (reporting Lehman stock up 8 percent).

Aug 12
SEC short sale
order expires

Aug 13
LEH stock
down 4%

and this trend continued during the first week of August 2008,[105] despite disappointing economic reports on jobs and manufacturing activity. On August 12, the SEC emergency order expired,[106] and the following day, Lehman stock closed down 4 percent, on the strength of analyst downgrades.[107] By August 19, Lehman stock closed down by more than 10 percent.[108] Despite some upticks,[109] Lehman stock had already lost 85 percent of its market value since early 2007.[110] Increasingly, it seemed to be "ripe for a hostile takeover."[111]

And so began Lehman's fruitless attempts to raise additional capital by a major sale of new equity to foreign investors – mainly Chinese and South

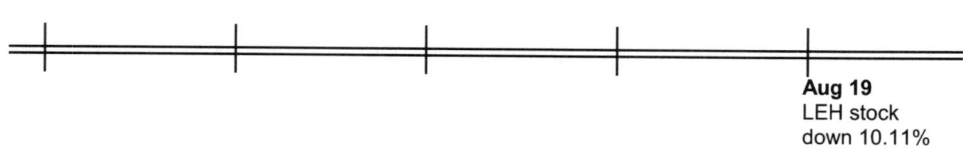

Aug 19
LEH stock
down 10.11%

105. *See, e.g.*, *A Rough Week with a Sedate Conclusion*, N.Y. TIMES, Aug. 2, 2008, at C7, *available at* 2008 WLNR 14409851 (reporting Lehman stock up 7.6 percent); Jeremy Lemer, *Wall Street Higher as Oil Prices Drop*, FT.com, Aug. 5, 2008 (reporting Lehman stock up 6.6 percent); Kaja Whitehouse, *Wall St. Whiplash – Dow Boomerangs Back up 302 Points, As Oil Sinks*, N.Y. POST, Aug. 9, 2008, at 21, *available at* 2008 WLNR 15014020 (reporting Lehman stock up 5 percent).

106. 73 Fed. Reg. at 45,257.

107. Jeremy Lemer, *Financials Lead Wall Street Down*, FT.com, Aug. 13, 2008.

108. Ben White, *Lehman Shares Slide on Fears Over Results*, FT.com, Aug. 19, 2008.

109. *See, e.g.*, Matthew Karnitschnig & Susanne Craig, *Fed Acted on Lehman Rumor – Amid Market Speculation in July, Credit Suisse Was Urged to Maintain*, WALL ST. J., Aug. 21, 2008, at C1 (reporting Lehman stock up 5.1 percent); Jenny Anderson, Landon Thomas Jr., Andrew Ross Sorkin & Choe Sang-Hun, *Lehman's Shares Gain on Signs of Raising Capital*, N.Y. TIMES, Aug. 23, 2008, at C2, *available at* 2008 WLNR 15936332 (reporting Lehman stock up 5 percent).

110. Henny Sender, *Lehman's Secret Talks Fail to Offload 50% Stake*, FT.com, Aug. 20, 2008.

111. Jenny Anderson, *Burdened by Mortgages, Lehman's Options Narrow*, N.Y. TIMES, Aug. 22, 2008, at C1, *available at* 2008 WLNR 15864855.

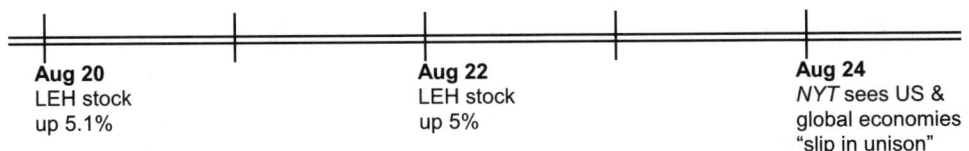

Aug 20
LEH stock
up 5.1%

Aug 22
LEH stock
up 5%

Aug 24
NYT sees US &
global economies
"slip in unison"

Korean investors.[112] This was to no avail – global economies were already beginning to "slip in unison."[113] The crisis had spread beyond the United States to major economies in Europe and Asia, threatening U.S. firms with the loss not only of foreign sales but also of investment that had become increasingly critical to their viability. The strain on Lehman in particular had reached the breaking point. On Thursday, August 28, Lehman announced that it had prepared to lay off an additional 1,500 employees, its fourth round of cutbacks in 2008.[114]

12. Time Spirals Out

Reports of a possible takeover of Lehman by the Korean Development Bank (KDB) persisted early in September 2008.[115] The KDB chairmen reportedly believed that the subprime crisis offered an opportunity for it to enter the global

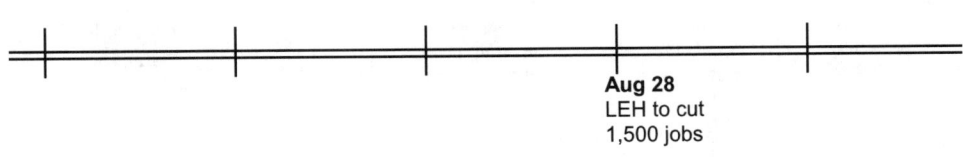

Aug 28
LEH to cut
1,500 jobs

---

112. *See, e.g.*, Henny Sender, *Lehman's Secret Talks Fail to Offload 50% Stake*, FT.com, Aug. 20, 2008 (detailing Lehman talks with South Korean and Chinese interests, failing due to reportedly high sales price); Jenny Anderson, Landon Thomas Jr., Andrew Ross Sorkin & Choe Sang-Hun, *Lehman's Shares Gain on Signs of Raising Capital*, N.Y. TIMES, Aug. 23, 2008, at C2, *available at* 2008 WLNR 15936332 (reporting Korean Development Bank considering buying Lehman); *Regulator Questions Korean Bank's Interest in Lehman*, N.Y. TIMES, Aug. 26, 2008, *available at* 2008 WLNR 16086231.

113. Peter S. Goodman; Keith Bradsher, Carter Dougherty & Heather Timmons, *U.S. and Global Economies Slipping in Unison*, N.Y. TIMES, Aug. 24, 2008, at A1, *available at* 2008 WLNR 15991497.

114. Jenny Anderson & Eric Dash, *For Lehman, More Cuts and Anxiety*, N.Y. TIMES, Aug. 29, 2008, at C1, *available at* 2008 WLNR 16331011.

115. Song Jung-a, *Lehman and KDB Edge Closer to Deal*, FT.com, Sept. 2, 2008 confirming KDB in talks with Lehman).

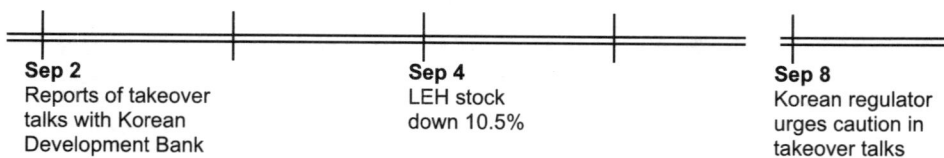

Sep 2
Reports of takeover
talks with Korean
Development Bank

Sep 4
LEH stock
down 10.5%

Sep 8
Korean regulator
urges caution in
takeover talks

banking market.[116] Aggressive negotiating on Lehman's part was apparently alienating KDB,[117] however, and by September 4 Lehman stock closed down a further 10.5 percent.[118]

The end was near. On Sunday, September 7, the Federal Housing Finance Agency placed Fannie Mae and Freddie Mac into conservatorship, following billions of dollars in losses by the two government-sponsored enterprises on securitized mortgages.[119] On Monday, the chairman of the Financial Services Commission – KDB's regulator in South Korea – publicly urged that the bank "take a cautious approach toward taking over Lehman," in light of domestic and international financial conditions.[120] This expression of views terminated the Lehman-KDB negotiations as a practical matter, and the market value of Lehman shares virtually collapsed.[121] By Wednesday, Lehman announced a third quarter net loss of $3.9 billion,[122] effectively wiping out the March investors in Lehman convertible preferred shares. As time spiraled out, Lehman

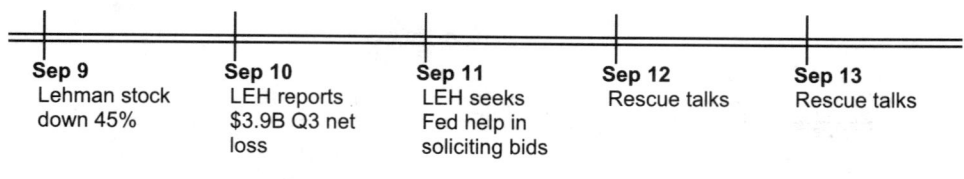

Sep 9
Lehman stock
down 45%

Sep 10
LEH reports
$3.9B Q3 net
loss

Sep 11
LEH seeks
Fed help in
soliciting bids

Sep 12
Rescue talks

Sep 13
Rescue talks

---

116. *See, e.g., South Korea and Wall Street: Deal or No Deal?*, THE ECONOMIST, Sept. 6, 2008, at 40, *available at* 2008 WLNR 16858798 (discussing attempts by Korean banks to restyle themselves as global players).

117. Mark McCambre, *Korea in the Fuld – Lehman Revamps Plan*, N.Y. POST, Sept. 3, 2008, at 35, *available at* 2008 WLNR 16652631.

118. Ben White & Jenny Anderson, *Lehman May Split Off Weak Holdings*, N.Y. TIMES, Sept. 5, 2008, at C1, *available at* 2008 WLNR 16818836.

119. Press Release, Henry M. Paulson, Jr., Sec'y of the Treasury, Statement by Secretary Henry M. Paulson, Jr. on Treasury and Federal Housing Finance Agency Action to Protect Financial Markets and Taxpayers (Sept. 7, 2008), available at http://www.treas.gov/press/releases/hp1129.htm.

120. Song Jung-a, *Korean Development Bank Warned Over Lehman Stake*, FT.com, Sept. 8, 2008.

121. Alistair Gray, *Lehman Shares Plunge*, FT.com, Sept. 9, 2008.

122. Peter Thal Larsen, *Lehman Brothers Loses $3.9bn in Third Quarter*, FT.com, Sept. 10, 2008.

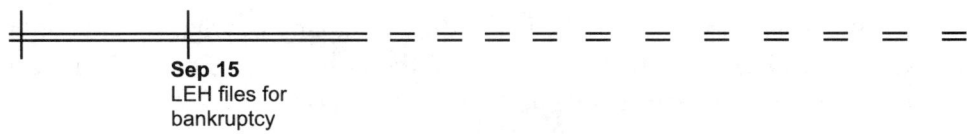

Sep 15
LEH files for
bankruptcy

explored selling off the "bad bank" portions of its business,[123] attracting another investor,[124] and soliciting the intervention of the Federal Reserve.[125]

The end arrived in mid-September. Federal Reserve officials and representatives of major U.S. financial institutions held two days of emergency meetings in an effort to devise a rescue plan for Lehman, but by Saturday evening, September 13, no agreement had emerged.[126] Failing to find a buyer or other substantial financial support, Lehman decided to file for bankruptcy.[127] The light had gone out at One William Street.

ANDREW ROSS SORKIN, *BIDS TO HALT FINANCIAL CRISIS RESHAPE LANDSCAPE OF WALL ST.*

N.Y. TIMES, Sept. 15, 2008, at A1,
available at 2008 WLNR 17497665

In one of the most dramatic days in Wall Street's history, Merrill Lynch agreed to sell itself on Sunday to Bank of America for roughly $50 billion to avert a deepening financial crisis, while another prominent securities firm, Lehman Brothers, said it would seek bankruptcy protection and hurtled toward liquidation after it failed to find a buyer. . . .

The stunning series of events culminated a weekend of frantic around-the-clock negotiations, as Wall Street bankers huddled in meetings at the behest of Bush administration officials to try to avoid a downward spiral in the markets stemming from a crisis of confidence. . . .

Early Monday morning, Lehman said it would file for Chapter 11 bank-

---

123. Ben White, *Pressure Builds as Lehman Faces Mounting Losses*, N.Y. TIMES, Sept. 11, 2008, at A1, *available at* 2008 WLNR 17213262.

124. Ben White, *Pressure Builds as Lehman Faces Mounting Losses*, N.Y. TIMES, Sept. 11, 2008, at A1, *available at* 2008 WLNR 17213262.

125. Jenny Anderson, Andrew Ross & Ben White, *As Options Fade, Lehman Is Said To Seek a Buyer*, N.Y. TIMES, Sept. 12, 2008, at A1, *available at* 2008 WLNR 17326260.

126. Eric Dash, Ben White, Jenny Anderson, Michael J. de la Merced, Louise Story & Landon Thomas Jr., *Leading Plan for Rescue Would Split Up Lehman*, N.Y. TIMES, Sept. 14, 2008, at A28, *available at* 2008 WLNR 17445286.

127. Andrew Ross Sorkin, Edmund L. Andrews, Eric Dash, Michael Barbaro, Michael J. de la Merced, Louise Story & Ben White, *Bids to Halt Financial Crisis Reshape Landscape of Wall St.*, N.Y. TIMES, Sept. 15, 2008, at A1, *available at* 2008 WLNR 17497665.

ruptcy protection in New York for its holding company in what would be the largest failure of an investment bank since the collapse of Drexel Burnham Lambert 18 years ago, the Associated Press reported.

Questions remain about how the market will react Monday, particularly to Lehman's plan to wind down its trading operations, and whether other companies, like A.I.G. and Washington Mutual, the nation's largest savings and loan, might falter.* Indeed, in a move that echoed Wall Street's rescue of a big hedge fund a decade ago this week, 10 major banks agreed to create an emergency fund of $70 billion to $100 billion that financial institutions can use to protect themselves from the fallout of Lehman's failure. . . .

The weekend that humbled Lehman and Merrill Lynch and rewarded Bank of America, based in Charlotte, N.C., began at 6 p.m. Friday in the first of a series of emergency meetings at the Federal Reserve building in Lower Manhattan.

The meeting was called by Fed officials, with Treasury Secretary Henry M. Paulson Jr. in attendance, and it included top bankers. The Treasury and Federal Reserve had already stepped in on several occasions to rescue the financial system, forcing a shotgun marriage between Bear Stearns and JPMorgan Chase this year and backstopping $29 billion worth of troubled assets – and then agreeing to bail out Fannie Mae and Freddie Mac.

The bankers were told that the government would not bail out Lehman and that it was up to Wall Street to solve its problems. Lehman's stock tumbled sharply last week as concerns about its financial condition grew and other firms started to pull back from doing business with it, threatening its viability.

Without government backing, Lehman began trying to find a buyer, focusing on Barclays, the big British bank, and Bank of America. . . .

Bank of America eventually pulled out of its talks with Lehman after the government refused to take responsibility for losses on some of Lehman's most troubled real-estate assets, something it agreed to do when JP Morgan Chase bought Bear Stearns to save it from a bankruptcy filing in March.

A leading proposal to rescue Lehman would have divided the bank into two entities, a "good bank" and a "bad bank." Under that scenario, Barclays would have bought the parts of Lehman that have been performing well, while a group of 10 to 15 Wall Street companies would have agreed to absorb losses from the bank's troubled assets, to two people briefed on the proposal said. Taxpayer money would not have been included in such a deal, they said.

Other Wall Street banks also balked at the deal, unhappy at facing potential losses while Bank of America or Barclays walked away with the potentially

---

*. They did. Washington Mutual's collapse is detailed in Chapter 3, *infra*.

profitable part of Lehman at a cheap price.

For Lehman, the end essentially came Sunday morning when its last potential suitor, Barclays, pulled out from a deal, saying it could not obtain a shareholder vote to approve a transaction before Monday morning, something required under London Stock Exchange listing rules, one person close to the matter said. Other people involved in the talks said the Financial Services Authority, the British securities regulator, had discouraged Barclays from pursuing a deal. Peter Truell, a spokesman for Barclays, declined to comment. Lehman's subsidiaries were expected to remain solvent while the firm liquidates its holdings, these people said. Herbert H. McDade III, Lehman's president, was at the Federal Reserve Bank in New York late Sunday, discussing terms of Lehman's fate with government officials.

Lehman's filing is unlikely to resemble those of other companies that seek bankruptcy protection. Because of the harsher treatment that federal bankruptcy law applies to financial-services firms, Lehman cannot hope to reorganize and survive. . . .

The weekend's events indicate that top officials at the Federal Reserve and the Treasury are taking a harder line on providing government support of troubled financial institutions.

While offering to help Wall Street organize a shotgun marriage for Lehman, both the Fed chairman, Ben S. Bernanke, and Mr. Paulson had warned that they would not put taxpayer money at risk simply to prevent a Lehman collapse.

The message marked a major change in strategy but it remained unclear until at least Friday what would happen. "They were faced after Bear Stearns with the problem of where to draw the line," said Laurence H. Meyer, a former Fed governor who is now vice chairman of Macroeconomic Advisors, a forecasting firm. "It became clear that this piecemeal, patchwork, case-by-case approach might not get the job done."

Both Mr. Paulson and Mr. Bernanke worried that they had already gone much further than they had ever wanted, first by underwriting the takeover of Bear Stearns in March and by the far bigger bailout of Fannie Mae and Freddie Mac.

Outside the public eye, Fed officials had acquired much more information since March about the interconnections and cross-exposure to risk among Wall Street investment banks, hedge funds and traders in the vast market for credit-default swaps and other derivatives. In the end, both Wall Street and the Fed blinked.

NOTES AND QUESTIONS

1. Immediately after Lehman's bankruptcy filing, Barclays and Lehman began negotiating Barclays' purchase of Lehman's North American broker-dealer operations and significant real estate holdings, including the Lehman Brothers headquarters building in New York City. This quickly resulted in the sale to Barclays, approved by the federal bankruptcy court on September 20, 2008, and completed two days later. The consequences of this transaction are explored in Chapter 4, *infra.*

2. *Did Lehman Have to Go?* There has been speculation that "the financial crisis would have been even worse had Lehman been rescued. Although nobody realized it at the time, Lehman Brothers had to die for the rest of Wall Street to live."[128] The idea seems to be that the Lehman failure gave Treasury and the Fed the kind of dramatic set piece they needed to persuade Congress to enact the Emergency Economic Stabilization Act of 2008 (EESA),[129] which created the Troubled Assets Relief Program (TARP) for the purchase of troubled assets of financial institutions. Among other things, the EESA granted the Secretary of the Treasury emergency authority to help restore liquidity and stability to the U.S. financial system. Does that sound like a realistic explanation for the failure of the federal authorities to rescue Lehman?

B. TRUTH AND CONSEQUENCES

The immediate impact of the Lehman collapse may seem obvious – turmoil in the markets, panic among investors, a dramatic contraction of credit – but the long term consequences have yet to be determined. This section attempts to identify some simple truths about the collapse and to suggest the likely consequences.

1. Short Selling as the Villain

Repeatedly, investment banks under market pressure during this crisis have insisted that negative movement in the market value of their stock was the result of market manipulation by short sellers – traders who borrow a target security, agree to a sale of the stock, and then purchase the target stock at the

---

128. Joe Nocera, *Lehman Had to Die, It Seems, So Global Finance Could Live*, N.Y. TIMES, Sept. 12, 2009, at A1.

129. Pub. L. No. 110-343, 122 Stat. 3765 (2008) (codified at scattered sections of, *inter alia*, 5, 12, 31 U.S.C.).

lower price resulting from the manipulation in order to complete the sale. Pushing this a little further, a "naked short sale" involves a situation in which the short seller *does not* borrow the target security in advance of the agreement to sell, and so the net proceeds of the manipulated sale increase, because there is no transactional cost associated with a borrowed security.

QUESTION

Is the investment banks' argument that short selling victimized their market value just a convenient excuse for their own overreaching behavior? Or was short selling a genuine villain in this story? The SEC certainly took the argument seriously. Consider the following excerpt from the SEC Emergency Order in answering the question.

SECURITIES AND EXCHANGE COMMISSION, EMERGENCY ORDER PURSUANT TO SECTION 12(K)(2) OF THE SECURITIES EXCHANGE ACT OF 1934 TAKING TEMPORARY ACTION TO RESPOND TO MARKET DEVELOPMENTS

73 Fed. Reg. 42,379 (July 21, 2008)

False rumors can lead to a loss of confidence in our markets. Such loss of confidence can lead to panic selling, which may be further exacerbated by "naked" short selling. As a result, the prices of securities may artificially and unnecessarily decline well below the price level that would have resulted from the normal price discovery process. If significant financial institutions are involved, this chain of events can threaten disruption of our markets.

The events preceding the sale of The Bear Stearns Companies Inc. are illustrative of the market impact of rumors. During the week of March 10, 2008, rumors spread about liquidity problems at Bear Stearns, which eroded investor confidence in the firm. As Bear Stearns' stock price fell, its counterparties became concerned, and a crisis of confidence occurred late in the week. In particular, counterparties to Bear Stearns were unwilling to make secured funding available to Bear Stearns on customary terms. In light of the potentially systemic consequences of a failure of Bear Stearns, the Federal Reserve took emergency action.

The Commission has taken a series of actions to address concerns about rumors. For example, in April, 2008, we charged Paul S. Berliner, a trader, with securities fraud and market manipulation for intentionally disseminating a false rumor concerning The Blackstone Group's acquisition of Alliance Data

Systems Corp ("ADS"). The Commission alleged that this false rumor caused the price of ADS stock to plummet, and that Berliner profited by short selling ADS stock and covering those sales as the false rumor caused the price of ADS stock to fall. See http://www.sec.gov/litigation/litreleases/2008/lr20537.htm.

As another example, on July 13, 2008, the Commission announced that the SEC and other securities regulators would immediately conduct examinations aimed at the prevention of the intentional spreading of false information intended to manipulate securities prices. . . . See http://www.sec.gov/news/press/2008/2008-140.htm.

We intend these and similar actions to provide powerful disincentives to those who might otherwise engage in illegal market manipulation through the dissemination of false rumors and thereby over time to diminish the effect of these activities on our markets. In recent days, however, false rumors have continued to threaten significant market disruption. For example, press reports have described rumors regarding the unwillingness of key counterparties to deal with certain financial institutions. There also have been rumors that financial institutions are facing liquidity problems.

As a result of these recent developments, the Commission has concluded that there now exists a substantial threat of sudden and excessive fluctuations of securities prices generally and disruption in the functioning of the securities markets that could threaten fair and orderly markets. Based on this conclusion, the Commission is exercising its powers under Section 12(k)(2) of the Securities Exchange Act of 1934.[1] Pursuant to Section 12(k)(2), in appropriate circumstances the Commission may issue summarily an order to alter, supplement, suspend, or impose requirements or restrictions with respect to matters or actions subject to regulation by the Commission.

In these unusual and extraordinary circumstances, we have concluded that requiring all persons to borrow or arrange to borrow the securities identified in Appendix A [reproduced at 62, *supra*] prior to effecting an order for a short sale of those securities is in the public interest and for the protection of investors to maintain fair and orderly securities markets, and to prevent substantial disruption in the securities markets. This emergency requirement will eliminate any possibility that naked short selling may contribute to the disruption of markets in these securities. We described in the releases in which we proposed and adopted Regulation SHO the bases for the current requirements Regulation SHO imposes. We believe, however, that the unusual

---

1. This finding of an "emergency" is solely for purposes of Section 12(k)(2) of the Exchange Act and is not intended to have any other effect or meaning or to confer any right or impose any obligation other than set forth in this Order.

circumstances we now confront require the temporarily enhanced requirements we are imposing today.

It is ordered that, pursuant to our Section 12(k)(2) powers, in connection with transactions in the publicly traded securities of substantial financial firms, which entities are identified in Appendix A, no person may effect a short sale[2] in these securities using the means or instrumentalities of interstate commerce unless such person or its agent has borrowed or arranged to borrow the security or otherwise has the security available to borrow in its inventory prior to effecting such short sale and delivers the security on settlement date.[3] . . .

2. Searching for Root Causes

Even if manipulative short selling played a role in the crisis, there were obviously other significant factors at work in the meltdown of the securities and credit markets worldwide. In the case of Lehman Brothers, what were the causes of its collapse? And what does that experience tell us about the future of the financial services markets? In answering these questions, consider the following account of Lehman's demise.

> **JOHN GAPPER, COST OF A WRONG TURN:**
> **THE BIG FREEZE PART 2 – THE FUTURE OF BANKING**

_____

FT.com, Aug. 5, 2008

On Friday August 3[, 2007,] last year, as US financial markets were approaching the summer doldrums and bankers began to head off for holidays on Long Island or Cape Cod, Bear Stearns held a conference call for investors.

Shares in the investment bank, the fifth largest in the world, had fallen as investors worried about the collapse of two hedge funds that it managed and its exposure to the troubled housing market. But few were prepared for the candour of Sam Molinaro, its chief financial officer. Instead of reassuring them about Bear Stearns' financial condition, he scared them even more: "I've been at this for 22 years. It's about as bad as I have seen it in the fixed income market during that period . . . [what] we have been seeing over the last eight weeks has been pretty extreme." . . .

---

2. The definition of "short sale" shall be the same definition used in Rule 200(a) of Regulation SHO and the requirements for marking orders "long" or "short" shall be the same as provided in Regulation SHO.

3. Short sales to be effected as a result of a put options exercise are subject to this Order. In addition, we note that short sales used to hedge would also be subject to this Order.

If all of this sounded bizarrely alarmist at the time, a year later it reads like a fair assessment of the havoc that was breaking out in financial markets as the liquidity that had washed through the US economy and the rest of the world abruptly froze.

As Americans defaulted on subprime mortgages in increasing numbers, bond markets became chaotic. Most of these mortgages had been securitised by banks and sold to investors in complex collateralised debt obligations, which were rated by credit agencies led by Moody's and Standard & Poor's. Investors knew that the lower-rated tranches would be at risk in any downturn, but few predicted the damage to investment grade securities. . . .

The chaos in the US housing market and structured finance rippled into the wholesale markets in which banks raise short-term finance. Trust evaporated as financial institutions hoarded cash and withdrew credit from others. The London interbank offered rate, the main measure of interbank lending rates, rose sharply.

The effect was devastating. Six weeks later, Northern Rock, the mortgage lender that relied on interbank funding, was rescued by the UK government after other institutions refused to lend to it. Seven months after Mr Molinaro's warning, Bear Stearns itself succumbed to the market crisis. It was given emergency funding by the Federal Reserve and forced to sell itself to JPMorgan Chase for $2.1bn [€1.3 billion, £1.1 billion], paying the ultimate price for the market's loss of confidence.

Financial institutions are still fighting to restore stability. Banks such as Citigroup, UBS and Merrill Lynch have made billions of dollars worth of asset writedowns, forced out chief executives and repeatedly raised new capital. Lehman Brothers has fought to persuade investors that it is more stable than Bear Stearns.

It is impossible yet to know the full damage from the credit crisis. Bank writedowns are estimated at $476 [billion] by the International Institute of Finance. This is still less than the $600 [billion] of US bank failures in the savings and loans crisis of the early 1990s but $1,600 [billion] has been cut from the global market capitalisation of banks.

Many bankers think the eventual bill will top the S&L crisis. . . . But, whatever the ultimate bill, the impact on investment banking and financial regulation will be profound. . . .

The crisis has called into question the existence of independent investment banks, the institutions that have been among the biggest winners of the past three decades of financial and trade liberalisation. Investment banks led by Goldman Sachs have grown rapidly and rewarded their employees lavishly: Wall Street banks paid bonuses of $33 [billion] last year.

But many analysts think that the crisis has shifted power in the direction of "universal" banks – those with retail as well as investment banking arms – and away from broker-dealers such as Goldman and Morgan Stanley. The latter may find it hard to keep on operating with small, highly leveraged balance sheets, relying on wholesale markets for funding. "It is pretty clear that retail deposit-taking institutions are in a stronger position . . . I think the business model will change significantly and there will be fewer independent investment banks," says James Wiener, a partner in Oliver Wyman, the financial consultancy.

Not surprisingly, the universal banks that have expanded into investment banking in the past decade – many by investing heavily in bond operations – agree with this. They think the crisis will give them an opportunity to grab business from the independents, or acquire them. "Stand-alone investment banks will struggle to operate in anything like the way they were before the crisis," says the head of investment banking at one commercial bank. "They are not going to be able to operate with the same degree of flexibility and leverage."

Investment banks have two challenges. One is to reassure investors that they are financially stable. Bear Stearns collapsed while it was making money and had, theoretically at least, a sound balance sheet. Its former leaders still complain that short-selling hedge funds spread false rumours to bring their institution down.

While they argue this point, however, the four remaining big investment banks have rushed to reduce their leverage and raise their capital reserves. Goldman Sachs, the strongest of them, now holds $90 [billion] in cash and liquid assets and its balance sheet debt has an average maturity of eight years. This makes them safer but it adds to their second challenge of making enough money to satisfy shareholders and keep their most highly valued employees from joining hedge funds or private equity groups.

Banks enjoyed a run from 1998 onwards (with a brief interruption after the September 11 2001 attacks) of rising profits and high ratings. They had been valued at one to 1.5 times their book value because of their earnings volatility but their share prices rose as they persuaded investors that they had learnt how to manage risk.

Few people believe that now and banks' share prices have fallen abruptly. Not only are their earnings back to being rated as they were before, but the banks have to find ways to replace the huge revenues from bond financing over the past decade. . . .

. . . The credit crisis has brought home once again the need for investment banks to have diverse earnings streams so that mishaps in one area can be offset elsewhere. In practice, only Goldman Sachs has had sufficient depth and breadth to ride out this crisis reasonably unscathed.

Before the crisis, others were trying to mimic Goldman's expertise in hedge funds and trading. Bear Stearns was trying to build its fund management arm, Merrill was continuing a long push to transcend its roots as a retail broker and Lehman was expanding outside fixed income. But Bear has gone and others have been set back.

Their capacity to bounce back is constrained by new limits on their balance sheets and freedom of manoeuvre. The market is imposing its own disciplines and regulators are likely to impose others. Bear Stearns' near-collapse prompted the biggest government intervention in the financial system since the splitting of banks and investment banks and the setting up of the Securities and Exchange Commission in the wake of the Great Depression.

The Federal Reserve has long provided a funding back-stop to banks that took retail deposits through its discount window, but investment banks were not given the same explicit backing. That policy changed during Bear's rescue, when the Treasury and the Fed judged that it was too central to the US financial system to be allowed to fail.

The Fed gave investment banks temporary access to the discount window and has since extended the guarantee. Even if it eventually closes off access, the precedent has been clearly established: in times of financial distress, the Fed will give financial backing to investment banks. . . .

Fed oversight of investment banks, instead of them being supervised mostly by the SEC, would come at a cost. . . .

When there was no implicit government guarantee, investment banks could run highly leveraged balance sheets, carry out a lot of proprietary trading and lend to hedge funds and private equity groups. Now they face scrutiny of, and perhaps curbs on, their most profitable activities.

Some investment bankers remain sanguine, arguing that the past few years was an era of super-profitability that is not likely to return in a hurry. They say that investment banks will be able to adapt after a year or two and resume as normal, albeit with lower revenues and share prices.

But the fear is that investment banks' advantages over their universal bank rivals have been eroded by this crisis. There are not many independents in any case. The disappearance of Bear leaves only Goldman, Morgan Stanley, Merrill Lynch and Lehman Brothers as big broker-dealers.

It may be that merchant banks such as Lazard, private equity groups such as Kohlberg Kravis Roberts, or hedge funds such as Citadel or Fortress will expand to fill the gap left by Bear. Consolidation in financial services has often prompted the rise of new players.

But there is another possibility: that investment banks such as Lehman and Merrill will give up the unequal struggle to match Goldman and be swallowed up into universal banks. Partners at Goldman, who have traditionally worried about being outsmarted by Morgan Stanley and others, now have another concern.

If their rivals cannot bounce back from the credit crisis of 2007, Goldman could end up as an industry of one. . . .

How risk refused to be sliced and diced

. . . [T]he irony is that CDOs [collateralised debt obligations, the structured finance vehicles that lay at the heart of the credit crisis] were designed to relieve banks of the necessity to hold loan risks on their balance sheets at all.

. . . [B]anks thought they had transformed themselves from lenders to intermediaries in credit markets, and investment banks believed they could lend money as effectively as commercial banks.

In practice, it did not work out that way. When the credit markets froze in August last year, many banks had not yet passed on the risk to others. Many were holding asset-backed securities in "warehouses" and were working on splicing them up into CDOs, getting them rated by a credit agency such as Moody's or Standard & Poor's.

This version of banking had developed over two decades with the evolution of credit derivatives and structured finance. Instead of a bank making loans and then either holding them on its balance sheet or syndicating them to others, it structured them into new securities.

This opened up the market for credit to all kinds of investors. The cashflow from a portfolio of mortgages could be spliced into a variety of securities with different interest rates, appealing to a wide range of buyers. Hedge funds and insurance companies became the holders of mortgage loans.

The collapse of the CDO market and recriminations among bankers, credit agencies, investors and regulators has called all of this into question. If the CDO market was riddled with such flawed assumptions and lax calculations, what does that say about the theory behind it? . . .

Indeed, the reason why banks moved first to loan syndication and then to securitisation was that they suffered so badly in past banking crises when the borrowers defaulted. Although CDOs failed to protect them, that was not entirely the fault of structured finance techniques.

For one thing, several banks were caught out not only because it took time to structure the securities but because they deliberately held on to what they regarded as "safe" tranches of loans. UBS was badly damaged by retaining "super-senior" CDO debt.

But banks will be a lot warier about treating structured finance as the cure-all for lending risk in future. They are unlikely to be given much choice:

investors in such securities will demand more transparency and may well require an originating bank to keep some exposure.

The ultimate lesson of the CDO collapse is that technology does not obviate the need to assess a borrower carefully. Neither banks nor credit agencies did this well enough on behalf of investors and it proved a painful experience for everyone.

3

WASHINGTON MUTUAL GOES UNDER

Washington National Building Loan and Investment Association was established in Seattle, Washington, exactly 119 years before it was placed in receivership – as Washington Mutual Bank – by the Office of Thrift Supervision (OTS).[1] Washington National changed its name to Washington Savings and Loan Association in June 1908 and eventually became Washington Mutual Savings Bank.

From as early as 1930, "WaMu" periodically grew by acquisition of other financial services firms, eventually becoming the third-largest mortgage lender in the United States. In 1983, it "demutualized" and acquired a brokerage firm, and by the end of the decade it had doubled in size. WaMu's 2001 acquisition of PNC Mortgage jump-started its residential mortgage business into the nation-wide market.[2] In October 2005, it acquired Providian, a subprime credit card issuer that had expanded into a more traditional credit card business, making WaMu the ninth-largest credit card company in the United States. Over the next few years, WaMu plunged itself into the subprime mortgage market, and the stage was set for its drowning in a flood of defaulting debt.

---

1. This historical summary is based largely upon a corporate history on http://Wamu.com, visited at various times during 2008. This website has since been coopted by http://Chase.com. *See* https://www.chase.com/wamuwelcome3/ (indicating migration of website).

2. *See* http://www.allbusiness.com/banking-finance/banking-lending-credit-services-mortgage/6048203-1.html (announcing acquisition from PNC Financial Services Group, Inc.).

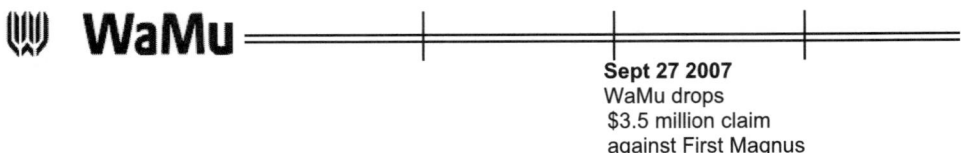

Sept 27 2007
WaMu drops
$3.5 million claim
against First Magnus

A. FROM "WHOO HOO" TO BOO HOO

1. Packed with Subprimes

WaMu's last year showed troubling signs almost from the start. In late September 2007, failed mortgage lender First Magnus Financial Corp. agreed in a bankruptcy court filing that it would drop its claims that WaMu be required to remit $1 billion in mortgage loans originated by First Magnus, and in return WaMu agreed to drop its claim to a separate pool of $3.15 million in First Magnus mortgages.[3] On September 30 came reports that WaMu was eliminating 1,000 employees, and that its investment portfolio was "packed with just the type of [subprime] home loans that are causing problems for homeowners and financial markets alike."[4]

2. Coming to Terms

As consumer anger about ambiguous or misunderstood mortgage loan terms and policies continued to grow,[5] WaMu announced that it had instituted a "key terms" policy that required mortgage brokers to explain material loan terms, such as the amount, term, variable rate and payment features, prepayment fees,

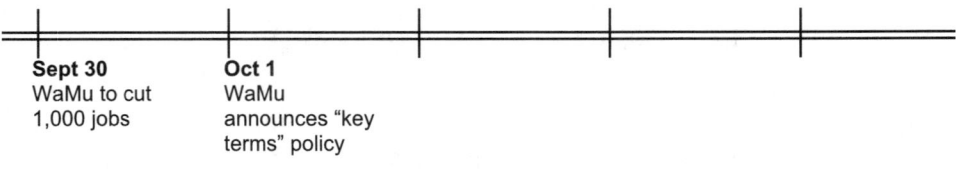

Sept 30
WaMu to cut
1,000 jobs

Oct 1
WaMu
announces "key
terms" policy

---

3. *First Magnus Has Deals with WaMu*, ARIZ. REPUBLIC, Sept. 27, 2007, at 3.

4. Danielle Reed, *WaMu Feels Subprime Pain, but Not as Deeply; Larger Deposit Base, Access to Low-Cost Funds Puts It on More Solid Footing Than Countrywide*, CHICAGO TRIB., Sept. 30, 2007, at C8.

5. *See, e.g.*, Vikas Bajaj & Miguel Helft, *The End of an American Dream: Creative Home Loans End in Lawsuits*, INT'L HERALD TRIB., Sept. 26, 2007, at 14 (reporting on suits by non-English speaking families against mortgage brokers and real estate agents for disclosure failures lack of translation of loan terms; noting WaMu role in providing some disputed loans).

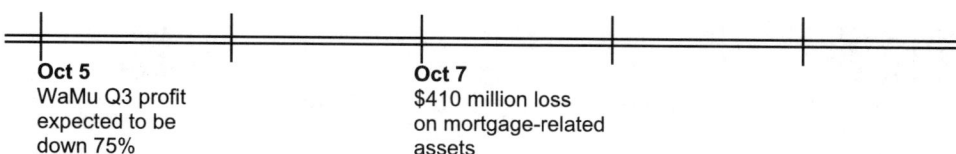

Oct 5
WaMu Q3 profit
expected to be
down 75%

Oct 7
$410 million loss
on mortgage-related
assets

and all loan points and fees.[6] WaMu even suggested that a representative might contact borrowers prior to loan closing "to review key loan terms."[7]

By October 5, 2007, there were reports in the press that WaMu third-quarter profit would be down by as much as 75 percent.[8] Two days later, WaMu acknowledged a $410 million dollar loss on mortgage-related assets.[9] By October 18, however, WaMu stock was down only 7.7 percent.[10]

Within a week, WaMu announced that it would commit $2 billion to refinance adjustable-rate mortgages.[11] The following day, market value of WaMu stock rose 4.7 percent in a trading session that saw some bounce in financial services stocks, generally.[12] The bounce was short-lived, however, as the financial crisis deepened and the New York Attorney General escalated his ongoing investigation into the causes and effects of the crisis in broadening civil and criminal probes.

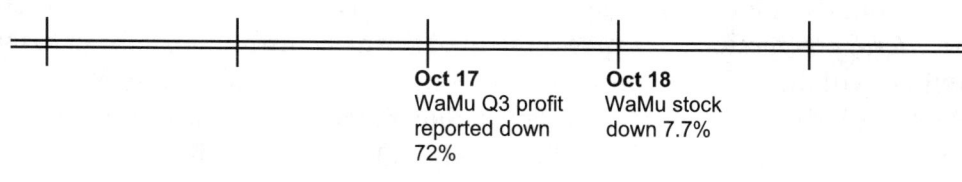

Oct 17
WaMu Q3 profit
reported down
72%

Oct 18
WaMu stock
down 7.7%

---

6. *WaMu Brokers to Explain Loan Terms in More Detail*, [Portland, OR] Bus. J., Oct. 1, 2007, *available at* 2007 WLNR 19212823.

7. *Id.*

8. Ben White & David Wighton, *Credit Squeeze Costs Banks $18bn*, FT.com, Oct. 5, 2008. When disclosed two weeks later, the loss amounted to a 72 percent decrease. Chris Bryant, *US Stocks Mixed as Economy Fears Grows*, FT.com, Oct. 17, 2007.

9. David Wighton, *JPMorgan and BofA Poised for Total $3bn Writedown*, FT.com, Oct. 7, 2007 (noting WaMu losses on mortgages held for sale, mortgage-backed securities and trading business).

10. *A Losing Session Ends on a Late Bounce*, N.Y. TIMES, Oct. 19, 2007, at C10, *available at* 2007 WLNR 20542525.

11. *Industry Leader Says It Will Work with Borrowers, and That Should Be Good for Everyone*, LAS VEGAS SUN, Oct. 25, 2007, at A4, *available at* 2007 WLNR 20998537.

12. E. Scott Reckard, *Earnings; Investors Look Beyond Loss at Countrywide; The Quarterly Deficit Is Worse Than Expected, but the Stock Shoots Up 32% After the Lender Says the Worst Is Over*, L.A. TIMES, Oct. 27, 2007, at C1.

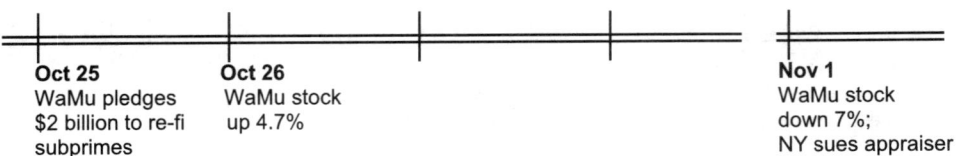

Oct 25
WaMu pledges
$2 billion to re-fi
subprimes

Oct 26
WaMu stock
up 4.7%

Nov 1
WaMu stock
down 7%;
NY sues appraiser

3. Cuomo and *Cuomo*

Crucial to the high volume and quick turn-over in the subprime mortgage market were the mortgage brokers, which trawled for prospective borrowers and processed the application paperwork, and the real estate appraisers, which routinely plugged in the right numbers to push the applications through to closing. Without the willing partners, the mortgage lenders might not have been able to sustain the pace that made subprimes the extraordinary growth market that they became. Accordingly, Attorney General Andrew M. Cuomo accused First American Corporation and its appraisal unit eAppraiseIT of inflating the value of homes that served as collateral for subprime mortgages under pressure from WaMu.[13] Although WaMu was not named as a defendant, market value of its stock immediately fell 7 percent, the culmination of a two-month loss of 30 percent of market value.[14]

Cuomo's tiptoeing around WaMu was largely due to the vexing problem of *federal* preemption of *state* regulation of financial institutions subject to the authority of the U.S. Comptroller of the Currency (as in the case of Wachovia Bank, N.A.[15]) or the Office of Thrift Supervision (as in the case of WaMu itself).[16] While the state official did publicly endorse stronger federal consumer financial protection and prohibitions against appraisal manipulation,[17] it was his expanding investigation of abuses in the residential mortgage market that

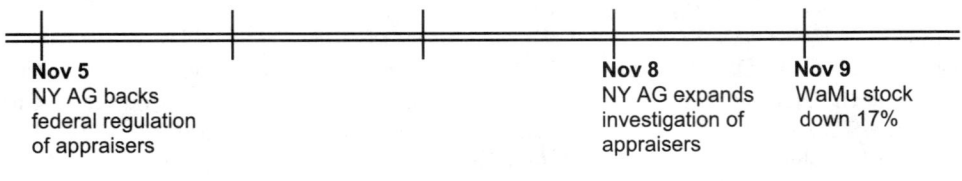

Nov 5
NY AG backs
federal regulation
of appraisers

Nov 8
NY AG expands
investigation of
appraisers

Nov 9
WaMu stock
down 17%

---

13. *Contagion Fears Grow on Subprime Writedowns*, FT.com, Nov. 1, 2007.

14. *Id.*

15. *See Watters v. Wachovia Bank, N.A.*, 550 U.S. 1 (2007) (preempting state regulation of mortgage lender that was subsidiary of national bank).

16. On the impact of preemption on the meltdown, see Chapter 5, *infra*, § A.

17. *Attorney General Cuomo Backs Federal Legislation Prohibiting Intimidation, Coercion of Appraisals*, US STATE NEWS, Nov. 5, 2007, *available at* 2007 WLNR 21890257.

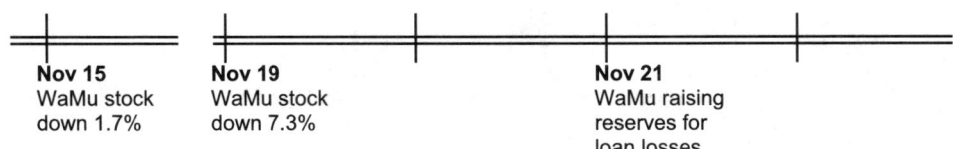

Nov 15
WaMu stock
down 1.7%

Nov 19
WaMu stock
down 7.3%

Nov 21
WaMu raising
reserves for
loan losses

would eventually lead to a significant amelioration of the preemption problem.[18] In the meantime, Cuomo continued to expand the investigation of the crisis, reaching into Fannie Mae and Freddie Mac files for information reflecting the "pattern of collusion between lenders and appraisers" in mortgage loans that the two government-sponsored enterprises had purchased from lenders like WaMu.[19]

On the day following news of the expanded investigation, WaMu stock closed down 17 percent, on reports that its expected 2007 losses would amount to almost $3 billion because of its exposure to subprime mortgages and other weak assets.[20] This market value trend continued over the next two weeks.[21] Finally, on November 21, 2007, it was reported that WaMu was raising its loan loss reserves in response to burgeoning delinquencies in its loan portfolio.[22]

What should have been reassuring news to the market turned out to be of no avail – the shadow of the appraiser investigation continued to color the market's perception of WaMu. News reports began comparing and contrasting the alleged WaMu-eAppraiseIT collusion over mortgage appraisals with such

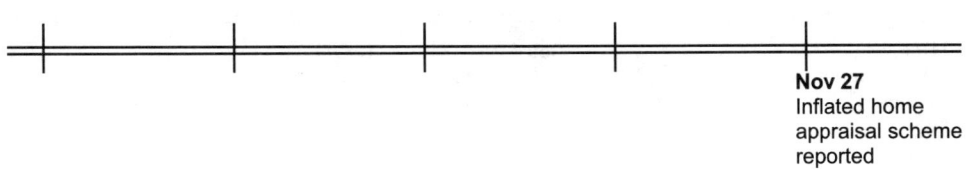

Nov 27
Inflated home
appraisal scheme
reported

---

18. *Cuomo v. Clearing House Ass'n*, — U.S. —, 129 S.Ct. 2710 (2009). For discussion of the impact of *Cuomo* on the application of preemption to state regulation of financial services, see Chapter 5, *infra*, § A.

19. *New York Widens Inquiry on Mortgages*, N.Y. TIMES, Nov. 8, 2007, at C8 *available at* 2007 WLNR 22022751.

20. Karen Talley, *Moving the Market: Capital One Leads Financials Downward; American Express, GM Also Tumble; Foster Wheeler Rises*, WALL ST. J., Nov. 9, 2007, at C7.

21. *See, e.g.*, Chris Bryant, *Wall Street Lower on JC Penny Warning*, FT.com, Nov. 15, 2007 (noting WaMu stock decline of 1.7 percent); Michael Mackenzie & Chris Bryant, *Wall Street Falls Amid Credit Fears*, FT.com, Nov. 19, 2007 (reporting WaMu market value decline of 7.3 percent).

22. *Thrifts' Quarterly Profits Tumble in Housing Downturn*, CHICAGO TRIB., Nov. 21, 2007, at C5.

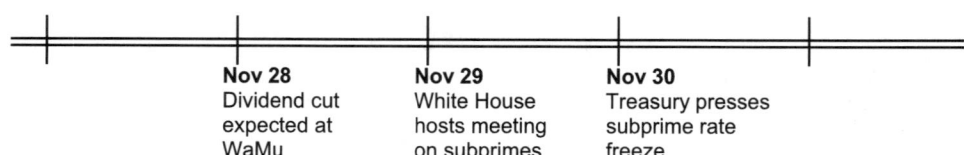

Nov 28
Dividend cut
expected at
WaMu

Nov 29
White House
hosts meeting
on subprimes

Nov 30
Treasury presses
subprime rate
freeze

past corporate corruption *causes célèbres* as Enron, Tyco, and WorldCom.[23] In an unfortunate collocation of events, the day after this story broke came news that WaMu was expected to cut its dividend.[24]

4. The Crisis Spreads

Matters quickly went from bad to worse – the Bush Administration tried to help. On Thursday, November 29, 2007, financial industry representatives, including JPMorgan Chase, WaMu, Wells Fargo, and Citigroup, met with Treasury Secretary Hank Paulson and FDIC Chairman Sheila Bair to discuss interest rates on distressed subprime loans, with particular attention to residential mortgagors who might default if their adjustable interest rates increased.[25] With many rates scheduled to pop by at least 30 percent, Treasury was pressing for a temporary freeze on subprime rates.[26] Participating firms would voluntarily help up to approximately 1.2 million mortgagors who may be anticipating difficulty paying subprime mortgages. In some cases, participating loan servicers would freeze mortgages at their low introductory rates; in

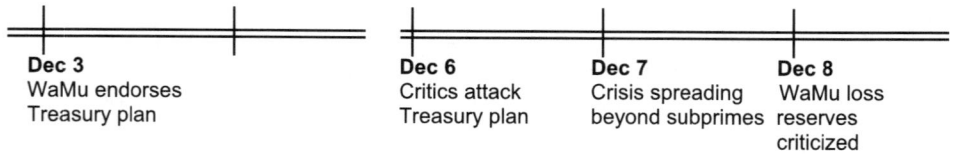

Dec 3
WaMu endorses
Treasury plan

Dec 6
Critics attack
Treasury plan

Dec 7
Crisis spreading
beyond subprimes

Dec 8
WaMu loss
reserves
criticized

---

23. *See, e.g.*, Barrie McKenna, *Shades of Enron, Tyco Allegations. Will the Results Be Different?*, GLOBE & MAIL (Can.), Nov. 27, 2007, at B18, *available at* 2007 WLNR 23395285 ("the alleged relationship between lenders and appraisers seems reminiscent of the analysts who didn't do their homework on once-high flying companies such as Tyco and WorldCom because it might jeopardize lucrative underwriting business"). For an excellent treatment of the implications of the Enron scandal, see NANCY B. RAPOPORT, JEFFREY D. VAN NIEL & BALA G. DHARAN (eds.), ENRON AND OTHER CORPORATE FIASCOS: THE CORPORATE SCANDAL READER (2d ed. 2009).

24. George Anders, *Business: Dividend Cut Shouldn't Be Death Sentence*, WALL ST. J., Nov. 28, 2007, at A2.

25. Ben White, Stephanie Kirchgaessner & Saskia Scholtes, *US Subprime Plan Faces Hurdles*, FT.com, Nov. 30, 2007.

26. Edmund L. Andrews, *U.S. Urges Freezing Some Rates on Loans*, N.Y. TIMES, Dec. 1, 2007, at C1, *available at* 2007 WLNR 23739065.

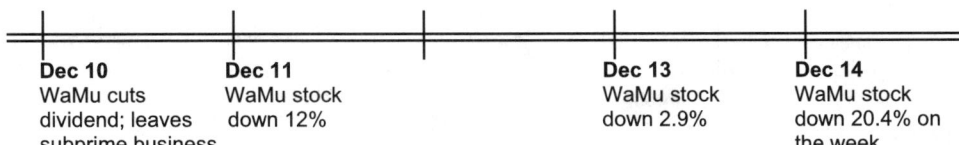

| Dec 10 | Dec 11 | | Dec 13 | Dec 14 |
| WaMu cuts dividend; leaves subprime business | WaMu stock down 12% | | WaMu stock down 2.9% | WaMu stock down 20.4% on the week |

others, participating credit counselors or loan servicers would assist mortgagors in the refinancing process. Under the plan there would be no relief for mortgagors who are already in foreclosure, who have already refinanced, or who have been more than 60 days delinquent on more than one payment over the past year. Ironically, the plan essentially excluded mortgagors with good credit scores or otherwise capable of affording higher reset rates over the next two years.

With rates tightening even for prospective mortgagors with good credit, on December 3, 2007, WaMu endorsed the Treasury plan,[27] but it brought no shelter to WaMu. Critics almost immediately began attacking the plan from every conceivable angle – it offered little or no assistance to the most distressed mortgagors; it would bail out reckless borrowers and prolong the crisis; it would constrict the creditworthy; it would violate the investment contracts of purchasers of securitized mortgage pools by denying them their expected rate of return.[28] Already the crisis was spreading beyond the subprime market, with "turmoil on Wall Street and . . . the specter of an economic slowdown. In the third quarter, home foreclosures hit their highest rate since at least 1972."[29]

WaMu's situation was also becoming significantly worse. On December 8, 2007, it was criticized for improperly valuing its loans for investment purposes and was reportedly suffering from "low quality income."[30] Two days later, WaMu announced that it was cutting its dividend and would eliminate an

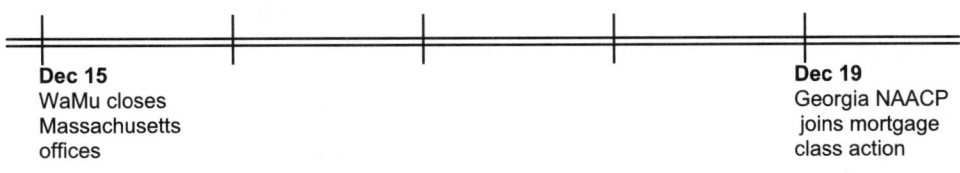

| Dec 15 | | | | Dec 19 |
| WaMu closes Massachusetts offices | | | | Georgia NAACP joins mortgage class action |

---

27. William Neikirk, *U.S. Puts Heat on Lenders to Freeze Rates; Hope to Avert Foreclosure Surge, Recession,* CHICAGO TRIB., Dec. 4, 2008, at C1.

28. Ben White, Saskia Scholtes, & Stephanie Kirchgaessner, *Critics from All Corners Quick on the Draw,* FT.com, Dec. 6, 2007.

29. Michael M. Philips, Serena Ng & John D. McKinnon, *Battle Lines Form Over Mortgage Plan,* WALL ST. J., Dec. 7, 2008, at A1.

30. Herb Greenberg, *MarketWatch Weekend Investor: This Game Theory Is Cautionary Tale,* WALL ST. J., Dec. 8, 2007, at B3.

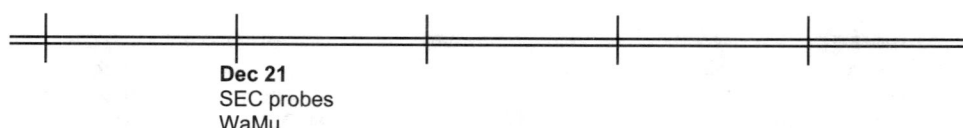

Dec 21
SEC probes
WaMu

additional 3,150 employees.[31] WaMu was also ending its involvement in subprime lending.[32] By December 11, WaMu stock closed down 12 percent.[33] It continued this free-fall and ended down 20.4 percent on the week.[34] It also abruptly closed all seven of its Massachusetts offices.[35]

WaMu's horizons were narrowing. On December 19, the Georgia State Conference of the NAACP filed an amended class action in the federal district court for the Central District of California against seventeen major national mortgage lenders, including WaMu, alleging that the lenders had made subprime mortgage loans to African American buyers, even when the mortgagors were qualified for more traditional loans.[36] Two days later, news reports indicated that the Securities and Exchange Commission was investigating whether WaMu had accurately disclosed to investors of mortgage-backed securities how the underlying mortgage loans were appraised and whether it properly accounted for its loans in its periodic disclosures to its shareholders.[37]

By the end of the month the crisis had spread beyond subprimes and into

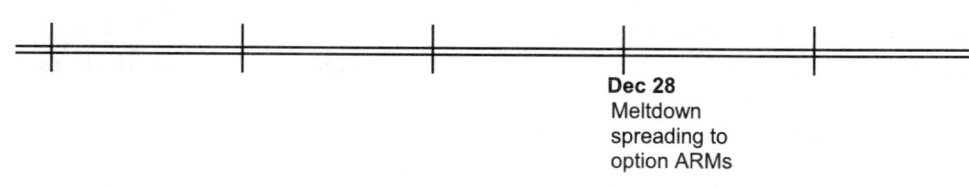

Dec 28
Meltdown
spreading to
option ARMs

---

31. Jad Mouawad, *Large Lenders Cutting Dividend and Jobs*, N.Y. TIMES, Dec. 11, 2007, at C8, *available at* 2007 WLNR 24413655.

32. *Id.*

33. Vikas Bajaj, *Shares Fall on a Rate Cut Considered a Disappointment to Fed Watchers*, N.Y. TIMES, Dec. 12, 2007, at C4, *available at* 2007 WLNR 24487899.

34. Chris Bryant, *Wall St Unease About Credit Squeeze Remains*, FT.com, Dec. 14, 2007.

35. Jerry Kronenberg, *Chase Offers Jobs to Laid-Off WaMu Workers*, BOSTON HERALD, Dec. 15, 2007, at 20.

36. Joe Rauch, Georgia NAACP Joins Class Action Suit Against Mortgage Lenders, Atlanta Bus. Chron., Dec. 20, 2007.

37. Amir Efrati, *SEC Probes WaMu on Appraisals – Regulator Checks Handling of Loans Possibly Based on Inflation Valuations*, WALL ST. J., Dec. 21, 2007, at A2.

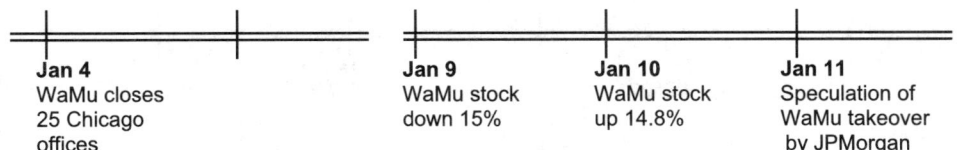

| Jan 4 | Jan 9 | Jan 10 | Jan 11 |
| WaMu closes 25 Chicago offices | WaMu stock down 15% | WaMu stock up 14.8% | Speculation of WaMu takeover by JPMorgan |

the pay-option adjustable-rate mortgages ("option ARMs"),[38] and even into prime mortgages.[39] At the beginning of the new year, WaMu announced that it was closing 25 of its last 146 Chicago-area branches, local offices, bringing its closings to 30 percent of its Chicago branches from their peak in 2006.[40]

5. Rumor Has It

By the second week in January 2008, WaMu stock was fluctuating significantly in value, on the strength of conflicting reports about likely future economic performance.[41] On Friday, January 11, a new rumor circulated, that WaMu *might* be the target of a *possible* takeover by JP Morgan Chase.[42] In that peculiar market climate, disclosure of a fourth quarter loss of $1.87 billion[43]

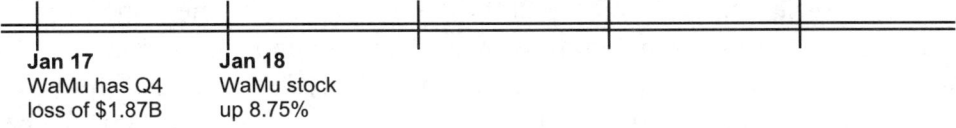

| Jan 17 | Jan 18 |
| WaMu has Q4 loss of $1.87B | WaMu stock up 8.75% |

---

38. An option ARM is a mortgage loan that "gives a borrower the option of paying less than the interest due, causing the loan balance to rise. If it rises too much – say, by 10% or 15% – the opportunity to make a low payment vanishes and the required payment skyrockets." E. Scott Reckard, *Mortgage Meltdown; Prime Loans Seeing Rise in Defaults; Delinquencies Among Holders of Risky Option ARMs Are Increasing as Their Minimum Payments Climb*, L.A. TIMES, Dec. 28, 2008, at C1.

39. *Id.*

40. Becky Yerak, *Washington Mutual to Cut 25 Branches; 150 Workers May Move to Other Units*, CHICAGO TRIB., Jan. 5, 2008, at C3.

41. *See, e.g.*, Daniel Pimlott, *Countrywide Shares Plunge on Foreclosure News*, FT.com, Jan. 9, 2008. (reporting on WaMu 15 percent decline on fears of rising mortgage defaults); Chris Bryant, *US Stocks Rally on Rate Cut Hopes*, FT.com, Jan. 10, 2008 (reporting on WaMu stock 14.8 percent rise on rumors of Fed rate action).

42. *See, e.g.*, David Reilly & Peter Eavis, *Beware, Investors, of Search for Countrywide-Like Deals*, WALL ST. J., Jan. 12, 2008, at B1, *available at* 2008 WLNR 788884 (reporting on speculation that WaMu was candidate for takeover); Jeff May, *Financial Firms Could Be Looking at Ugly Week; The Week Ahead*, STAR-LEDGER (Newark), Jan. 13, 2008, at 1, *available at* 2008 WLNR 720787 (reporting on speculation that JPMorgan would bid for WaMu).

43. *Loss Hits $1.87 Billion in Quarter at WaMu*, N.Y. TIMES, Jan. 18, 2008, at C4, *available at* 2008 WLNR 1016398.

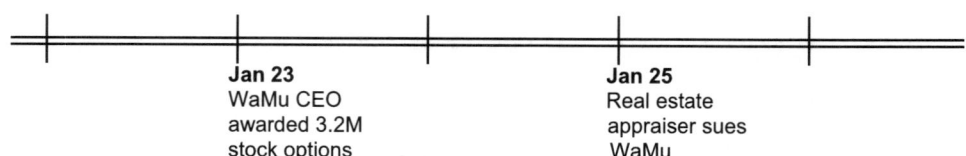

Jan 23
WaMu CEO
awarded 3.2M
stock options

Jan 25
Real estate
appraiser sues
WaMu

was followed by an 8.75 percent rise in the market value of WaMu stock the day after the loss was reported in the press.[44] Three days later came reports that WaMu had awarded CEO Kerry Killinger 3.2 million stock options for 2008.[45]

This serene situation began to fray around the edges. Jennifer Wertz, a California real estate appraiser, brought suit against WaMu, claiming that she had been blacklisted for refusing to provide favorable appraisals despite declining market conditions.[46] Two days later came reports that Clayton Holdings, a Connecticut firm that analyzed the quality of securitized home mortgages for investment banks, had agreed to provide information to New York state prosecutors about the risks posed by subprime mortgages, information that could have prevented the collapse of mortgage-backed securities but had been withheld from investors.[47]

Still, by the end of January 2008 there were still some hopeful signs. Financial institutions – including WaMu – had begun to pump up many ATM and other service fees to generate income to offset market losses.[48] In the last trading days of January, WaMu stock was trending up.[49] It closed up 35.4 percent on the week.[50]

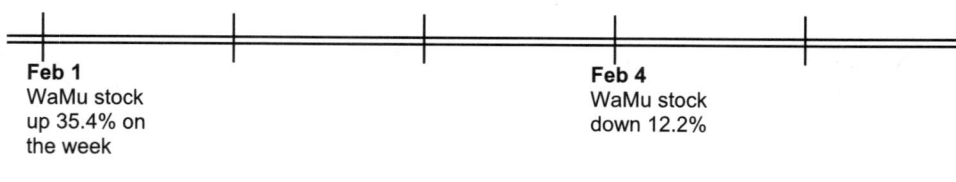

Feb 1
WaMu stock
up 35.4% on
the week

Feb 4
WaMu stock
down 12.2%

---

44. *Deal Talk Lifts WaMu*, CHICAGO SUN TIMES, Jan. 20, 2008, at A34, *available at* 2008 WLNR 3388597.

45. *WaMu Awards CEO Options*, L.A. TIMES, Jan. 23, 2008, at C9.

46. Kenneth R. Harney, *Appraiser's Lawsuit Puts Lenders on Notice*, WASH. POST, Jan. 26, 2008, at F1.

47. Jenny Anderson & Vikas Bajaj, *Reviewer of Subprime Loans Agrees to Aid Inquiry of Banks*, N.Y. TIMES, Jan. 27, 2008, at A1.

48. David Enrich, *Ailing Banks Begin to Raise Fees; Housing Slump Tied to Increases; ATM Charges, Other Nuisance Fees Go Up*, SEATTLE TIMES, Jan. 29, 2008, at E1.

49. *Stocks Buoyed by Reports; Strong Earnings Data Help Calm Investors' Recession Fears as They Wait for a Rate Cut*, L.A. TIMES, Jan. 30, 2008, at C4 (noting 6.8 percent rise in WaMu stock market value, following CEO's prediction that 2008 net interest income would exceed company forecast).

50. Chris Bryant, *Wall Street Rises in Volatile Week*, FT.com, Feb. 1, 2008.

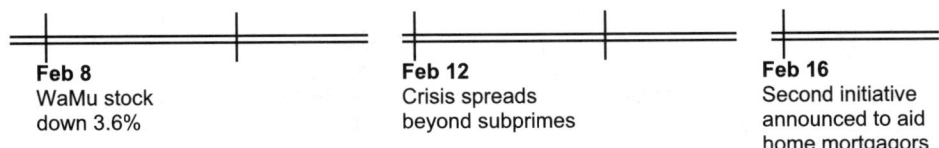

Feb 8
WaMu stock
down 3.6%

Feb 12
Crisis spreads
beyond subprimes

Feb 16
Second initiative
announced to aid
home mortgagors

6. A Falling Market

The good news dried up in February 2008. On the first Monday of the month, WaMu stock lost 12.2 percent in market value, on fears that rising unemployment would hurt the retail credit market.[51] This trend continued throughout the week.[52] The prime mortgage market was beginning to collapse into the crisis that began in the subprimes.[53]

By mid-February, the Bush Administration was promoting a new initiative to help struggling homeowners. "Project Lifeline" called for a 30-day moratorium on foreclosures for any mortgagor at least three months behind on payments.[54] Despite its endorsement of the new initiative, there appeared to be little upside for WaMu.

A week later, there were reports that WaMu CEO Killinger had declined his 2007 bonus,[55] and two days later Goldman Sachs cut WaMu stock from "neutral" to "sell," on fears that mortgage losses would increase as housing prices continued to decline.[56] By the end of February, WaMu had announced the closure of 40 more branches nationwide.[57]

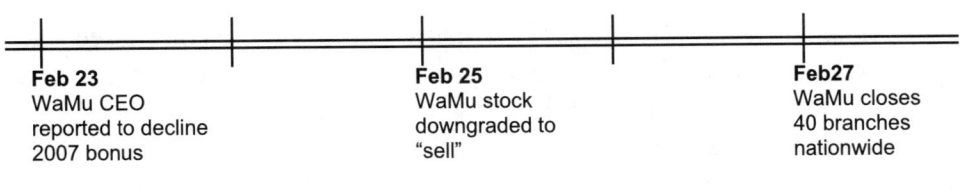

Feb 23
WaMu CEO
reported to decline
2007 bonus

Feb 25
WaMu stock
downgraded to
"sell"

Feb 27
WaMu closes
40 branches
nationwide

---

51. Chris Bryant, *US Stocks Retreat as Investors Lock in Profits*, FT.com, Feb. 4, 2008.

52. *See, e.g.*, *Financials Bearing the Brunt of Latest Sell-Off*, MIDNIGHT TRADER, Feb. 8, 2008, *available at* 2008 WLNR 2478457 (reporting 3.6 percent decline in WaMu market value).

53. Vikas Bajaj & Louise Story, *Mortgage Crisis Spreads Beyond Subprime Loans*, N.Y. TIMES, Feb. 12, 2008, at A1, *available at* 2008 WLNR 2676886.

54. *Another Positive Step to Help Homeowners; Government, Private Sector Are Working with Borrowers*, STAR TRIB. (Minneapolis), Feb. 16, 2008, at 16A.

55. Erin White, *Executive Pay: Lavishly Rewarded Trio Faces an Embarrassing Day*, WALL ST. J., Feb. 23, 2008, at A2.

56. Stacey-Marie Ishmael, *Wall St Rallies as Monolines Retain Rating*, FT.com, Feb. 25, 2008.

57. *Fed Auction Pumps Another 30B into Banks*, ST. PETERSBURG TIMES (Fla.), Feb. 27, 2008, at 2D, *available at* 2008 WLNR 383011.

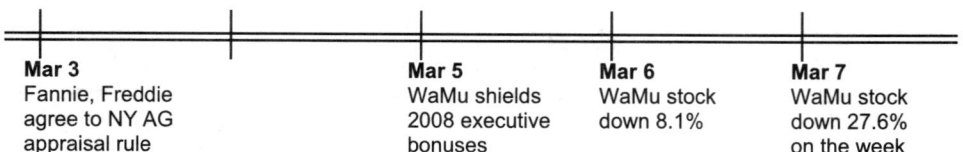

Mar 3		Mar 5	Mar 6	Mar 7
Fannie, Freddie agree to NY AG appraisal rule		WaMu shields 2008 executive bonuses	WaMu stock down 8.1%	WaMu stock down 27.6% on the week

7. A Bad Month Ends Well

March 2008 was a particularly harrowing month for WaMu, as the appraiser controversy continued. Responding to the continuing state investigation of appraisers, on Monday, March 3, 2008, Fannie Mae and Freddie Mac entered into an agreement with the New York Attorney General in which they pledged to buy mortgages only from lenders that used independent appraisers.[58] This shift, which was essentially a repudiation of the appraisal practices of large lenders like Countrywide Financial and WaMu, was coldly received by the Office of Thrift Supervision, WaMu's federal regulator.[59]

Two days later, new reports illustrated WaMu's peculiar approach to damage control. The WaMu board of directors had set compensation targets for CEO Killinger and more than 100 other WaMu executives that would "exclude" – board-speak for "ignore" – some costs tied to mortgage losses and foreclosures in calculating 2008 bonuses.[60] Quantitative approaches to performance evaluation would not factor in the negative impact of loan-loss provisions for mortgages or foreclosure costs. In SEC filings, the board's human resources committee stressed "the need to evaluate performance across a wide range of factors."[61] In these crisis conditions, the committee said it would "subjectively evaluate company performance in credit risk management and other strategic actions"[62] in deciding on bonuses.

The market's reaction to these developments was markedly negative. For the first week of March, WaMu stock was down 27.6 percent, with its credit

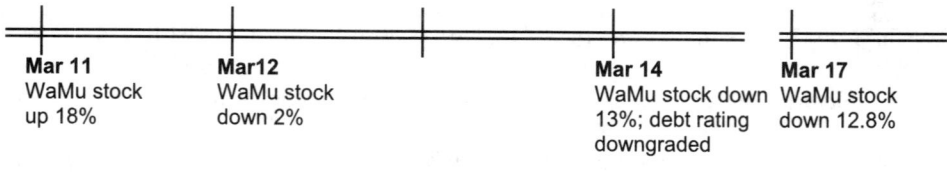

Mar 11	Mar12		Mar 14	Mar 17
WaMu stock up 18%	WaMu stock down 2%		WaMu stock down 13%; debt rating downgraded	WaMu stock down 12.8%

---

58. Vikas Bajaj, *In Deal with Cuomo, Mortgage Giants Accept Appraisal Standards*, N.Y. TIMES, March 4, 2008, at C3, *available at* 2008 WLNR 4264666.

59. *Id.*

60. Valerie Bauerlein & Ruth Simon, *WaMu Board Shields Executives' Bonuses*, WALL ST. J., March 5, 2008, at A3.

61. *Id.*

62. *Id.*

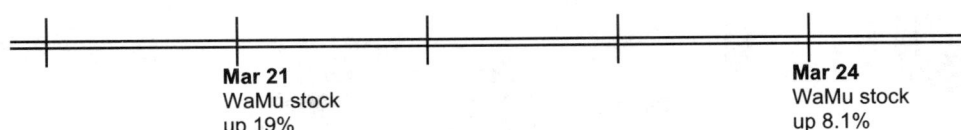

rating cut and further downgrading anticipated.[63] With the exception of a substantial one-day rally,[64] prompted by rumors of possible new investors, WaMu stock took a beating during the next two weeks.[65] On Friday, March 14, after Moody's cut WaMu's credit rating again due to "rapid deterioration of the residential housing sector in the first quarter," WaMu stock declined 13 percent.[66]

Efforts by regulators to prompt more trading by Fannie Mae and Freddie Mac momentarily came to the aid of mortgage-related firms like WaMu. By the next Friday, WaMu stock responded by closing up 19 percent.[67] This hopeful trend continued during the remainder of March,[68] but bad news was about to eclipse this market optimism.

8. A Good Month Ends Badly

With analysts predicting that WaMu would not see profitability until 2010, on April 4, 2008, WaMu stock closed down 11.5 percent.[69] However, by the end

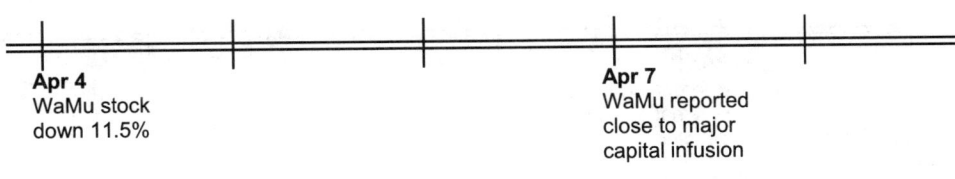

63. Stacey-Marie Ishmael & Michael Mckenzie, *Wall Street Hit by Surprise Decline in Jobs*, FT.com, March 7, 2008.

64. *See* Vikas Bajaj & Michael M. Grynbaum, *Fed Steps in, and Stocks Take Off, Dow Up 416*, N.Y. TIMES, March 12, 2008, at C1, *available at* 2008 WLNR 4807580 (noting effect of rumors).

65. *See, e.g., A Day After a Big Gain, Markets Turn Wary Again*, N.Y. TIMES, March 13, 2008, at C8, *available at* 2008 WLNR 4882758 (noting weakened financial sector); Jenny Anderson, *Aftershocks of a Collapse, with a Bank at the Epicenter*, N.Y. TIMES, March 18, 2008, at C1, *available at* 2008 WLNR 5259395 (noting decline in Lehman Brothers and WaMu market value following collapse of Bear Stearns and its fire sale to JP Morgen Chase).

66. *Credit Crunch: In Brief*, WALL ST. J., March 15, 2008, at B6.

67. Geoffrey Rogow, *Lehman, Goldman, Morgan Stanley Rise – Citigroup Climbs with Layoff News; GE Gets an Upgrade*, WALL ST. J., March 21, 2008, at C8.

68. Jeremy Lemer, *Wall St Higher on Housing Data*, FT.com, March 24, 2008.

69. *Best Week for Nasdaq Since '06*, N.Y. TIMES, April 5, 2008, at C6.

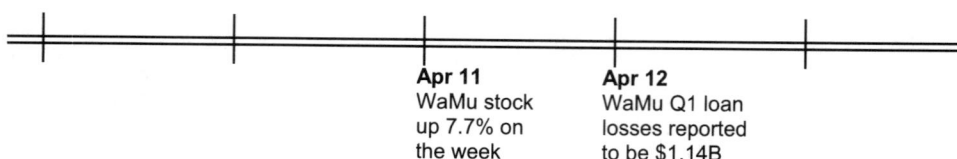

Apr 11
WaMu stock
up 7.7% on
the week

Apr 12
WaMu Q1 loan
losses reported
to be $1.14B

of the first week of the month, there were reports that the firm might be close to obtaining a $5 billion capital injection from new investors, including the private equity group TPG.[70] WaMu in fact secured a $7 billion capital infusion, diluting existing shareholder equity by 50 percent and making steep dividend cuts almost inevitable.[71] Still, WaMu stock closed up 7.7 percent on the week.[72]

The following day came reports that WaMu had suffered first quarter loan losses of $1.14 billion.[73] Three days later, WaMu shareholders exacted a revenge of sorts by forcing the resignation of the director who served as the chair of the WaMu board's finance committee.[74] By the end of the month, WaMu stock resumed its steep decline.[75]

9. Closing Down and Closing In

The drumbeat could now be heard rather clearly. On May 1, 2008, came reports that WaMu would close a mortgage division and would eliminate 1,000 employees.[76] And with that, WaMu continued its decline.[77] By mid-May, there

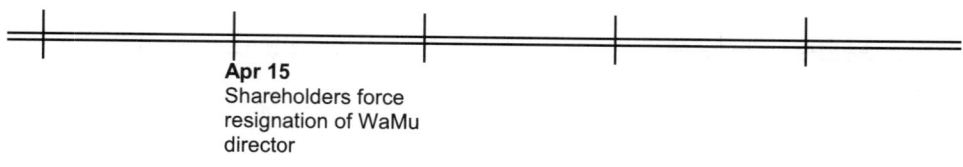

Apr 15
Shareholders force
resignation of WaMu
director

70. *WaMu's Injection*, FT.com, April 7, 2008.

71. *American Banks: Not So Thrifty*, THE ECONOMIST, April 12, 2008, at 37.

72. Jeremy Lemer, *Wall Street Soured by Poor GE Results*, FT.com, April 11, 2008.

73. *American Banks, supra* note 71.

74. Ben White & Francesco Guerrera, *WaMu Board Director Forced Out*, FT.com, April 16, 2008.

75. *See, e.g.,* Jeremy Lemer, *Wrigley Bid Eases Credit Fears on Wall St.*, FT.com, Aug. 28, 2008, (noting WaMu market value decline of 4.3 percent in Monday trading).

76. Michael Andrews, *Efficiency Ratios Take a Hit*, AM. BANKERS ASS'N BANKING J., May 1, 2008, at 8, *available at* 2008 WLNR 25525476.

77. *See, e.g.,* Rob Curran, *Fannie, Citigroup, WaMu Give Back Gains – AIG Drops 6.9% as Merrill Declines; Disney Rises 2.9%*, WALL ST. J., May 8, 2008, at C5 (reporting WaMu 5.7 percent loss of market value on May 7, 2008); Rob Curran, *Freeport, Unilever, Alcoa Post Solid Gains – Fannies, AIG Lead Financials Lower; Barr Tumbles 23%*, WALL ST. J., May 9, 2008, at C6. (reporting WaMu 4 percent loss of market value on May 8, 2008).

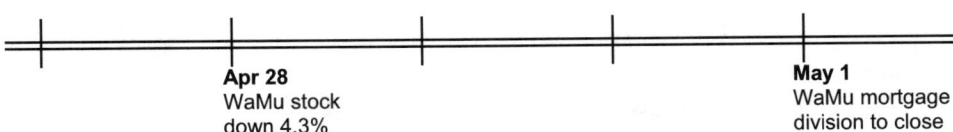

Apr 28
WaMu stock
down 4.3%

May 1
WaMu mortgage
division to close

were reports that WaMu, among others, was freezing lines of credit nationwide as housing values plunged.[78] By May 19, WaMu stock was burdened with a "sell" rating by analysts.[79] It seemed that WaMu was heading for a fire sale, like Bear Stearns before it.[80]

10. Spiraling Downwards

With its stock having lost some 80 percent of market value in a year, WaMu announced that CEO Killinger was stepping down as chairman of the board.[81] The following day WaMu stock closed down 2.8 percent.[82] By the end of the week, it posted another 12.5 percent loss.[83] This downward trend continued with substantial daily losses in market value throughout the rest of the month. Confirming these developments, the NEW YORK TIMES reported on June 21

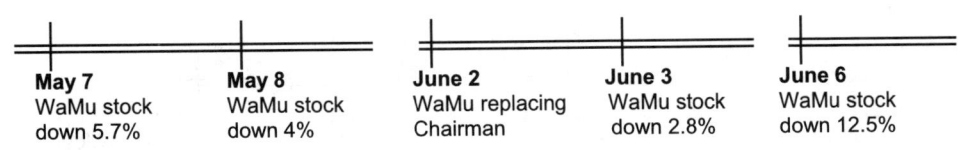

May 7
WaMu stock
down 5.7%

May 8
WaMu stock
down 4%

June 2
WaMu replacing
Chairman

June 3
WaMu stock
down 2.8%

June 6
WaMu stock
down 12.5%

---

78. Vivien Lou Chen, *Bank of America, Other Lenders Act: Credit Lines Are Vanishing as Property Values Plunge; Countrywide Suspends Almost All Home-Equity Lines in Las Vegas*, CHARLOTTE OBSERVER, May 10, 2008, at 4D *available at* 2008 WLNR 8800136.

79. *See, e.g.*, Stephanie Chen, *Best on the Street (A Special Report): 2008 Analysts Survey – Thrifts*, WALL ST. J., May 19, 2008, at R10 (reporting analyst advice to "run away" from savings association stocks, including WaMu).

80. Kate Kelly, *The Fall of Bear Stearns: Lost Opportunities Haunt Final Days of Bear Stearns – Executives Bickered over Raising Cash, Cutting Mortgages*, WALL ST. J., May 27, 2008, at A1 (reporting growing belief that WaMu was headed in same direction as Bear Stearns, purchased by JPMorgan Chase for $2 a share). On the demise of Bear Stearns, see *supra* at 34-35.

81. Jeremy Lemer, *Wall St Down Amid Fears over Bank*, FT.com, June 2, 2008.

82. Rob Curran, *Lehman, WaMu Both Lose Ground – Tyson Foods, Boeing Also Post Declines; Toll Brothers Gains*, WALL ST. J., June 4, 2008, at C7.

83. Jeremy Lemer, *Jump in Jobless Rate Pummels Wall Street*, FT.com, June 6, 2008.

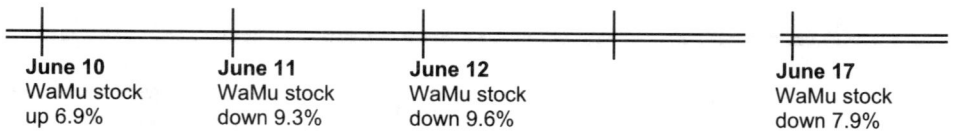

that WaMu had cut credit lines by 10 percent in the first quarter.[84] It seemed effectively to be putting itself out of business.

11. Hope Evaporates

A slight uptick in the market at the beginning of July 2008 gave a momentary glimmer of hope to WaMu stock,[85] but this quickly evaporated. NAACP claims of predatory lending on the part of WaMu and other lenders continued to attract media attention.[86] By July 5, there were reports predicting "substantial loan writedowns in excess of what the market is expecting."[87]

In this market climate, WaMu stock value fell to its lowest level in 16 years, with almost a 90 percent decline in the last year.[88] At the end of the second week in July, WaMu stock declined 5.7 percent on the day.[89] The following Monday, fears generated by the performance of financial stock dragged the entire market lower, with WaMu stock experiencing a further scary plunge of 34.7 percent on the day.[90]

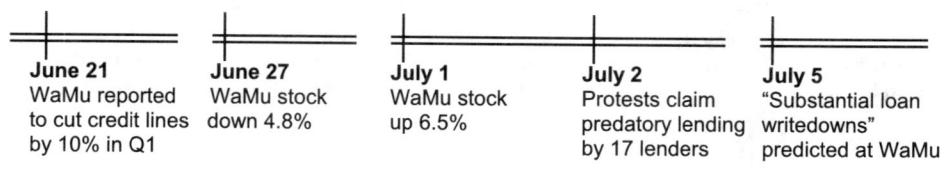

84. Eric Dash, *Banks Trim Credit Lines, and It Hurts,* N.Y. TIMES, June 21, 2008, at C1 *available at* 2008 WLNR 11712783.

85. *See GM Sales Report Reverse Dow Slide*, L.A. TIMES, July 2, 2008, at C5 *available at* 2008 WLNR 12386596 (reporting WaMu stock up 6.5 percent).

86. Andrew Kipkemboi, *Bias Seen in Mortgages; NAACP Accuses Lenders, Blames Rise in Foreclosures on Predatory Actions*, BALTIMORE SUN, July 3, 2007, at 3B, *available at* 2008 WLNR 12466096.

87. Whitney Tilson, *Buy Prudently and Be a Fan of Fear to Reduce Risk*, FT.com, July 5, 2007.

88. Andy Stern, *Keep Private Equity Away from our Banks*, WALL ST. J., July 7, 2008, at A13.

89. Rob Curran, *Large Stock Focus: Fannie and Freddie Lead Stocks Down – GE Stays in Green; Rohm & Haas Rise 66% on Week*, WALL ST. J., July 12, 2008, at B3.

90. Jeremy Lemer, *Wall Street Falls on Fears over Financials*, FIN. TIMES, July 14, 2008.

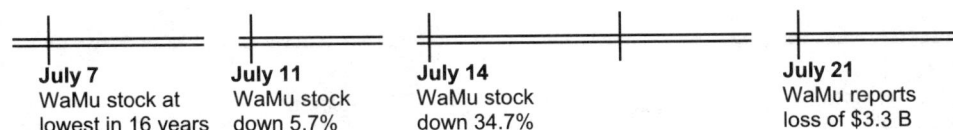

July 7	July 11	July 14		July 21
WaMu stock at	WaMu stock	WaMu stock		WaMu reports
lowest in 16 years	down 5.7%	down 34.7%		loss of $3.3 B

So dire were the circumstances, that investors were actually encouraged when WaMu reported a second-quarter loss of *only* $3.3 billion.[91] WaMu's market value rose on the day by 6.2 percent.[92] A brief "bank rally" in the market at the end of the month moved WaMu stock up by 12.4 percent on the day,[93] but the final word for the month was ominous – a trader for Deutsche Bank was reported as warning that WaMu was "twice as risky" as Lehman Bros.[94]

12. Profits of Doom [95]

On the first Monday in August 2008, WaMu began what would be its final slide into receivership, with its stock closing down 8.5 percent on the day.[96] A week later, some value was recaptured, as investors moved in to pick up some bargains.[97] Optimism was short-lived, however; five days later came reports

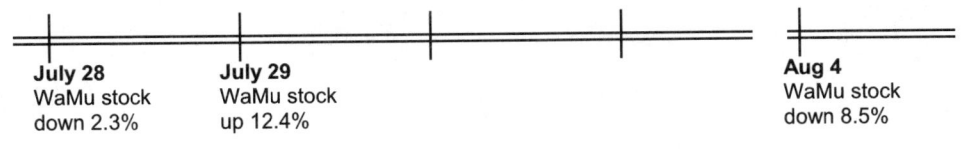

July 28	July 29			Aug 4
WaMu stock	WaMu stock			WaMu stock
down 2.3%	up 12.4%			down 8.5%

---

91. Eric Dash, *Refilling with Hope*, N.Y. TIMES, July 23, 2008, at C1, *available at* 2008 WLNR 13701099.

92. *Id.*

93. Paul Tharp, *Bank Rally Ignites Rest of Market*, N.Y. POST, July 30, 2008, at 35, *available at* 2008 WLNR 14190967.

94. Henny Sender, *Canny Buyer in the Debt Market*, FT.com, July 31, 2008 (quoting Boaz Weinstein of Deutsche Bank). We should keep in mind that at that precise moment, Lehman was pulling out of a very discouraging July and was experiencing a momentary upturn in market value of its stock. *See supra* at 52-55.

95. With apologies to "Buttonwood" of THE ECONOMIST. *See* Buttonwood, *Profits of Doom*, THE ECONOMIST, Aug. 2, 2008, at 36 ("The biggest area of [corporate finance] business is bank capital-raising, and success there may be a mixed blessing, given recent underwriting losses").

96. Rob Curran, *Large Stock Focus: Exxon Mobil Leads Commodities Bust – Selloff Hits Mosiac, Range Resources and Consol Energy*, WALL ST. J., Aug. 5, 2008, at C5.

97. *See* Jeremy Lemer, *US Stocks Up as Investors Cheer Drop in Oil*, FT.com, Aug. 11, 2008 (reporting 3.5 percent rise in WaMu stock).

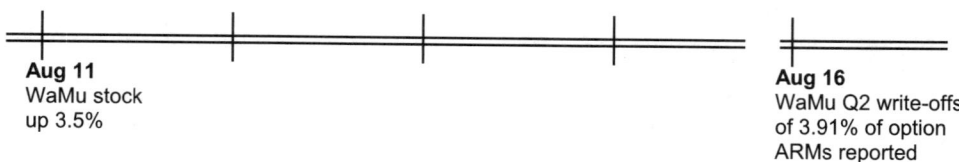

Aug 11
WaMu stock
up 3.5%

Aug 16
WaMu Q2 write-offs
of 3.91% of option
ARMs reported

that WaMu had begun writing off delinquent option ARMs[98] at an increasing rate – up to 3.91 percent in the second quarter.[99] Far worse news was in the offing, with many mortgages set to "recast" their payment terms, forcing mortgagors into full-payment status.[100] A dramatic wave of recasts was expected to hit in two to three years, increasing typical monthly payments on residential mortgages by as much as 60 to 80 percent.[101] This spelled doom for WaMu.

The situation was desperate. WaMu and other lenders were forced to offer higher rates to depositors in order to scramble for liquidity.[102] Dividends were slashed.[103] Under these circumstances, it was becoming increasingly unlikely that WaMu could find a white knight to negotiate with on its own terms.[104] On the last Monday in August, WaMu stock closed down 6 percent of market value.[105] There were few, if any, alternatives open to WaMu.

With losses piling up, the Vice-Chairman of WaMu, a 26-year veteran of the company, retired at the beginning of September.[106] On Thursday, Septem-

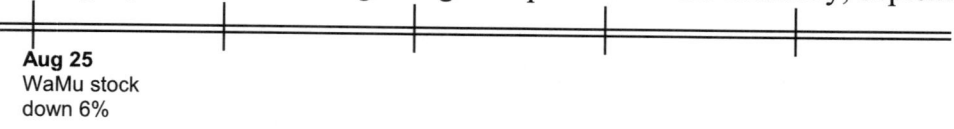

Aug 25
WaMu stock
down 6%

---

98. For an explanation of option ARMs, see note 38, *supra.*

99. *American Housing 2: Ticking Time Bomb*, THE ECONOMIST, Aug. 16, 2008, at 41.

100. *Id.*

101. *Id.*

102. Kathy M. Kristof, *Personal Finance; Cash-Hungry Lenders Paying More to Savers; Rates on Certificates of Deposit Are Up Since April. Some Big Banks Offer Better Than 4%*, L.A. TIMES, Aug. 23, 2008, at C1, *available at* 2008 WLNR 15940844.

103. Janet Kidd Stewart, *Restricted Flow Slows Dividends; As Payouts Decline, Investors Can Do More Than Pull Out*, CHICAGO TRIB., Aug. 24, 2008, at C3, *available at* 2008 WLNR 15994865.

104. *See, e.g.,* Francesco Guerrera, *Wells Fargo 'Unlikely' to Pursue Larger Rival*, FT.com, Aug. 25, 2008 (commenting on sluggish acquisitions market in financial services sector). TPG, the institutional investor that had previously come to WaMu's rescue, had been steadily losing money on the investment. *Private Equity and Banks: Loan Rangers*, THE ECONOMIST, Aug. 30, 2008, at 12.

105. Catherine Rampell, *Worries About Major Banks Drag Down the Market*, N.Y. TIMES, Aug. 26, 2008, at C6, *available at* 2008 WLNR 16085895.

106. Joe Adler, *Wamu Vice Chairman Longbrake Retires*, AM. BANKER, Sept. 3, 2008, at 20, *available at* 2008 WLNR 16601512.

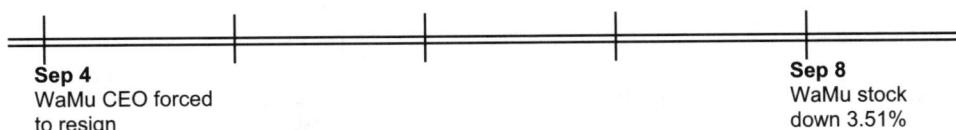

Sep 4
WaMu CEO forced
to resign

Sep 8
WaMu stock
down 3.51%

ber 4, 2008, the WaMu board demanded that CEO Killinger retire.[107] Coincidentally, on the day that Killinger's ouster was publicly confirmed, the Federal Government took over the troubled mortgage giants Fannie Mae and Freddie Mac.[108] The markets rose markedly in response to news of the takeover, but WaMu stock closed down 3.51 percent on the day.[109]

With Fannie and Freddie under government wraps, and Lehman Brothers feverishly looking for federal assistance in its search for a merger partner to rescue it, investor attention was becoming focused on the next big disaster – WaMu, which had been placed under special supervision by the Office of Thrift Supervision.[110] Two days after the announcement of the Killinger resignation, WaMu stock closed down a staggering 30 percent on the day.[111] Over the next week, it fluctuated up and down by double-digit percentages.[112]

On September 17, 2008 – two days after Lehman Brothers filed for bankruptcy – there were reports that WaMu was looking to for a buyer.[113] By the crazy logic of the market, this news pushed the market value of WaMu stock

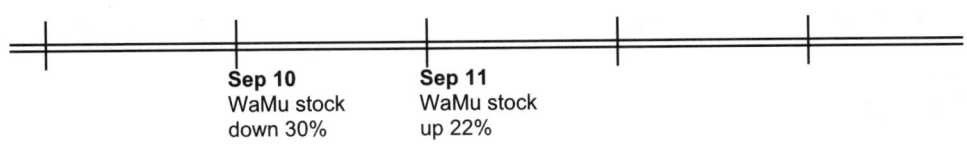

Sep 10
WaMu stock
down 30%

Sep 11
WaMu stock
up 22%

---

107. Eric Dash, *Chief Forced Out at Washington Mutual*, N.Y. TIMES, Sept. 8, 2008, at A20, *available at* 2008 WLNR 17003259.

108. *See* Vikas Bajaj & Keith Bradsher, *Stocks Soar on Takeover Plans*, N.Y. TIMES, Sept. 9, 2008, at C1, *available at* 2008 WLNR 17070106.

109. *Id.*

110. *See* Eric Dash, *Washington Mutual Stock Falls on Investor Fears*, N.Y. TIMES, Sept. 11, 2008, at C1, *available at* 2008 WLNR 17213561 (characterizing WaMu as "the next weakest link after Lehman Brothers").

111. *Id.*

112. *See, e.g.*, Eric Dash, *Washington Mutual Acts to Shore Up Stock*, N.Y. TIMES, Sept. 12, 2008, at C7, *available at* 2008 WLNR 17326250 (reporting 22 percent rise in market value of WaMu stock, on poor performance better than expected ("BTE") by the market); Stephen Labaton, *Wall St. in Worst Loss Since '01 Despite Reassurance by Bush*, N.Y. TIMES, Sept. 16, 2008, at A1, *available at* 2008 WLNR 17576130 (reporting WaMu stock closing down by 27 percent on the day that Lehman Brothers filed for bankruptcy).

113. Geraldine Fabrikant, *Mutual Is Said to Consider Sale*, N.Y. TIMES, Sept. 18, 2008, at A33, *available at* 2008 WLNR 17703984.

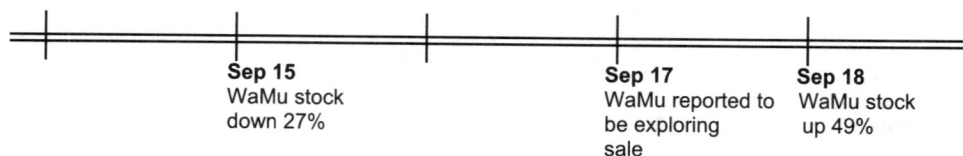

up 49 percent on the following day.[114]

By the following week, the media was already linking WaMu's search for a partner with the rising tide of financial sector failures.[115] On September 23, it was reported to be in preliminary acquisition talks with five banks – JP Morgan Chase, Wells Fargo, Citigroup, HSBC, and Banco Santander.[116] It was still unclear whether any of these suitors was really ready to make a bid.[117] Apparently, no one wanted to make a move without a clear signal that government financial assistance would be available – and no such signals were being transmitted as the federal government struggled to put together the terms of the Emergency Economic Stabilization Act of 2008 (EESA),[118] to respond to the growing crisis. Unfortunately, EESA would not be enacted until October 2008, and with it the creation of the Troubled Assets Relief Program (TARP) to provide $700 billion in appropriated funds for the purchase of troubled assets from financial institutions.[119] With its finances unraveling, WaMu seemed no closer to serious talks with any of the suitors than when it started the search. On September 25, 2008, the OTS determined that WaMu had insufficient liquidity to meet its obligations, and was therefore "in an unsafe and unsound

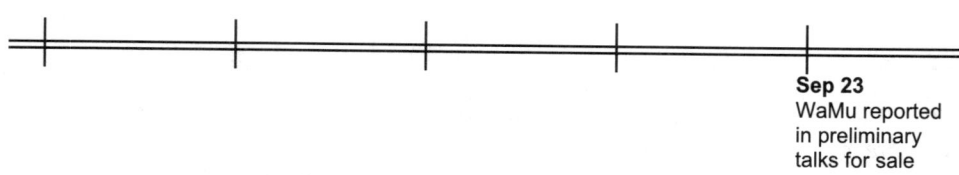

---

114. Vikas Bajaj, *Investors, Hungry for Hope, Send Dow Up 410*, N.Y. TIMES, Sept. 19, 2008, at C1, *available at* 2008 WLNR 17805017.

115. *See, e.g.*, Paul J. Lim, *A Rally Built on a Government Rescue: Can It Last?*, N.Y. TIMES, Sept. 21, 2008, at B6, *available at* 2008 WLNR 17942024 (noting 11 failures representing $40 billion, with "Washington Mutual . . . exploring a sale and there are, no doubt, more failures coming").

116. Saskia Scholted & Julie MacIntosh, *WaMu's Suitors Line Up for Talks*, FT.com, Sept. 23, 2008.

117. *Id.*

118. Pub. L. No. 110-343, 122 Stat. 3765 (2008) (codified at scattered sections of, *inter alia*, 5, 12, 15, 31 U.S.C.).

119. For discussion of TARP, see *infra* at 282-286, 295-296.

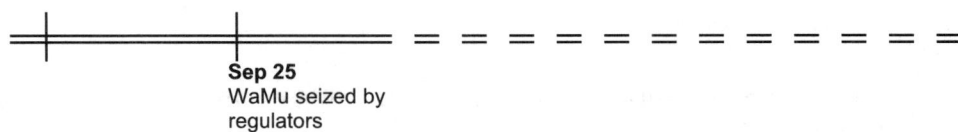

Sep 25
WaMu seized by
regulators

condition to transact business."[120] Accordingly, the OTS placed WaMu in receivership and JPMorgan Chase immediately closed a deal for its acquisition. While the receivership might, technically, persist for some time, and the bankruptcy proceedings of its holding company may drag on, business operations continued seamlessly. WaMu's seizure and handover "will have no impact on the bank's depositors or other customers. Business will proceed uninterrupted. . . ."[121]

B. TAKING RESPONSIBILITY (AND HIDING IT IN THE CLOSET)

Many factors contributed to the meltdown of the mortgage market and the attendant crisis in the securities markets. In the federal government's official inquiry into the causes of the crisis, much time and energy has been expended in attempts at avoiding responsibility for the meltdown. Still, the following features would seem to be necessary ingredients in the sequence of events:

- Demand for subprime mortgages was stoked by traditional lenders and by affiliated and unaffiliated mortgage bankers and brokers.

- The dramatic increase in the volume of subprimes was abetted by real estate appraisers with blind eyes, and by credit rating agencies and investment banks eager to push securitized mortgage products onto high and low investors with little or no disclosure of risks.

- At their core, the subprimes underlying these products were grossly over-inflated and unsustainable, making a crash all but inevitable – particularly once the subprime rates and payment terms reset after an initial promotional period, typically two to three years out.

- Federal supervisors of the safety and soundness of depository institutions like WaMu offered no substantive guidance, and appeared to be nonfeasant, perhaps

---

120. *OTS Fact Sheet on Washington Mutual Bank* (Sept. 25, 2008), *available at* http://files. ots.treas.gov/730021.pdf
121. *Id.*

intentionally so.[122]

This section examines some of the factors that might be responsible for these critical events.

1. Pumping up Demand

Where did all of the funding for the expanding mortgage market come from? Eventually, of course, it flowed in from the net proceeds of sales of securitized pools of mortgages, but was the institutional system of mortgage regulation itself instrumental in the phenomenal growth of the mortgage market? Consider the following excerpt.

ERIC DASH, FEDERAL MORTGAGE SUCCESS STORIES

N.Y. Times, Sept. 10, 2008, 2008 WLNR 17148626

The government's takeover of Fannie Mae and Freddie Mac, the nation's largest mortgage finance companies, is training a spotlight on a part of the American financial system that rarely gets much attention: the vast network of federal agencies and quasi-governmental lenders that helps keep credit flowing through the economy.

So far, these government-linked lenders – including other, smaller Maes and Macs – have come through the credit crisis largely unscathed. Some of them, in fact, are even prospering. . . .

Still, some worry that the rapid growth of other government-sponsored enterprises, most prominently the 12 Federal Home Loan Banks, eventually might create headaches for the financial industry and American taxpayers.

The Federal Home Loan Banks, which like Fannie Mae and Freddie Mac help finance housing, are like the troubled mortgage giants in at least one crucial respect: size. The F.H.L.B. system is enormous – and getting bigger. Over the last year alone, the combined value of these institutions' balance sheets has ballooned by 30 percent.

And, like Fannie and Freddie, the 12 banks borrow large amounts of money in the bond markets. Their debt outstanding totals about $1.3 trillion.

---

122. More troubling, perhaps, would be the pursuit by the OTS and the Comptroller of the Currency of an aggressive policy of preempting any attempts by state supervisors to address abuses in the mortgages practices of market participants that were federal savings associations or national banks – or even affiliated with such associations and banks. For extensive treatment of the connection between this "preemption initiative" and the meltdown, see *infra* at 179-212.

Over the last year or so, the Federal Home Loan Bank System, which is run as a cooperative by the nation's banks, rather than as a public company, has been a crucial source of funding for lenders. The home loan banks borrow money in the capital markets, securing low rates because of their implied backing by the federal government, and then lend that money to banks. That has been crucial during the current crisis as traditional sources of funding have dried up. . . .

Eleven of the 12 home loan banks have been profitable lately, although one, the Federal Home Loan Bank of Chicago, recently lost money when some of its hedges on mortgage investments went awry. . . .

[T]he home loan banks, which were created during the Depression amid a wave of bank failures, have lent billions of dollars to banks and thrifts that are themselves exposed to troubled home loans.

Washington Mutual, the nation's largest savings and loan, nearly doubled its borrowing from the Federal Home Loan Bank System over the last year, to $47.7 billion, according to government filings. The Wachovia Corporation has also ramped up its borrowing, in part because of its acquisition of Golden West, a big California lender. In 2007, before it was sold to Bank of America, the Countrywide Financial Corporation took out more than $53.2 billion as it fought to stay afloat.

Collectively, the home loan banks have never reported a loss in the system's 76-year history. Many experts say the risk that lenders will fail to pay back the home loan banks is small, particularly because the loans are secured by collateral in the form of high-quality mortgages and other protections.

Still, the explosive growth of the system concerns some analysts, who worry that the loan banks enable overly aggressive lenders to continue to make loans.

"The accusation is that they are the ones that continue to provide alcohol to the alcoholic borrower that just can't get off the sauce," said Gary Townsend, a manager of a hedge fund oriented toward the financial sector who spent seven years as the chief examiner of the F.H.L.B. system. "They continue to entice the borrower to borrow more and more."

The costs, if any, ultimately might be borne by the [Federal Deposit Insurance Corporation] and, by extension, taxpayers. When a lender fails, the home loan banks are repaid before the F.D.I.C., which guarantees checking and savings accounts.

"Any financial institution that is involved in the housing market could be in risk if home prices continue to plunge and the housing crisis doesn't start to abate," said Jaret Seiberg, a banking policy analyst at the Stanford Group in Washington. Even so, the risk to the loan banks appears small. . . .

2. Intermediaries and Gatekeepers

It may seem self-evident to lay the blame for the meltdown on the firms that so actively generated and sustained feverish growth in the mortgage market. Likewise, the banking and investment executives who stood to pull down mind-boggling salaries and bonus payments may seem complicit.[123] But how much blame should be allocated to the many secondary parties who made the mortgage market hum? These would include the systemic gatekeepers like investment banks marketing mortgage-backed securities and credit rating agencies that qualified the securities and intermediaries like real estate brokers and appraisers. Consider the following excerpt.

Eric Dash, So Many Ways to Almost Say "I'm Sorry"

N.Y. Times, Apr. 18, 2010, at WK4
available at 2010 WLNR 8014905

The parade of bankers called to account for the financial crisis continued last week when Kerry K. Killinger, head of Washington Mutual, the largest bank ever to fail, apologized, sort of, as have many before him. But he also said that his firm "should have been given a chance." Here are some of those mea culpa moments.

Angelo R. Mozilo
Co-founder, former chairman and chief executive, Countrywide Financial
QUOTE "No single entity or industry sector is responsible for the collapse in housing prices. . . . The issue is not so much the products, but the housing market."
BLAME In testimony before a House panel in March 2008, he faulted real estate speculators, rating agencies, a sharp decline in investor appetite for certain mortgages, and market psychology.
TOTAL COMPENSATION $530.9 million. . . .

---

123. Efforts are already underway to contain executive compensation practices in the financial services sector. *See, e.g.,* Federal Deposit Insurance Corporation, *Incorporating Employee Compensation Criteria Into the Risk Assessment System,* 75 Fed. Reg. 2823 (2010) (to be codified at 12 C.F.R. pt. 327) (proposing to amend FDIC risk-based deposit insurance assessment system to account for risks posed by certain employee compensation programs). *See generally* Devin Leonard, *Bargains in the Boardroom?* N.Y. Times, Apr. 4, 2010, at B1, *available at* 2010 WLNR 6962134 (detailing government efforts to scrutinize compensation at firms like troubled insurance giant AIG, Bank of America, Chrysler, Citigroup, and General Motors).

Kerry K. Killinger

Former chief executive, Washington Mutual

QUOTE "As C.E.O., I accept responsibility for our performance and am deeply saddened by what happened."

BLAME In his testimony before a Senate panel, he also said that federal regulators and Wall Street's "too clubby to fail" culture contributed to WaMu's demise. "For those outside the club, the penalty was severe," he said.

TOTAL COMPENSATION $95.7 million

Robert E. Rubin

Former chairman of the executive committee and board member, Citigroup

QUOTE "We all bear responsibility for not recognizing this, and I deeply regret that."

BLAME In testimony before the Financial Crisis Inquiry Commission on April 8, Mr. Rubin stopped short of accepting personal responsibility for Citigroup's troubles. He blamed at least a dozen forces – from trade imbalances to a surge in the use of complex derivatives.

TOTAL COMPENSATION $101 million

E. Stanley O'Neal

Former chairman and chief executive, Merrill Lynch

QUOTE "The bottom line is, despite our best efforts, a lot of money was lost in this one area" – mortgage securities – "and I, as the chief executive of the firm, was held accountable," he told THE NEW YORKER in a written statement in March 2008. "At the same time, the record over all is that we – the firm under my leadership – did a lot of things that benefited Merrill Lynch greatly and will continue to benefit the firm in the years ahead."

BLAME In testimony before a House committee in March 2008, Mr. O'Neal blamed an "unprecedented meltdown in the credit market" and noted that credit rating agencies failed to foresee the magnitude of the risk. In the latest issue of FORTUNE magazine, Mr. O'Neal said he recognized Merrill's mortgage problems in August 2007 but failed to persuade Merrill's directors to sell the company at the time. (Bank of America bought it a year later at a much lower price.)

TOTAL COMPENSATION $201.9 million.

Lloyd C. Blankfein

Chairman and chief executive, Goldman Sachs

QUOTE "We participated in things that were clearly wrong and have reason to regret and apologize for," he said at a conference last November in a response to a question about impact the crisis has had on the firm's image. "Some of this is real and some of this is extrapolated."

BLAME In an appearance before the financial crisis panel in mid-January, Mr. Blankfein said overdependence on credit ratings, risk models that substituted data for judgment, and a fundamental mispricing of risk also contributed to the crisis.

TOTAL COMPENSATION $391.2 million

Alan Greenspan
Former chairman of the Federal Reserve
QUOTE "I was right 70 percent of the time but I was wrong 30 percent of the time."
BLAME In testimony before the Financial Crisis Inquiry Commission on April 7, Mr. Greenspan pointed to an undercapitalized banking system and inadequate risk management by banks. He said that the Fed's limited powers restricted it from doing more to stop abusive lending practices.
TOTAL COMPENSATION $2.6 million.

Richard S. Fuld
Former chairman and chief executive, Lehman Brothers
QUOTE "I take full responsibility for the decisions that I made and for the actions that I took," he told a House committee in October 2008. "I feel horrible about what has happened to the company and its effects on so many – my colleagues, my shareholders, my creditors, and my clients."
BLAME Mr. Fuld said he acted prudently but Lehman was done in by higher borrowing costs, naked short attacks, accounting rules that forced the bank to mark down the value of its assets, and credit rating agency downgrades. He suggested that the Federal Reserve was unwilling to save the firm.
TOTAL COMPENSATION $167.5 million. (He lost about $900 million in stock when his firm went bankrupt.)

Charles O. Prince III
Former chairman and chief executive, Citigroup
QUOTE "Let me start by saying I'm sorry. I'm sorry the financial crisis has had such a devastating impact for our country. I'm sorry about the millions of people, average Americans, who lost their homes. And I'm sorry that our management teams, starting with me, like so many others could not see the unprecedented market collapse that lay before us."
BLAME In his testimony before the financial crisis commission on April 8, he also said that other factors – from rating agencies, to patchwork regulation, to the explosive growth of securitization – contributed to the crisis.
TOTAL COMPENSATION $132.7 million. . . .

3. Bubbles Pop

It now seems obvious that the market for mortgage-backed securities – and by extension the securities market as a whole – was much more vulnerable than it may have appeared to investors at the crest of its expansion. This was an investment bubble, and bubbles pop. What could have been done to prevent this? Preventive measures were no longer a viable remedy; conditions had already gone too far. As it began to realize the volatility of the market, the Securities and Exchange Commission attempted to contain it by issuing the following emergency order. Knowing what we now know of the meltdown, how likely do you think it was that this response could have prevented the bubble bursting?

SECURITIES AND EXCHANGE COMMISSION, EMERGENCY ORDER PURSUANT TO SECTION 12(K)(2) OF THE SECURITIES EXCHANGE ACT OF 1934 TAKING TEMPORARY ACTION TO RESPOND TO MARKET DEVELOPMENTS

73 Fed. Reg. 55,169 (2008)

The Commission is aware of the continued potential of sudden and excessive fluctuations of securities prices and disruption in the functioning of the securities markets that could threaten fair and orderly markets. In our recent publication of an emergency order under Section 12(k) of the Exchange Act (the "Act"),[1] for example, we were concerned about the possible unnecessary or artificial price movements based on unfounded rumors regarding the stability of financial institutions and other issuers exacerbated by "naked" short selling.[a] Our concerns, however, are no longer limited to just the financial institutions that were the subject of the July Emergency Order. Recent market conditions have made us concerned that short selling in the securities of a wider range of financial institutions may be causing sudden and excessive fluctuations of the prices of such securities in such a manner so as to threaten fair and orderly markets.

Given the importance of confidence in our financial markets as a whole, we have become concerned about recent sudden declines in the prices of a wide range of securities. Such price declines can give rise to questions about the underlying financial condition of an issuer, which in turn can create a crisis of confidence, without a fundamental underlying basis. This crisis of confidence can impair the liquidity and ultimate viability of an issuer, with potentially broad market consequences. Our concerns are no longer limited to the financial institutions that were the subject of the July Emergency Order.

As a result of these recent developments, the Commission has concluded that there continues to exist the potential of sudden and excessive fluctuations of securities prices generally and disruption in the functioning of the securities markets that could threaten fair and orderly markets. Based on this conclusion, the Commission is exercising its powers under Section 12(k)(2) of the Act....

In these unusual and extraordinary circumstances, we have concluded that, to prevent substantial disruption in the securities markets, temporarily prohibiting any person from effecting a short sale in the publicly traded

---

1. [*See supra* at 64-66 (excerpting earlier order).]

a. For a definition of "short sale," see *supra* at 52 n.81. On "naked short selling," see *supra* at 53 n.91.

securities of certain financial firms [identified in an appendix to the order as "Included Financial Firms," including WaMu] is in the public interest and for the protection of investors to maintain or restore fair and orderly securities markets.

This emergency action should prevent short selling from being used to drive down the share prices of issuers even where there is no fundamental basis for a price decline other than general market conditions.

It is ordered that, pursuant to our Section 12(k)(2) powers, all persons are prohibited from short selling any publicly traded securities of any Included Financial Firm.

Similar to the Amended July Emergency Order, we are providing a limited exception for certain bona fide market makers. We believe this narrow exception is necessary because such market makers may need to facilitate customer orders in a fast moving market without possible delays associated with complying with the requirements of this Order.

It is therefore ordered that, pursuant to our Section 12(k)(2) powers, the following entities are excepted from the requirements of the Order: Registered market makers, block positioners, or other market makers obligated to quote in the over-the-counter market, in each case that are selling short a publicly traded security of an Included Financial Firm as part of bona fide market making in such security.

In addition, we are providing an exception to allow short sales that occur as a result of automatic exercise or assignment of an equity option held prior to effectiveness of this Order due to expiration of the option.

It is therefore ordered that, pursuant to our Section 12(k)(2) powers, the requirements of this Order shall not apply to any person that effects a short sale in any publicly traded security of any Included Financial Firm as a result of automatic exercise or assignment of an equity option held prior to effectiveness of this Order due to expiration of the option.

Finally, to facilitate the expiration of options on September 20th, options market makers are excepted from the requirements of this Order until 11:59 p.m. on September 19th when selling short as part of bona fide market making and hedging activities related directly to bona fide market making in derivatives on the publicly traded securities of any Included Financial Firm.

4. Supervisory Shortfall

Fed Chairman Ben Bernanke probably said it best, at a January 2010 meeting of the American Economic Association. "[T]he best response to the housing bubble would have been regulatory, not monetary. Stronger regulation and supervision aimed at problems with [loan] underwriting practices and lenders' risk management would have been a more effective and surgical approach to constraining the housing bubble than a general increase in interest rates."[124] None of the federal regulators effectively intervened.[125] Worse yet, OCC and the OTS policies may have exacerbated the impact of abuses and missteps in the mortgage market. These two agencies actively shielded federal participants in the subprime market (and even their non-federal affiliates) from state intervention in their hazardous activity.[126]

---

124. *Quoted in* Aaron Lorenzo, *Bernanke Defends Fed Policy, Joins Other Officials with Guarded Forecasts*, BNA BANKING DAILY (Jan. 5, 2010), *available at* http://bna.com. For the full text of Bernanke's remarks, see http://www.federalreserve.gov.

125. *See, e.g.*, Jewel Edwards, *Federal Regulators Say Regulatory System Failed to Detect Risky Investment Practices*, BNA BANKING DAILY (Jan. 15, 2010), *available at* http://www.bna.com (reporting on testimony of federal regulators before Financial Crisis Inquiry Commission (FCIC) that faulty federal regulatory system allowed high-risk activities without adequate oversight) For information on the FCIC, see http://fcic.gov.

126. *Cf.* note 122, *supra* (discussing impact of preemption initiative).

CHAPTER 4

ASHES AND THE PHOENIX

Two iconic firms fail, punctuating the growing financial crisis. As a matter of historical accident, one is categorized as an investment bank, the other a depository institution. This taxonomy leads to concrete, critical differences in the way in which each failure is treated. The investment bank ends in ashes; the depository institution reconstitutes like a phoenix. This chapter explores the differences between these two experiences.

A. BANKRUPTCY AND LIQUIDATION

1. Breaking Up

Lehman filed a petition in the U.S. Bankruptcy Court for the Southern District of New York under Bankruptcy Code Chapter 11 on September 15, 2008. The following excerpt describes the events immediately surrounding the bankruptcy filing. Does the downfall seem inevitable in the retelling?

STEPHEN JOYCE, ONE YEAR AFTER LEHMAN FAILURE, NEED FOR FINANCIAL REFORM SEEN AS STILL URGENT

BNA BANKING DAILY (Sept. 14, 2009),
available at http://pubs.bna.com

Downfall of Storied Firm

Lehman executives decided to file for bankruptcy Sept. 14, 2008, a Sunday, after it incurred large losses related to nonperforming assets on its balance sheet and was unable to raise fresh capital or identify a firm to acquire it to mitigate those losses. The bankruptcy filing of the 158 year-old firm, which formally occurred Sept. 15, provided an endnote to the significant role large independent U.S. investment banks played for decades in U.S. financial matters.

The bankruptcy occurred during a run of days that proved to be among the current economic downturn's darkest moments: the Federal Housing Finance Agency's placement of government sponsored enterprises Fannie Mae and Freddie Mac in conservatorship, Merrill Lynch & Co. Inc.'s quick decision to sell itself to Bank of America Corp., and a government lifeline thrown to the American International Group Inc. in the form of an $85 billion loan in exchange for 79.9 percent of the company's common stock.

The Lehman bankruptcy and the financial drama surrounding it signaled to many U.S. citizens, for the first time since the current economic downturn began in the summer of 2007, that the domestic economy was in serious trouble, Financial Services Roundtable senior vice president of government affairs Scott Talbott told BNA Sept. 10. "This was a real, tangible event," he said. . . .

Effects of Bankruptcy

The bankruptcy had immediate, direct effects on the economy. Many money market mutual funds, commonly known as money funds, held large positions in Lehman debt securities that essentially became worthless with Lehman's failure, which led to a wave of rapid redemption requests to money funds – historically an extremely conservative investment – by panicked investors.

With the money funds short of cash, the funds could not buy short term debt instruments issued by corporations to fund the corporations' day-to-day operations, a typical and traditional money fund short term investment. Corporations suddenly found themselves unable to raise cash needed to run their organizations in the so-called commercial paper markets[,] and credit markets began to freeze.

Indeed, an "environment of paralysis" regarding short-term corporate debt securities occurred, Investment Company Institute President and Chief

Executive Officer Paul Schott Stevens told BNA Sept. 10.

NOTES AND QUESTIONS

1. *After the Fall.* Immediately after the filing, the U.K. firm Barclays Capital Inc. and Lehman executives began negotiating a transaction under which Barclays would purchase Lehman's North American broker-dealer operations and related support systems and significant real estate holdings including the Lehman Brothers headquarters building in New York City. The negotiations swiftly resulted to the sale of the assets to Barclays, and the deal was approved by the federal bankruptcy court on September 20, 2008, and completed two days later. Does this seem like an appropriate outcome? At the time, Barclays claimed that no other bidders were willing to purchase Lehman in the wake of the bankruptcy filing, and that its transaction would avert "hundreds of billions of dollars" in losses to Lehman creditors and rescue thousands of former Lehman employees from the threat of unemployment.

2. *All Over but the Lawyers.* Apparently huge losses and plenty of unemployment still awaited the large segments of the Lehman business not picked up by Barclays. As of mid-November 2009, the ongoing Lehman bankruptcy proceedings included more than 5,800 separate court filings or document entries.[1] As the following case illustrates, third parties who had dealt with Lehman pre-petition, but who were not picked up by Barclays or one of the smaller players, often found themselves inextricably tied to Lehman's fate. With the Barclays-acquired assets out of the picture, what is the likelihood that Lehman creditors will see a positive outcome?

IN RE LEHMAN BROTHERS HOLDINGS INC.

416 B.R. 392 (Bkrtcy. S.D.N.Y. Sept. 25, 2009)

JAMES M. PECK, Bankruptcy Judge.

[A pre-petition borrower brought adversary proceedings against two Lehman entities and State Street Bank & Trust, a bank that had purchased the borrower's loan as part of a pool of commercial loans transferred pre-petition pursuant to a master repurchase agreement (MRA). The borrower sought a declaratory judgment that the loan agreements constituted an integrated loan and that the bank necessarily acquired all three loans in exercising its rights as

---

1. *See* Stephen Joyce, *Lehman Claims Barclays Received $5 Billion in Secret Payment in Asset Sale Transaction*, BNA BANKING DAILY (Nov. 19, 2009), *available at* http://pubs.bna.com (reporting on Lehman-Barclays dispute in bankruptcy proceedings).

a counterparty under the MRA and taking possession of the commercial loans. The defendants moved to dismiss. The court granted the motion in part and denied it in part, holding that (*i*) the bank did not assume funding obligations associated with the loans that were not included in the pool of acquired assets; and, (*ii*) the question whether the borrower's loans could be split could not be decided on a motion to dismiss.]

Introduction

This dispute involves one of the loans held by State Street Bank and Trust Company ("State Street") that is part of a pool of commercial loans transferred pursuant to the terms of [the MRA]. Under the MRA, State Street paid approximately $1 billion to purchase this portfolio of financial assets from Lehman Brothers Commercial Paper, Inc. ("LCPI"). The transaction evidenced by the MRA contemplated that LCPI would repurchase these assets and repay State Street in accordance with the agreement, but LCPI filed for relief under chapter 11 and has defaulted under the MRA. The result is that State Street now owns these assets, including the loan in question made to LH 1440 LLC ("LH 1440") as borrower.

Plaintiff LH 1440 complains that the transfer of this loan to State Street adversely impacted its rights under other contemporaneous loan documentation. In substance, LH 1440 contends that it entered into three integrated loans that were intended to function as a unified financing package for the acquisition and improvement of certain commercial real estate. It claims that its expectations have been frustrated due to the sale of only one of these loans to State Street under the terms of the MRA. The splitting up of the financing and the selection of one loan for inclusion in the pool of loans sold to State Street allegedly has exposed Plaintiff to the risk of a mortgage foreclosure action at a time when it is unable to obtain advances needed to support the project under the remaining loans still held by LCPI. Plaintiff argues that State Street, as purchaser of this pool of assets, should be placed in the shoes of the original lender and be required to advance funds to LH 1440 even though financing documents for these other loans were not included within the pool of assets acquired by State Street.

As it relates to State Street, the issues presented lead to an examination of the applicable loan documentation with respect to the project and of the rights and obligations of a non-defaulting counterparty under a repurchase agreement. State Street contends that in exercising its rights upon the occurrence of a default under the MRA, it cannot be forced to fulfill the role of lender in relation to another loan that was not expressly designated and made a part of the pool of assets. Accordingly, State Street has brought a motion to dismiss the complaint . . . for failure to state a claim under Rule 12(b)(6) of the Federal Rules of Civil Procedure and Rule 7012(b) of the Federal Rules of Bankruptcy

Procedure ("Bankruptcy Rules"). Lehman Brothers Holdings, Inc. ("LBHI") and LCPI join in the Motion on the basis of unambiguous language providing that there were three separate loans, each of which was individually transferable. LBHI and LCPI assert that given this language, the loan in question was properly transferred to State Street pursuant to the MRA.

As discussed below, the Motion is granted as to State Street and denied as to LBHI and LCPI, but LH 1440 shall be allowed to amend its complaint.

Background

On June 8, 2007, LH 1440, as borrower, and LBHI, as lender, entered into real estate financing arrangements documented by means of two separate loan agreements, the Acquisition and Project Loan Agreement and the Building Loan Agreement. In addition, the parties executed a Consolidated, Amended and Restated Acquisition Loan Mortgage and Security Agreement, and an Option Agreement referencing three loans: 1) the Acquisition Loan of $15,649,568.31; 2) the Project Loan of $6,232,323.69; and 3) the Building Loan of $4,875,819.00. The loans were secured by three separate promissory notes. A single Participation Fee of 28.5% and a single Interest Rate Cap of $26,757,711.00 applied to the loans.

The Acquisition Loan was used to acquire certain real property located at 1440 Story Avenue in the Bronx, New York. The Project and Building Loans have been used to maintain and improve the acquired property and to fund interest payments on the Acquisition Loan. The Acquisition Loan is fully funded, and the Project and Building Loans have future funding obligations. Thus, the holder of the Acquisition Loan is under no direct obligation to advance funds to LH 1440. At some point, LCPI acquired the above referenced loans from LBHI.

On May 1, 2007, State Street entered into the MRA with LCPI, and as evidenced by a July 2007 confirmation letter, purchased a pool of commercial loans for $1 billion. Pursuant to the MRA, LCPI was entitled to substitute loans, as long as the value of those assets, in the aggregate, exceeded $1 billion. On September 17, 2008, State Street gave LCPI a notice of default under the MRA. When LCPI failed to repurchase the loans, State Street took possession of the mortgages and promissory notes for those assets. At that time, the promissory note for the Acquisition Loan was one of thirty-six commercial loans within the pool of assets held by State Street, but the promissory notes for the Project Loan and the Building Loan were not included among those assets.

On March 31, 2009, LH 1440 filed this adversary proceeding to obtain a declaratory judgment that the loan agreements together constitute an integrated loan to LH 1440 and that State Street necessarily acquired the Acquisition Loan, Project Loan, and Building Loan when it exercised its rights as counterparty under the MRA and took possession of the commercial loans described in the MRA. Thereafter, on May 1, 2009, State Street filed the Motion based on the failure to state a claim upon which relief may be granted. LBHI and LCPI have joined in the Motion. Following oral argument, the Court reserved judgment.

Discussion

. . . As Collier explains, "a repurchase agreement is an agreement by a bank or dealer in securities to transfer securities to a counterparty against a transfer of funds by the counterparty to the bank or dealer, with a simultaneous agreement by the parties for the counterparty to retransfer the securities to the bank or dealer at a future time against a transfer of funds by the bank or dealer to the counterparty." 1 COLLIER ON BANKRUPTCY ¶ 101.47 (15th Ed. Rev.). "Repo transactions are used in the marketing and trading of debt securities, including federal, state and municipal government obligations. They enable parties to invest available revenues in income generating instruments on a short-term basis. The recovery of investments in these transactions, in a timely fashion, is essential to the smooth functioning of these markets." 3 COLLIER ON BANKRUPTCY ¶ 362 .05[7] (15th Ed. Rev.).

Repo agreements, such as the MRA, are essential sources of market liquidity and have become important components of a smoothly running financial system. The designation of those assets that are being transferred to a counterparty in consideration for the transfer of funds is a basic element of every repo agreement. The repo market is a vital and vibrant source of liquidity for the financial system as a whole. Cash and financial assets are exchanged between financial institutions in the ordinary course of business based on standard documentation with the understanding that the assets being sold are otherwise unrestricted and may be converted to cash without the overhang and delay of litigation risk. This is a market that is fueled by the unfettered transferability of financial assets.

It is undisputed that in connection with the financing granted to LH 1440 and the subsequent transfer of identified financial assets pursuant to the MRA, State Street as transferee acquired only the promissory note for the Acquisition Loan, and not the promissory notes attached to the Project Loan or Building Loan. This note transfer to State Street was proper, because the transfer provisions, along with the splitting clause in each of the loan agreements, establish that each of the loans was individually transferable. There is, as a result, a disconnect between what the documentation expressly allows and the allegations of LH 1440 as to what it understood or expected when it entered into the underlying loan transactions.

Separate transfers plainly are authorized under the applicable documentation. Section 13 of the Consolidated, Amended and Restated Acquisition Loan

Promissory Note states unambiguously that the lender may at any time assign or otherwise transfer its right to payment of principal, interest or any other right or benefit under the Note. Importantly, the Acquisition Loan has its own promissory note and is individually transferable. This right to liberally assign and transfer the loans separately is without restriction and is not conditioned upon or tied in any way to the transfer of any other loans.

Each loan agreement has its own transfer provision that gives a great deal of flexibility and discretion to the lender to transfer the loans in whole or in part. The Acquisition and Project Loan Agreement and the Building Loan Agreement provide in section 18.1 that the lender may, at any time, sell, transfer or assign any of the loan documents and any or all related servicing rights. Section 7.4 of the Acquisition and Project Loan Agreement also gives the lender the ability to split or divide the indebtedness into two or more separate notes or agreements. Accordingly, even if all three loans were deemed to be one loan, pursuant to this provision, that single loan could be split under section 7.4, and then transferred under section 18.1.

Given the express language in the loan documents allowing for splitting and free transferability of the loans, LH 1440 is unable to state a claim upon which relief may be granted as to State Street. State Street paid one billion dollars in exchange for a pool of specified assets that, for all practical purposes, functioned in the same manner as collateral for a secured one billion dollar loan. By entering into such a conventional repurchase agreement (albeit for a significant sum), State Street did not thereby agree to take on exposure to funding obligations that attach to assets that were never designated to be included in the pool.

As to State Street, no facts have been alleged to support LH 1440's claim that a counterparty to a repurchase agreement that is in the process of attempting to recover value from a pool of acquired assets after a default somehow can be forced to assume funding obligations associated with another closely related loan that never was part of the underlying pool of assets. State Street's rights and obligations as counterparty are set forth in the MRA and related documents governing the commercial relationship between the seller, LCPI, and the purchaser, State Street, of a defined set of assets. As purchaser of a pool of specified assets, State Street cannot have any legally binding and enforceable obligations in relation to another asset that was not subject to the transaction documents and that was left behind with the seller. A purchaser cannot have liabilities with respect to an asset that it neither purchased nor agreed to purchase.

The only conceivable exceptions to this general proposition would be those situations in which the purchaser of assets under a repurchase agreement was on notice of an ongoing funding obligation, a restriction or some other condition impacting the right of a seller to freely transfer a particular asset.

The Court believes that a purchaser under a repurchase agreement should be treated in a manner comparable to a good faith purchaser for value. A repo counterparty should not be exposed to adverse claims by a third party with respect to any asset subject to a repurchase agreement unless there are circumstances sufficient to place a reasonable market participant on actual notice or inquiry notice regarding liabilities or infirmities that might attach to such asset.

The complaint fails to allege that State Street had actual notice that the three loans made to LH 1440 were interrelated and may not have been separable when it purchased the Acquisition Loan. Therefore, it becomes necessary to examine whether the circumstances alleged were sufficient to place State Street on inquiry notice, such that it was required to make further inquiries.

In the Second Circuit, the test for determining whether a party is placed on inquiry notice is objective. *See In re Bayou Group, LLC,* 396 B.R. 810, 848 (Bankr.S.D.N.Y.2008); *In re Integrated Res. Real Estate Ltd. P'ships Secs. Litig.,* 815 F.Supp. 620, 637 (S.D.N.Y.1993). Whether a party is deemed to be on inquiry notice depends on whether the facts known by that party would induce a reasonable actor in a similar position to investigate the matter further. *See Nat'l W. Life Ins. Co. v. Merrill Lynch, Pierce, Fenner & Smith Inc.,* 89 F. Appx. 287 (2d Cir.2004) (discussing inquiry notice in the context of a securities fraud case). Parties on inquiry notice who do not make diligent inquiry are charged with knowledge of the facts they would have learned upon making such inquiry. *Armstrong v. McAlpin,* 699 F.2d 79, 88 (2d Cir.1983). However, nothing has been alleged in the complaint to indicate that State Street knew or had any reason to suspect that there were other allegedly related loans between LBHI and LH 1440 that could not be separated from the Acquisition Loan, or that State Street as counterparty had any duty to inquire further with respect to any loan within the pool.[2]

Although LH 1440 may have reasonably believed that it was entering into a single financing arrangement, State Street, as a counterparty to the MRA, would be indifferent to the expectations of the parties at the time of origination with respect to a particular loan within a diverse pool of assets. In the ordinary course of an efficient market involving sophisticated financial institutions, counterparties such as State Street would not be expected to undertake a

---

2. The complaint implies, but fails to specifically allege, that State Street knew or should have known of the link between the three loans and the possibility that they may not be separable. While the complaint alleges that State Street acquired all three loans, and that State Street may not choose the rights and remedies that it prefers, it does not state that State Street knew about the interrelation of the three loans or that State Street had any obligation to investigate further based on the knowledge that it had.

detailed investigation with respect to the underwriting of the Acquisition Loan Note or the authority of the seller, here LCPI, to freely transfer that Note. The smooth functioning of the financing markets depends upon easy execution of transactions such as the MRA. The market is structured to foster the orderly and prompt exchange of dollars and financial assets between market participants. Restrictions on transfer of financial assets or the existence of undisclosed and perhaps unknowable incremental liabilities would interfere with that model and make it both more cumbersome and more costly to obtain access to needed short term financing.

The Court concludes that it would be inconsistent with customary market practices to expect the counterparty in a repo transaction to conduct a time consuming investigation regarding the assets that are included in the transaction. This is particularly true in consideration of the fact that other assets often can be substituted, and the focus of the transaction is on the aggregate value of the assets, rather than the specific assets within the pool. LH 1440 has not alleged that State Street as repo counterparty had any reason to know about or a duty to discover the alleged connection between the Acquisition Loan Note and other instruments executed by LH 1440 and LBHI. The complaint as to State Street seeks a remedy from a party that owes no duty to LH 1440 and fails to state a claim that rises above the speculative level. For that reason, the Motion is granted as to State Street, but LH 1440 shall be granted the opportunity to reformulate its allegations in an amended complaint.

The Motion is denied as to LBHI and LCPI. While the transfer provisions and the splitting clause establish that the loans were separately transferable, the underlying documents indicate that the transaction appears to have been intended to function as an interrelated loan. The loans were to be used in tandem; the Acquisition Loan, now fully funded, provided funds to purchase the property, while the Project and Building Loans, with ongoing funding obligations, would allow the borrower to maintain and improve the acquired property. The single Participation Fee and the single Interest Rate Cap Agreement also may be indicative of a single loan transaction.

LH 1440 has alleged that the loans are tied together and should be given the opportunity to move beyond the pleading stage and take discovery that may help clarify the role of LBHI in originating the loan and the proper characterization of the loan. Pending the completion of discovery, it is unclear whether the transactions between LBHI and LH 1440 may or may not have constituted an integrated transaction and what the parties actually intended.

One thing does seem clear, however. LH 1440 claims to have suffered as a consequence of the transfer of one of its promissory notes to State Street and now is exposed to unanticipated transactional risks. LH 1440 should have an opportunity to develop its thesis that the loan should not have been split to its detriment and to explore facts in support of its claims relating to the structuring of the financing by LBHI.

NOTES AND QUESTIONS

1. *The Repo Transaction.* What kind of transaction did State Street and LCPI enter into? Does the court's reference to COLLIER ON BANKRUPTCY, *supra*, clear up the terms of a "repurchase agreement" (or "repo") for you? On its own terms, the transaction involved LCPI "selling" or "transferring" the Acquisition Loan to State Street, with an obligation to "repurchase" it under certain specified circumstances. The traditional repo agreement, now referred to as a "wholesale repo,"[2] is typically used to increase the liquidity of the "seller," and it has the following characteristics: (*i*) it usually has a relatively short duration, often overnight or a few days; (*ii*) it involves relatively large amounts (*e.g.*, $1 million); (*iii*) it is privately negotiated rather than mass-marketed; and, (*iv*) it involves an entire security, often a government-issued debt instrument that may be delivered directly to the "purchaser." SEC Release No. 33-6351, 1 Fed. Sec. L. Rep. (CCH) ¶ 2024, at 2559-64 (Sept. 25, 1981). While commonly characterized as a "sale" subject to an obligation to "repurchase," the repo is in economic reality "essentially a short-term collateralized loan, and the parties to these transactions tend to perceive them as such."[3] The Acquisition Loan involved in *In re Lehman Brothers Holdings Inc.* is therefore the *collateral* for a loan that State Street made to LCPI. Does this fact make it clearer why State Street might not be considered the successor to any loan or funding obligations owed by LCPI to the borrower LH 1440?

2. *Barclays Capital Inc.: To the Rescue or to the Max?* In mid-November 2009, Lehman Brothers Holdings Inc. filed an adversary complaint in bankruptcy alleging that Barclays Capital Inc. had received an illegal payment of at least $5 billion as part of the transaction that sold Lehman components to Barclays after Lehman's voluntary declaration of bankruptcy on Sept. 15,

---

2. Beginning in the mid-1970's, a number of commercial banks began to market to the public an investment that came to be known as a "retail repurchase agreement" or "retail RP," which were initially marketed as smaller-denomination "participations" in a large-denomination government security or pool of securities "sold" to individual investors subject to "repurchase." *See* Michael P. Malloy & James T. Pitts, *Post-Mortem on Retail Repurchase Agreements: Where Were the Regulators?* 3 ANN. REV. BANKING L. 89 (1984) (tracing development of retail repo).

3. *SEC v. Miller*, 495 F.Supp. 465, 457 (S.D.N.Y. 1980), *citing* M. STIGUM, THE MONEY MARKET: MYTH, REALITY, AND PRACTICE 328 (Dow Jones-Irwin 1978); *United States v. Erickson*, 601 F.2d 296, 300 n.4 (7th Cir. 1979), *cert. denied*, 444 U.S. 979 (1980).

2008.[4] In a previous filing in the bankruptcy proceedings, Barclays had stated that the terms of the sale were clearly outlined in the documentation and willingly signed by Lehman executives.[5] While it is conceivable that Lehman's adversary complaint might prevail, that would not resurrect its business, nor is it likely that the sale itself would be rolled back at this point.

2. Retrospective

1. *After the Fall – One Year Out.* As of the first anniversary of Lehman Brothers Holdings Inc.'s declaration of bankruptcy, in September 2009, significant regulatory reform – necessary to prevent a similar crisis in the future – still had not materialized.[6] Ironically, many industry experts are now concerned that complacency might "dull a sense of urgency that should be attached to the pace of industry and regulatory reforms."[7] The next chapter will analyze what steps the Congress and the regulators have taken to address the crisis.

2. *After the Fall – An Industry Perspective.* Whatever significant supervision exists in the wake of the Lehman collapse is still largely a matter of market forces. How has the private sector responded to the financial crisis? Are these responses anywhere near adequate to deal with any future market crisis? Consider the following excerpt.

STEPHEN JOYCE, ONE YEAR AFTER LEHMAN FAILURE, NEED FOR FINANCIAL REFORM SEEN AS STILL URGENT

BNA BANKING DAILY (Sept. 14, 2009),
available at http://pubs.bna.com

Indirect Consequences

The Lehman failure had several indirect negative consequences . . . , including an eroding market confidence in the financial system generally. With relatively safe bets such as money funds experiencing difficulties, financial

---

4. *Lehman Brothers Holdings Inc. v. Barclays Capital Inc. (In re Lehman Brothers Holdings Inc.),* Bankr. S.D.N.Y., Adv. No. 09-01731 (JMP), No. 08-13555 (JMP), (*adversary complaint filed* Nov. 16, 2009).

5. *See* Stephen Joyce, *Lehman Claims Barclays Received $5 Billion in Secret Payment in Asset Sale Transaction,* BNA BANKING DAILY (Nov. 19, 2009), *available at* http://pubs.bna.com (reporting on dispute).

6. *See* Stephen Joyce, *One Year After Lehman Failure, Need for Financial Reform Seen as Still Urgent,* BNA BANKING DAILY (Sept. 14, 2009), *available at* http://pubs.bna.com (reporting on situation one year after Lehman collapse).

7. *Id.*

firms began to contemplate risks associated with other, seemingly conservative financial transactions, such as interbank lending, as well.

Relatively exotic financial products once viewed as creative vehicles offering investors high yields fell from favor with investors as purchasers wrote down their value, in some cases were forced to do so because of accounting rules. The assets themselves became hard to sell, further reducing their value. Investors pulled money out of the equities markets, particularly bank stocks, and sought refuge in the relative safety of government-backed debt. . . .

Firms Apply Lessons Learned

Financial specialists said the Lehman bankruptcy taught the financial services industry a few key lessons, which in turn has changed certain practices without new regulatory impositions. . . .

The financial services sector, meantime, has learned to better account for risk without the demands of new regulation, the sources said. For example, the firms have improved internal risk-management controls and taken more practical steps, such as tightening credit standards to borrowers, including mortgage applicants, Talbott said.

And many of the risk-taking practices exercised by institutions at the beginning of the current economic downturn have been eliminated, he said.

ICI's Stevens said financial firms are assuming more defensive positions when managing their portfolios. And managers are looking at credit conditions more closely, he said. "I do think that their risk limitations are more robust now than in the past," he said.

Bank Holding Companies Proliferate

Another development since the Lehman failure that has made the financial sector safer is the conversion of investment banks such as Goldman Sachs Group Inc. and Morgan Stanley to bank holding companies, O'Melveny & Myers LLP senior counsel Demetrios Xistris told BNA Sept. 11.

While the conversion provides the banks with greater access to government funds in the event of a financial crisis, it also increases state and federal government oversight of the entities, said Xistris, who previously worked at U.S. and French banks managing legal, regulatory, and enforcement activities.

Other nongovernment initiatives have helped, too. A total of 15 large derivatives dealers announced Sept. 8[, 2009,] they will increase their use of central counterparties to clear certain over-the-counter derivatives. The move will help disperse risk, making it less concentrated in just a few market participants, Xistris said.

Market Innovation Still Desirable

Another development since the Lehman bankruptcy has involved product development, sources said. For the first six to nine months after the Lehman failure, "simpler was better" for investors such as state treasurers, Xistris said. "Innovation was put to the side while people had to deal with real credit issues. . . . But I do think innovation will continue in financial markets. I don't think that will change," he said.

Xistris and others said the financial services sector will continue to develop innovative products, including complex instruments, to help investors hedge other investments or realize pricing efficiencies. Talbott said risk is inherent to an innovative market economy, and such economies will inevitably experience financial booms and busts. . . .

"Complex products have an important role to play and will continue to play a role in the future," Talbott said. And while the appetite for such products is currently weak, they are "absolutely coming back," he said

Others agreed. Despite market turmoil caused by exotic financial instruments in the runup to the Lehman failure, investors will continually seek innovative products that provide handsome returns. "I think there will always be investors out there who will buy these things," Kelley Drye & Warren LLP partner and financial specialist Thomas Kinzler told BNA. . . .

NOTES AND QUESTIONS

1. *What We Learned.* When the financial services industry says that the Lehman bankruptcy has taught it "a few key lessons," is that its way of trying to avoid new, presumably stricter "regulatory impositions"? There has been much talk, post-Lehman, about "improved internal risk-management controls," but does that mean mortgage lenders and investment banks are actually going to assess the realistic market value of assets they hope to sell to investors? Does it mean that they will actually disclose, fully and fairly, the material information about the risks of assets backing up securitized interests that they market? Or are we just talking about superficial "tightening credit standards" until the next new financial craze gets underway?

2. *Déjà Vu All Over Again?* Many industry experts are already signaling impatience with suggested regulatory changes. Many argue openly that the government should not impede the ability of financial services firms to develop innovative financial products. Some criticize legislative policy makers for trying to interfere with the financial services industry, the favored example being proposals to impose guidelines discouraging excessive executive compensation. With the sting of the crisis slowly abating – and with regulatory reform efforts already well past their shelf date – how likely is it that the post-crisis financial services market will be safer or more stable that it was before

the Lehman collapse?

B. RECEIVERSHIP

The WaMu experience has been rather different from the fate of Lehman Brothers. While Lehman (and its creditors and investors) painfully make their way through Chapter 11 bankruptcy and liquidation, most of WaMu's branches are back up and running as part of JPMorgan Chase. In the depository institutions sector, the process is one of insolvency and receivership, which is largely a fast-track administrative process.

1. Contrast and Compare

The savings bank subsidiaries of WaMu's holding company, Washington Mutual, Inc. (WMI), were closed by the Office of Thrift Supervision and placed into FDIC receivership. The FDIC arranged for the WaMu business to be acquired by JP Morgan Chase in a "purchase and assumption" transaction, in which Chase agreed to purchase specified assets of WaMu and to assume specified liabilities, with the FDIC holding Chase harmless with respect to any other prior claims against WaMu. Thereafter, WMI filed for Chapter 11 bankruptcy where, as in the case of Lehman, creditors and investors of the holding company have little expectation of a positive outcome.

NOTES AND QUESTIONS

1. The acquisition of WaMu's business by JPMorgan Chase has not been without its human cost. In February 2009, Chase reported that "integration of operations" would result in an expected workforce reduction of approximately 12,000 WaMu employees.[8] Integration would save approximately $2 billion, including a likely $1.35 billion in compensation and other employee-related costs.[9]

2. How does a purchase and assumption work? And what other options are available to the FDIC in resolving the affairs of a failed depository institution? The following excerpt explores these issues.

---

8. *Integration with WaMu Will Reduce Head Count by 12,000, JPMorgan Says*, BNA BANKING DAILY (March 3, 2009), *available at* http://www.bna.com.
9. *Id.*

3 Michael P. Malloy, Banking Law and Regulation

§§ 11.3-11.3.2, 11.3.4-11.3.4.2 (Aspen 2004 & Cum. Supps.)[a]

. . . As in the case of the bankruptcy of a general business corporation, a depository institution failure usually involves a situation of insolvency.[3] However, the process for failing depository institutions is to be distinguished from that applicable in a general business bankruptcy.

First, it should be kept in mind that depository institutions are not subject to the general federal law with respect to bankruptcy.[4] Determination of insolvency (default) by the depository institution's primary regulator is in this

---

a. Some footnotes have been renumbered for the convenience of the reader.

3. *See, e.g.,* [12 U.S.C. §§191(1) (grounds for appointment of receiver of national bank, referring to §1821(c)(5)); 1821(c)(5)(A) (depository institution's obligations greater than assets); 1821(c)(5)(F) (inability to meet obligations as they come due); 1821(c)(5)(G) (depletion of capital); 1821(c)(5)(H) (violation of law or regulation, or unsafe or unsound practice or condition likely to cause insolvency or the like). Other grounds for the appointment of a receiver or conservator do not directly relate to a condition of insolvency. These grounds are:

> 1. Substantial dissipation of assets or earnings due to violation of any statute or regulation or any unsafe or unsound practice (12 U.S.C. §1821(c)(5)(B));
> 2. Unsafe or unsound condition to transact business (12 U.S.C. §1821(c)(5)(C));
> 3. Willful violation of a final cease-and-desist order (12 U.S.C. §1821(c)(5)(D));
> 4. Concealment of the institution's books, papers, records, or assets, or any refusal to submit the institution's books, papers, records, or affairs for inspection to any examiner or to any lawful agent of the appropriate federal or state supervisor (12 U.S.C. §1821(c)(5)(E));
> 5. Consent to the appointment by resolution of board of directors or of shareholders or members (12 U.S.C. §1821(c)(5)(1); *see also id.* §1821(c)(12) (directors not liable for such consent or acquiescence));
> 6. Cessation of insured status of the institution (12 U.S.C. §1821(c)(5)(J));
> 7. Undercapitalization, under specified circumstances (12 U.S.C. §1821(c)(5)(K)); or
> 8. Critical undercapitalization or substantially insufficient capital (12 U.S.C. §1821(c)(5)(L).

In situations of undercapitalization (grounds (7) and (8), supra), additional authority exists for the appropriate federal banking agency to appoint the FDIC as conservator or receiver of any insured state depository institution. *See id.* §1821(c)(9). *See also id.* §1821(c)(11) (FDIC opportunity to appoint itself as receiver before appropriate federal banking agency may appoint a conservator). The FDIC has additional authority to appoint itself as conservator or receiver under any of the grounds identified if such appointment is necessary to reduce or prevent a loss to the deposit insurance fund. *See id.* §1821(c)(10). Appointment of a conservator or receiver does not violate the Fifth Amendment takings clause, because those who enter the banking industry do so voluntarily. *California Hous. Sec. v. United States*, 959 F.2d 955, 958 (Fed. Cir. 1992), *cert. denied*, 506 U.S. 916. Use of the appointment authority is "entitled to a presumption of regularity," and judicial review is narrow. *Franklin Sav. Assn. v. Director, Office of Thrift Supervision*, 934 F.2d 1127, 1141 (10th Cir. 1991), *cert. denied*, 503 U.S. 937 (1992).

4. *See* 11 U.S.C. §109 (expressly exempting banks and other depository institutions from recourse to bankruptcy protection).

regard exclusive and results in the institution being placed into receivership[5] or conservatorship.[6]

Second, it should be remembered that a holding company of a depository institution is itself subject to the general federal bankruptcy laws.[7] Because the financial condition of the principal operating subsidiary of such a holding company (that is, its subsidiary bank or savings association) is likely to be the cause of the parent's insolvency, however, the situation will naturally be a very complicated one, with the parent subject to the Bankruptcy Code and the principal subsidiary subject exclusively to federal statutes governing the default of depository institutions.[8] For the sake of clarity, the discussion that follows will focus exclusively on the regulatory regime applicable to the failing depository institutions alone.

§ 11.3.2. Approaches to Resolution of Failed Institutions

The ultimate liability of the federal government in a situation involving a failed depository institution is the obligation for insured deposits of the institution.[1] In fact, the way in which the FDIC has handled failures has varied from situation to situation, and at least since 1945 the insured deposit payoff approach has not been favored.[2] . . .

a. *Insured deposit payoff.* Originally, the FDIC tended to resolve failures by either paying off its deposit insurance obligation or by allowing the failing bank to be acquired by another institution. In a deposit payoff transaction, the FDIC as receiver would hold any net assets of the failed institution, against which uninsured depositors, other unsecured creditors, and the FDIC itself as insurer became general creditors. . . .

b. *Modified insured deposit payoff.* In 1984, the FDIC initiated a "modified

---

5. *See, e.g.,* 12 U.S.C. §§191-199 (receivership rules for national bank), *as amended,* Riegle Community Development and Regulatory Improvement Act of 1994 (CDRIA), Pub. L. No. 103-325, Sept. 23, 1994, §602(e)(36), (g)(11)-(13), 108 Stat. 2160, 2292, 2294 (1994) (codified at 12 U.S.C. §192, 194, 196; *repealing id.* §195) (technical amendments). *See also id.* §§91 (transfers in contemplation of insolvency).

6. *See, e.g., id.* §§202-206, 209, 211 (conservatorship rules for national bank).

7. *Cf.* 11 U.S.C. §109 (exemption does not explicitly apply to holding company). *See generally MCorp Fin., Inc. v. Board of Governors,* 900 F.2d 852 (5th Cir. 1990), *aff'd in part and rev'd in part on other grounds,* 502 U.S. 32 (1991) (discussing §109 of the Bankruptcy Code).

8. *See, e.g., MCorp Financial, supra* note 7 (illustrating the complications inherent in the failure of depository institutions and their holding company parent).

1. *See* 12 U.S.C. §1821(a)(1) (insurance of deposit to a maximum of $100,000).

2. *See generally* U.S. Department of the Treasury, *Modernizing the Financial System,* Discussion Chapter I, at I-30-I-45 (Feb. 1991), *reprinted in* Fed. Banking L. Rep. (CCH) No. 1377, Pt. II (Feb. 14, 1991) (discussing FDIC treatment of bank failures). *But cf. No Buyer for Utah Bank; FDIC to Mail Checks; Va. Bank Takes Over Failed Maryland Thrift* , BNA Banking Daily (Feb. 2, 2009)), available at http://www.bna (reporting on FDIC decision to perform insured deposit payout as to closed MagnetBank of Salt Lake City Utah). . . .

payoff" approach as a variation on the traditional insured deposit payoff. Under this approach, insured deposits would be paid off, and a sum equal to a conservative estimate of the funds to be realized from the assets left in receivership would be paid out to the uninsured deposits, with additional payments to be made in the future if collections exceeded the conservative estimate. This approach eventually led to the development of the "insured deposit transfer," in which an acquiring bank would pay a premium for insured deposits and certain assets of a failed bank that would otherwise be subject to an insured deposit payoff.

c. *Purchase and assumption.* Originally, the typical acquisition transaction involving a failed bank was not a merger, strictly speaking, but was in fact structured as a purchase of assets (that is, loans) and assumption of liabilities (that is, deposits) of the failing bank by the acquiring bank, with the FDIC making up the shortfall between the value of liabilities assumed and assets purchased. Before the 1960s, these resolutions took place without the creation of a receivership, so approval of the shareholders and the chartering authority of the acquired bank would be required. During the latter part of the 1960s, the FDIC adopted a different approach to these transactions: It would first place the institution into receivership, so that the FDIC as receiver could proceed with the transaction without the costly delays of shareholder and chartering authority approval. . . .

If successful, the effect of these transactions was very much like a payoff of all depositors, not just insured depositors. On the other hand, assuming that the cost of the "sweetener" provided by the FDIC to the acquiror bank was less than the potential total insured depositor liability, the purchase and assumption method could be less costly to the FDIC. (However, almost inevitably, the FDIC as receiver was left with a nearly worthless shell within the receivership.) Furthermore, from 1968, the FDIC sought premiums from potential acquiror banks in proposed purchase and assumption transactions through an explicit bidding process.[10]

d. *"Open bank" assistance.* In many of the approaches adopted by the FDIC,[11] one goal has been to avoid the rigors of insured deposit payoff and the resulting disruption of the local economy that the closing of a bank would

---

10. ... *Cf.* 70 Fed. Reg. 60,015 (2005) (to be codified at 12 C.F.R. §§307.1-307.3, app. A, B) (proposing revision to regulation addressing certification to FDIC of assumption of deposits and notification to depositors of change in insured status).

11. For a recent case discussing alternative methods of fulfilling the FDIC's obligation to depositors, including deposit payoffs and purchase-and-assumption transactions, see *NCNB Texas Natl. Bank v. Cowden*, 895 F.2d 1488 (5th Cir. 1990).

cause. An important device in this regard, not used until 1971,[12] is "open-bank assistance."[13] This approach proceeds on the assumption that it will be less costly to the FDIC to lend financial assistance to a troubled bank than to close and liquidate it in receivership.

e. *Other variations*. Two variations on this "walking dead" approach to failing-bank resolution should be mentioned. One was the "capital forbearance" program, in which capital and other supervisory requirements were not enforced against financially troubled institutions viewed as viable by the FDIC. This approach has been severely criticized as increasingly the ultimate cost of unavoided (and possibly unavoidable) collapse of such viable but troubled institutions.

Until recently, the other "walking dead" approach involved an FDIC equity investment in the troubled institution.[16] This often involved extreme, and often questionable measures, such as the 75 to 80 percent equity interests assumed by the FDIC in large, failing regional banks such as the MCorp subsidiary and Continental Illinois. . . .

§ 11.3.4. Current Statutory Approaches . . .

§ 11.3.4.1. *Financial Assistance*

To prevent the default of an insured depository institution,[1] to restore a closed insured bank to normal operation,[2] or to lessen the risk to the FDIC from the instability of a significant number of insured depository institutions or of institutions with significant financial resources,[3] the FDIC has the sole

---

12. *See* U.S. Department of the Treasury, *Modernizing the Financial System*, Discussion Chapter I, at I-34 (Feb. 1991), reprinted in Fed. Banking L. Rep. (CCH) No. 1377, Pt. II (Feb. 14, 1991) (discussing FDIC treatment of bank failures).

13. *See* 12 U.S.C. § 1823(c), *as amended*, Riegle Community Development and Regulatory Improvement Act of 1994 (CDRIA), Pub. L. No. 103-325, Sept. 23, 1994, §602(a)(34)-(35), 108 Stat. 2160, 2289-2290 (1994) (codified at 12 U.S.C. §1823(c)(1)(B), (c)(2)(A)) (technical amendments); Economic Growth and Regulatory Paperwork Reduction Act, Pub. L. No. 104-208, title II, §2704(d)(14)(M) 110 Stat. 3009 (1996) (codified at 12 U.S.C. §1823) (technical and conforming amendment in light of prospective merger of BIF and SAIF into DIF). . . .

16. *See id.* at I-38–I-39. *But see* 12 U.S.C. §1823(c)(5), (i)(11) (limiting FDIC authority to make equity investments).

1. 12 U.S.C. §1823(c)(1)(A), *as amended*, Economic Growth and Regulatory Paperwork Reduction Act (EGRPR Act), Pub. L. No. 104-208, title II, §2704(d)(14)(M) 110 Stat. 3009 (1996) (codified at 12 U.S.C. § 1823) (prospective merger of BIF and SAIF into DIF).

2. *Id.* § 1823(c)(1)(B), as amended, Riegle Community Development and Regulatory Improvement Act of 1994 (CDRIA), Pub. L. No. 103-325, Sept. 23, 1994, §602(a)(34), 108 Stat. 2160, 2289 (1994) (codified at 12 U.S.C. § 1823(c)(1)(B)) (technical amendment); EGRPR Act, supra note 1.

3. *Id.* § 1823(c)(1)(C), as amended.

authority and discretion to give financial assistance to such institutions.[4] Such assistance may take the form of loans to, deposits in, purchase of assets or securities of, assumption of liabilities of, or contributions to any such institution.[5] FDIC financial assistance may also take the form of assistance to facilitate a merger, consolidation, or other acquisition of a troubled or closed insured depository institution by another insured institution.[6] FDIC decisions to render assistance are generally subject to a requirement that the FDIC make a determination that the assistance provided be "necessary to meet the obligation of the [FDIC] to provide insurance coverage,"[7] and that it be the least-cost approach to resolving the problem – that is, that

> the total amount of the expenditures by the [FDIC] and obligations incurred by the [FDIC] (including any immediate and long-term obligation of the [FDIC] and any direct or contingent liability for future payment by the [FDIC]) in connection with the exercise of any such [assistance] authority with respect to such institution is the least costly to the deposit insurance fund of all possible methods for meeting the [FDIC's] obligation....[8]

The FDIC may not use its assistance authority to purchase voting or common stock of an insured depository institution.[9] Assistance provided may be made

---

4. *Id.* § 1823(c)(1). For a discussion of the implications of an open-bank assistance arrangement, see *Senior Unsecured Creditors' Committee v. FDIC*, 749 F. Supp. 758 (N.D. Tex. 1990). In December 1992, the FDIC published a policy statement indicating the circumstances under which it would extend assistance to a troubled insured depository institution that was still open. 57 Fed. Reg. 60,203 (1992). In July 1996, the FDIC published a proposed revision of the policy statement. 61 Fed. Reg. 34,814 (1996).

5. 12 U.S.C. § 1823(c)(1). On purchase of assets by the FDIC, see *id.* § 1823(d). On parallel FDIC assistance authority for savings associations, see *id.* §1823(k)(5). Section 111 of the Garn-St Germain Act, Public Law 97-320, §111, 96 Stat. 1469 (1982), fundamentally amended the formerly narrow option presented by 12 U.S.C. § 1823(c). Previously, § 1823(c) had only authorized loans, deposits, and purchase of assets by the FDIC to prevent closing or to reopen a bank. The amended section also explicitly authorized the FDIC to engage in a range of actions in order to facilitate a merger or consolidation of an insured bank or to arrange a purchase and assumption transaction. *See* 12 U.S.C. § 1823(c)(2), *as amended*, CDRIA, §602(a)(35), 108 Stat. at 2289-2290 (codified at 12 U.S.C. § 1823(c)(2)(A)) (technical amendment).

6. 12 U.S.C. § 1823(c)(2). . . .

7. 12 U.S.C. § 1823(c)(4)(A)(i).

8. *Id.* § 1823(c)(4)(A)(ii). *See* 58 Fed. Reg. 67,662 (1993) (codified at 12 C.F.R. pt. 360) (FDIC least-cost resolution rules, implementing §141). See also Federal Deposit Insurance Corporation, Statement of Policy on Assistance to Operating Insured Depository Institutions, reprinted in 58 Fed. Reg. 60,203 (1993) (FDIC policy with respect to statutory cost test for FDIC-assisted resolutions, and requirements for FDIC assistance to operating institutions prior to appointment of conservator or receiver).

9. [12 U.S.C.] § 1823(c)(5).

subordinate to the rights of depositors and other creditors.[10]

§11.3.4.2. *Appointment of Conservator or Receiver*

It is generally within the discretion of the chartering authority[1] of a failing depository institution to determine whether or not to place it in conservatorship or receivership.[2] In a conservatorship, the basic statutory assumption is that the

---

10. *Id.* § 1823(c)(9).

1. *But see id.* § 1821(c)(4) (FDIC appointment of itself as conservator or receiver, notwithstanding other state or federal law, under specified statutory conditions). On judicial review of these FDIC self-appointments, see *id.* § 1821(c)(7). On FDIC replacement of itself as conservator in such situations, see *id.* § 1821(c)(8). *See also id.* § 1821(c)(10) (other grounds for FDIC self-appointment as conservator or receiver of insured depository institution). Heightened involvement of the regulators in the burgeoning thrift crisis beginning in the early 1980s placed additional strains on the regulatory system and raised questions about the discretion and good faith of the regulators themselves. For a case considering a challenge to federal regulatory discretion in the face of claims of basic property rights of thrift owners, see *Biscayne Fed. S.&L. v. Federal Home Loan Bank Bd.*, 720 F.2d 1499 (11th Cir. 1983), *cert. denied*, 467 U.S. 1215 (1984). *Cf. Hindes v. F.D.I.C.*, 137 F.3d 148 (3d Cir. 1998) (barring actions affecting FDIC exercise of powers as receiver, where claims based on allegedly improper notification by FDIC in corporate capacity that bank was operating in unsafe and unsound condition); *Auction Co. of America v. F.D.I.C.*, 132 F.3d 746 (D.C. Cir. 1998), clarified on denial of rehearing, 141 F.3d 1198 (allowing breach of contract action where auction company was to auction assets of failed thrifts for FDIC receiver; reading statutory reference to FDIC "as receiver" to mean as receiver for specific institution, not situation under auctioneer's contract); *Bolduc v. Beal Bank*, SSB, 994 F. Supp. 82 (D.N.H. 1998) (allowing certain affirmative claims of debtors' invalid indorsement relating to transfers arising long after FDIC received promissory notes at issue).

2. *See, e.g.*, 12 U.S.C. §§ 191 (Comptroller; declaration with respect to national bank), 1464(d)(2)(A) (DOTS; declaration with respect to federal savings association). On the grounds for the appointment of a receiver or conservator, see § 11.3.1, text and accompanying note 3, *supra*. On the procedures governing a conservatorship, see generally *In re Conservatorship of Wellsville Natl. Bank*, 407 F.2d 223 (3d Cir. 1969), *cert. denied sub nom. Miller v. Camp*, 396 U.S. 832, *reh'g denied*, 396 U.S. 949. *See also Central W. Rental Co. v. Horizon Leasing*, 740 F. Supp. 1109 (E.D. Pa. 1990) (challenge to conservator's actions, despite § 1464(d)(7)(C) prohibition on judicial action restraining or affecting conservator's power). On the procedures governing the decision to place an institution in receivership, see generally *Federal Deposit Ins. Corp. v. McKnight*, 769 F.2d 658 (10th Cir. 1985), *cert. denied*, 475 U.S. 1010. The receivership process has primarily been an administrative one, with a limited role for courts. *See Shemonsky v. Office of Thrift Supervision*, 733 F. Supp. 892 (M.D. Pa. 1990), *aff'd*, 922 F.2d 833 (3d Cir.), *cert. denied*, 499 U.S. 965 (1991); *Matter of Receivership of Penn Square Bank, N.A.*, 556 F. Supp. 494 (D. Okla. 1983). On conservatorship and liquidation procedures for insured credit unions, see, e.g., 66 Fed. Reg. 40,574 (2001) (codified at 12 C.F.R. §§ 709.0, 709.12) (clarifying that, as conservator or liquidating agent of federally insured credit union, NCUA will honor claim for prepayment fees by FHLBank under specified circumstances); 68 Fed. Reg. 32,355 (2003) (codified at 12 C.F.R. § 709.13) (amending NCUA involuntary liquidation regulation to designate swap agreements as "qualified financial contracts," limiting swap counterparty exposure when federally-insured credit union is placed in involuntary liquidation or conservatorship).

institution may well return to the transaction of its business.[3] In a receivership, the basic statutory assumption is that the institution will be merged with or otherwise acquired by a healthy depository institution or liquidated.[4] In either event, a conservator or receiver, respectively, will be appointed. Almost inevitably in either case, this will be the FDIC.[5]

The statutory rules governing the appointment of the FDIC in either capacity override any contrary provision of federal law, state constitution, or state law.[6] In the case of federal depository institutions,[7] appointment of the FDIC as conservator is within the discretion of the institution's supervisor.[8] Appointment of the FDIC as receiver is mandatory whenever the institution's supervisor decides to place it in receivership.[9] When acting as conservator or receiver, the FDIC is not subject to the direction or supervision of any other state or federal agency in the exercise of its rights, powers, or privileges.[10] However, in the conservatorship context, the institution in conservatorship itself remains subject to the supervision of its appropriate federal banking agency—that is, the Comptroller (for national banks and district banks) and the Director of the Office of Thrift Supervision (for federal savings associations).[11]

---

3. *See, e.g.*, 12 U.S.C. § 205(a)(1) (termination of conservatorship of a national bank permitting the bank "to resume the transaction of its business subject to such terms, conditions, and limitations as the Comptroller may prescribe"). *See also Minichello v. Saxon*, 337 F.2d 75 (3d Cir. 1964), *cert. denied*, 380 U.S. 952, 393 U.S. 849, *reh'g denied*, 393 U.S. 992 (Comptroller's authority and minority shareholder rights). *Cf.* 12 U.S.C. § 1821(d)(2)(D) (general power of FDIC as conservator to put institution on sound and solvent condition and to conserve its assets). *But see* note 4, *infra*.

4. *See, e.g.*, 12 U.S.C. § 1821(c)(2)(A)(ii) (appointment of FDIC as receiver "for the purpose of liquidation or winding up the affairs of an insured Federal depository institution"). *See also id.* § 1821(d)(2)(E) (general power of FDIC as receiver to place institution in liquidation). Despite its starting assumption (see text and accompanying note 3, supra), a conservatorship may also ultimately conclude with the liquidation or winding up of the affairs of the institution in conservatorship. *See* 12 U.S.C. § 205(a)(2).

5. *See generally* 12 U.S.C. § 1821(c) (appointment of FDIC as conservator or receiver).

6. *See id.* § 1821(c)(1).

7. For these purposes, the term federal depository institution is defined by the FDIA to mean "any national bank, any Federal savings association, and any Federal branch" of a foreign bank. *Id.* § 1813(c)(4). On the meaning of federal savings association, see *id.* § 1813(b)(2). On the meaning of the term federal branch, see *id.* § 1813(s)(2).

8. *Id.* § 1821(c)(2)(A)(i) (in general), (c)(6)(A) (DOTS appointment of FDIC or RTC as conservator; FDIC acceptance of appointment). *But see id.* § 1821(c)(11) (FDIC opportunity to appoint itself as receiver, under certain conditions, before federal agency may appoint a conservator).

9. *Id.* § 1821(c)(2)(A)(ii) (in general), (c)(6)(B)(i)-(ii) (DOTS appointment of RTC during threexyear period beginning August 9, 1989; DOTS appointment of FDIC thereafter).

10. *Id.* § 1821(c)(2)(C).

11. *Id.* § 1821(c)(2)(D).

In the case of insured state depository institutions,[12] appointment of the FDIC as conservator or receiver is within the discretion of the appropriate state authority.[13] When acting as conservator or receiver under appointment by the state authority, the FDIC is not subject to the direction or supervision of any other state or federal agency in the exercise of its rights, powers, or privileges.[14] However, in the conservatorship context, the institution in conservatorship itself remains subject to the supervision of its state authority.[15]

As conservator or receiver, the FDIC has a wide range of statutory powers.[16] The FDIC gains control of the entity as its successor by operation of law.[17] As such, the FDIC has full authority to operate the institution.[18] Whether serving as conservator or receiver, it also has the power to effect the merger

---

12. For these purposes, the term *insured state depository institution* is derived from two terms defined by the FDIA: "insured depository institution," defined to mean "any bank or savings association the deposits of which are insured by the [FDIC]" and "state depository institution," defined to mean "any State bank, any State savings association and any insured branch which is not a Federal branch" of a foreign bank. *Id.* § 1813(c)(2), (c)(4). On the meaning of the term state bank, see *id.* §1813(a)(2). On the meaning of the term state savings association, see *id.* §1813(b)(3). On the meaning of the term insured branch, see *id.* §1813(s)(3).

13. *Id.* § 1821(c)(3)(A). In the past, this discretionary aspect of the appointment of a federal agency as receiver has occasionally created tension between the state authority and the federal agency. *See, e.g., Fidelity Sav. & Loan Assn. v. Federal Home Loan Bank*, 689 F.2d 803 (9th Cir. 1982) (describing tension between California Savings and Loan Commissioner and now defunct FSLIC). For grounds for appointment of FDIC as conservator or receiver of state depository institution by its appropriate *federal* banking agency (after consultation with the state authority), see 12 U.S.C. § 1821(c)(9).

14. 12 U.S.C. § 1821(c)(3)(C).

15. *Id.* § 1821(c)(3)(D).

16. This grant of authority includes all incidental powers "as shall be necessary to carry out [its] powers" as conservator or receiver. *Id.* § 1821(d)(2)(I). *See also id.* § 1821(c)(2)(B), (c)(3)(B) (additional powers available to FDIC as conservator or receiver), (c)(13) (additional powers where FDIC is self-appointed under § 1821(c)(4), appointed by the DOTS under § 1821(c)(6), appointed because of undercapitalization under § 1821(c)(9), or self-appointed because of potential loss to deposit fund under § 1821(c)(10)). The FDIC resolution and receivership rules are contained in 12 C.F.R. pt. 360. For a case discussing the applicability of pt. 360, see *Waterview Management Co. v. FDIC*, 257 F. Supp. 2d 31 (D.D.C. 2003) (holding judgment awarding customer of savings bank in receivership prejudgment interest not superseded by FDIC claim-prioritizing regulation; requiring FDIC to pay customer post-judgment interest).

17. 12 U.S.C. § 1821(d)(2)(A).

18. *Id.* § 1821(d)(2)(B), *as amended,* CDRIA, §602(a)(22), 108 Stat. at 2289 (codified at 12 U.S.C. § 1821(d)(2)(B)(iii)) (technical amendment). On the functions of the institution's directors, officers, and shareholders by FDIC regulation or order, see id. § 1821(d)(2)(C). In operating the institution, the FDIC also has the responsibility to pay all valid obligations of the institutions "in accordance with the prescriptions and limitations of [the FDIA]." *Id.* § 1821(d)(2)(H).

of the institution with another insured depository institution,[19] or arrange a purchase or assumption transaction with another insured depository institution.[20] Where it determines that it is "practicable, efficient, and cost effective"[21] the FDIC may utilize the resources of the private sector to carry out its responsibilities for management and disposition of the assets of an insured depository institution. In addition to these general powers, there is also a range of specific powers available to the FDIC in either of its capacities.

As conservator, the FDIC has the power to take any action necessary to put the institution in a sound and solvent condition.[22] It also has the power to take any action appropriate to carry on the institution's business and to preserve or conserve the institution's assets.[23]

As receiver, the FDIC has the power to liquidate the institution and realize on the institution's assets, "having due regard [for] the conditions of credit in the locality" of the institution.[24] In this respect, the FDIC may organize a new savings association,[25] a new national bank,[26] or a transitional "bridge bank"[27] to take over assets and liabilities of the institution in receivership, as it deems appropriate.

The growth of interstate banking and branching over the past two decades and the increasing complexity of bank products and practices (such as sweep accounts[28]) has made the determination of closing account balances much

---

19. *Id.* § 1821(d)(2)(G)(i)(I).

20. *Id.* § 1821(d)(2)(G)(i)(II). *See SCFC ILC, Inc. v. Visa USA, Inc.*, 936 F.2d 1096, 1099-1100 (11th Cir. 1991) (interpreting statute). This transaction would be subject to the approval of the appropriate federal banking agency that supervises the acquiring institution. 12 U.S.C. § 1821(d)(2)(G)(ii). The FDIC also has the authority to purchase assets of an insured depository institution in default from any conservator, receiver or liquidator, including itself, or to take assets as security for loans from the FDIC. *Id.* § 1823(d)(2)(D).

21. 12 U.S.C. § 1821(d)(2)(K).

22. *Id.* § 1821(d)(2)(D)(i).

23. *Id.* § 1821(d)(2)(D)(ii).

24. *Id.* § 1821(d)(2)(E). On the status of the FDIC as receiver, see id. §1822.

25. *See id.* § 1821(d)(2)(F)(i).

26. *See id.* § 1821(d)(2)(F)(ii), (m).

27. *See id.* § 1821(d)(2)(F)(ii), (n). *See generally Bell & Murphy & Assoc., Inc. v. Interfirst Bank Gateway, N.A.*, 894 F.2d 750 (5th Cir.), *cert. denied*, 498 U.S. 895 (1990) (discussing role of bridge banks).

28. *See* 73 Fed. Reg. 2364, 2366 (2008):

> Most agreements between sweep customers and a depository institution expressly provide that the institution's liability, once the sweep occurs [from a designated account], is not a deposit (as defined in [12 U.S.C. § 1813(*l*)]) and that the institution will pay interest (typically overnight) while the liability remains a non-deposit liability. These sweep agreements allow an institution to pay interest without violating the statutory prohibition on the payment of interest on demand deposits. [*See, e.g.*, 12 U.S.C. §§ 371a, 1828(g) (so providing); *see also* 12 C.F.R. pts. 217; 329 (implementing regulations).] These sweep agreements also relieve insured institutions from having to maintain reserve requirements for the swept liabilities under the

more complicated for the receiver. The industry is more concentrated than in the past, and increasingly, consolidated financial institutions are much larger, factors further complicating the determination. Among other things, these complications make it more difficult for the FDIC to determine potential deposit insurance liability quickly and accurately in the event of a bank closing. In July 2008, the FDIC adopted a final rule requiring the largest insured depository institutions to adopt mechanisms that would, in the event of the institution's failure, provide the FDIC with standard deposit account and other customer information; and allow the placement and release of holds on liability accounts, including deposits.[29] The requirement applies only to insured depository institutions having at least $2 billion in domestic deposits[30] and either more than 250,000 deposit accounts[31] (currently estimated to be 152 institutions) or total assets over $20 billion, regardless of the number of deposit accounts[32] (currently estimated to be seven institutions). Subject to exceptions indicated in the final rule,[33] institutions subject to this final rule will have 18 months from the effective date of the final rule to implement the requirements,[34] or 18 months following the end of the second calendar quarter for which it first meets the criteria for a covered institution,[35] or 18 months after a merger in which the surviving institution is a covered institution.[36] However, under specified circumstances on a case-by-case basis, the FDIC may accelerate, upon notice, the implementation time frame of all or part of the requirements for a covered institution.[37]

---

regulations issued by the Board of Governors of the Federal Reserve System. [12 C.F.R. pt. 204.] In addition, the agreements relieve institutions from having to pay deposit insurance assessments (or premiums) on the swept liabilities, since only deposits are included in the base upon which institutions pay assessments. [*Id.* § 327.5.]

29. 73 Fed. Reg. 41,180 (2008) (codified at 12 C.F.R. § 360.9, apps. A-H).

30. 12 C.F.R. § 360.9(b)(1).

31. *Id.* § 360.9(b)(1)(i).

32. *Id.* § 360.9(b)(1)(ii).

33. *See id.* § 360.9(e)(7), (f)-(g) (providing for exception and requests for exemptions).

34. *Id.* § 360.9(e)(1). The effective date of the final rule is August 18, 2008. 73 Fed. Reg. at 41,180.

35. 12 C.F.R. § 360.9(e)(2).

36. *Id.* § 360.9(e)(3)-(5).

37. *Id.* § 360.9(e)(6). The specified circumstances involve any covered institution that

Has a composite rating of 3, 4, or 5 under the Uniform Financial Institution's Rating System, or in the case of an insured branch of a foreign bank, an equivalent rating; is undercapitalized, as defined under the prompt corrective action provisions of 12 CFR part 325; or is determined by the appropriate Federal banking agency or the FDIC in consultation with the appropriate Federal banking agency to be experiencing a significant deterioration of capital or significant funding difficulties or liquidity stress, notwithstanding the composite rating of the institution by its appropriate Federal banking agency in its most recent report of examination.

The final rule also requires that covered institutions have in place practices and procedures for providing the FDIC in a standard format upon the close of any day's business with required depositor and customer data for all deposit accounts held in domestic and foreign offices and interest-bearing investment accounts connected with sweep and automated credit arrangements.[38] At the same time, the FDIC adopted an interim rule establishing practices for determining deposit and other liability account balances at a failed insured depository institution.[39] In February 2009, the FDIC published a final version of that rule.[40] For the most part, the practices defined in the rule represent "a continuation of long-standing FDIC procedures in processing such balances,"[41] though it does initiate disclosure requirements with respect to sweep accounts. The rule is effective March 4, 2009.[42]

NOTES AND QUESTIONS

1. If making an equity investment in a troubled institution has proven to be a risky – and very expensive – approach to resolution of a failed depository institution, and is now statutorily limited,[10] then why has the Treasury Department been so anxious to pour billions of dollars into troubled institutions during the current financial crisis? This program – the Troubled Assets Relief Program, or "TARP" – is examined in the next chapter.

2. FDIA was also amended in August 1993 to provide a national depositor preference for amounts realized from the liquidation or other resolution of FDIC-insured depository institutions.[11] The amendment requires that distribu-

---

Id. In implementing this provision, the FDIC is required to consult with the institution's primary federal regulator and to consider the following factors:

> Complexity of the institution's deposit systems and operations, extent of the institution's asset quality difficulties, volatility of the institution's funding sources, expected near-term changes in the institution's capital levels, and other relevant factors appropriate for the FDIC to consider in its roles as insurer and possible receiver of the institution.

Id.

38. *Id.* § 360.9(d)(1). Such data files must be created "through a mapping of pre-existing data elements and internal institution codes into standard data formats. Deposit account and customer data provided must be current as of the close of business for that day."*Id.*

39. *See* 73 Fed. Reg. 41,170 (2008) (codified at 12 C.F.R. § 360.8).

40. 74 Fed. Reg. 5797 (2009) (codified at 12 C.F.R. § 360.8).

41. 74 Fed. Reg. at 5797.

42. *Id.*

10. *See* 12 U.S.C. §1823(c)(5), (i)(11) (limiting FDIC authority to make equity investments).

11. Pub. L. 103-66, 107 Stat. 312 (1993) (codified at 12 U.S.C. § 1821(d)(11)).

tions from all future receivership estates be made in the following order:

1. administrative expenses of the receiver;
2. deposit liability claims;
3. other general or senior liabilities of the institution, other than subordinated obligations or shareholder claims;
4. subordinated obligations; and,
5. shareholder claims.[12]

The legislation applies to all receiverships of insured institutions initiated after its enactment date (August 10, 1993),[13] and it supersedes any inconsistent state or other federal distribution provisions.[14] In practical terms, what does this mean for shareholders of WMI? For purchasers of securitized interest in WaMu mortgage pools? For former WaMu depositors?

3. In *Adagio Investment Holding Ltd. v. FDIC*,[15] a case involving the national deposit preference system, the FDIC was appointed as the receiver of the failed Connecticut Bank of Commerce. On the night of the bank's failure, in accordance with its customary practice, the FDIC "completed the day's business," which involved processing pending transactions, including approximately $20.2 million that had allegedly been authorized to be "swept" (*i.e.,* automatically transferred) from a demand deposit account in the bank to a non-insured, non-deposit account in the bank's international banking facility ("IBF").[16] Because deposits in an IBF are not "deposits" for purposes of the Federal Deposit Insurance Act § 3(*l*),[17] pursuant to the national deposit

---

12. *Id.*

13. 12 U.S.C. § 1821 note.

14. *Id.* § 1821(d)(11). For FDIC rules interpreting and implementing the amendment, see 58 Fed. Reg. 43,069 (1993) (codified at 12 C.F.R. pt. 360) (interim rule); 58 Fed. Reg. 67,662 (1993) (redesignating 12 C.F.R. §§ 360.1-360.3 as §§ 360.2-360.4) (final rule), *as amended,* 60 Fed. Reg. 35,487 (1995) (codified at 12 C.F.R. §§ 360.3(f), 360.4). For discussion of the applicability of sections 1821(d) and (e), see *Battista v. FDIC*, 195 F.3d 1113 (9th Cir. 1999), *cert. denied,* 531 U.S. 812 (2000) (holding that severance pay claims arising from FDIC repudiation, as receiver, of insolvent bank's employment contracts were subject to distribution priority scheme under section 1821(e), not distribution priority under section 1821(d)(11)(A)); *Bank of New York v. F.D.I.C.*, 453 F. Supp. 2d 82 (D.D.C. 2006) (upholding broad FDIC power to repudiate contracts of bank in receivership). *See also* 67 Fed. Reg. 34,385 (2002) (codified at 12 C.F.R. § 360.7) (providing for payment of post-insolvency interest in receiverships with surplus funds). *Cf. Golden Pacific Bancorp. v. FDIC*, 375 F.3d 196 (2d Cir. 2004) (holding that FDIC, as insured depositors' subrogee, was entitled to post-insolvency interest on funds previously paid to cover insurance obligations).

15. 338 F. Supp. 2d 71 (D.D.C. 2004).

16. For discussion of IBFs, deposit entries treated as off-shore obligations, see 3 MICHAEL P. MALLOY, BANKING LAW AND REGULATION §12.3.1, text and accompanying notes 4-5 (Aspen 1994 & Cum. Supps.).

17. 12 U.S.C. §1813(*l*).

preference statute the FDIC issued the holders of these "deposits" receivership certificates as general creditors, rather than according them priority status as depositors. The creditors, claiming that the receiver did not have authority to permit the sweeps, sued the FDIC. The federal district court for the District of Columbia concluded that the sweep should not have been performed in light of the lack of "any provision in either the statute or regulations that would permit the sweep that occurred."[18] Adagio then moved for summary judgment. In reading the following excerpt from the court's decision, consider carefully how the court characterizes the legal issues before it. Why does the FDIC lose on this motion?

ADAGIO INVESTMENT HOLDING LTD. V. FDIC

338 F. Supp. 2d 85 (D.D.C. 2004)

HUVELLE, District Judge.

Plaintiff Elver Capital Ltd. ("Elver") alleges that FDIC improperly classified Elver's certificate of deposit ("CD") held at the Connecticut Bank of Commerce ("CBC") when it failed in June 2002. . . . [B]efore the Court is plaintiff's partial motion for summary judgment. [T]he Court concludes that plaintiff's motion should be granted because FDIC, contrary to its regulations, failed to rely on the bank's records, which, along with the testimony of CBC officials, establish that Elver's CD was a garden-variety CD, and not an IBF CD.

BACKGROUND

On July 5, 2001, Elver, a British Virgin Islands corporation, completed CBC's International Account Opening Documentation ("IAOD"), checking three boxes: "checking" (also known as a demand deposit account or "DDA"), "International Banking Facility Deposit-Non-Bank Customer" (also known as an "IBF") and "Certificate of Deposit." . . . The bank established three different account numbers corresponding to each type of account that Elver had opened. . . . Elver's checking account statements reflect funds flowing daily between the checking and IBF accounts, and they also indicate the quarterly maturing and contemporaneous issuance of a replacement ninety-day $250,000 CD in Elver's name.

After CBC was closed by order of the Connecticut Superior Court on June 26, 2002, FDIC accepted appointment as the bank's receiver and began the process of determining which accountholders' funds qualified for deposit

18. *Adagio Investment*, 338 F. Supp. 2d at 81.

insurance and how claims against CBC's receivership estate were to be prioritized. FDIC ultimately concluded that Elver's CD was an IBF CD, rather than an ordinary CD. Had the latter been the case, FDIC, in its corporate capacity, would have paid Elver $100,000 in deposit insurance, and pursuant to the National Depositor Preference Act ("NDPA"), 12 U.S.C. § 1821(d)(11), FDIC, in its capacity as receiver for CBC, would have issued a Class 2 receivership certificate for the CD's remaining $150,000.[2] However, having been classified as an owner of an IBF CD, Elver received no deposit insurance and was issued a Class 3 receivership certificate, which as a practical matter has no monetary value.

Thus, the issue presented is whether FDIC violated the Federal Deposit Insurance Act, 12 U.S.C. §§ 1811 *et seq.* ("FDI Act"), and related regulations when it designated Elver's CD as an IBF CD account, as opposed to an insured and NDPA-preferred ordinary certificate of deposit account.

LEGAL ANALYSIS . . .

In addressing plaintiff's motion, FDIC correctly notes that, "[i]n making the [CD] insurance determinations, FDIC is entitled to rely exclusively on the deposit account records of a failed institution." . . . Indeed, FDIC is *required* to rely on them, unless it finds them ambiguous. 12 C.F.R. § 330.5(a)(1). *See also FDIC v. Fedders Air Conditioning, USA, Inc.,* 35 F.3d 18, 22-23 (1st Cir.1994) (relying on bank records as evidence to support a claim of a deposit denied by FDIC). This principle, which FDIC purportedly followed in classifying Elver's CD as an IBF CD, guides this Court's analysis. However, because the Court cannot agree Elver's money was deposited in an IBF CD in light of CBC's unambiguous records, it grants partial summary judgment in favor of Elver.

First, plaintiff's IAOD clearly reflected Elver's choice to open three separate types of account, including a "certificate of deposit" that made no reference to an international banking facility. . . . Moreover, . . . an international customer's decision to open an IBF in addition to a checking account did not transform all facets of the customer's banking relationship with CBC into an IBF. . . . Rather, Elver – like twenty-four other similarly-situated plaintiffs – had separate DDA and IBF accounts. This same reasoning applies to Elver's decision to open a CD in addition to a DDA and an IBF – the IAOD clearly reflects Elver's intent to open a CD, but in no way supports the notion that the CD was an IBF CD. . . . Therefore, since the IAOD filled out by Elver indicates its intent to open an ordinary CD, there is no basis to argue that the IAOD established an IBF CD, which is itself such an obscure financial instrument that the FDIC claims agent in charge of CBC's closure had only

---

2. To date, such receivership certificates have been paid sixty-one cents on the dollar. . . .

encountered it once before. . . .

Second, Elver's account statements confirm that CBC in fact established the three account types requested on the IAOD. Elver's DDA statement shows numerous wire transfers, the IBF overnight sweeps, and the quarterly maturing of a $250,000 CD, with corresponding interest, and the contemporaneous issuance of a replacement ninety-day CD for $250,000, with an interest rate of 2.6% as of May 7, 2002. . . . Nothing in the statement would signal to Elver, FDIC, or this Court that Elver's CD was anything other than a regular CD. Rather, the statement simply reflects a "Deposit from closed CD," giving the certificate number and amount, and later that day shows a "Transfer to CD Acct.," giving a new certificate number, the date of maturity, and the interest rate. There is no reference to an IBF in the CD line items. By contrast, the IBF sweep is clearly listed as "Transfer into IBF/Transfer Cdt. [credit]" and "Transfer From IBF/Transfer Dr. [debit]." Therefore, Elver's account statement does not support, and indeed refutes, FDIC's attempt to merge Elver's CD with its IBF.

Third, there is no evidence to support the contention that Elver's CD was somehow linked to its IBF, thereby rendering the CD an IBF CD. Elver's CD had a different account number from its IBF . . . , and it received a higher rate of interest on the funds in the CD, as compared to the IBF. . . . And, although funds from Elver's CD and its IBF accounts were deposited in Elver's DDA checking account on the day each quarter when the CD matured, a new CD was always purchased contemporaneously in precisely the same amount as the CD that had just matured. . . .

In addition to these bank records, the testimony of CBC officials also refutes FDIC's theory that an IBF CD was offered to the bank's customers. Carmen Gomez, an international account officer at CBC, stated emphatically that the bank did not offer IBF CDs. . . . So did CBC's Senior Vice President, Benjamin Canto. . . . Moreover, Joseph Bush, Jr., FDIC's Senior Financial Management Analyst in charge of numerous FDIC functions with respect to the closing of CBC . . . , conceded that, despite his assertion that CBC offered IBF CDs to its customers, Ms. Gomez's and Mr. Canto's knowledge of what products CBC offered would "trump" his own. . . .

Thus, FDIC has not shown that Elver chose to, or was even able to, open an IBF CD. The bank records that relate specifically to plaintiff's account demonstrate unequivocally that Elver's CD was a regular CD, not an IBF CD. Bank officials in a position to know what products they offered customers also testified that CBC did not offer IBF CDs. Therefore, as required by 12 C.F.R. § 330.5(a)(1), the Court must conclude that the bank's records clearly show that Elver's CD was not an IBF CD, and, indeed, customer IBF CDs were a fiction first created by FDIC after it assumed control of the bank.

Despite the compelling and unrebutted evidence from the bank's account documents relating to Elver and from CBC officials, FDIC argues that CBC's internal records and its general ledger show that Elver's CD was in "Branch 31" and that this somehow rendered the CD part of Elver's IBF account. While it is true that Elver's CD was reflected in Branch 31 on CBC's books and records . . . , the leap that Branch 31 was equivalent to a customer IBF CD account is simply inconsistent with the evidence.

As FDIC argues, CBC, for internal bookkeeping purposes, treated Elver's CD as part of "Branch 31," which was not a physical bank branch, but rather was a category used by CBC to refer to "IBF/Correspondent Banking CD Offshore > 100K." . . . Elsewhere, Branch 31 was referred to simply as "IBF/Correspondent Banking." . . . But the moniker in and of itself proves nothing. Rather, it is necessary to examine the records relating to Branch 31 to understand the error made by FDIC. For, as is clear from FDIC's own records, Branch 31 contained *CBC's* IBF money, and this money was invested by CBC with a correspondent bank (M & T Bank) in Buffalo, New York. In other words, there was an IBF CD, but it belonged to CBC, not its customers, and it was funded by foreign investors' funds, some of which were customers' IBF funds, while others were ordinary insured deposits like CDs.

As correctly argued by Elver, this is the only reasonable interpretation of the bank's internal records. . . .

In addition to its incorrect interpretation of the meaning of Branch 31, FDIC relies on the deposition testimony of Mercedes Braida, a CBC foreign exchange trader, who stated that some IBFs were made up of certificates of deposit. . . . Yet, Ms. Braida's testimony does not justify an inference that Elver's CD was an IBF CD. Rather, it supports the undisputed proposition that the Branch 31 account included customers' certificates of deposit, but it in no way indiscriminately lumps those CDs with the IBFs of these same customers, as FDIC attempts to do here. . . .

CONCLUSION

In sum, the evidence before the Court indicates that the only reasonable inference is that Elver's CD was not an IBF CD. FDIC violated the FDI Act and its own regulations by characterizing Elver's CD as an uninsured and NDPA non-preferred bank liability, when in fact the bank's own records clearly showed it to be a CD that was an insured deposit for FDI Act purposes. *See* 12 U.S.C. § 1813(*l*). Accordingly, FDIC is directed to pay plaintiff deposit insurance up to the legal limit ($100,000) on Elver's CD and to issue a Class 2 "excess deposit" receivership certificate for the remainder.

NOTES AND QUESTIONS

1. *Adagio Investment* would seem to be a clear "win" for depositors of a

failed depository institution in receivership, but consider carefully the issue before the court and the standard of judicial review that the court applies in reviewing the FDIC's decision not to classify Elver's claim as an insured deposit. The issue before the court is whether "the FDIC, contrary to its regulations, failed to rely on the bank's records, which, along with the testimony of CBC officials, establish that Elver's CD was a garden-variety CD." The standard is whether there is a "reasonable inference" supporting the FDIC's decision. In the typical situation, this is a strategic advantage for an administrative agency like the FDIC. It must show only that there is a reasonable inference to be drawn from the record in support of its position, not that its position is unavoidable. Had the bank records been at all ambiguous, it is quite possible that the FDIC's decision would have been upheld.

2. One feature of the FDIC's resolution process that may promote efficiency is the administrative process for third parties – not just depositors – who have claims to assert against the depository institution in receivership. Prior to 1989, resolving the problems of a failing depository institution could be considerably complicated, and the costs markedly increased, by the claims of third parties that had dealt with the institution. The now defunct Federal Home Loan Bank Board and the Federal Savings & Loan Insurance Corporation (FSLIC) tried to implement an expedited administrative process for claims against insolvent savings & loan associations (S&Ls), but this was struck down by the Supreme Court in 1988, on the grounds that the FSLIC did not have statutory authority to exercise exclusive adjudicatory power over creditors' claims against insolvent S&Ls in FSLIC receivership.[19] In response to the savings & loan crisis of the 1980s, however, the FDIC as receiver was given explicit statutory authority to determine the validity of claims against the institution in an exclusive administrative process subject to an elaborate statutory procedure.[20]

3. There are three major types of claimants that can be particularly troubling in the resolution of a failed bank. One, of course, is the group of depositors, all of whom are clamoring for insurance coverage or assumption of the deposit by an acquiring bank. A second set of claimants is the bank's

---

19. *Coit Independence Joint Venture v. FSLIC*, 489 U.S. 561 (1988). *See also Carrollton-Farmers Branch Indep. Sch. Dist. v. Johnson & Cravens*, 889 F.2d 571 (5th Cir. 1989) (rehearing on claims following *Coit*); *Triland Holding & Co. v. Sunbelt Serv. Corp.*, 884 F.2d 205 (5th Cir. 1989) (remand under *Coit*); *Central W. Rental Co. v. Horizon Leasing*, 740 F. Supp. 1109 (E.D. Pa. 1990) (applying *Coit*). *See generally* Baxter, *Life in the Administrative Track: Administrative Adjudication of Claims Against Savings Institution Receivers*, 1988 DUKE L.J. 422 (discussing *Coit* and making recommendations for reform).

20. *See* 12 U.S.C. §1821(d)(3)-(10). On the adjudication of creditor claims involving federally insured credit unions in liquidation, see 12 U.S.C. §1787(c); 12 C.F.R. pt. 709, as amended, 66 Fed. Reg. 11,229 (2001) (codified at 12 C.F.R. §§ 709.0, 709.12).

investors – with equity investors given the least favorable preference under 12 U.S.C. § 12 U.S.C. § 1821(d)(11), and debt holders placed behind the FDIC's administrative expenses and the depositors. Depending upon the terms of the debt instrument, which may be subordinated to other general or senior creditors, debt holders may even be behind a third set of claimants – other customers of the bank, for example, borrowers with claims out of the loan agreement or the performance of its terms.

2. Investors as Claimants

Adagio Investment gives us an example of what can happen in the context of claims by depositors. The next two case excerpts deal with the second type of claimants – equity investors (including WaMu's former holding company) in the first excerpt, and bond holders in the second.

WASHINGTON MUTUAL, INC. V. FDIC

— F.Supp.2d —, 2009 WL 3164419 (D.D.C. 2009)

ROSEMARY M. COLLYER, District Judge.

[Claimants brought an action against the FDIC both as "corporation" and as receiver for WaMu, seeking judicial review of the FDIC's sale of certain assets that allegedly belonged to WMI, the former WaMu holding company that was also one of the claimants. JPMorgan Chase, as purchaser of the disputed assets, moved to intervene. The district court granted the motion, holding that: (*i*) the purchaser was entitled to intervene as of right and had Article III standing; and, (*ii*) an automatic stay in WMI's Chapter 11 bankruptcy proceeding did not bar the purchaser from intervening and asserting its counterclaim.]

Plaintiffs Washington Mutual, Inc. ("WMI"), and WMI Investment Corp. have filed this action against the Federal Deposit Insurance Corporation ("FDIC") in its separate capacities as a corporation and as receiver for Washington Mutual Bank, Henderson, Nevada ("WMB"), a federal savings bank owned by WMI. WMI brings this case pursuant to the Federal Deposit Insurance Act, 12 U.S.C. § 1811 *et seq.,* which allows a party to seek judicial review of its claims after such claims are disallowed by the receiver. *See* 12 U.S.C. § 1821(d)(6). The Complaint effectively alleges that the FDIC, as receiver for WMB, purported to sell certain assets to J.P. Morgan Chase ("JPMC") but that such assets belonged to Plaintiffs, not to WMB, and that the FDIC owes Plaintiffs billions of dollars in compensation. . . . JPMC seeks to intervene as a defendant. . . . As explained below, the motion to intervene will be granted.

I. FACTS

On September 25, 2008, the Director of the Office of Thrift Supervision ("OTS") appointed the FDIC as receiver for WMB ("FDIC-Receiver"). FDIC-Receiver immediately sold "substantially all the assets of WMB" to JPMC pursuant to a Purchase and Assumption Agreement ("P & A Agreement") dated September 25, 2008. . . . The following day, Plaintiffs filed for bankruptcy protection pursuant to chapter 11 of title 11 of the United States Code (the "Bankruptcy Code") in the United States Bankruptcy Court for the District of Delaware (the "Bankruptcy Court"). . . . In the schedules of assets submitted to the Bankruptcy Court, WMI claimed it owned or otherwise held interests in certain WMB assets acquired by JPMC from the FDIC as receiver for WMB under the P & A. . . . Similarly, WMI submitted claims against the FDIC-Receiver asserting that it owned or held interests in certain assets purportedly sold to JPMC pursuant to the P & A Agreement. . . .

The FDIC-Receiver disallowed WMI's claims on January 23, 2009, on the grounds that, *inter alia,* WMI's claims lacked sufficient documentation, failed to state claims against the receivership, and appeared to assert claims against third parties. Thereafter, WMI filed this action pursuant to 12 U.S.C. §1821(d)(6). On March 24, 2009, JPMC initiated an adversary proceeding against WMI in the Bankruptcy Court, and on March 30, 2009, JPMC filed a motion to intervene in this case, in both instances seeking to assert and protect its ownership interests in the assets it purportedly purchased from the FDIC-Receiver. . . .

III. ANALYSIS

[T]he Court finds that JPMC is entitled to intervene in this action. . . . First, JPMC's motion to intervene was timely, having been filed only ten days after Plaintiffs commenced this action. Second, JPMC has an interest in the property or transaction which is the subject of the action. The Court agrees with JPMC that Plaintiffs' claims are "premised on the allegation that assets sold by the FDIC to JPMC . . . belong to WMI." . . . In Count 4 of the Complaint, for example, Plaintiffs allege that "property taken into the Receivership that (a) belonged to Plaintiffs rather than WMB, (b) was improperly transferred to WMB, and/or (c) is property that otherwise should be returned to Plaintiffs under applicable law." . . . The property to which Plaintiffs refer is the very same property JPMC purportedly purchased under the P & A Agreement. "An intervenor's interest is obvious when he asserts a claim to property that is the subject matter of the suit." *Foster v. Gueory,* 655 F.2d 1319, 1324 (D.C.Cir. 1981).

The third element required for intervention of right . . . is that the disposition of the action may impair the movant's ability to protect his interests. That element is met here, as WMI is asking the Court to find that it was the owner of the property FDIC-Receiver purported to sell to JPMC or, at the very least, that its claim of ownership is colorable and the FDIC-Receiver was wrong to disallow it. Such a finding would likely impair JPMC's interests under the P & A Agreement. Finally, the Court notes none of the current parties adequately represents JPMC's interests in this matter. Plaintiffs' interests are directly opposed to those of JPMC, and the FDIC, as a government entity, must serve the public interest and adhere to federal law. The FDIC "would be shirking its duty were it to advance [JPMC's] narrower interest at the expense of its representation of the general public interest." *Dimond v. District of Columbia,* 792 F.2d 179, 192-93 (D.C.Cir.1986); *see also Fund for Animals, Inc. v. Norton,* 322 F.3d 728, 736 (D.C.Cir.2003) (granting intervention where, although federal defendant and movant's initial positions were similar, it was not unlikely that their interests "might diverge during the course of litigation" due to their differing obligations). Therefore, JPMC has met the criteria for intervention of right in this action.

JPMC also meets the requirements for Article III standing. JPMC asserts that WMI seeks to divest it of its ownership interest in assets it purportedly purchased under the P & A Agreement. . . . WMI argues that it merely seeks monetary damages from the FDIC; however, the Complaint clearly alleges that WMI had an ownership interest in some or all of the property the FDIC Receiver purported to transfer to JPMC. . . . Plaintiffs also made these allegations in WMI's claims to the FDIC, which WMI asks the Court to declare valid. . . . Thus, JPMC asserts an impending injury, caused by Plaintiffs, redressable by this Court.

Plaintiffs argue, however, that the automatic stay in the bankruptcy proceeding bars JPMC from intervening and asserting a counterclaim in this matter. . . . The Bankruptcy Code imposes an automatic stay prohibiting any entity from commencing or continuing any action with respect to a claim against the debtor if such claim arose prior to the filing of the bankruptcy petition and prohibiting "any act to obtain possession of property of the estate . . . or to exercise control over property of the estate." 11 U.S.C. 362(a)(1) and (3). However, JPMC is not attempting to bring a claim against the debtor – rather, the debtor has brought claims that implicate JPMC's interests. Thus, WMI's claim that the automatic stay applies to JPMC's proposed intervention must fail. As the Seventh Circuit noted,

> [T]he automatic stay is inapplicable to suits by the bankrupt.... The fundamental purpose of bankruptcy ... is to prevent creditors from trying to steal a march on each other, and the automatic stay is essential to accomplishing this purpose. There is, in contrast, no policy of preventing persons whom the bankrupt has sued from protecting their legal rights.

Martin-Trigona v. Champion Federal Sav. & Loan Ass'n., 892 F.2d 575, 577 (7th Cir.1989); *see also Gordon v. Whitmore (In re Merrick*), 175 B.R. 333, 338 (B.A.P. 9th Cir.1994) ("The automatic stay should not tie the hands of a defendant while the plaintiff debtor is given free rein to litigate."); *Justus v. Financial News Network (In re Financial News Network),* 158 B.R. 570, 573 (S.D.N.Y.1993) ("Since [the Bankruptcy Code] mandates a stay only of litigation against the debtor . . . it does not prevent entities against whom the debtor proceeds in an offensive posture – for example, by initiating a judicial or adversarial proceeding – from protecting their legal rights.") (internal citation and quotation marks omitted).

Nor does the automatic stay apply to JPMC's counterclaim seeking a declaratory judgment finding that WMI does not own the property at issue. JPMC does not seek to take possession of or assert control over WMI's cause of action here, which is rightfully part of the estate. *See* 11 U.S.C. 541(a)(1); *Martin-Trigona,* 892 F.2d at 577 ("True, the bankrupt's cause of action is an asset of the estate; but as the defendant in the bankrupt's suit is not, by opposing that suit, seeking to take possession of it, [the automatic stay does not apply]."). Additionally, JPMC's counterclaim did not arise until after WMI filed for bankruptcy, when WMI asserted an ownership interest in the property JPMC purportedly purchased via the FDIC as receiver of WMB. The automatic stay provision of the Bankruptcy Code only applies to those claims arising prior to the filing of a bankruptcy petition. *See* 11 U.S.C. § 362(a)(1); *see also United States v. Inslaw, Inc.,* 932 F.2d 1467, 1473 (D.C.Cir.1991) (finding that a cause of action that arises post-petition is not stayed, and therefore is not an "act to obtain possession of property of the estate" in violation of 11 U.S.C. § 362(a)(3), because to find otherwise would require finding a violation "whenever someone already in possession of property mistakenly refuses to capitulate to a bankrupt's assertion of rights in that property").

NOTES AND QUESTIONS

1. Among other things, this case highlights the peculiar strains in federal policy with respect to insolvencies – a bank is not subject to the generally applicable bankruptcy laws, but its holding company is. While as an operating enterprise, there was a more or less complete practical identity between the holding company and what is typically its principal operating subsidiary, once insolvency occurs, they are treated like strangers or – worse yet – as adversaries. Since the financial condition of that subsidiary is likely to be the cause of the parent holding company's insolvency, the situation will naturally be a very complicated one. *See e.g., MCorp Financial, Inc. v. Board of Governors,* 900 F.2d 852 (5th Cir. 1990), *reversed on other grounds,* 502 U.S. 32 (1991) (illus-

trating complications inherent in failure of depository institutions and their holding company parent). How should this tension be resolved? Apparently not by progressive development of the case law; the Supreme Court missed an opportunity to work towards such an interpretive solution in *MCorp Financial*. In its decision in *MCorp Financial*, the Fifth Circuit had refused to allow the Federal Reserve Board to pursue administrative proceedings to force the holding company to act as a "source of strength" for its ailing operating subsidiary banks. On certiorari, the Supreme Court invalidated the Fifth Circuit's decision enjoining the "source of strength" proceeding, but on narrow grounds that did not determine the validity of the "source of strength" doctrine. Rather, the Court focused on the independence of these administrative proceedings from judicial intervention under 12 U.S.C. § 1818(i). Thus, the tension remains between bank regulatory enforcement in the failing bank context and federal bankruptcy law, generally applicable to the holding company of a failing bank.[21]

2. In *Washington Mutual*, the court noted one inherent conflict of interest in the FDIC's involvement in failing bank litigation: "the FDIC, as a government entity, must serve the public interest and adhere to federal law. The FDIC "would be shirking its duty were it to advance [JPMC's] narrower interest at the expense of its representation of the general public interest," citing *Dimond*. This is inherent in its position as the "Corporation." There is another inherent conflict that the court does not discuss – the conflict between the FDIC's role as *corporation*, a government regulator, and its role as *receiver*, which succeeds to the rights and obligations of the failed depository institution and has an obvious interest in seeing the purchase and assumption transaction upheld intact. Notice that it was in its role as receiver that the FDIC negotiated the purchase and assumption agreement with Chase. Notice also that WMI and WMI Investment Corp. sued the FDIC both as corporation and as receiver. Why are *both* capacities relevant to the claims of the plaintiffs? *Cf. United States v. Winstar Corporation*, 518 U.S. 839 (1996) (plurality opinion) (holding that apparently governmental role of regulator/receiver does not prevent contractual liability arising out of subsequent regulatory actions).

---

21. *But see FDIC v. Hirsch (In re Colonial Realty Co.)*, 980 F.2d 125 (2d Cir. 1992) (holding that automatic stay in bankruptcy applied to FDIC and barred it from exercising power to avoid asset transfers previously made by debtor). *See generally* John R. Ashmead, *In re Colonial Realty Co.: Second Circuit harmonizes bankruptcy and bank insolvency law (rejecting established bankruptcy case law in the process)*, 60 Brook. L. Rev. 517 (1994) (discussing *Hirsch* and suggesting that harmony between the two bodies of law was feasible).

WASHINGTON MUTUAL, INC. v. FDIC

— F.Supp.2d —, 2009 WL 3273880 (D.D.C. 2009)

ROSEMARY M. COLLYER, District Judge.

The plaintiffs in this case are Washington Mutual, Inc. ("WMI") . . . and WMI's affiliate, WMI Investment Corp. They complain that the FDIC disallowed their claims against WMB as asserted creditors of the Bank. Pending before the Court is a motion to intervene as a defendant, filed by the holders of senior notes issued by WMB (the "Bank Bondholders"),[1] which motion is opposed by the FDIC and the plaintiffs. For the reasons set forth below, the Court will grant the motion.

I. BACKGROUND

Although this is complex litigation, the immediate issue is not so complicated once the parties and their relationships are understood. WMB was closed by the Office of Thrift Supervision on September 25, 2008 and the FDIC was appointed to act as its receiver ("FDIC-Receiver"). Under the Federal Deposit Insurance Act (as amended, *inter alia,* by the Financial Institutions Reform, Recovery and Enforcement Act of 1989, Pub.L. No. 101-73, 103 Stat. 183 ("FIRREA")), the FDIC-Receiver succeeded to "all rights, titles, powers, and privileges of" WMB, 12 U.S.C. § 1821(d)(2)(A) (i); it was empowered to operate or liquidate WMB, *id.* §§ 1821(d)(2)(B), (E); and it was charged with the responsibility for determining claims against the receivership, *id.* § 1821(d)(3). In accordance with its statutory responsibilities, FDIC-Receiver established December 30, 2008 as the deadline for filing claims.

WMI filed a proof of claim on December 30, 2008, asserting itself as a creditor of WMB. The FDIC-Receiver disallowed the claim in a letter dated January 23, 2009. . . . WMI filed its complaint against this disallowance on

---

1. The Bank Bondholders are Bank of Scotland plc; Fir Tree Capital Opportunity Master Fund, L.P.; Fir Tree Mortgage Opportunity Master Fund, L.P.; Fir Tree Value Master Fund, L.P.; HFR ED Select Fund IV Master Trust; Lyxor/York Fund Limited; Marathon Credit Opportunity Master Fund, Ltd.; Marathon Special Opportunity Master Fund, Ltd.; Permal York Ltd.; Quintessence Fund L.P.; QVT Fund LP; The Governor and Company of the Bank of Ireland; The Varde Fund, L.P.; The Varde Fund VI-A, L.P.; The Varde Fund VII-B, L.P.; The Varde Fund VIII, L.P.; The Varde Fund IX, L.P.; The Varde Fund IX-A, L.P.; Varde Investment Partners (Offshore), Ltd.; Varde Investment Partners, L.P.; York Capital Management, L.P.; York Credit Opportunities Fund, L.P.; York Credit Opportunities Master Fund, L.P.; York Investment Master Fund, L.P.; York Select, L.P.; and York Select Master Fund, L .P.

March 20, 2009. . . . [*S*]*ee* 12 U.S.C. § 1821(d)(6)(A). In contrast, the Bank Bondholders assert that their senior notes have been recognized by the FDIC-Receiver as "a legitimate liability of the receivership," and that they will be issued receivership certificates reflecting this determination. . . .

III. ANALYSIS

The FDIC-Receiver and WMI contend that intervention by the Bank Bondholders is barred by FIRREA's jurisdictional bar that provides "no court shall have jurisdiction over any claim or action . . . seeking a determination of rights with respect to, the assets of" a failed bank as to which the FDIC has been appointed receiver or that "relat[es] to any act or omission" of the FDIC as receiver. 12 U.S.C. § 1821(d)(13)(D)(I); *see Freeman v. FDIC,* 56 F.3d 1394, 1402 (D.C.Cir.1995) (§ 1821(d) is a bar that "extends to all claims and actions against, and actions seeking a determination of rights with respect to, the assets of failed financial institutions for which the FDIC serves as receiver").

The Bank Bondholders respond that this argument is "invent[ed] out of whole cloth" because they do not want to sue the FDIC but, rather, defend the FDIC's disallowance of WMI's claim to be a creditor of WMB. . . . While they admittedly have no statutory right to intervene, the Bank Bondholders insist that they have an interest relating to WMI's claim against WMB because it could imperil their own chances of any recovery. Furthermore, the FDIC does not adequately represent the Bank Bondholders' interest in this action, because, as a government entity, it must serve the public interest and adhere to federal law, *see Dimond v. District of Columbia,* 792 F.2d 179, 192-93 (D.C.Cir.1986), and as receiver to WMB, it merely stands in the shoes of the failed bank. *See O'Melveny & Myers v. FDIC,* 512 U.S. 79, 86 (1994); 12 U.S.C. § 1821(d)(2)(A)(i).

The Court recognizes that Congress has given the FDIC full authority to make allowance determinations in these circumstances but also believes . . . the Bank Bondholders are not attempting to bring any "claim or action" that would otherwise be barred by § 1821(d)(13)(D)(I). They are seeking only to be heard with respect to their defenses to WMI's claims against the receivership estate, which claims the FDIC-Receiver and WMI concede are properly before the Court. Thus, even if the Bank Bondholders could not intervene as of right . . . the Court may permit them to intervene pursuant to [Fed.R.Civ.P. 24(a)]. The Court will grant the Bank Bondholders' motion with great caution, finding that the circumstances of this case – wherein the owners of a failed bank posit themselves as creditors against other creditors with claims in the receivership – warrant full explication of the law and facts.

NOTES AND QUESTIONS

1. Notice that WMI and the FDIC are both opposed to the bondholders' motion to intervene. Does the court seem more aware in this opinion than in the prior one of the potential conflict of interests involved in the FDIC's dual roles as corporation and receiver? If the bondholders' claims have in fact been recognized by the FDIC as "a legitimate liability of the receivership" – unlike WMI's claims – why is the FDIC joining WMI's opposition to the motion?

2. By granting the bondholders' motion, has the court in fact allowed a claim "seeking a determination of rights with respect to, the assets of" WMB, contrary to 12 U.S.C. § 1821(d)(13)(D)(I)? If it ultimately rejects WMI's claim because the bondholders' claims are superior to it, would that be "a determination of rights with respect to" WMB's assets still in receivership?

3. If, as the court admits, "Congress has given the FDIC full authority to make allowance determinations" in receivership situations, what is this litigation all about?

3. Third-Party Claimants

We now turn to the class of claimants consisting of other customers of the bank. As receivership claimants, they stand behind the FDIC's administrative expenses and the claims of depositors.[22] How likely is it that those who have contractual claims against WaMu or its affiliates would be able to make themselves whole by "following the money" – *i.e.*, suing the reconstituted parts of WaMu's business now in other hands? The following case excerpt explores the possibilities in that regard.

PUNZALAN V. FEDERAL DEPOSIT INSURANCE CORPORATION

---

633 F.Supp.2d 406 (W.D.Tex. 2009)

PHILIP R. MARTINEZ, District Judge.

[A group of mortgagors tried to bring a class action against a Texas bank and its mortgage-banking subsidiary in state court for wrongful foreclosure, because the foreclosure procedures did not comply with Texas law. In the meantime, WaMu had succeeded to the mortgages. When WaMu failed, and the FDIC was appointed receiver, the FDIC removed the case to federal district court and moved to dismiss the case for lack of subject matter jurisdiction

---

22. 12 U.S.C. § 1821(d)(11).

under the Financial Institutions Reform, Recovery, and Enforcement Act of 1989 (FIRREA). The district court granted the motion, holding that the mortgagors' failure to exhaust the administrative claims procedure established by FIRREA deprived the court of jurisdiction.]

I. Factual and Procedural Background . . .

B. FDIC's appointment as receiver and Chase
   Bank's purchase of Washington Mutual

On September 25, 2008, during the pendency of the Punzalans' appeal, the Office of Thrift Supervision (OTS) – acting pursuant to its authority under the [FIRREA] – closed Washington Mutual and appointed FDIC as its Receiver. . . . Contemporaneous with the appointment of FDIC as Receiver, J.P Morgan Chase Bank, National Association (Chase Bank) entered into a contract entitled "Purchase and Assumption Agreement" (the P & A Agreement) with FDIC. . . . Under Section 2.5 of the P & A Agreement, Chase Bank purchased Washington Mutual on the condition that FDIC remain responsible for any "Borrower Claims" against Washington Mutual "related in any way to any loan or commitment to lend made by [Washington Mutual] prior to failure . . . or otherwise arising in connection with the Washington Mutual's lending or loan purchase activities[.]" . . . In exchange, pursuant to Section 2.1 of the P & A Agreement, Chase Bank promised to assume responsibility for all other liabilities, specifically including "all mortgage servicing rights and obligations of [Washington Mutual]." . . .

C. FDIC's attempt to comply with FIRREA's notice requirements

On December 18, 2008, while the Court of Appeals considered FDIC's motions for stay and substitution, FDIC attempted to mail individual notice of FIRREA's administrative-claims procedure to the Punzalans. . . . In that notice, FDIC advised the Punzalans that they had to submit their claims against Washington Mutual to FDIC for administrative review by March 18, 2009, the "claims bar date." . . . Additionally, FDIC published and re-published similar notice in various newspapers of wide distribution, as required by FIRREA. . . .

The Punzalans never filed an administrative claim with FDIC.

D. FDIC's removal to federal court and its motion to dismiss . . .

In its motion, FDIC "requests that the Court dismiss Plaintiffs' action for lack of subject matter jurisdiction because Plaintiffs have failed to exhaust the mandatory administrative claims process set forth in 12 U.S.C. §§ 1821(d)(3) through (13)." . . . In response, the Punzalans first argue that their particular claim is one assumed by Chase Bank under Section 2.1 of the P & A

Agreement because their loan was one that was "serviced," and not owned by Washington Mutual. Alternatively, the Punzalans argue that, even if Washington Mutual did own the Punzalans' loan and FDIC thus assumed their claim under Section 2.5 of the P & A Agreement, FDIC may not subject their claim to FIRREA's administrative-claims procedure because FDIC mailed the Punzalans' notice to the wrong address, failing to satisfy FIRREA's mailing requirements. . . .

III. ANALYSIS

A. The Punzalan's claim that FDIC failed to provide them notice

. . . The Punzalans specifically argue that FDIC incorrectly mailed the Punzalans' notice to the zip code of 79902 instead of 79901, the allegedly correct zip code for their attorney's law firm, Firth Johnston Martinez. . . . The Punzalans have claimed no other deficiency in FDIC's notice aside from this one-digit variation in the zip code.

For FDIC to successfully invoke the administrative-claims procedure as to pre-receivership claims like the Punzalans', FDIC must comply with FIRREA's extensive notice requirements. Under these requirements, FDIC must both publish and mail notice to any creditors and claimants of the failed depository institution, instructing them to present their claims for FDIC's determination. *See* 12 U.S.C. § 1821(d)(3)(B)-(C) (requiring FDIC to publish notice and mail notice, respectively). Regarding the mailing requirement, FIRREA provides that "[t]he receiver shall mail a notice . . . to any creditor shown on the institution's books (i) at the creditor's last address appearing in such books; or (ii) upon discovery of the name and address of a claimant not appearing on the institutions books within 30 days after the discovery of such name and address." 12 U.S.C. § 1821(d)(3)(C)(i)-(ii).

The Court concludes for two reasons that FDIC complied with FIRREA's notice requirements, and thereby rejects the Punzalans' claim that FDIC's mailed notice was fatally deficient under § 1821(d)(3)(C).

First, . . . [n]either the Punzalans nor the FDIC have presented evidence as to what address, if any, appeared on Washington Mutual's "books." *See* 12 U.S.C. § 1821(d)(3)(C)(i) (providing for notice to be mailed to "any creditor shown on the institution's books at the creditor's last address appearing in such books").

However, the Court finds persuasive that in nearly all of the five years' worth of documents filed by Mr. Firth in Texas state court, Mr. Firth's very own signature block recites 79902 as the proper zip code for Firth Johnston Martinez's offices. . . . Moreover, as FDIC correctly notes, 79902 remains the zip code that is listed on the Court's docket for Firth Johnston Martinez. . . .

Second, and in the alternative, even if FDIC did affix the incorrect zip code on the Punzalans' notice, such an error would not render FDIC's notice fatally deficient under the standards of FIRREA. . . .

   B. The Punzalans' claim that its lawsuit is one assumed by
      Chase Bank . . .

While the Punzalans concede that "the only claim against [WaMu] at present is that of the Punzalans," they continue to seek the inclusion of FDIC as a defendant in this lawsuit based solely on speculation that "in the event a class is certified, there potentially are claims against [WaMu] as to mortgages it serviced, which would be subject to the receivership." . . . The Punzalans' argument only further counsels for the dismissal of their lawsuit as filed against FDIC. The Punzalans concede that the potential claims of any putative, unnamed plaintiffs would still be subject to FIRREA's exhaustion requirements. . . .

NOTES AND QUESTIONS

   1. *On the Same Page?* The majority of circuits have recognized the preclusive effect of the administrative claims provision, and they have adopted the view that a claimant's failure to exhaust administrative remedies results in disallowance of the claim and prevents courts from asserting subject matter jurisdiction over the claim. *Hindes v. F.D.I.C.*, 137 F.3d 148 (3d Cir. 1998); *Brady Dev. Co. v. RTC*, 14 F.3d 998 (4th Cir. 1994); *Village of Oakwood v. State Bank and Trust Co*, 539 F.3d 373 (6th Cir. 2008); *Maher v. F.D.I.C.*, 441 F.3d 522 (7th Cir. 2006); *Bueford v. RTC*, 991 F.2d 481 (8th Cir. 1993); *McCarthy v. F.D.I.C.*, 348 F.3d 1075 (9th Cir. 2003) *RTC v. Mustang Partners*, 946 F.2d 103 (10th Cir. 1991); *Decrosta v. Red Carpet Inns Int'l, Inc.*, 767 F. Supp. 694 (E.D. Pa. 1991). *See* Barry S. Zisman, Banks & Thrifts: Government Enforcement and Receivership § 23.04 (1994) (endorsing preclusive view); Jeffery S. Rosenblum, *The RTC's Quest for Exclusive Federal Court Jurisdiction Under FIRREA*, 24 MEM. ST. U. L. REV. 725 (1994) (same). *Cf. Marquis v. FDIC*, 965 F.2d 1148 (1st Cir.1992) (rejecting sweeping FDIC claims as to preclusion; confirming that federal courts retain jurisdiction of pre-receivership claims but expecting courts would usually stay proceedings pending administrative exhaustion of claims); *Yeomalakis v. F.D.I.C.*, 562 F.3d 56 (1st Cir. 2009) (following *Marquis*; calling FIRREA "a procedural muddle"); *Carlyle Towers Condominium Ass'n, Inc. v. F.D.I.C.*, 170 F.3d 301 (2d Cir. 1999) (recognizing requirement of exhaustion of administrative claims procedure; allowing litigation of post-bar date claim); *IndyMac Bank, F.S. B. v. MacPherson*, — F.Supp.2d —, 2009 WL 4289945 (E.D.N.Y. 2009) (holding court lacked subject matter jurisdiction over mortgagor's counterclaims against FDIC as receiver of a failed bank in

foreclosure action because of failure to exhaust administrative remedies under FIRREA). *But see Whatley v. RTC*, 32 F.3d 905, 910 (5th Cir. 1994) (holding pre-receivership claimants not required to exhaust administrative remedies because statute differentiates between pre- and post-receivership claims); *F.D.I.C. v. Lacentra Trucking, Inc.*, 157 F.3d 1292 (11th Cir. 1998) (interpreting statute to allow receiver option of adjudicating prereceivership claims in pending litigation or of following FIRREA administrative claims procedures).

2. *Turning the Clock Back.* To put the Punzalans' claim in perspective, consider what would have happened if they had received and appropriately responded to the FDIC notice. Chances are, *they would not have been in federal district court.* Assuming – as the court does – that the FDIC properly invoked the administrative-claims procedure as to pre-receivership claims like the Punzalans' claim,[23] the administrative claims procedure would have been their exclusive remedy as a practical matter. The FDIC has the statutory authority as receiver to "determine claims."[24] The key language in this regard provides that

> In the handling of receiverships of insured depository institutions, to maintain essential liquidity and to prevent financial disruption, the Corporation may, after the declaration of an institution's insolvency, settle all uninsured and unsecured claims on the receivership with a final settlement payment which shall constitute full payment and disposition of the Corporation's obligations to such claimants.[25]

The final settlement payment is likely to be a proportional amount of the total claims determined by the FDIC, with the ratio represented by a statutorily mandated "amount equal to the product of the final settlement payment rate and the amount of the uninsured and unsecured claim on the receivership."[26] If the FDIC disallows the claim, the statute bars judicial review of the determination.[27]

---

23. 12 U.S.C. § 1821(d)(3)(B)-(C).

24. *Id.* § 1821(d)(3)(A).

25. *Id.* § 1821(d)(4)(B)(i).

26. *Id.* § 1821(d)(4)(B)(ii). For these purposes, the "final settlement payment rate" is defined as "a percentage rate reflecting an average of the Corporation's receivership recovery experience, determined by the Corporation in such a way that over such time period as the Corporation may deem appropriate, the Corporation in total will receive no more or less than it would have received in total as a general creditor standing in the place of insured depositors in each specific receivership." *Id.* § 1821(d)(4)(B)(iii).

27. *Id.* § 1821(d)(5)(E).

5

PARABLES AND LESSONS

The events surrounding the meltdown of the financial services markets are replete with stories of rise and fall, of challenges and tragedies, of pridefulness humbled. The critical question for policy makers now is: what lessons are to be drawn from these parables? This chapter will relate some of these parables and suggest some lessons.

A. FINANCIAL FALLOUT

1. The Preemption Initiative

One story that serves as a backdrop to the unfolding financial crisis is the preemption initiative undertaken by the Office of the Comptroller of the Currency (OCC) and the Office of Thrift Supervision (OTS) beginning with the first decade of the new century. The initiative sought to remove states from the supervision of the financial services markets. In a February 2003 notice of proposed rulemaking, the OCC proposed revisions to the interpretive provisions of its regulations that would have the effect of strengthening preemption, by invoking the exclusive "visitorial" powers of the federal regulator under 12 U.S.C. §484.[1] It would be fair to say that the discussion of the proposed revisions to § 7.400 in the Supplementary Information section of the notice reads like the final draft of an amicus brief in favor of generally applicable preemption of state law with respect to national banks and their operating subsidiaries.[2] In January 2004, the Comptroller adopted regulations asserting broad preemptive authority based on his "visitorial" powers,[3] and under his substantive regulatory authority.[4] Likewise, in an October 2004 legal opinion,[5] the OTS Chief Counsel took the position that federal law preempted

---

1. *See Rules, Policies and Procedures for Corporate Activities*, 68 Fed. Reg. 6363 (2003) (to be codified at, *inter alia*, 12 C.F.R. §7.400(a)(3)(i)-(ii), (b)). On the Comptroller's exclusive visitorial authority over national banks and its relationship to the dual banking system, see 69 Fed. Reg. 1895, 1896-1900 (2004). On visitorial powers generally, see *Watters v. Wachovia Bank, N.A.*, 550 U.S. 1 (2007) (holding that OCC did not exceed its authority under NBA by promulgating regulation limiting application of state visitorial powers to national bank operating subsidiaries to same extent as those laws' application to banks themselves was limited, that conflict preemption existed as to state statutes regulating mortgage lenders, when applied to bank's subsidiary, and that Tenth Amendment was not offended by OCC regulation); *National City Bank of Indiana v. Turnbaugh*, 463 F.3d 325 (4th Cir. 2006), *cert. denied*, 550 U.S. 913; *Wachovia Bank, N.A. v. Burke*, 414 F.3d 305 (2d Cir. 2005), *cert. denied*, 550 U.S. 913 (holding that NBA and OCC regulations preempted application of certain Connecticut banking laws to operating subsidiary of national bank, and holding that state's attempt to regulate operating subsidiary did not give rise to action by bank under 42 U.S.C. §1983); *Clearing House Ass'n, L.L.C. v. Spitzer*, 394 F. Supp.2d 620 (S.D.N.Y. 2005) (barring state enforcement of Fair Housing Act fair lending provisions against national banks or operating subsidiaries thereof; holding, inter alia, state parens patriae capacity to enforce Act constituted visitorial authority preempted by NBA), *aff'd in part and rev'd in part and remanded sub nom. Clearing House Ass'n, L.L.C. v. Cuomo*, 510 F.3d 105 (2d Cir. 2007), *aff'd in part and rev'd in part*, — U.S. —, 129 S.Ct. 2710 (2009); *Office of Comptroller of Currency v. Spitzer*, 396 F. Supp. 2d 383 (S.D.N.Y. 2005) (upholding OCC regulation asserting exclusive authority to enforce state laws regulating national bank authorized banking activities as reasonable construction of NBA provision limiting state visitorial powers over national bank; preempting state enforcement of state anti-discrimination law against national bank), *aff'd in part and rev'd in part and remanded sub nom. Clearing House Ass'n, L.L.C. v. Cuomo*, 510 F.3d 105 (2d Cir. 2007), *aff'd in part and rev'd in part*, — U.S. —, 129 S.Ct. 2710 (2009).

2. *Compare* 68 Fed. Reg. at 6366-6370 (arguing for exclusive, preemptive authority of OCC under visitorial provisions of 12 U.S.C. §484) *with Wells Fargo Bank, N.A. v. Boutris*, 252 F. Supp. 2d 1065 (E.D. Cal. 2003), *aff'd in part and rev'd in part*, 419 F.3d 949 (9th Cir. 2005) (granting preliminary injunction against enforcement of state law against national bank operating subsidiary; discussing OCC amicus brief preemption arguments).

3. 69 Fed. Reg. 1895 (2004) (codified at 12 C.F.R. §7.4000(a)(3), (b)).

4. 69 Fed. Reg. 1904 (2004) (codified at 12 C.F.R. §§ 7.4007-7.4009, 34.3(a)-(c), 34.4) (identifying types of state laws preempted and types generally not preempted with respect to national bank lending, deposit-taking, and other operations; adopting supplemental anti-predatory lending standard for national bank lending activities).

5. P-2004-7, Oct. 25, 2004 (released Nov. 5, 2004), available at http://www.ots.treas.gov/docs/5/560404.pdf.

state restrictions on business agents of federal savings associations with respect to any agent with an exclusive relationship with an association, if the agent agrees to significant supervision by it and works to advance the association's deposit and lending activities.[6] The following case excerpt represents the typical preemption argument raised by a federally chartered depository institution – Washington Mutual – prior to the onset of the financial crisis.

WEISS V. WASHINGTON MUTUAL BANK

147 Cal.App.4th 72, 53 Cal.Rptr.3d 782 (Ct. App. 2007)

VOGEL, Acting P.J.

[Borrowers brought suit against WaMu challenging a prepayment penalty and raising claims for fraud, unlawful restraint on alienation of real property, unfair and deceptive business practices, and unjust enrichment. WaMu moved for judgment on the pleadings, on the ground that complaint was preempted by federal law. The trial court granted the motion without leave to amend. On appeal, the court of appeal affirmed, holding that (*i*) the borrowers' suit against WaMu was preempted; and, (*ii*) a claim against a WaMu loan officer was also preempted.]

The question on this appeal is whether a lawsuit challenging a federal savings and loan association's prepayment penalty formula is preempted by the Home Owners' Loan Act (HOLA) and the regulations promulgated by the Office of Thrift Supervision (OTS). (12 U.S.C. § 1461 et seq.; 12 C.F.R. §§ 560.2, 560.34). Our answer is yes.

FACTS

A.

In July 2003, Mitchell Weiss (and others included in our references to Weiss) borrowed about $4 million from Washington Mutual Bank and signed two 10-year promissory notes – one for $1.175 million plus interest at 5.33 percent per annum and with monthly payments of $6,546.74 (secured by real property in Los Angeles), the other for $2.85 million plus interest at 5.33 percent per annum and with monthly payments of $15,879.32 (secured by real property in Beverly Hills). A prepayment addendum to each note set forth a

---

6. For a discussion of the effects of current federal preemption policy on lending, see Dreher & Anstaett, *Preemption Developments Impacting Interstate Lending by Federally Regulated Financial Institutions*, 58 Consumer Fin. L.Q. Rep. 8 (2004).

formula for calculating the "prepayment premium" due in the event Weiss prepaid his obligations under the notes. Weiss negotiated the loans with Jeffrey Monahan, a Washington Mutual loan officer.

When Weiss read the prepayment addenda, he believed the prepayment penalty would be "below two percent" of the unpaid balance or, if higher than 2 percent, only by a "small margin." In fact, the addenda provided for a prepayment penalty of up to 10 percent of the unpaid balance (depending on the time of prepayment). In October and November 2004, Weiss prepaid both notes, including prepayment penalties of roughly 10 percent of the unpaid balances ($286,740.35 on the $2.85 million loan, and $116,509.98 on the $1.175 million loan).

B.

[Weiss alleged] that Washington Mutual had not disclosed that the prepayment penalty formula could yield a penalty rate as high as 10 percent of the unpaid balance of the loan, that he would not have borrowed from Washington Mutual had he not been misled. . . .

DISCUSSION

Weiss contends his claims are not preempted. We disagree.

A.

OTS has the exclusive authority to regulate the operations of federal savings associations such as Washington Mutual (12 C.F.R. § 560.2; *Fidelity Federal Sav. & Loan Assn. v. de la Cuesta* (1982) 458 U.S. 141, 144-145) and with Congress's authorization (12 U.S.C. §§ 1463(a), 1464(a)) has preempted any state law that even incidentally affects prepayment penalties (12 C.F.R. § 560.2(b)(5) ["the types of state laws preempted . . . include . . . state laws purporting to impose requirements regarding . . . [l]oan-related fees, including . . . prepayment penalties"]; 12 C.F.R. § 560.34 [authorizing prepayment fees]).[2] Because all of Weiss's claims against Washington Mutual seek relief

---

2. As relevant, 12 C.F.R. § 560.2 provides:

> "(a) *Occupation of field.* . . . OTS hereby occupies the entire field of lending regulation for federal savings associations. OTS intends to give federal savings associations maximum flexibility to exercise their lending powers in accordance with a uniform federal scheme of regulation. Accordingly, federal savings associations may extend credit as authorized under federal law . . . without regard to state laws purporting to regulate or otherwise affect their credit activities, except to the extent provided in paragraph (c) of this section or § 560.110 of this part. For purposes of this section, 'state law' includes any state statute, regulation, ruling, order or judicial decision.
>
> (b) *Illustrative examples.* Except as provided in § 560.110 of this part, *the types of state laws preempted by paragraph (a) of this section include, without limitation, state laws purporting to impose requirements regarding . . .*

that if granted would necessarily impose requirements on Washington Mutual's prepayment penalty provisions, all of those claims are preempted. . . . *Washington Mutual Bank v. Superior Court* (2002) 95 Cal.App.4th 606, 610, 115 Cal.Rptr.2d 765; . . . *Silvas v. E*Trade Mortg. Corp.* (S.D.Cal.2006) 421 F.Supp.2d 1315, 1321. . . .

B.

To avoid this conclusion, Weiss contends his claims against Washington Mutual and, in particular, his fraud claim against Monahan are exempt from HOLA's preemption because they "only incidentally affect [Washington Mutual's] lending operations . . . or are otherwise consistent with the purposes" of HOLA. (12 C.F.R. § 560.2(c).) We disagree.

Although 12 C.F.R. § 560.2(c) exempts state tort laws that only incidentally affect the lending operations of federally regulated institutions, the "incidentally affect" analysis is triggered only when dealing with an activity that is not listed in 12 C.F.R. § 560.2(b). According to the OTS, "[w]hen analyzing the status of state laws under § 560.2, the first step will be to determine whether the type of law in question is listed [among the illustrative examples of preempted state laws] in paragraph (b) [of 12 C.F.R. § 560.2]. *If so, the analysis will end there; the law is preempted. . . . Any doubt should be resolved in favor of preemption.*" (61 Fed.Reg. 50951, 50966-50967 (Sept. 30, 1996), emphasis added.) It is only if the law is not covered by paragraph (b) that the inquiry continues to determine whether the particular state law affects lending. (*Ibid.*) As noted above and in footnote 2, *ante,* prepayment penalty provisions are listed among the illustrations in 12 C.F.R. § 560.2(b). For this reason, our inquiry ends here (and we thus do not discuss Weiss's contention

---

(5) Loan-related fees, including without limitation, . . . prepayment penalties . . .

(c) *State laws that are not preempted.* State laws of the following types are not preempted to the extent that they only incidentally affect the lending operations of Federal savings associations or are otherwise consistent with the purposes of paragraph (a) of this section:

(1) Contract and commercial law;

(2) Real property law;

(3) Homestead laws . . . ;

(4) Tort law;

(5) Criminal law; and

(6) Any other law that OTS, upon review, finds:

(i) Furthers a vital state interest; and

(ii) Either has only an incidental effect on lending operations or is not otherwise contrary to the purposes expressed in paragraph (a) of this section."

(Emphasis added; and see *Fidelity Federal Sav. & Loan Assn. v. de la Cuesta, supra,* 458 U.S. at p. 155 ["Federal regulations have no less preemptive effect than federal statutes. . . . A preemptive regulation's force does not depend on express congressional authorization to displace state law. . . ."].)

that the relief he seeks would not affect Washington Mutual's "operations" or "lending activities"). (*Rosenberg v. Washington Mut. Bank* (2004) 369 N.J.Super. 456, 849 A.2d 566, 572 [tort action preempted because it sought injunctive relief and money damages that would have inserted a form of state regulation by compelling a different type of billing statement disclosure].)

We reject Weiss's suggestion that his claim against Monahan is unaffected by the preemption doctrine. Weiss's complaint expressly alleges that Monahan was at all relevant times acting solely within the course and scope of his employment by Washington Mutual and not for any personal purpose. He thus cannot be personally liable to Weiss (*Self-Insurers' Security Fund v. ESIS, Inc.* (1988) 204 Cal.App.3d 1148, 1163, 251 Cal.Rptr. 693), and stands in the same shoes as his employer (*Shoemaker v. Myers* (1990) 52 Cal.3d 1, 25, 276 Cal.Rptr. 303, 801 P.2d 1054; *Black v. Bank of America* (1994) 30 Cal.App.4th 1, 6, 35 Cal.Rptr.2d 725; *Shaw v. Hughes Aircraft Co.* (2000) 83 Cal.App.4th 1336, 1347, 100 Cal.Rptr.2d 446). In short, claims preempted as against the employer are necessarily preempted against the employee who acted within the course and scope of his employment.

C.

We summarily reject Weiss's contention that the trial court should have granted him leave to amend his complaint. He did not tell the trial court, and he has not told us, what allegations he could add that would possibly salvage his complaint from Washington Mutual's claim of preemption. Under these circumstances, leave to amend would not accomplish anything.[5]

---

5. The Attorney General, as amicus curiae in support of Weiss's appeal, asks us to allow Weiss to enforce California's unfair competition law (the UCL, Bus. & Prof.Code, § 17200 et seq.). There are at least two problems with the Attorney General's position. First, the case relied on by the Attorney General, *McKell v. Washington Mutual, Inc.* (2006) 142 Cal.App.4th 1457, 1484, 49 Cal.Rptr.3d 227, does not consider the express preemptions found in subdivision (b) of 12 C.F.R. § 560.2 (*id.* at p. 1496, fn. 4, 49 Cal.Rptr.3d 227, dissenting opn. of Vogel, J.) and thus offers no authority for the conclusion proposed by the Attorney General in this case. (*Chevron U.S.A., Inc. v. Workers' Comp. Appeals Bd.* (1999) 19 Cal.4th 1182, 1195, 81 Cal.Rptr.2d 521, 969 P.2d 613 [a case is not authority for a proposition not considered].) The case that *is* on point is *Washington Mutual Bank v. Superior Court, supra,* 95 Cal.App.4th at pp. 620-621, 115 Cal.Rptr.2d 765, in which Division Two of our court held that an action under the UCL challenging pre-closing interest charges on home loans was expressly preempted by 12 C.F.R. § 560.2(b). (See also *Silvas v. E*Trade Mortg. Corp., supra,* 421 F.Supp.2d at p. 1321.) Second, the presumption against preemptive intent relied on by the Attorney General is irrelevant in light of the express statement of preemptive intent found in 12 C.F.R. § 560.2(b). (*Cipollone v. Liggett Group, Inc.* (1992) 505 U.S. 504, 517.)

NOTES AND QUESTIONS

1. For cases considering conduct unrelated to § 560.2(b) and deciding whether a state statute's prohibition of the conduct "only incidentally affect[s] the lending operations" of a savings association, see *Fenning v. Glenfed, Inc.* 40 Cal.App.4th 1285, 1289-1290, 47 Cal.Rptr.2d 715 (1995) (challenging Glenfed's general advertising and sales practices); *Gibson v. World Savings & Loan Assn.* 103 Cal.App.4th 1291, 1303, 128 Cal.Rptr.2d 19 (2002) (challenging World's "forced order insurance" practices).

2. Thus, the battle lines were drawn for the Supreme Court's 5-3 decision in *Watters v. Wachovia Bank, N.A.* in April 2007. As we shall see, this decision – capping a line of case law involving consumer protection – has direct relevance to the financial crisis that would shortly emerge.

WATTERS V. WACHOVIA BANK, N.A.

550 U.S. 1 (2007)

JUSTICE GINSBURG delivered the opinion of the Court.

[Wachovia, a national bank, and its non-bank mortgage company subsidiary sued the Michigan Commissioner of Insurance and Financial Services for declaratory and injunctive relief from state registration and inspection requirements, claiming preemption of the state law by the National Bank Act (NBA). The district court granted summary judgment for the plaintiffs, and the Sixth Circuit affirmed. On certiorari, the Supreme Court affirmed, holding, *inter alia*, that under the NBA Wachovia's mortgage business – whether conducted by the bank itself or by its subsidiary – was subject to supervision by the OCC, and was not subject to the licensing, reporting, or visitorial regimes of the states in which the subsidiary operated.]

Business activities of national banks are controlled by the National Bank Act (NBA or Act), 12 U.S.C. § 1 et seq., and regulations promulgated thereunder by the Office of the Comptroller of the Currency (OCC). *See* §§ 24, 93a, 371(a). As the agency charged by Congress with supervision of the NBA, OCC oversees the operations of national banks and their interactions with customers. *See NationsBank of N. C., N.A. v. Variable Annuity Life Ins. Co.*, 513 U.S. 251, 254, 256 (1995). The agency exercises visitorial powers, including the authority to audit the bank's books and records, largely to the exclusion of other governmental entities, state or federal. *See* § 484(a); 12 CFR § 7.4000 (2006). . . .

Respondent Wachovia Bank, a national bank, conducts its real estate lending business through Wachovia Mortgage Corporation, a wholly owned, state-chartered entity, licensed as an operating subsidiary by OCC. It is uncontested in this suit that Wachovia's real estate business, if conducted by the national bank itself, would be subject to OCC's superintendence, to the exclusion of state registration requirements and visitorial authority. The question in dispute is whether the bank's mortgage lending activities remain outside the governance of state licensing and auditing agencies when those activities are conducted, not by a division or department of the bank, but by the bank's operating subsidiary. In accord with the Courts of Appeals that have addressed the issue,[1] we hold that Wachovia's mortgage business, whether conducted by the bank itself or through the bank's operating subsidiary, is subject to OCC's superintendence, and not to the licensing, reporting, and visitorial regimes of the several States in which the subsidiary operates.

I

Wachovia Bank is a national banking association chartered by OCC. Respondent Wachovia Mortgage is a North Carolina corporation that engages in the business of real estate lending in the State of Michigan and elsewhere. Michigan's statutory regime exempts banks, both national and state, from state mortgage lending regulation, but requires mortgage brokers, lenders, and servicers that are subsidiaries of national banks to register with the State's Office of Insurance and Financial Services (OIFS) and submit to state supervision. Mich. Comp. Laws Ann. §§ 445.1656(1), 445.1679(1)(a) (West 2002), 493.52(1), and 493.53a(d) (West 1998).[2] From 1997 until 2003, Wachovia Mortgage was registered with OIFS to engage in mortgage lending. As a registrant, Wachovia Mortgage was required, inter alia, to pay an annual operating fee, file an annual report, and open its books and records to inspection by OIFS examiners. §§ 445.1657, 445.1658, 445.1671 (West 2002), 493.54, 493.56a(2), (13) (West 1998).

Petitioner Linda Watters, the commissioner of OIFS, administers the State's lending laws. She exercises "general supervision and control" over registered lenders, and has authority to conduct examinations and investigations and to enforce requirements against registrants. See §§ 445.1661, 445.1665, 445.1666 (West 2002), 493.58, 493.56b, 493.59, 493.62a (West

---

1. *National City Bank of Indiana v. Turnbaugh,* 463 F.3d 325 (C.A.4 2006); *Wachovia Bank, N.A. v. Burke,* 414 F.3d 305 (C.A.2 2005); 431 F.3d 556 (C.A.6 2005) (case below); *Wells Fargo Bank N.A. v. Boutris,* 419 F.3d 949 (C.A.9 2005).

2. Michigan's law exempts subsidiaries of national banks that maintain a main office or branch office in Michigan. Mich. Comp. Laws Ann. §§ 445.1652(1)(b) (West Supp.2006), 445.1675(m) (West 2002), 493.53a(d) (West 1998). Wachovia Bank has no such office in Michigan.

1998 and Supp.2005). She also has authority to investigate consumer complaints and take enforcement action if she finds that a complaint is not "being adequately pursued by the appropriate federal regulatory authority." § 445.1663(2) (West 2002).

On January 1, 2003, Wachovia Mortgage became a wholly owned operating subsidiary of Wachovia Bank. Three months later, Wachovia Mortgage advised the State of Michigan that it was surrendering its mortgage lending registration. Because it had become an operating subsidiary of a national bank, Wachovia Mortgage maintained, Michigan's registration and inspection requirements were preempted. Watters responded with a letter advising Wachovia Mortgage that it would no longer be authorized to conduct mortgage lending activities in Michigan.

Wachovia Mortgage and Wachovia Bank filed suit against Watters, in her official capacity as commissioner, in the United States District Court for the Western District of Michigan. . . . The NBA and regulations promulgated thereunder, they urged, vest supervisory authority in OCC and preempt the application of the state-law controls at issue. Specifically, Wachovia Mortgage and Wachovia Bank challenged as preempted certain provisions of two Michigan statutes – the Mortgage Brokers, Lenders, and Services Licensing Act and the Secondary Mortgage Loan Act. The challenged provisions (1) require mortgage lenders – including national bank operating subsidiaries but not national banks themselves – to register and pay fees to the State before they may conduct banking activities in Michigan, and authorize the commissioner to deny or revoke registrations . . . ; (2) require submission of annual financial statements to the commissioner and retention of certain documents in a particular format . . . ; (3) grant the commissioner inspection and enforcement authority over registrants . . . ; and (4) authorize the commissioner to take regulatory or enforcement actions against covered lenders. . . .

In response, Watters argued that, because Wachovia Mortgage was not itself a national bank, the challenged Michigan controls were applicable and were not preempted. She also contended that the Tenth Amendment to the Constitution of the United States prohibits OCC's exclusive superintendence of national bank lending activities conducted through operating subsidiaries.

The District Court granted summary judgment to the banks in relevant part. . . . Invoking the two-step framework of *Chevron U.S.A. Inc. v. Natural Resources Defense Council, Inc.*, 467 U.S. 837 (1984), the court deferred to the Comptroller's determination that an operating subsidiary is subject to state regulation only to the extent that the parent bank would be if it performed the same functions[,] citing, e.g., 12 CFR §§ 5.34(e)(3), 7.4006 (2004)). The court also rejected Watters' Tenth Amendment argument. . . .

II

A

. . . The Act vested in nationally chartered banks enumerated powers and "all such incidental powers as shall be necessary to carry on the business of banking." 12 U.S.C. § 24 Seventh. To prevent inconsistent or intrusive state regulation from impairing the national system, Congress provided: "No national bank shall be subject to any visitorial powers except as authorized by Federal law. . . ." § 484(a).

In the years since the NBA's enactment, we have repeatedly made clear that federal control shields national banking from unduly burdensome and duplicative state regulation. *See, e.g., Beneficial Nat. Bank v. Anderson*, 539 U.S. 1, 10 (2003) (national banking system protected from "possible unfriendly State legislation" (*quoting Tiffany v. National Bank of Mo.*, 18 Wall. 409, 412 (1874))). Federally chartered banks are subject to state laws of general application in their daily business to the extent such laws do not conflict with the letter or the general purposes of the NBA. *Davis v. Elmira Savings Bank*, 161 U.S. 275, 290 (1896). *See also [Atherton v. FDIC*, 519 U.S. 213, 223 (1997)]. For example, state usury laws govern the maximum rate of interest national banks can charge on loans, 12 U.S.C. § 85, contracts made by national banks "are governed and construed by State laws," *National Bank v. Commonwealth*, 9 Wall. 353, 362 (1870), and national banks' "acquisition and transfer of property [are] based on State law," ibid. However, "the States can exercise no control over [national banks], nor in any wise affect their operation, except in so far as Congress may see proper to permit. Any thing beyond this is an abuse, because it is the usurpation of power which a single State cannot give." *Farmers' and Mechanics' Nat. Bank v. Dearing*, 91 U.S. 29, 34 (1875) (internal quotation marks omitted).

We have "interpret[ed] grants of both enumerated and incidental 'powers' to national banks as grants of authority not normally limited by, but rather ordinarily pre-empting, contrary state law." *Barnett Bank of Marion Cty., N.A. v. Nelson*, 517 U.S. 25, 32 (1996). *See also Franklin Nat. Bank of Franklin Square v. New York*, 347 U.S. 373, 375-379 (1954). States are permitted to regulate the activities of national banks where doing so does not prevent or significantly interfere with the national bank's or the national bank regulator's exercise of its powers. But when state prescriptions significantly impair the exercise of authority, enumerated or incidental under the NBA, the State's regulations must give way. *Barnett Bank*, 517 U.S., at 32-34 (federal law permitting national banks to sell insurance in small towns preempted state statute prohibiting banks from selling most types of insurance); *Franklin Nat. Bank*, 347 U.S., at 377-379 (local restrictions preempted because they burdened exercise of national banks' incidental power to advertise).

The NBA authorizes national banks to engage in mortgage lending, subject to OCC regulation. . . .

Beyond genuine dispute, state law may not significantly burden a national bank's own exercise of its real estate lending power, just as it may not curtail or hinder a national bank's efficient exercise of any other power, incidental or enumerated under the NBA. *See Barnett Bank*, 517 U.S., at 33-34; *Franklin*, 347 U.S., at 375-379. *See also* 12 CFR § 34.4(a)(1) (2006) (identifying preempted state controls on mortgage lending, including licensing and registration). In particular, real estate lending, when conducted by a national bank, is immune from state visitorial control: The NBA specifically vests exclusive authority to examine and inspect in OCC. 12 U.S.C. § 484(a) ("No national bank shall be subject to any visitorial powers except as authorized by Federal law.").

Harmoniously, the Michigan provisions at issue exempt national banks from coverage. Mich. Comp. Laws Ann. § 445.1675(a) (West 2002). This is not simply a matter of the Michigan Legislature's grace. . . . For, as the parties recognize, the NBA would have preemptive force, *i.e.*, it would spare a national bank from state controls of the kind here involved. . . . State laws that conditioned national banks' real estate lending on registration with the State, and subjected such lending to the State's investigative and enforcement machinery would surely interfere with the banks' federally authorized business: National banks would be subject to registration, inspection, and enforcement regimes imposed not just by Michigan, but by all States in which the banks operate.[6] Diverse and duplicative superintendence of national banks' engagement in the business of banking, we observed over a century ago, is precisely what the NBA was designed to prevent: "Th[e] legislation has in view the erection of a system extending throughout the country, and independent, so far as powers conferred are concerned, of state legislation which, if permitted to be applicable, might impose limitations and restrictions as various and as numerous as the States." *Easton v. Iowa*, 188 U.S. 220, 229 (1903). Congress did not intend, we explained, "to leave the field open for the States to attempt to promote the welfare and stability of national banks by direct legislation. . . . [C]onfusion would necessarily result from control possessed and exercised by two independent authorities." *Id.*, at 231-232.

Recognizing the burdens and undue duplication state controls could produce, Congress included in the NBA an express command: "No national bank shall be subject to any visitorial powers except as authorized by Federal

---

6. *See* 69 Fed.Reg. 1908 (2004) ("The application of multiple, often unpredictable, different state or local restrictions and requirements prevents [national banks] from operating in the manner authorized under Federal law, is costly and burdensome, interferes with their ability to plan their business and manage their risks, and subjects them to uncertain liabilities and potential exposure.").

law. . . ." 12 U.S.C. § 484(a). . . . "Visitation," we have explained "is the act of a superior or superintending officer, who visits a corporation to examine into its manner of conducting business, and enforce an observance of its laws and regulations." *Guthrie v. Harkness,* 199 U.S. 148, 158 (1905) (internal quotation marks omitted). *See also* 12 CFR § 7.4000(a)(2) (2006) (defining "visitorial" power as "(i) [e]xamination of a bank; (ii) [i]nspection of a bank's books and records; (iii) [r]egulation and supervision of activities authorized or permitted pursuant to federal banking law; and (iv)[e]nforcing compliance with any applicable federal or state laws concerning those activities"). Michigan, therefore, cannot confer on its commissioner examination and enforcement authority over mortgage lending, or any other banking business done by national banks.[7]

B

While conceding that Michigan's licensing, registration, and inspection requirements cannot be applied to national banks, . . . Watters argues that the State's regulatory regime survives preemption with respect to national banks' operating subsidiaries. Because such subsidiaries are separately chartered under some State's law, Watters characterizes them simply as "affiliates" of national banks, and contends that even though they are subject to OCC's superintendence, they are also subject to multistate control. . . . We disagree.

Since 1966, OCC has recognized the "incidental" authority of national banks under § 24 Seventh to do business through operating subsidiaries. *See* 31 Fed. Reg. 11459-11460 (1966); 12 CFR § 5.34(e)(1) (2006) ("A national bank may conduct in an operating subsidiary activities that are permissible for

---

7. Ours is indeed a "dual banking system." . . . But it is a system that has never permitted States to license, inspect, and supervise national banks as they do state banks. The dissent repeatedly refers to the policy of "competitive equality" featured in *First Nat. Bank in Plant City v. Dickinson,* 396 U.S. 122, 131 (1969). . . . Those words, however, should not be ripped from their context. *Plant City* involved the McFadden Act (Branch Banks), 44 Stat. 1228, 12 U.S.C. § 36, in which Congress expressly authorized national banks to establish branches "only when, where, and how state law would authorize a state bank to establish and operate such [branches]." 396 U.S., at 130. *See also id.,* at 131 ("[W]hile Congress has absolute authority over national banks, the [McFadden Act] has incorporated by reference the limitations which state law places on branch banking activities by state banks. Congress has deliberately settled upon a policy intended to foster competitive equality. . . . [The] Act reflects the congressional concern that neither system ha[s] advantages over the other in the use of branch banking." (*quoting First Nat. Bank of Logan v. Walker Bank & Trust Co.,* 385 U.S. 252, 261 (1966))). "[W]here Congress has not expressly conditioned the grant of 'power' upon a grant of state permission, the Court has ordinarily found that no such condition applies." *Barnett Bank of Marion Cty., N.A. v. Nelson,* 517 U.S. 25, 34 (1996). The NBA provisions before us, unlike the McFadden Act, do not condition the exercise of power by national banks on state allowance of similar exercises by state banks. . . .

a national bank to engage in directly either as part of, or incidental to, the business of banking. . . ."). That authority is uncontested by Michigan's commissioner. . . . OCC licenses and oversees national bank operating subsidiaries just as it does national banks. § 5.34(e)(3) ("An operating subsidiary conducts activities authorized under this section pursuant to the same authorization, terms and conditions that apply to the conduct of such activities by its parent national bank.");[8] United States Office of the Comptroller of the Currency, *Related Organizations: Comptroller's Handbook* 53 (Aug.2004) (hereinafter Comptroller's Handbook) ("Operating subsidiaries are subject to the same supervision and regulation as the parent bank, except where otherwise provided by law or OCC regulation.").

. . . For supervisory purposes, OCC treats national banks and their operating subsidiaries as a single economic enterprise. . . . OCC oversees both entities by reference to "business line," applying the same controls whether banking "activities are conducted directly or through an operating subsidiary."[10]

. . . Watters seeks to impose state regulation on operating subsidiaries over and above regulation undertaken by OCC. But just as duplicative state examination, supervision, and regulation would significantly burden mortgage lending when engaged in by national banks, . . . so too would those state controls interfere with that same activity when engaged in by an operating subsidiary.

We have never held that the preemptive reach of the NBA extends only to a national bank itself. Rather, in analyzing whether state law hampers the

---

8. The regulation further provides:

> "If, upon examination, the OCC determines that the operating subsidiary is operating in violation of law, regulation, or written condition, or in an unsafe or unsound manner or otherwise threatens the safety or soundness of the bank, the OCC will direct the bank or operating subsidiary to take appropriate remedial action, which may include requiring the bank to divest or liquidate the operating subsidiary, or discontinue specified activities." 12 CFR § 5.34(e)(3) (2006).

10. For example, "for purposes of applying statutory or regulatory limits, such as lending limits or dividend restrictions," *e.g.,* 12 U.S.C. §§ 56, 60, 84, 371d, "[t]he results of operations of operating subsidiaries are consolidated with those of its parent." Comptroller's Handbook 64. Likewise, for accounting and regulatory reporting purposes, an operating subsidiary is treated as part of the member bank; assets and liabilities of the two entities are combined. *See* 12 CFR §§ 5.34(e)(4)(i), 223.3(w) (2006). OCC treats financial subsidiaries differently. A national bank may not consolidate the assets and liabilities of a financial subsidiary with those of the bank. Comptroller's Handbook 64. It cannot be fairly maintained "that the transfer in 2003 of [Wachovia Mortgage's] ownership from the holding company to the Bank" resulted in no relevant changes to the company's business. . . . On becoming Wachovia's operating subsidiary, Wachovia Mortgage became subject to the same terms and conditions as national banks, including the full supervisory authority of OCC. This change exposed the company to significantly more federal oversight than it experienced as a state nondepository institution.

federally permitted activities of a national bank, we have focused on the exercise of a national bank's powers, not on its corporate structure. *See, e.g., Barnett Bank*, 517 U.S., at 32. And we have treated operating subsidiaries as equivalent to national banks with respect to powers exercised under federal law (except where federal law provides otherwise). . . . *See also Clarke v. Securities Industry Assn.*, 479 U.S. 388 (1987) (national banks, acting through operating subsidiaries, have power to offer discount brokerage services).[11]

Security against significant interference by state regulators is a characteristic condition of the "business of banking" conducted by national banks, and mortgage lending is one aspect of that business. *See, e.g.,* 12 U.S.C. § 484(a); 12 CFR § 34.4(a)(1) (2006). . . . That security should adhere whether the business is conducted by the bank itself or is assigned to an operating subsidiary licensed by OCC whose authority to carry on the business coincides completely with that of the bank. *See Wells Fargo Bank, N.A. v. Boutris*, 419 F.3d 949, 960 (C.A.9 2005) (determination whether to conduct business through operating subsidiaries or through subdivisions is "essentially one of internal organization").

Watters contends that if Congress meant to deny States visitorial powers over operating subsidiaries, it would have written § 484(a)'s ban on state inspection to apply not only to national banks but also to their affiliates. She points out that § 481, which authorizes OCC to examine "affiliates" of national banks, does not speak to state visitorial powers. This argument fails for two reasons. First, one cannot ascribe any intention regarding operating subsidiaries to the 1864 Congress that enacted §§ 481 and 484, or the 1933 Congress that added the provisions on examining affiliates to § 481 and the definition of "affiliate" to § 221a. That is so because operating subsidiaries were not authorized until 1966. . . . Over the past four decades, during which operating subsidiaries have emerged as important instrumentalities of national banks, Congress and OCC have indicated no doubt that such subsidiaries are "subject to the same terms and conditions" as national banks themselves. . . .

C

. . . A national bank has the power to engage in real estate lending through an operating subsidiary, subject to the same terms and conditions that govern the national bank itself; that power cannot be significantly impaired or impeded by state law. *See, e.g., Barnett Bank,* 517 U.S., at 33-34; 12 U.S.C. §§ 24 Seventh, 24a(g)(3)(A), 371.

---

11. *Cf. Marquette Nat. Bank of Minneapolis v. First of Omaha Service Corp.,* 439 U.S. 299, 308, and n. 24 (1978) (holding that national bank may charge home State's interest rate, regardless of more restrictive usury laws in borrower's State, but declining to consider operating subsidiaries).

The NBA is thus properly read by OCC to protect from state hindrance a national bank's engagement in the "business of banking" whether conducted by the bank itself or by an operating subsidiary, empowered to do only what the bank itself could do. . . . The authority to engage in the business of mortgage lending comes from the NBA, § 371, as does the authority to conduct business through an operating subsidiary. *See* §§ 24 Seventh, 24a(g)(3)(A). That Act vests visitorial oversight in OCC, not state regulators. § 484(a). State law (in this case, North Carolina law), all agree, governs incorporation-related issues, such as the formation, dissolution, and internal governance of operating subsidiaries. And the laws of the States in which national banks or their affiliates are located govern matters the NBA does not address. . . . But state regulators cannot interfere with the "business of banking" by subjecting national banks or their OCC-licensed operating subsidiaries to multiple audits and surveillance under rival oversight regimes. . . .

JUSTICE THOMAS took no part in the consideration or decision of this case.

JUSTICE STEVENS, with whom the CHIEF JUSTICE and JUSTICE SCALIA join, dissenting.

Congress has enacted no legislation immunizing national bank subsidiaries from compliance with nondiscriminatory state laws regulating the business activities of mortgage brokers and lenders. Nor has it authorized an executive agency to preempt such state laws whenever it concludes that they interfere with national bank activities. Notwithstanding the absence of relevant statutory authority, today the Court endorses an agency's incorrect determination that the laws of a sovereign State must yield to federal power. The significant impact of the Court's decision on the federal-state balance and the dual banking system makes it appropriate to set forth in full the reasons for my dissent. . . .

II

Although the dual banking system has remained intact, Congress has radically transformed the national bank system from its Civil War antecedent and brought considerably more federal authority to bear on state-chartered institutions. Yet despite all the changes Congress has made to the national bank system, and despite its exercise of federal power over state banks, it has never preempted state laws like those at issue in this case.

Most significantly, in 1913 Congress established the Federal Reserve System to oversee federal monetary policy through its influence over the availability of credit. Federal Reserve Act §§ 2, 9, 38 Stat. 252, 259. The Act required national banks and permitted state banks to become Federal Reserve member banks, and subjected all member banks to Federal Reserve regulations and oversight. Ibid. Also of signal importance, after the banking system collapsed during the Great Depression, Congress required all member banks to obtain deposit insurance from the newly established Federal Deposit Insurance Corporation. Banking Act of 1933 (or Glass-Steagall Act), § 8, 48 Stat. 168; see also Banking Act of 1935, 49 Stat. 684. Although both of these steps meant that many state banks were subjected to significant federal regulation, "the state banking system continued along with the [national] banking system, with no attempt to exercise preemptive federal regulatory authority over the activities of the existing state banks." M. Malloy, Banking and Financial Services Law 48 (2d ed.2005).

In addition to these systemic overhauls, Congress has over time modified the powers of national banks. The changes are too various to recount in detail, but two are of particular importance to this case. First, Congress has gradually relaxed its prohibition on mortgage lending by national banks. . . . While these changes have enabled national banks to engage in more evenhanded competition with state banks, they certainly reflect no purpose to give them any competitive advantage.[9]

Second, Congress has over the years both curtailed and expanded the ability of national banks to affiliate with other companies. In the early part of the century, banks routinely engaged in investment activities and affiliated with companies that did the same. . . .

A scant two years later, Congress forbade national banks from owning the shares of any company because of a similar fear that such ownership could undermine the safety and soundness of national banks. . . . That provision remains on the books today. *See* 12 U.S.C. § 24 Seventh. . . .

III . . .

The NBA . . . provides in 12 U.S.C. § 484(a) that "[n]o national bank shall be subject to any visitorial powers except as authorized by Federal law." Although this exemption from state visitorial authority has been in place for more than 140 years, . . . it is significant that Congress has never extended 12 U.S.C. § 484(a)'s preemptive blanket to cover national bank subsidiaries. . . .

---

9. It is noteworthy that the principal cases that the Court cites to support its conclusion that the federal statute itself preempts the Michigan laws were decided years before Congress authorized national banks to engage in mortgage lending and years before the Office of the Comptroller of the Currency (OCC) authorized their use of operating subsidiaries. . . .

NOTES AND QUESTIONS

1. On Friday, September 26, 2008 – one day after the failure of Washington Mutual – the listed price of Wachovia stock lost 27 percent in value.[7] By the following Monday Wachovia agreed to break the company apart, with Citigroup acquiring its banking operations with FDIC assistance and a standalone public company, still called Wachovia and based in Charlotte, NC, retaining its brokerage, asset management and insurance units.[8]

2. *A Systemic Threat?* The OCC and the OTS adopted policies targeting state transactional and consumer protection laws that affect national bank and federal savings association operations, as well as their affiliates and subsidiaries. Do you think such policies go too far? At the September 2005 meeting of the American Bankers Association, the FDIC Chairman criticized the OCC initiative to assert preemptive powers as a symptom of the problem threatening the viability of the dual banking system.[9] What is the attitude of the majority in *Watters* towards this threat to the viability of the dual banking system? What is attitude of the dissent?

3. *The President Intervenes – sort of.* Not surprisingly, the aggressive preemption initiative endorsed by *Watters* continued apace.[10] However, after a dramatic appeal from the nation's state attorneys general in March 2009,[11] in May 2009 President Obama signed a Memorandum directed to the heads of executive departments and agencies stating "the general policy of [his] Administration that preemption of State law by executive departments and agencies

7. Rick Rothacker, *Stunningly Swift Fall for Wachovia: Sale to Citigroup Technically Keeps Bank from Failing, but Thousands of Layoffs Are Still Likely*, CHARLOTTE OBSERVOR, http://www.charlotteobserver.com/408/story/222685.html (posted Sep. 30, 2008).

8. *Id.*

9. *See* Richard Cowden, *Powell Says Falling State Bank Asset Share Highlights Inequities in Dual Banking System*, BNA BANKING DAILY (Sept. 27, 2005), available at http://pubs.bna.com/ip/BNA/bbd.nsf/is/A0B1M9Z5H3 (reporting on speech). For vigorous critiques of OCC preemption policies, see Fisher, *Toward a Basal Tenth Amendment: A Riposte to National Bank Preemption of State Consumer Protection Laws*, 29 Harv. J.L. & Pub. Pol'y 981 (2006); Arthur E. Wilmarth, Jr., *The OCC's Preemption Rules Exceed the Agency's Authority and Present a Serious Threat to the Dual Banking System and Consumer Protection*, 23 Ann. Rev. Banking & Fin. L. 225 (2004).

10. *See, e.g., State Farm Bank v. Reardon*, 539 F.3d 336 (6th Cir. 2008) (holding that OTS preemption regulation, 12 C.F.R. § 560.2, preempted application of Ohio Mortgage Broker Act to federal savings association independent contractor agent).

11. Martha Kessler, *State AGs Call on Obama Administration to Restore State Authority Over Lending*, BNA BANKING DAILY (Mar. 13, 2009), available at http://www.bna (reporting on letter to President Obama from all 50 state attorneys general asking Administration to restore state authority to regulate national bank lending, credit cards and rules relating to predatory lending, banking and credit card practices by national banks).

should be undertaken only with full consideration of the legitimate preroga-
tives of the States and with a sufficient legal basis for preemption."[12] By its
own terms, the Memorandum does not revoke any rules or policies, including
the current OCC and OTS preemption policies. Furthermore, the Memorandum
states that it "is not intended to, and does not, create any right or benefit,
substantive or procedural, enforceable at law or in equity by any party against
the United States, its departments, agencies, or entities, its officers, employees,
or agents, or any other person, and does not give any party grounds to
challenge the validity of an agency action. Any repeal of preemptive actions
that the OCC or OTS have taken will have to come from the agencies
themselves."[13] There has been some speculation that state officials and
consumer advocates might use the Memorandum as an argumentative basis for
lobbying federal financial services agencies to roll back the preemption
initiative.[14]

    4. *Historical Perspective.* Throughout the majority and dissenting opinions
in *Watters*, there is a continuing battle over the historical roots – and
limitations – of preemption with respect to national banks. The following
excerpt offers some perspective on this issue. As you review the excerpt
consider whether the majority or dissent has the better understanding of the
appropriate role of preemption in banking.

1 MICHAEL P. MALLOY, BANKING LAW AND REGULATION

§ 1.3.9 (Aspen 2004 & Cum. Supps.)

Federal preemption is a constitutional doctrine with broad application far
beyond bank regulatory policy.[1] However, application of the doctrine in an

---

    12. Presidential Memorandum: Preemption, 74 Fed. Reg. 24,693 (May 20, 2009).

    13. *Id.*

    14. *See* David L. Beam, *Obama Order on Preemption Could Expose Banks to State Regula-
tion*, BNA Banking Daily (May 29, 2009), available at http://news.bna.com ("state officials,
consumer advocates, and other preemption critics will no doubt encourage the agencies to scale
back their preemption regulations"). Beam's view, however, is that the Memorandum does not
"require either the OCC or the OTS to repeal or reverse any preemptive actions they have taken
in the past." *Id.*

    1. *See, e.g., Crosby v. National Foreign Trade Council,* 530 U.S. 363 (2000) (applying
preemption doctrine to Massachusetts law barring state contractors from dealing with Burma;
collecting cases).

area of traditional state law competence, like bank regulation,[2] raises particularly unsettling concerns. There is a strong argument to be made that broad federal preemption of the application of state law and policy to national banks and even to their nonbanking operating subsidiaries significantly threatens the continuing viability of the balanced state-federal structure known as the dual banking system.[3] . . .

From the 1830s (when the federal charter of the second Bank of the United States expired), until the early 1860s, the federal government had no direct involvement in regulating U.S. banking. The national crisis of the Civil War pushed the federal government to reenter bank regulation. The national banking system that resulted from these exigent circumstances has outlasted the Civil War and has become a central feature of the modern U.S. bank regulatory system. Thus, by creating the national bank system, the National Bank Act (NBA)[6] established the federal-state "dual banking system" that has been a characteristic of U.S. commercial banking ever since.[7] . . .

Today, . . . the [Gramm-Leach-Bliley Act of 1999 (GLBA)[10]] requires the Comptroller, in addition to his or her many other responsibilities, to supervise: the expanded "financial services activities" of operating subsidiaries of national banks; the privacy of nonpublic personal information of customers of national banks; and consumer protection with respect to insurance sales by

---

2. The Supreme Court has long acknowledged that "banking and related financial activities are of profound local concern." *Lewis v. B.T. Inv. Managers, Inc.*, 447 U.S. 27, 38 (1980). The Court went on to explain that

> sound financial institutions and honest financial practices are essential to the health of any State's economy and to the well-being of its people. Thus, it is not surprising that ever since the early days of our Republic, the States have chartered banks and have actively regulated their activities.

Id.

3. On the dual banking system generally, *see, e.g.*, Wilmarth, *The Expansion of State Bank Powers, the Federal Response, and the Case for Preserving the Dual Banking System*, 58 FORDHAM L. REV. 1133 (1990); Frankel, *The Dual State-Federal Regulation of Financial Institutions—A Policy Proposal*, 53 BROOKLYN L. REV. 53 (1987); Lybecker, *The "South Dakota" Experience and the Bush Task Group's Report: Reconciling Perceived Overlaps in the Dual Regulation of Banking*, 53 BROOK. L. REV. 71 (1987); Lovett, *Federalism, Boundary Conflicts and Responsible Financial Regulation*, 18 LOYOLA L.A. L. REV. 1053 (1985); Scott, *Patchwork Quilt: State and Federal Roles in Bank Regulation*, 32 STAN. L. REV. 687 (1980); Fein, *Fragmented Depository Institutions Systems: A Case for Unification*, 29 AM. U. L. REV. 633 (1980); Scott, *Dual Banking System: Model of Competition in Regulation*, 30 STAN. L. REV. 1 (1977).

6. 12 Stat. 670 (1863), *amended by* 13 Stat. 111 (1864).

7. Scott, *Dual Banking System, supra* note 3.

10. Pub. L. No. 106-102, Nov. 12, 1999, 113 Stat. 1338 (1999) (codified at scattered sections of 12, 15, 16, 18 U.S.C.).

national banks. Thus, in sharp contrast to the period before the emergence of the dual banking system, the federal government has expanded its regulatory reach – and its potential preemptive effects – into a vast array of financial services.[11]

---

11. *Cf., e.g., Watters v. Wachovia Bank, N.A.*,550 U.S. 1 (2007) . . . ; *American Bankers Ass'n v. Lockyer*, 541 F.3d 1214 (9th Cir. 2008) (severing preempted application of state statute governing information sharing by financial institutions, excluding state regulation of "consumer report information," as defined by FCRA); *Silvas v. E*Trade Mortg. Corp.*, 514 F.3d 1001 (holding that HOLA, through OTS regulations, preempted the entire field of lending regulation); *Rose v. Chase Bank USA, N.A.*, 513 F.3d 1032 (9th Cir. 2008) (holding state-required disclosure concerning credit card "convenience checks" preempted by NBA and OCC rules); *Discover Bank v. Vaden*, 489 F.3d 594 (4th Cir. 2007) (holding state law claims of credit cardholder against state-chartered, federally insured bank preempted by 12 U.S.C. §1831d(a)); *National City Bank of Indiana v. Turnbaugh*, 463 F.3d 325 (4th Cir. 2006), *cert. denied*, 550 U.S. 913 (holding that NBA and OCC regulations preempted state laws permitting Maryland Commissioner of Financial Regulation to exercise visitorial powers over national bank subsidiary operating as mortgage lender and to restrict prepayment penalties on adjustable rate mortgage loans); *American Bankers Ass'n. v. Gould*, 412 F.3d 1081 (9th Cir. 2005) (holding that federal Fair Credit Reporting Act affiliate-sharing preemption clause preempted California Financial Information Privacy Act (SB1) regulating communication of information between affiliates, to extent that SB1 purported to regulate communication between affiliates of "information," as defined in the FCRA); *Ass'n of Banks in Ins., Inc. v. Duryee*, 270 F.3d 397 (6th Cir. 2001) (preempting state insurance "principal purpose" licensing restrictions and related restrictions); *Guadagno v. E*Trade Bank*, 592 F.Supp.2d 1263 (C.D. Cal. 2008) (holding claim for injunction under state Unfair Competition Law against online bill payment process of federal savings bank preempted by HOLA and accompanying OTS regulations), *citing Bank of Am. v. City & County of S.F.*, 309 F.3d 551, 558 (9th Cir. 2002); *Capital One Bank (USA), N.A. v. McGraw*, 563 F. Supp. 2d 613 (S.D.W.Va. 2008) (holding that state investigation of consumer complaints regarding banking practices of national bank was unenforceable exercise of visitorial powers); *Pacific Capital Bank, N.A. v. Milgram*, — F. Supp. — 2008 WL 700180 (D.N.J. 2008) (preempting state statute limiting national bank in offering, facilitating, and making refund anticipation loans); *State Farm Bank, F.S.B. v. Burke*, 445 F. Supp. 2d 207 (D. Conn. 2006) (holding OTS regulations preempted Connecticut bank licensing and registration requirements, as applied to lending activities of exclusive agents of federal savings association chartered under HOLA); *Wells Fargo Bank, N.A. v. Boutris*, 252 F. Supp. 2d 1065 (E.D. Cal. 2003), *aff'd in part and rev'd in part*, 419 F.3d 949 (9th Cir. 2005) (holding that OCC acted within its authority in promulgating regulation providing for preemption of state laws purporting to regulate operating subsidiaries of national banks; that NBA preempted state exercise of visitorial authority over national bank operating subsidiaries; that state mortgage-lending licensing requirements, as applied to national bank operating subsidiaries, were field-preempted by OCC licensing regulations; and that Depository Institutions Deregulation and Monetary Control Act did not preempt state per diem loan-interest statute); *National Bank of Indiana v. Boutris*, — F. Supp. 2d —, 2003 WL 21536818 (E.D. Cal. 2003) (holding that NBA and related federal regulations preempted state exercise of state visitorial powers over operating subsidiary of national bank); *Bank of America v. Sorrell*, 248 F. Supp. 2d 1196 (N.D. Ga. 2002) (holding state prohibition of non-account holder fees for check cashing preempted by NBA incidental powers provision); *American Bankers*

Two early NBA decisions by the U.S. Supreme Court helped to set the tone for any future consideration of the relationship between state and federal regulation of financial services. In *Tiffany v. National Bank of Missouri*,[12] decided some nine years after the enactment of the NBA, Justice Strong observed in passing that "National banks are National favorites."[13] In this simple truism we may discover the heart of the current controversy over federal preemption of state financial services policy. In the circumstances of the actual case, Strong's observation seems straightforward. The NBA provided that the maximum rate to be charged on loans extended by a national bank was the rate of interest allowed by the laws of the state where the bank was located, or the rate allowed by the state to banks. Missouri had a generally applicable rate of 10 percent, and a special rate of 8 percent for banks.[14] What rate could a national bank in Missouri charge?

The Court viewed the problem before it as simply one of statutory interpretation, involving "the fair construction of the act of Congress, entirely consistent with its words and with its spirit."[15] The "spirit" of this interpretation was, in Justice Strong's view, one of national favoritism. If there was a reasonable interpretation of the words of the statute that would seem to favor the national bank, that was the interpretation to be adopted. This approach leads to a "most favored lender" policy in favor of national banks: whatever rate might apply to state banks, the rate applicable to national banks should be the most favorable rate available under state law for the particular type of lending transaction. Thus, a national bank would be subject to the 10 percent rate applicable to Missouri lenders generally, while state banks would be subject to the more restrictive 8 percent rate.

Ass'n v. Lockyer, 239 F. Supp. 2d 1000 (E.D. Cal. 2002) (preempting California statute requiring credit card issuers to provide "minimum payment" warnings and disclosures in monthly bills); *Weiss v. Washington Mut. Bank*, 53 Cal. Rptr. 3d 782 (Cal. Ct. App. 2007) (holding borrowers' challenge to federal savings and loan association's prepayment penalty preempted by HOLA and OTS regulations). *See generally Phipps v. FDIC*, 417 F.3d 1006 (8th Cir. 2005) (holding that NBA preempted claims to recover allegedly unlawful fees charged on second mortgage loans under the Missouri Second Mortgage Loan Act); *Flagg v. Yonkers Sav. and Loan Ass'n, FA*, 396 F.3d 178 (2d Cir. 2005), *cert. denied*, 546 U.S. 817 (holding, *inter alia*, that OTS regulations under HOLA, removing all legal obligations that federal savings associations might otherwise have to pay interest on mortgage escrow accounts, and allowing such matters to be governed by loan contract, preempted New York law requiring payment of interest on escrow funds); *Massachusetts Bankers Ass'n, Inc. v. Bowler*, 392 F. Supp. 2d 24 (D. Mass. 2005) (preempting state statute restricting bank ability to solicit insurance sales to loan applicants, citing GLBA).

12. 85 U.S. (18 Wall.) 409 (1873).

13. *Id.* at 413.

14. *Id.* at 411.

15. *Id.* at 411-412.

One might extrapolate from this case in two entirely different directions. On the one hand, this case could be viewed as an example of the "model of competition"[16] that results from – and should be encouraged by – the dual banking system. State and national bank systems make different regulatory policy choices, which are allowed to play out competitively. On the other hand, however, the case could be viewed as an early illustration of the skewing of regulatory choices in favor of the national bank system. In this sense, national favoritism, whether explicitly undertaken by statute or implicit in the application of the preemption doctrine, leads to results that subordinate state policy choices to federal ones.

The Supreme Court's 1875 NBA decision in *Farmers' & Mechanics' National Bank v. Dearing*[17] . . . express[ed] the view that the national banks created under the act's authority were to be accorded a degree of national favor, and that has largely been their experience ever since. The national banking system now enjoys, in addition to basic banking powers like lending and accepting deposits, flexible power to engage in a broad range of incidental powers – including data processing services, lease financing of automobiles, municipal bond insurance, securities activities, and selling variable annuities, among many others. . . .

For much of the history of the dual banking system, the full implications of national favoritism were muted by the happenstance that federal and state bank regulation tended to be institutional or corporate in its orientation. For the most part, regulation focused on corporate issues like chartering, branching, core operational powers and resolution of institutional failures, each of which was within the exclusive purview of the chartering authority of the institution. By default, ordinary transactional issues tended to be resolved by generally applicable transaction law, which meant state law. Thus, a balance was struck in the early stages of the dual banking system, in which state and national banks were equally and entirely subject to state law governing such issues as collection of debts, transactions in commercial paper, bank deposits, and contract law generally. For national banks, the one important exception to this rule was that federal law, primarily that administered by the OCC, determined the rights and obligations of national banks as corporate entities.[23] It is this balance of generally applicable state transactional law and fundamental, federal corporate law that defined the framework in which banks operated. Hence, it had long been accepted that national banks

---

16. Scott, *Dual Banking System, supra* note 3.

17. 91 U.S. (1 Otto) 29 (1875). . . .

23. *See, e.g.*, 12 U.S.C. §24 (concerning powers of national banking associations). *See also Easton v. Iowa*, 188 U.S. 220 (1903) (recognizing sole power of Congress to define powers of national banks); *Bullard v. National Eagle Bank*, 85 U.S. (18 Wall.) 589 (1873).

are subject to the laws of the State, and are governed in their daily course of business far more by the laws of the State than of the Nation.... It is only when the state law incapacitates the banks from discharging their duties to the government that it becomes unconstitutional.[24]

This basic principle was invoked by the Supreme Court in *Atherton v. FDIC*,[25] holding that fiduciary duties of bank management were derived from state common law, not federal general common law.[26] However, federal statutory and regulatory law have continued to play an increasingly important role in the powers of depository institutions, state and federal, to engage in particular types of transactions.[27] There are a number of reasons for this development. First, and most importantly, despite the dual nature of the depository institutions industry, it has become markedly federalized, primarily due to the fact that virtually all depository institutions are subject to federal supervision through the federal deposit insurance system.[28] Hence, despite occasional suggestions that the dual system should be modified in one way or another, the fact is that the system has already been significantly modified over time, due to the prevalence of federal deposit insurance.[29] Second, at a technical level, standards of conduct in banking transactions are subject to a distinctive federal regime. The authority of state-chartered banks to engage in activities not permitted to national banks has been significantly curtailed by the enactment of the Federal Deposit Insurance Corporation Improvements Act (FDICIA).[30] With certain specified exceptions, FDICIA generally requires that insured state banks not engage in any type of activity not permissible for national banks.[31]

The burgeoning federal role in the operation of state-chartered institutions

---

24. *First Nat'l Bank v. Kentucky*, 76 U.S. (9 Wall.) 353, 362 (1870). *See also Davis v. Elmira Sav. Bank*, 161 U.S. 275, 283 (1896); *McClellan v. Chipman*, 164 U.S. 347, 356-357 (1896).

25. 519 U.S. 213 (1997).

26. *See id.* at 222 (noting that "federally chartered banks are subject to state law").

27. For an excellent discussion of the development of the contemporary environment for banking, *see* Arthur E. Wilmarth, *The Transformation of the U.S. Financial Services Industry, 1975-2000: Competition, Consolidation, and Increased Risks*, 2002 U. ILL. L. REV. 215

28. On the prevalence and significance of federal deposit insurance as a feature of the contemporary banking market, *see* Helen Garten, *Banking on the Market: Relying on Depositors to Control Bank Risks*, 4 YALE J. ON REG. 129 (1986).

29. *See, e.g.*, 12 U.S.C. §1818(b) (subjecting all FDIC-insured depository institutions to administrative enforcement power of appropriate federal regulators with respect to violations of law, violations of regulatory agreements and unsafe and unsound practices).

30. Pub. L. No. 102-242, Dec. 19, 1991,105 Stat. 2236 (1991) (codified at scattered sections of 12 U.S.C.).

31. FDICIA §303 (codified at 12 U.S.C. §1831a).

has been complemented by a growing insulation of federally chartered institutions from any corresponding state role in the operation of federally chartered institutions. This growing imbalance is largely the result of the increasing significance of the doctrine of incidental powers. In general, when examining the powers of any depository institution to engage in particular types of transactions, one must keep in mind that these institutions are creatures of their constitutive statutes. This principle has traditionally been interpreted by the courts as defining the limits of the institution's power to engage in transactions.[33] Banks generally have authority only to exercise express statutory powers and powers necessarily incident to such express powers.[34] Typical express powers include the power to adopt a corporate seal; to make contracts; to sue and be sued; to elect and appoint executive management; to adopt bylaws; and to carry on the business of banking.

Carrying on the business of banking—and in particular the exercise of incidental powers in that regard—is the key to contemporary preemption. In the case of national banks, the statutory language begins simply enough, with the mandate that a national bank has the power "[t]o exercise ... subject to law, all such incidental powers as shall be necessary to carry on the business of banking."[41] Beginning in the mid-1950s, the Supreme Court has consistently held that attempts by state authority to intrude into the exercise of these powers are constitutionally preempted as inconsistent with the fundamental governance of federally chartered depository institutions.[42]

---

33. *See, e.g., City of Yonkers v. Downey*, 309 U.S. 590 (1940) (using statutory provisions as measure of bank's powers); *Texas & Pac. Ry. v. Pottorff*, 291 U.S. 245 (1934), *amended sub nom. Texas Pac. Ry. v. First Nat'l Bank of El Paso, Tex.*, 291 U.S. 649 (1934), *reh'g denied sub nom.Texas & Pac. Ry. v. Pottorff*, 292 U.S. 600 (1934) (using statutory provisions as measure of bank's powers); *First Nat'l Bank of St. Louis v. Missouri*, 263 U.S. 640 (1924) (limiting national banks to express statutory powers and necessary incidental powers); *Easton, supra* note 23; *California Sav. Bank v. Kennedy*, 167 U.S. 362 (1897) (limiting banks to express statutory powers and necessary incidental powers); *Logan County Nat'l Bank v. Townsend*, 139 U.S. 67 (1890) (limiting national banks to express statutory powers and necessary incidental powers); *Kimen v. Atlas Exch. Nat'l Bank of Chicago*, 92 F.2d 615 (7th Cir. 1937), *cert. denied sub nom. Awotin v. Healy*, 303 U.S. 650 (1938); *Berylwood Inv. Co. v. Graham*, 43 Cal. App. 2d 659, 111 P.2d 467 (1941); *Commonwealth Trust Co. v. First–Second Nat'l Bank*, 260 Pa. 223, 103 A. 598 (Pa. 1918), *cert. denied*, 246 U.S. 675.

34. *Williams v. Merchants' Nat'l Bank of St. Cloud*, 42 F.2d 243 (D. Minn. 1930); *Suburban Trust Co. v. Nat'l Bank of Westfield*, 211 F. Supp. 694 (D. N.J. 1962); *Bank of Calif. v. Portland*, 157 Or. 203, 69 P.2d 273 (1937), *cert. denied*, 302 U.S. 765.

41. [12 U.S.C. § 24(Seventh).]

42. *See, e.g., Franklin Nat'l Bank v. New York*, 347 U.S. 373 (1954) (preempting state law governing advertisement of accounts in light of national bank powers under 12 U.S.C. § 24); *Fidelity Fed. Sav. & Loan Ass'n v. De la Cuesta*, 458 U.S. 141 (1982) (preempting state law governing due-on-sale clauses applicable to savings associations).

Federal preemption doctrine has become increasingly important as a tool for consolidation of federal authority over bank regulatory policy. The 1954 decision of the Supreme Court in *Franklin National Bank v. New York*[43] invoked the federal statutory authority of national banks to engage in incidental powers as an obvious basis for preempting a state consumer protection provision that would have prohibited a national bank from characterizing itself in its advertising as a "savings" bank. This approach was cited with approval in *Barnett Bank of Marion County, N.A. v. Nelson,*[44] and is frequently utilized to preempt a widening range of state regulatory law that would otherwise be applicable to national banks and their operating subsidiaries. Furthermore, it would be disingenuous to ignore the concerted effort by the OCC to pursue a generally applicable strategy of preemption with respect to such state laws. . . .

The broadening invocation of preemption in the financial services context obviously raises serious concerns for the effectiveness and equity of state financial services and consumer protection policies. To the extent that national banks and their operating subsidiaries are significant participants in a state's financial services market, application of a state's policy is rendered markedly less effective when federal preemption intervenes. Furthermore, the application of the state policy to state-chartered institutions may, after federal preemption, be an inequitable competitive burden on those state institutions; this competitive consequence invites elimination of the policy or flight by the state institutions to federal charters. Can there be an effective response on the part of the state that preserves the values underlying its policies without completely compromising their effectiveness and competitive equity? A number of paths to resolution of this problem may be suggested.

One obvious possibility is, of course, to continue the vigorous litigation and appeal of these issues. The results in [the preemption cases in the lower courts], or even *Watters*, are not necessarily ineluctable.[67] The disadvantage

---

43. 347 U.S. 373 (1954).

44. 517 U.S. 25 (1996).

67. *See, e.g., Bernhard v. Whitney Nat'l Bank*, 523 F.3d 546 (5th Cir. 2008) (holding Electronic Funds Transfer Act not completely preemptive of bank customers' state law claims for unauthorized transfers); *State Farm Bank, F.S.B. v. Reardon*, 512 F. Supp. 2d 1107 (S.D. Ohio 2007) (holding Ohio mortgage broker law not preempted by OTS regulations; opinion letter drafted by OTS counsel regarding licensing of independent insurance agents as mortgage brokers for federal savings association not preemptive of Ohio law); *Quicken Loans, Inc. v. Wood*, 449 F.3d 944 (9th Cir. 2006), *cert. denied sub nom. Quicken Loans, Inc. v. DuFauchard*, 549 U.S. 1096 (holding that California "per diem" loan-interest statute, precluding mortgage interest during certain pre-recordation periods, not preempted by federal law, citing *Wells Fargo Bank N.A. v. Boutris, supra*); *Binetti v. Washington Mut. Bank*, 446 F. Supp. 2d 217 (S.D.N.Y. 2006) (holding New York consumer fraud statute not preempted by Home Owners'

of this approach is that preemption decisions in favor of exclusive OCC authority are based on a wide range of possible preemption grounds – including a range of NBA express or incidental powers – and involve a wide variety of regulatory subjects – including state consumer protection laws, ATM nondepositor fee prohibitions, branching rules, and the like. *Watters* confirms the breadth of the preemptive approach. From the perspective of a state attacking these varied issues, there are few economies of scale in such litigation, but the argument on the federal side is essentially the same in each case.

There may be greater economies of scale in seeking congressional action to clarify the legitimate interests of states in regulatory issues that affect national banks and their operating subsidiaries. The difficulty here is that Congress has spoken with conflicting voices concerning the status of the dual banking system over the years, and sometimes at the same time. Let us not forget that the preemption strategy currently being pursued by the OCC is grounded in the provisions of federal legislation, however general or vague that language may be. If experience is any guide, a congressional response to the problem of broad preemption in the regulation of financial services is likely to be piecemeal – a legislative reversal of a particular judicial decision here or there – which will leave states still confronting the broader problem.

It must be admitted that one practical difficulty in defending state policy against federal preemption in cases like *Watters* . . . is the dramatic impact that the state policies would have on the operations of the affected national banks and their affiliated enterprises. Whether it is the millions of dollars that compliance with state policy would inflict on an individual bank in start-up costs alone,[68] or the financial and personnel costs of conducting manual audits of more than 300,000 mortgage loans,[69] significant burdens on national banks and their affiliated enterprises may well be viewed as creating impermissible obstructions on national policy with respect to the safe and sound operation of national banks. This consideration certainly swayed the *Watters* Court.

Can more modest, incremental regulation by the state avoid preemption

---

Loan Act, as state commercial law only incidentally affecting lending operations of federal savings associations); *BankWest, Inc. v. Baker*, 324 F. Supp. 2d 1333 (N.D. Ga. 2004) (holding that FDIA provision allowing insured state banks to "export" home state interest rates to borrowers in other states on same basis as national banks, did not impliedly preempt Georgia legislation prohibiting "payday lending"); *Charter One Mortgage Corp. v. Condra*, 847 N.E.2d 207 (Ind. Ct. App. 2006) (holding that state supreme court's jurisdiction over unauthorized practice of law was not preempted by NBA or regulations promulgated thereunder, in case alleging that fee charged by nonbank operating subsidiary of national bank for preparation of deed and mortgage documents violated state law and constituted unjust enrichment).

68. *American Bankers Ass'n*, 239 F. Supp. 2d at 1005-1006.

69. *Wells FargoBank, N.A., supra* at note 11.

and still serve its policy objectives? Some suggestion of this incremental approach is apparent in *American Bankers* itself. There the court noted that "[i]n order to survive preemption, [the state law in question] must not prevent or significantly interfere with national banks' powers under the NBA."[70] In fact, the court argued that a state disclosure requirement imposed on national bank credit card issuers involving a "generic Minimum Payment Warning" might be "insufficiently burdensome to warrant preemption"[71] and might "well be de minimis and 'salutary'...."[72] Unfortunately, the court held, this provision was not severable from the unduly burdensome aspects of the state law.[73]

Close and focused legislative consideration of the preemption implications of proposed legislation might counsel enactment of a more modest state policy, leading to incremental benefits that escape federal preemption. Explicit consideration should be given to such incremental regulation in legislative deliberations.[74] Of course, it may be that the more modest result of incremental regulation may simply be inadequate to serve the policy objectives identified by the legislature. The risks of preemption litigation or the uncertainties of congressional lobbying may be unavoidable.

One bold approach to the problem of federal preemption may be based on an historical insight that is blandly endorsed by all the decisions, but usually ignored once analysis begins. The NBA notwithstanding, national banks are generally subject to state transactional law.[75] It is on this basis that *American Bankers* blithely states that:

> States are not without any authority to impose regulations upon national banks. They do "retain some power to regulate national banks in areas such as contracts, debt collection, acquisition and transfer of property, and taxation, zoning, criminal, and tort law." *Bank of America* [*v. City & County of San Francisco*], 309 F.3d [551,] 559 [(9th Cir. 2002)] (citing cases). However, because there is a "'history of significant federal presence' in national banking, the presumption against preemption of state law is inapplicable." Id. (*citing United States v. Locke*, 529 U.S. 89, 108, 120 S.Ct. 1135, 146 L.Ed.2d 69 (2000)).[76]

Preemption conflicts typically involve an attempt by a state to impose an

---

70. *American Bankers Ass'n*, 239 F. Supp. 2d at 1016, *citing Barnett Bank, supra* note 44.

71. *Id.* at 1019.

72. *Id.* at 1020.

73. *Id.* at 1021.

74. The absence of such express deliberation reflected in the legislative history of the credit card legislation was a significant factor in the court's holding that the Minimum Payment Warning was not severable from the preempted portions of the Cal. Civ. Code §1748.13. *American Bankers Ass'n*, 239 F. Supp. 2d at 1021.

75. *See supra* text and accompanying note 24.

76. *American Bankers Ass'n*, 239 F. Supp. 2d at 1008.

external regulatory or supervisory framework on the transactional behavior of federally regulated entities. In light of the historical position endorsed by the case law, how likely is federal preemption if, instead, the state "regulation" in substance and in form consisted of principles of ordinary contract law? Aside from such transborder activities as international contracts for the sale of goods,[77] there is no federal law of contracts—historically significant or otherwise. Thus, there is no reason to expect that normal presumptions against preemption would not apply.[78]

Consider a situation like *American Bankers*, involving policy concerns about the treatment of unsophisticated credit card holders who may be passively encouraged to pay only the minimum monthly required amount on their credit card accounts. If, instead of imposing a set of regulatory requirements on credit card issuers, the state were to enact legislation making specified credit card agreements unconscionable and unenforceable, the subsequent preemption argument would begin at the question of whether or not state legislation with respect to traditional contract concepts was entitled to a presumption of validity.[79] Obviously, the use of traditional contract concepts will not be adaptable to every issue of state policy that might confront a federal preemption argument, but for some issues contract law may be a useful alternative to a direct regulatory confrontation. Invocation of traditional common law doctrines are not necessarily fool-proof either.

---

77. *See, e.g.*, U.N. Convention on Contracts for the International Sale of Goods, GENERAL A/CONF.97/18 (Apr. 10, 1980), 15 U.S.C.A. App. (providing contract law with respect to private contracts between nationals of states party to the convention).

78. *Cf. United States v. Locke*, 529 U.S. at 108 (discussing presumption against preemption).

79. *See* 12 C.F.R. § 557.13(a)(1) ("The OTS has not preempted the following types of state law, to the extent that the law only incidentally affects your deposit-related activities or is otherwise consistent with the purposes of § 557.11: (1) Contract and commercial law…"). *But see Guadagno v. E*Trade Bank*, 592 F. Supp. 2d 1263 (C.D. Cal. 2008):

> However, if a law of general application requires a thrift and savings bank to affirmatively change its practices, it is preempted. *See Reyes v. Downey Sav. & Loan Ass'n*, 541 F.Supp.2d 1108, 1113 (C.D.Cal.2008); *see also Wash. Mut. Bank v. Superior Court*, 95 Cal. App. 4th 606, 115 Cal. Rptr. 2d 765, 776 (2002); *Boursiquot v. Citibank*, 323 F. Supp. 2d 350, 355-56 (D. Conn. 2004) (holding that HOLA and OTS regulations preempted Connecticut's Unfair Trade Practices Act as applied because plaintiffs' claim would have required federal savings and loan association to alter lending practices). Thus, even if Guadagno's UCL injunctive relief claim was not explicitly preempted by 12 C.F.R. 557.12(b) and (d), it would nonetheless be preempted because it would require E*Trade to affirmatively change its deposit-related practices.

The referenced § 557.11 is the OTS field preemption provision with respect to regulation of federal savings association deposit-related activities.

2. A Different Strategy for Consumer Protection

Obviously, the transactional law (contracts, creditor's rights, checks and commercial paper, bank collections) relevant to banking remains largely state law. *Watters* does not really dispute this basic historical principle, and *Atherton* may even demand it. Can courts apply these transactional rules to blunt the effect of the preemption initiative?

NOTES AND QUESTIONS

1. *Turning the Tide.* A fresh intimation of a possible turn in the post-*Watters* preemption tide comes from the Court itself in *Cuomo v. Clearing House Ass'n, L.L.C.*, excerpted *infra*. Returning to the familiar ground of *Watters*, *Cuomo* holds that an OCC regulation interpreting the visitorial powers provision of the NBA was not a reasonable interpretation, since it appeared to preclude state officials from using the courts to enforce compliance by national banks with non-preempted state law.

2. *The Strategy Applied?* In a sense, *Cuomo* explores the implications of the alternative suggested at the beginning of this section – that one should look for ordinarily applicable concepts from state law when confronting the preemption initiative of the federal bank regulators. As you read the following excerpt from *Cuomo*, consider whether the case actually vindicates the suggested alternative strategy.

CUOMO V. CLEARING HOUSE ASS'N, L.L.C.

— U.S. —, 129 S.Ct. 2710 (2009)

Justice SCALIA delivered the opinion of the Court.

In 2005, Eliot Spitzer, Attorney General for the State of New York, sent letters to several national banks making a request "in lieu of subpoena" that they provide certain non-public information about their lending practices. He sought this information to determine whether the banks had violated the State's fair-lending laws. Spitzer's successor in office, Andrew Cuomo, is the petitioner here. Respondents, the federal Office of the Comptroller of the Currency ("Comptroller" or "OCC") and the Clearing House Association, a banking trade group, brought suit to enjoin the information request, claiming that the Comptroller's regulation promulgated under the National Bank Act prohibits that form of state law enforcement against national banks.

The United States District Court for the Southern District of New York entered an injunction in favor of respondents, prohibiting the attorney general from enforcing state fair-lending laws through demands for records or judicial proceedings. The United States Court of Appeals for the Second Circuit affirmed. . . . The question presented is whether the Comptroller's regulation purporting to pre-empt state law enforcement can be upheld as a reasonable interpretation of the National Bank Act.

I . . .

Section 484(a) of Title 12, U.S.C., a provision of the National Bank Act, 13 Stat. 99, reads as follows:

> "No national bank shall be subject to any visitorial powers except as authorized by Federal law, vested in the courts of justice or such as shall be, or have been exercised or directed by Congress or by either House thereof or by any committee of Congress or of either House duly authorized."

The Comptroller, charged with administering the National Bank Act, adopted, through notice-and-comment rulemaking, the regulation at issue here designed to implement the statutory provision. Its principal provisions read as follows:

> § 7.4000 Visitorial powers.
> "(a) *General rule.* (1) Only the OCC or an authorized representative of the OCC may exercise visitorial powers with respect to national banks, except as provided in paragraph (b) of this section. State officials may not exercise visitorial powers with respect to national banks, such as conducting examinations, inspecting or requiring the production of books or records of national banks, or prosecuting enforcement actions, except in limited circumstances authorized by federal law. However, production of a bank's records (other than non-public OCC information under 12 CFR part 4, subpart C) may be required under normal judicial procedures.
> "(2) For purposes of this section, visitorial powers include:
> "(i) Examination of a bank;
> "(ii) Inspection of a bank's books and records;
> "(iii) Regulation and supervision of activities authorized or permitted pursuant to federal banking law; and
> "(iv) Enforcing compliance with any applicable federal or state laws concerning those activities." 12 CFR § 7.4000 (2009).

By its clear text, this regulation prohibits the States from "prosecuting enforcement actions" except in "limited circumstances authorized by federal law."

Under the familiar *Chevron* framework, we defer to an agency's reasonable interpretation of a statute it is charged with administering. *Chevron U.S.A. Inc. v. Natural Resources Defense Council, Inc.,* 467 U.S. 837 (1984). There is necessarily some ambiguity as to the meaning of the statutory term "visitorial powers," especially since we are working in an era when the prerogative writs – through which visitorial powers were traditionally enforced – are not in vogue. The Comptroller can give authoritative meaning to the statute within the bounds of that uncertainty. But the presence of some uncertainty does not expand *Chevron* deference to cover virtually any interpretation of the National Bank Act. We can discern the outer limits of the term "visitorial powers" even through the clouded lens of history. They do not include, as the Comptroller's expansive regulation would provide, ordinary enforcement of the law. Evidence from the time of the statute's enactment, a long line of our own cases, and application of normal principles of construction to the National Bank Act make that clear.

A

Historically, the sovereign's right of visitation over corporations paralleled the right of the church to supervise its institutions and the right of the founder of a charitable institution "to see that [his] property [was] rightly employed," 1 W. Blackstone, Commentaries on the Laws of England 469 (1765). By extension of this principle, "[t]he king [was] by law the visitor of all civil corporations," *ibid.* A visitor could inspect and control the visited institution at will.

When the National Bank Act was enacted in 1864, "visitation" was accordingly understood as "[t]he act of examining into the affairs of a corporation" by "the government itself." 2 J. Bouvier, A Law Dictionary 790 (15th ed. 1883). Lower courts understood "visitation" to mean "the act of a superior or superintending officer, who visits a corporation to examine into its manner of conducting business, and [to] enforce an observance of its laws and regulations." *First Nat. Bank of Youngstown v. Hughes,* 6 F. 737, 740 (C.C.N.D.Ohio 1881). A State was the "visitor" of all companies incorporated in the State, simply by virtue of the State's role as sovereign: The "legislature is the visitor of all corporations founded by it." *Guthrie v. Harkness,* 199 U.S. 148, 157 (1905) (internal quotation marks omitted).

This relationship between sovereign and corporation was understood to allow the States to use prerogative writs – such as mandamus and *quo warranto* – to exercise control "whenever a corporation [wa]s abusing the power given it, . . . or acting adversely to the public, or creating a nuisance." H. Wilgus, Private Corporations, in 8 American Law and Procedure § 157, pp. 224-225 (1910). State visitorial commissions were authorized to "exercise a general supervision" over companies in the State. I. Wormser, Private Corporations § 80, pp. 100, 101, in 4 Modern American Law (1921).

B

Our cases have always understood "visitation" as this right to oversee corporate affairs, quite separate from the power to enforce the law. In the famous *Dartmouth College* case, Justice Story, describing visitation of a charitable corporation, wrote that Dartmouth was "subject to the controlling authority of its legal visitor, who . . . may amend and repeal its statutes, remove its officers, correct abuses, and generally superintend the management of [its] trusts," and who are "liable to no supervision or control." *Trustees of Dartmouth College v. Woodward,* 4 Wheat. 518, 676, 681, 4 L.Ed. 629 (1819) (concurring opinion). This power of "genera[l] superintend[ence]" stood in contrast to action by the court of chancery, which acted "not as itself possessing a visitorial power . . . but as possessing a general jurisdiction . . . to redress grievances, and frauds." *Id.,* at 676.

In *Guthrie, supra,* we held that a shareholder acting in his role as a private individual was not exercising a "visitorial power" under the National Bank Act when he petitioned a court to force the production of corporate records, *id.,* at 159. "[C]ontrol in the courts of justice," we said, is not visitorial, and we drew a contrast between the nonvisitorial act of "su[ing] in the courts of the State" and the visitorial "supervision of the Comptroller of the Currency," *id.,* at 159, 157, 26 S.Ct. 4.

In *First Nat. Bank in St. Louis v. Missouri,* 263 U.S. 640 (1924), we upheld the right of the Attorney General of Missouri to bring suit to enforce a state anti-bank-branching law against a national bank. We said that only the United States may perform visitorial administrative oversight, such as "inquir[ing] by *quo warranto* whether a national bank is acting in excess of its charter powers." *Id.,* at 660, 44 S.Ct. 213. But if a state statute of general applicability is not substantively pre-empted, then "the power of enforcement must rest with the [State] and not with" the National Government, *ibid.*

Our most recent decision, *Watters v. Wachovia Bank, N.A.,* 550 U.S. 1 (2007), does not, as the dissent contends, . . . "suppor[t] OCC's construction of the statute." To the contrary, it is fully in accord with the well established distinction between supervision and law enforcement. *Watters* held that a State may not exercise " 'general supervision and control' " over a subsidiary of a national bank, 550 U.S., at 8, because "multiple audits and surveillance under rival oversight regimes" would cause uncertainty, *id.,* at 21. "[G]eneral supervision and control" and "oversight" are worlds apart from law enforcement. All parties to the case agreed that Michigan's general oversight regime could not be imposed on national banks; the sole question was whether operating subsidiaries of national banks enjoyed the same immunity from state visitation. The opinion addresses and answers no other question.

The foregoing cases all involve enforcement of state law. But if the Comptroller's exclusive exercise of visitorial powers precluded law enforcement by the States, it would also preclude law enforcement by federal agencies. Of course it does not. See, *e.g., Bank of America Nat. Trust & Sav.*

Assn. v. Douglas, 105 F.2d 100, 105-106 (CADC 1939) (Securities Exchange Commission investigation of bank fraud is not an exercise of "visitorial powers"); *Peoples Bank of Danville v. Williams,* 449 F.Supp. 254, 260 (W.D.Va.1978) (same).

In sum, the unmistakable and utterly consistent teaching of our jurisprudence, both before and after enactment of the National Bank Act, is that a sovereign's "visitorial powers" and its power to enforce the law are two different things. There is not a credible argument to the contrary. And contrary to what the Comptroller's regulation says, the National Bank Act pre-empts only the former.

C

The consequences of the regulation also cast doubt upon its validity. No one denies that the National Bank Act leaves in place some state substantive laws affecting banks. . . . But the Comptroller's rule says that the State may not *enforce* its valid, non-pre-empted laws against national banks. *Ibid.* The bark remains, but the bite does not. . . .

. . . As the Court said in *St. Louis:*

> "To demonstrate the binding quality of a statute but deny the power of enforcement involves a fallacy made apparent by the mere statement of the proposition, for such power is essentially inherent in the very conception of law." 263 U.S., at 660.

In sharp contrast to the "unusual" reading propounded by the Comptroller's regulation, reading "visitorial powers" as limiting only sovereign oversight and supervision would produce an entirely commonplace result – the precise result contemplated by our opinion in *St. Louis,* which said that if a state statute is valid as to national banks, "the corollary that it is obligatory *and enforceable* necessarily results." *Id.,* at 659-660 (emphasis added). Channeling state attorneys general into judicial law-enforcement proceedings (rather than allowing them to exercise "visitorial" oversight) would preserve a regime of exclusive administrative oversight by the Comptroller while honoring in fact rather than merely in theory Congress's decision not to pre-empt substantive state law. This system echoes many other mixed state/federal regimes in which the Federal Government exercises general oversight while leaving state substantive law in place. See, *e.g., Wyeth v. Levine,* 555 U.S. —, 129 S.Ct. 1187 (2009).

This reading is also suggested by § 484(a)'s otherwise inexplicable reservation of state powers "vested in the courts of justice." As described earlier, visitation was normally conducted through use of the prerogative writs of mandamus and *quo warranto.* The exception could not possibly exempt that manner of exercising visitation, or else the exception would swallow the rule.

Its only conceivable purpose is to preserve normal civil and criminal lawsuits. To be sure, the reservation of powers "vested in the courts of justice" is phrased as an exception from the prohibition of visitorial powers. But as we have just discussed, it cannot possibly be that, and it is explicable only as an attempt to make clear that the courts' ordinary powers of enforcing the law are not affected.[3]

On a pragmatic level, the difference between visitation and law enforcement is clear. If a State chooses to pursue enforcement of its laws in court, then it is not exercising its power of visitation and will be treated like a litigant. An attorney general acting as a civil litigant must file a lawsuit, survive a motion to dismiss, endure the rules of procedure and discovery, and risk sanctions if his claim is frivolous or his discovery tactics abusive. Judges are trusted to prevent "fishing expeditions" or an undirected rummaging through bank books and records for evidence of some unknown wrongdoing. In New York, civil discovery is far more limited than the full range of "visitorial powers" that may be exercised by a sovereign. Courts may enter protective orders to prevent "unreasonable annoyance, expense, embarrassment, disadvantage, or other prejudice," N.Y. Civ. Prac. Law Ann. § 3103(a) (West 2005), and may supervise discovery *sua sponte,* § 3104(a). A visitor, by contrast, may inspect books and records at any time for any or no reason.

II

The Comptroller's regulation, therefore, does not comport with the statute. Neither does the Comptroller's *interpretation* of its regulation, which differs from the text and must be discussed separately.

Evidently realizing that exclusion of state enforcement of *all* state laws against national banks is too extreme to be contemplated, the Comptroller sought to limit the sweep of its regulation by the following passage set forth in the agency's statement of basis and purpose in the Federal Register:

> "What the case law *does* recognize is that 'states retain some power to regulate national banks in areas such as contracts, debt collection, acquisition and transfer of property, and taxation, zoning, criminal, and tort law.' [citing a Ninth Circuit case.]

---

3. We reject respondents' contention that the Riegle-Neal Interstate Banking and Branching Efficiency Act of 1994, § 102(f)(1)(B), 108 Stat. 2349, 2350, 12 U.S.C. § 36(f)(1)(B), establishes that the Comptroller's visitorial power pre-empts state law enforcement. That provision states that some state laws respecting bank branching "shall be enforced" by the Comptroller. We need not decide here whether converting the Comptroller's visitorial *power* to assure compliance with all applicable laws, . . . into an *obligation* to assure compliance with certain state laws preempts state enforcement of those particular laws. Even if it had that effect it would shed no light on the meaning of "visitorial powers" in the National Bank Act, a statute that it does not refer to and that was enacted more than a century earlier.

Application of these laws to national banks and their implementation by state authorities typically does not affect the content or extent of the Federally-authorized business of banking . . . but rather establishes the legal infrastructure that surrounds and supports the ability of national banks . . . to do business." 69 Fed.Reg. 1896 (2004) (footnote omitted).

This cannot be reconciled with the regulation's almost categorical prohibition in 12 CFR § 7.4000(a)(1) of "prosecuting enforcement actions." . . .

III

The dissent fails to persuade us. Its fundamental contention – that the exclusive grant of visitorial powers can be interpreted to preclude state enforcement of state laws – rests upon a logical fallacy. The dissent establishes, . . . (and we do not at all contest), that in the course of exercising visitation powers the sovereign can compel compliance with the law. But it concludes from that . . . that any sovereign attempt to compel compliance with the law can be deemed an exercise of the visitation power. That conclusion obviously does not follow. . . .

States . . . have always enforced their general laws against national banks – and have enforced their banking-related laws against national banks for at least 85 years, as evidenced by *St. Louis,* in which we upheld enforcement of a state anti-bank-branching law, 263 U.S., at 656, 44 S.Ct. 213. See also *Anderson Nat. Bank v. Luckett,* 321 U.S. 233, 237 (1944) (state commissioner of revenue may enforce abandoned-bank-deposit law against national bank through "judicial proceedings"); *State by Lord v. First Nat. Bank of St. Paul,* 313 N.W.2d 390, 393 (Minn.1981) (state treasurer may enforce general unclaimed-property law with "specific provisions directed toward" banks against national bank); *Clovis Nat. Bank v. Callaway,* 69 N.M. 119, 130-132, 364 P.2d 748, 756 (1961) (state treasurer may enforce unclaimed-property law against national bank deposits); *State v. First Nat. Bank of Portland,* 61 Or. 551, 554-557, 123 P. 712, 714 (1912) (state attorney general may enforce bank-specific escheat law against national bank). . . .

IV

Applying the foregoing principles to this case is not difficult. "Visitorial powers" in the National Bank Act refers to a sovereign's supervisory powers over corporations. They include any form of administrative oversight that allows a sovereign to inspect books and records on demand, even if the process is mediated by a court through prerogative writs or similar means. The Comptroller reasonably interpreted this statutory term to include "conducting examinations [and] inspecting or requiring the production of books or records of national banks," § 7.4000, when the State conducts those activities in its capacity as supervisor of corporations.

When, however, a state attorney general brings suit to enforce state law against a national bank, he is not acting in the role of sovereign-as-supervisor, but rather in the role of sovereign-as-law-enforcer. Such a lawsuit is not an exercise of "visitorial powers" and thus the Comptroller erred by extending the definition of "visitorial powers" to include "prosecuting enforcement actions" in state courts, § 7.4000. . . .

Justice THOMAS, with whom the CHIEF JUSTICE, Justice KENNEDY, and Justice ALITO join, concurring in part and dissenting in part.

The Court holds that the term "visitorial powers" as used in the National Bank Act (NBA), 12 U.S.C. § 484(a), refers only "to a sovereign's supervisory powers over corporations," which are limited to "administrative oversight" including "inspect[ion of] books and records on demand." . . . Based on this definition, the Court concludes that § 484(a) does not pre-empt a "state attorney general['s] . . . suit to enforce state law against a national bank." *Ibid.* I would affirm the Court of Appeals' determinations that the term "visitorial powers" is ambiguous and that it was reasonable for the Office of the Comptroller of the Currency (OCC) to interpret the term to encompass state efforts to obtain national bank records and to enforce state fair lending laws against national banks. Accordingly, I respectfully concur in part and dissent in part.

NOTES AND QUESTIONS

1. *Disposition of the Case. Cuomo* arose out of an investigation by the New York Attorney General's office into possible violations of New York fair-lending laws, in which the Attorney General sent letters to several national banks requesting, "in lieu of a subpoena," that they provide certain non-public information about their lending practices. On certiorari, the Court concluded that the OCC regulation excluding state enforcement of *all* state laws against national banks did not reasonably interpret the statute:

> The Comptroller reasonably interpreted this statutory term [visitorial powers] to include "conducting examinations [and] inspecting or requiring the production of books or records of national banks," § 7.4000, when the State conducts those activities in its capacity as supervisor of corporations.
>
> When, however, a state attorney general brings suit to enforce state law against a national bank, he is not acting in the role of sovereign-as-supervisor, but rather in the role of sovereign-as-law-enforcer. Such a lawsuit is not an exercise of "visitorial powers" and thus the Comptroller erred by extending the definition of "visitorial

powers" to include "prosecuting enforcement actions" in state courts, § 7.4000.[15]

The problem presented by the facts of the case, however, is that the Attorney General took a middle ground that was not actually available to him – to attempt to enforce state law by resort to (or the threat of resort to) his *administrative* subpoena power, rather than judicial compulsory process. This administrative process was "not the exercise of the power of law enforcement 'vested in the courts of justice' which 12 U.S.C. § 484(a) exempts from the ban on exercise of supervisory power."[16] Accordingly, although the case is a triumph in principle for the dual banking system – the injunction is vacated to the extent that it would prohibit the Attorney General from commencing judicial proceedings – the injunction was affirmed by the Court as applied to the nascent administrative subpoenas.

2. *Reconciling Watters and Cuomo.* How should we reconcile the holdings in *Watters* and *Cuomo*? In *Cuomo*, Justice Scalia argues that the two decisions are in harmony – "[*Watters*] is fully in accord with the well established distinction between supervision and law enforcement." The implication seems to be that *Watters* concerned a question of "supervision" – and thus the state statute was preempted, whereas *Cuomo* involved "law enforcement," and state law properly pursued in state courts would not be preempted. The following case potentially pits the two cases against one another, with the majority using *Watters* to preempt a state garnishment statute and the dissent using *Cuomo* to insulate the statute from preemption. Which opinion seems persuasive to you?

MONROE RETAIL, INC. V. RBS CITIZENS, N.A.

589 F.3d 274 (6th Cir. 2009)

JULIA SMITH GIBBONS, Circuit Judge.

[Judgment creditors in Ohio had sought to collect on their judgments by garnishing the judgment debtors' deposits at various banks. The banks routinely imposed garnishment fees on customer accounts prior to full recovery of the amounts owed. The garnishor-creditors brought suit against the banks in state court. After removal, the U.S. district court granted the banks' motions to dismiss. The Sixth Circuit affirmed the dismissal, holding that: (*i*) the garnishors had standing; (*ii*) NBA preempted the garnishor-creditors' conversion claims brought pursuant to Ohio garnishment statutes; and, (*iii*) the

---

15. *Cuomo*, — U.S. at —, 129 S.Ct. at 2721
16. *Id.*

principle of setoff, invoked by the district court, did not apply as between the banks and the garnishors.]

Plaintiffs-appellants Monroe Retail, Inc.; Jerome Phillips, Esq.; and Leo Marks, Inc. ("the Garnishors") appeal the district court's dismissal of their claim against defendants-appellees RBS Citizens, N.A. (formerly known as Charter One Bank, N.A.); The Huntington National Bank; Huntington Bancshares, Inc.; JPMorgan Chase Bank, N.A.; JPMorgan Chase & Co.; Keybank; N.A.; Keycorp; National City Bank; National City Corporation; Sky Bank; U.S. Bank, N.A.; and U.S. Bancorp ("the Banks"). . . .

I.

The relevant facts are not in dispute. The Garnishors are garnishor-creditors in Ohio who obtain judgments against debtors when debts are not repaid. The Garnishors often collect these judgments by garnishing the debtors' bank accounts. Ohio Revised Code ("ORC") § 2716.12 provides that a garnishment action must be accompanied by a one dollar fee to the garnishee, in this case, the Banks who hold the debtors' funds in customer accounts. The Banks charge an additional $25 to $80 service fee to the debtors for the garnishment process. When debtors have insufficient funds to satisfy both the service fee and the garnishment order, the Banks extract the service fees from the garnished funds before releasing the remainder of the funds to the Garnishors.

The Garnishors filed a class action suit against the Banks in the Court of Common Pleas of Lucas County, Ohio, on August 31, 2006, alleging three causes of action against the Banks. First, the Garnishors claimed that the service fees charged by the Banks amount to additional garnishment fees beyond the one dollar fee authorized by ORC § 2716.12 and therefore violate that section, causing the Garnishors to have lost at least $5,000,000. Second, the Garnishors claimed that by deducting these service fees, the Banks were illegally converting funds belonging to the Garnishors for their own use in violation of the garnishment process prescribed by ORC § 2716.13(B) and § 2716.21(D). Third, the Garnishors sought injunctive relief to prevent the Banks from continuing to deduct service fees from funds in the debtors' accounts. The Banks all responded by filing dispositive motions. . . .

III. . . .

[T]he only issue before us is whether the Garnishors' conversion claim can survive a motion for judgment on the pleadings and a motion to dismiss. The Garnishors claim that the Banks have wrongfully converted $25 to $80 per garnishment to their own use in violation of ORC § 2716.13(B)[3] and ORC § 2716.21(D).[4] . . . The Garnishors interpret these regulations [*sic*] to require the Banks to relinquish debtors' funds before deducting service fees for the garnishment process. The Banks argue that the Garnishors do not state a claim because the National Bank Act, 12 U.S.C. § 24 (Seventh) ("NBA"), permits them to charge fees and preempts any claim to the contrary.[5]

Ordinarily, a presumption against preemption applies. *See United States v. Locke,* 529 U.S. 89, 108 (2000). . . . In the context of national banking, however, the Supreme Court has held that the general presumption against preemption does not apply. *See Watters v. Wachovia Bank, N.A.,* 550 U.S. 1, 12 (2007); *Locke,* 529 U.S. at 108 ("[A]n 'assumption' of nonpre-emption is not triggered when the State regulates in an area where there has been a history of significant federal presence."); *Barnett Bank of Marion County, N.A. v. Nelson,* 517 U.S. 25, 32 (1996).

. . . The Officer [*sic*] of the Comptroller of the Currency ("OCC"), which has regulatory and supervisory power over national banks, has issued regulations defining the "incidental powers" a national bank may exercise without state interference. *See, e.g., NationsBank of N.C., N.A. v. Variable Annuity Life Ins. Co.,* 513 U.S. 251, 25658 (1995). The OCC's interpretation of the NBA is entitled to substantial deference:

> It is settled that courts should give great weight to any reasonable construction of a regulatory statute adopted by the agency charged with the enforcement of that statute.

---

3. The pertinent language in ORC § 2716.13(B) states: "The [garnishment] order shall bind the property in excess of four hundred dollars, other than personal earnings, of the judgment debtor in the possession of the garnishee at the time of service."

4. The text of ORC § 2716.21(D) provides:

> A garnishee shall pay the personal earnings owed to the judgment debtor or the money or value of the property or credits, other than personal earnings, of the judgment debtor in the garnishee's possession or under the garnishee's control at the time of service of the order of garnishment, or so much thereof as the court orders, into court. The garnishee shall be discharged from liability to the judgment debtor for money so paid and shall not be subjected to costs beyond those caused by the garnishee's resistance of the claims against the garnishee. A garnishee is liable to the judgment creditor for all money, property, and credits, other than personal earnings, of the judgment debtor in the garnishee's possession or under the garnishee's control or for all personal earnings due from the garnishee to the judgment debtor, whichever is applicable, at the time the garnishee is served with the order under section 2716.05 or 2716.13 of the Revised Code.

5. The Garnishors brought claims against both national and state banks before the district court. The Huntington National Bank; JPMorgan Chase Bank, N.A.; Keybank N.A.; Keycorp; National City Bank; U.S. Bank N.A.; and Charter One are national banks, and Sky Bank was a state bank. As noted at oral argument, however, Huntington Bancshares has since acquired Sky Bank. Therefore, all of the defendants are now national banks, and we need not bifurcate the analysis.

The [OCC] is charged with the enforcement of banking laws to an extent that warrants the invocation of this principle with respect to [its] deliberative conclusions as to the meaning of these laws.

Clarke v. Secs. Indus. Ass'n, 479 U.S 388, 403-04 (1987) (citation omitted) (quoting *Investment Co. Institute v. Camp,* 401 U.S. 617, 62627 (1971), and collecting cases).

The OCC has specifically defined the ability to charge fees as an "incidental power" of a national bank. The OCC promulgated § 7.4002(a) of Title 12 of the Code of Federal Regulations, which gives national banks explicit "[a]uthority to impose charges and fees." 12 C.F.R. § 7.4002(a). Both parties have stipulated that the Banks have authority pursuant to such federal regulation to charge contractual fees to their customers. They disagree, however, as to whether the NBA's grant of authority to charge fees includes the service fees for the garnishment process and preempts the Garnishors' conversion claim.

The Banks contend that the NBA permits them to charge the Garnishors the service fees when debtors have insufficient funds in their accounts to satisfy the fees. According to the OCC's regulations, a national bank is authorized to "charge its customers non-interest charges and fees, including deposit account service charges." *Id.* The Banks argue that this language permits them to collect service fees from debtors' accounts, even if the funds in the accounts are subject to garnishment by the Garnishors. In response, the Garnishors argue that their right to the funds is protected by Ohio's garnishment statute, *see* ORC §§ 2716.13(B), 2716.21(D), and that Ohio garnishment law is explicitly exempt from preemption and the Banks' broad authority under 12 C.F.R. § 7.4007(c)(4), which exempts state laws governing the "rights to collect debts" from preemption. The Banks contend that this language exempts only state laws governing the *Banks'* rights to collect debts from preemption, not the Garnishors' rights, and further argue that any interpretation of Ohio debt collection law that would allow the Garnishors' claim to proceed is preempted by the NBA.

We find that the NBA does not preempt general state laws governing the rights of all entities, not just Banks, to collect debts; but we conclude that the Garnishors' specific conversion claim pursuant to the Ohio garnishment statute is nevertheless preempted by the NBA's grant of authority to the Banks to charge and collect fees.

A. "Rights to Collect Debts"

. . . The first question before us is whether the NBA saves all state laws governing "rights to collect debts" from preemption, or, as the Banks contend, merely laws governing the Banks' rights to collect debts. The text of the pertinent regulation states:

> State laws that are not preempted. State laws on the following subjects are not inconsistent with the deposit-taking powers of national banks and apply to national banks to the extent that they only incidentally affect the exercise of national banks' deposit-taking powers:
> (1) Contracts;
> (2) Torts;
> (3) Criminal law;
> (4) Rights to collect debts;
> (5) Acquisition and transfer of property;
> (6) Taxation;
> (7) Zoning;
> (8) Any other law the effect of which the OCC determines to be incidental to the deposit-taking operations of national banks or otherwise consistent with the powers set out in paragraph (a) of this section.

12 C.F.R. § 7.4007(c) (footnote omitted).

The Banks claim that this language clearly refers only to the Banks' rights to collect debts and thus that all other laws governing the rights to collect debts, including ORC § 2716.13(B) and § 2716.21(D), are preempted by the NBA. . . .

[The court reasoned that the NBA did not purport to preempt state laws of general applicability that did not target banks. It rejected the banks' narrow interpretation and found that the NBA did not preempt general state debt collection laws, including those regulating both banks' and others' rights to collect debts.]

B. Banks' Authority to Charge Fees

This finding, however, does not end our inquiry. We must now examine whether the Garnishors' specific conversion claim pursuant to Ohio's garnishment statute is preempted. As mentioned above, state laws, including those governing "rights to collect debts," are only exempted from preemption "to the extent that they only incidentally affect the exercise of national banks' deposit-taking powers." 12 C.F.R. § 7.4002(c)(4). The Supreme Court has held that states may not "prevent or significantly interfere with the national bank's exercise of its powers." *Barnett Bank*, 517 U.S. at 33. When state laws "significantly impair the exercise of authority, enumerated or incidental under the NBA," the state laws "must give way." *Watters*, 550 U.S. at 12. We have found that the level of "interference" that gives rise to preemption under the NBA is not very high. *See Ass'n of Banks in Ins., Inc. v. Duryee*, 270 F.3d 397, 409 (6th Cir.2001) (rejecting as "unpersuasive" an "attempt to redefine 'significantly interfere' as 'effectively thwart'"). Although the Garnishors have withdrawn their statutory claim, the Banks argue that any interpretation of

Ohio's garnishment laws that would allow the Garnishors' conversion claim to proceed would interfere with their ability to collect fees, as authorized by 12 C.F.R. § 7.4002(a), and is thus preempted.

The Banks . . . solicited the OCC's opinion on this matter. In [an] opinion letter, the OCC declared that the service fee for the garnishment process was a "fee" within the meaning of 12 C.F.R. § 7.4002 and therefore that the Banks were authorized to collect these fees. . . . Attendant to this authority to charge fees is the authority and discretion to determine the amount and method of charging those fees. *See* 12 C.F.R. § 7.4002(b)(2) ("The establishment of non-interest charges and fees, their amounts, and the method of calculating them are business decisions to be made by each bank, in its discretion, according to sound banking judgment and safe and sound banking principles."). By preventing the banks from exacting a fee for processing the garnishment orders through freezing the accounts, the Ohio garnishment laws "significantly interfere" with this fundamental national bank function by *de facto* mandating a $1 fee and the method by which that fee is extracted.

Moreover, the OCC stated that a "bank's authorization to establish fees pursuant to § 7.4002(a) includes the authorization to determine the order in which the fees are posted to a depositor's account." . . . As explained by the OCC, "[t]he garnishment fee and the Bank's process of debiting it first are intended to reduce the Bank's costs and compensate the Bank for other potential risks in connection with the legal requirement to process garnishments served on the Bank." . . . Accordingly, if the Banks are authorized to charge the service fee and similarly authorized to post the service fee in whatever order they determine, the OCC argued that the Banks are consequently authorized to collect the service fee even if this process has the effect of reducing the funds that the Garnishors receive. . . .

We find this argument persuasive. The requirement that banks freeze accounts immediately upon receipt of a garnishment order is unduly burdensome on national banks because it mandates the order in which those banks carry out their daily account-balancing and account-management functions. The OCC has consistently interpreted § 7.4002(a) as including the authorization to determine the order in which banks may post fees to an account. . . . Likewise, we note that this proposition is consistent with Ohio law, which grants state banks the power to decide that "items may be accepted, paid, certified, or charged to the indicated account of its customer in any order." Ohio Rev.Code, § 1304.29(B).

We find the OCC's interpretation sensible as it permits the Banks to complete the daily account-balancing tasks that all banks must undertake, both as a general operational matter and specifically in the context of responding to a garnishment notice served on debtors' accounts. The Garnishors cite the Ohio garnishment statute, which states that garnishees are liable "at the time of service of the order" of garnishment. ORC § 2716.21(D). Relying on this statutory language, the Garnishors claim that Ohio law requires the Banks to freeze the funds in the debtors' accounts at the time of service of the garnishment order and thus that Ohio law prohibits them from further deducting service fees after receiving the garnishment order. We agree with the Banks that the Garnishors' contention that the Banks must immediately "freeze" the garnished accounts is overly simplistic as the Banks must first undertake a number of procedures to assess what funds are available to be garnished.

Thus the Garnishors' interpretation would allow ORC § 2716.13(B) and § 2716.21(D) to "significantly interfere" not only with the Banks' ability to collect and set their service fees, but also with the Banks' federal authority to complete other transactions and balance their accounts. *See Duryee,* 270 F.3d at 409. We therefore find that any interpretation of the Ohio garnishment statute that would allow the Garnishors' claim to proceed is preempted by the NBA's grant of authority to the Banks to collect fees without interference. The Garnishors have thus failed to state a claim upon which relief can be granted. *See* Fed.R.Civ.P. 12(b)(6), (c). . . .

COLE, Circuit Judge, dissenting.

. . . The garnishment law at issue is a law of general applicability that only incidentally affects national banks, with negligible effect on their ability to perform their business. Both Supreme Court precedent and the plain language of the OCC regulation's savings clause strongly suggest that preemption is inappropriate here.

A. Supreme Court precedent clearly weighs against preemption

The majority opinion rests on several cases that it claims support a finding of preemption, but it does not discuss the substance of those cases, nor does it address the two Supreme Court decisions on which Monroe Retail principally relies. The cases cited by the majority do not weigh in favor of preemption here because those cases involved much more significant intrusions into the business of national banks – intrusions that bear little resemblance to the Ohio statute before us. On the other hand, the cases cited by Monroe Retail dealt with state statutes similar to Ohio's garnishment law, and both held those statutes not to be preempted by national banking laws.

The majority relies on *Watters v. Wachovia Bank, N.A.,* 550 U.S. 1, 21 (2007), in which the Court held that state regulators could not exercise corporate visitorial powers, such as the right to inspect books and records, over national banks' operating subsidiaries. The state conceded that the NBA preempts state visitorial powers over the national banks themselves, but

claimed that the same was not true of bank subsidiaries (specifically at issue were subsidiaries in the mortgage-lending business). *Id.* at 15. The Court disagreed and held that the NBA preempted the state from exercising its visitorial powers over the subsidiaries: "[S]tate regulators cannot interfere with the 'business of banking' by subjecting national banks or their OCC-licensed operating subsidiaries to multiple audits and surveillance under rival oversight regimes." *Id.* at 21. Thus, the intrusion into the business of banking at issue in *Watters* – "multiple audits [by state regulators] and surveillance under rival oversight regimes" – was far more significant than Ohio's garnishment law.
. . .

[T]he cases cited by the majority offer limited guidance because they entail far more significant intrusions into the business of national banks than the statute before us. The majority does not mention two cases raised by Monroe Retail in which the Supreme Court declined to find preemption with respect to state statutes similar to the one at issue here. Those decisions held that such statutes are not preempted because they do *not* significantly impair national banks' functions.

In *Anderson National Bank v. Luckett,* 321 U.S. 233, 236 (1944), the Supreme Court found that a state law directing banks, both state and national, to "turn over to the state, deposits which have remained inactive and unclaimed for a specified period" was not preempted by national banking laws. The Court stated: "This Court has often pointed out that national banks are subject to state laws, unless those laws infringe the national banking laws or impose an undue burden on the performance of the banks' functions." *Id.* at 248. With respect to the requirement that banks, including national banks, turn over abandoned funds, the Court stated: "It has never been suggested that non-discriminatory laws of this type are *so burdensome* as to be inapplicable to the accounts of depositors in national banks." *Id.* (emphasis added). We are not at liberty to ignore the holding of this binding authority. I doubt the majority would contend that if the state law at issue in *Luckett* had also specified that banks were required to turn over *all* of the abandoned property, without first deducting an "abandoned-property-turnover fee," like the one at issue in the present case, the *Luckett* Court would have changed course and deemed the state law to be preempted. *Luckett* was cited by the Supreme Court several months ago, and there is no indication that it is no longer good law. *See Cuomo v. Clearing House Ass'n, L.L. C.,* 129 S.Ct. 2710, 272122 (2009). In light of *Luckett,* I fail to see how we can fairly hold that Ohio's garnishment law is preempted.

The Supreme Court engaged in similar analysis and reached the same result in *McClellan v. Chipman,* 164 U.S. 347, 358 (1896). In that case, a national bank argued that a federal statute that allowed national banks to accept real property in satisfaction of a debt preempted a state statute that forbade preferential transfers of property to creditors on the eve of insolvency. The Court rejected this argument, stating:

> [There is nothing] in the statutes of the State of Massachusetts, here considered, which in any way impairs the efficiency of national banks or frustrates the purpose for which they were created. No function of such banks is destroyed or hampered by allowing the banks to exercise the power to take real estate, provided only they do so under the same conditions and restrictions to which all the other citizens of the State are subjected, one of which limitations arises from the provisions of the state law which in case of insolvency seeks to forbid preferences between creditors.

Id. This case, too, presents a much more analogous state law to the one under our consideration than any of the cases upon which the majority relies, further demonstrating that preemption should not apply here.

The above cases stand for the following proposition: a non-discriminating state law of general applicability that has an incidental effect on national banks but does not "frustrate[ ] the purpose for which they were created," *McClellan,* 164 U.S. at 358, "impose an undue burden on the performance of [their] functions," *Luckett,* 321 U.S. at 248, or "prevent or significantly interfere with the [ ] exercise of [their] powers," *Barnett,* 517 U.S. at 33, is not preempted by federal banking laws. . . .

3. Impact on the Subprime Mortgage Market

The federal regulators' aggressive preemption initiative against state regulation of financial services may have blunted any "early warning response" that state regulation might have provided.[17] *Watters* threw uncertainty on the viability of state consumer protection legislation as applied to mortgage banking activities, but *Cuomo* appears to have readjusted the federal-state balance.

In the meantime, some state courts have offered opportunities directly to mortgagors to combat questionable mortgage lending and servicing practices. The following case illustrates how state consumer protection regulation – here vindicated in private litigation – would apply to subprime mortgage programs.

---

17. On the effect of federal preemption policies on state financial services regulation, see Mark E. Budnitz, *The Federalization and Privatization of Public Consumer Protection Law in the United States: Their Effect on Litigation and Enforcement,* 24 GA. ST. U. L. REV. 663 (2008).

LaSalle Bank, N.A. v. Shearon

---

19 Misc.3d 433, 850 N.Y.S.2d 871 (N.Y.Sup. 2008)

Joseph J. Maltese, J.

This court has denied the plaintiff bank's summary judgment motion in a mortgage foreclosure action because it has found that the original lender has violated the "predatory lending" statutes found in New York Banking Law § 6L. As a result of the findings of violations of the predatory lending sections of the New York Banking Law this court grants the defendant home owner summary judgment wherein he may be entitled to damages to include the voiding of the mortgage and loan, along with the return of all mortgage payments, the expenses of obtaining the loans and attorney fees.

Facts

In the summer of 2005, after living in a rental home for three years, the Shearons, as first time home buyers, decided to purchase a house in Staten Island, New York. After searching for the "right" home, they executed a contract of sale for real property located at 33 Westport Lane in Staten Island, New York.

To locate this home, the Shearons utilized the services of a real estate agent from Coldwell Banker. After finding their home, they utilized the services of Glen DeLuca and Michael Farber, mortgage brokers associated with Liberty Capital Mortgage [doing business as (d/b/a) HCI Mortgage Company located in Lake Ariel, Pennsylvania], to provide them with all necessary financial information and potential lenders in order to obtain financing for the purchase. In August and September 2005, Michael Farber advised the Shearons that they would qualify for traditional loan products with fixed interest rates and that he was "shopping around for the best rates." At the time the Shearons were applying for financing, as husband and wife, in connection with purchasing their home, David Shearon's credit score was 696 and Karen Shearon's credit score was 760 on a scale where 800 is the maximum score.

The Shearons presented a joint tax return which shows a combined adjusted gross income of $29,567. On October 17, 2005 the Shearons entered into a contract of sale to purchase the house for $335,000. However, the Contract listed a purchase price of $355,100 with a "Seller's Concession" of $20,100. At the execution of the contract, the Shearons deposited $5,000 with the seller's attorneys, which would leave a balance of $350,100. But the financing was for the full $355,000, implying that it would be a "no money down" purchase at closing where arguably that amount should have reflected a deduction of the $5,000 deposit that the Shearons paid at the contract signing.

From the time of the contract until closing in January 2006, Michael Farber advised the Shearons that WMC Mortgage Corp. would be able to finance the entire $355,100 of the purchase price in two loans. The plaintiff, LaSalle Bank, N.A., (hereinafter "lender") was the trustee and successor for WMC. The first mortgage was for $284,000 and the second mortgage was for $71,000. . . . However, David Shearon was listed as the sole purchaser and sole borrower on all closing documents.

Shearon, in his answer alleges that he has been the victim of "*Predatory Lending*" practices by the mortgage brokers and the lender regarding the finance of his home. . . .

New York Banking Law

Predatory lending practices are prohibited by both New York State and Federal laws. Here, the "home loans"[3] in question are governed by New York Banking Law § 6-L(1)(d) which governs "High Cost Home Loans" which are classified as such by the scheme provided for in Banking Law § 6-L(1)(g). New York Banking Law § 6-L(2) prohibits certain practices by lending institutions when offering High Cost Loans. The statute also provides for a six year statute of limitations accruing from the origination of the loan, as well as remedies for violations of the statute. A court may also award reasonable attorneys fees to the prevailing borrower. And the Court may grant the borrower injunctive, declaratory, and such other equitable relief to enforce compliance with this section.

However, the most drastic remedies provided are found in Banking Law §§ 10 and 11 of the statute. Banking Law § 6-L(10) states:

> "Upon a finding by the court of an intentional violation by the lender of this section, or regulation thereunder, the home loan agreement shall be rendered void, and the lender shall have no right to collect, receive or retain any principal, interest, or other charges whatsoever with respect to the loan, and the borrower may recover any payments made under the agreement."

New York Banking Law 6-L(11) states: "Upon a judicial finding that a high-cost home loan violates any provision of this section, whether such violation is raised as an affirmative claim or as a defense, the loan transaction may be rescinded. Such remedy of rescission shall be available as a defense without time limitation."

---

3. "Home Loans" are defined in N.Y. Banking Law § 6-L(1)(e).

Discussion

... Shearon alleges that he was given excessive financing on a High Cost Loan without the lenders inquiry as to his ability to pay, which is mandated by N.Y. Banking Law § 6-L(2)(k). The lender alleges that loans of 7.65% and 10.5% are less than the 16% usury statute and hence are not "high cost" loans. But the home loans were considered high cost loans by the lender because the lender prepared the following forms dated December 8, 2005: a New York High Cost Loan Disclosure; New York High Cost Loan Payment Disclosure; and New York High Cost Loan Insurance.

It is undisputed that Shearon was given $355,000 to finance the purchase of a $335,000 house, where the extra $20,000 or 6% of the purchase price was used to pay points and fees associated with the closing on the property. Specifically, when examining the HUD-1 closing statement prepared at the time of closing, it is apparent that $19,145.69 was used to pay all costs and fees associated with securing the High Cost Loans. These monies were paid from financing received above and beyond the contract price of $335,000. This ultimately left Shearon with negative equity in the property.

The financing of the fees and points associated with the loan is also a violation of Banking Law 6-L(2)(m) which states:

> "In making a high-cost home loan, a lender shall not, directly or indirectly, finance any points and fees as defined in paragraph (f) of subdivision one of this section, in an amount that *exceeds three percent* of the principal amount of the loan" (emphasis added).

Here, the amount financed to cover the fees are in violation of the statute because the points and fees exceed 3% of the principal amount of the loan. Three percent of the loan equates to $10,650. However, the expenses of the loan were $19,145.69, which equates to about 5.4% ($19,145.69 / $355,000 = .0539) which is more than the 3% allowed by the statute. What is more egregious is that $19,145.69 in expenses is 5.72% of the original cost of the $335,000 house ($19,145.69 / $335,000 = .0572).

Shearon also alleges that the Lender did not conduct a "due diligence" or any inquiry into their ability to repay the High Cost Loan. The plaintiff argues in its motion for summary judgment that David Shearon stated that he reported $7,200 as monthly income when he first applied for the loan. The plaintiff then states in paragraph 25 of their attorney's affirmation that Mr. Shearon "cannot argue that his annual income of $86,400 places him in a category of low-income."

If David Shearon and his wife stated on the original loan application that their monthly income was $7,200, the lender's statutory requirement is to make an inquiry as to the truth of the statement and the borrower's ability to repay the loan. While this court will not condone fraud by the borrower, New

York Banking Law § 6-L(2)(k) states that:

"A lender or mortgage broker shall not make or arrange a high-cost home loan without due regard to repayment ability, based upon consideration of the resident borrower or borrowers' current and expected income, current obligations, employment status, and other financial resources (other than the borrower's equity in the dwelling which secures repayment of the loan), *as verified by detailed documentation of all sources of income and corroborated by independent verification.*" (*emphasis added*).

Here, plaintiff's counsel states in both the moving papers and reply papers that "Based on Defendant's income, credit history, and the low interest rate on the Mortgage loan, along with the Defendant's lack of evidence supporting predatory lending, the Defendant is precluded from alleging the same. As such, the Defendant's mortgage loan was in compliance with all applicable laws, including, but not limited to, all anti-predatory lending laws ."

While statements contained in an attorney's affirmation are not proper evidence before the court, the plaintiffs do not offer one scintilla of evidence as to their required "due diligence" inquiry regarding David Shearon's ability to pay, which is a violation of New York's Banking Law governing High Cost Loans.

Shearon also alleges that he and his wife were intentionally placed into a sub-prime loan product. He bases the argument upon two facts. First, David Shearon and his wife originally applied jointly for the loans where he had a credit score of 696 and his wife had a score of 760 on a scale of 800. The Shearons jointly were considered "A paper," a term given to those loan applicants that are deemed to have the highest level of credit-worthiness.[9] Shortly before the closing, Karen Shearon was removed as a borrower for the loans. The Lender claimed that since no loan terms were modified, the application was not subject to any new underwriting or analysis and the closing occurred without any apparent change to the entire financing process. However, removing the higher rated borrower from the loan would require a new underwriting inquiry, but none was conducted. Therefore, the Shearons argue that they were intentionally placed into a sub-prime loan product.

The second factor that the Lender used to place the Shearons into a sub-prime product was an adjustable rate mortgage. Throughout the process, Michael Faber from Liberty Capital stated that the Shearons would be placed into a traditional loan product with fixed interest rates. However, when Shearon closed title, he obtained the First Loan with a 7.59% rate for the first 2 years, which would thereafter re-adjust and rise to no more than 10.59% in February 2008. However, every six (6) months thereafter it was subject to increase with a ceiling of 14.09% with anticipated finance charges over the life

---

9. *See EMC Mortg. Corp. v. Batista* 15 Misc.3d 1143(A) [Sup.Ct. Kings County].

of the loan of $682,821.49. The Second Loan had a fixed rate of 10.750% for the life of the loan with anticipated finance charges over the life of the loan of $121,861.87. Therefore, Shearon would be obligated to pay up to $804,683.36 for a house that sold for $335,000. At the time of closing, these loans were considered sub-prime products, even though they had qualified for traditional fixed loan products at lower rates, because of their "A paper" credit worthiness.

Shearon also alleges a violation of Banking Law § 6-L(2)(l)(I), which has been dubbed the "*Counseling Statute.*" This section provides that a lender or mortgage broker must deliver, place in the mail, fax or electronically transmit the following notice in at least twelve point type[a] to the borrower at the time of application: "You should consider financial counseling prior to executing loan documents. The enclosed list of counselors is provided by the New York State Banking Department." Banking Law § 6-L(2)(l)(ii) requires that the lender or mortgage broker within three days after determining that the loan is a high-cost loan, but no less that ten days before closing, give the "Consumer Caution and Home Ownership Counseling Notice" to the borrower. This was not done. . . .

. . . [T]he plaintiff fails to provide any evidence of the required disclosure in any of their papers. Their attorney simply states that their loans were sold in compliance with the various regulating statutes including *RESPA, TILA, HOEPA, New York State Banking Law and Federal Statutory Law* prohibiting predatory lending. . . .

[The court granted summary judgment in favor of Shearon on his counter claims for violations of N.Y. Banking Law §§ 6-L(2)(k); 6-L(2)(l)(I); and 6-L(2)(m). The finding of these violations triggered the remedy and damages provisions of N.Y. Banking Law § 6-L(7) through § 6-L(10).]

In this case, the defendant David Shearon demonstrated by a preponderance of the evidence that the Lender violated the anti-predatory lending statutes of New York's Banking Law. Therefore, David Shearon may be entitled to receive: actual, consequential and incidental damages, as well as all of the interest, earned or unearned, points, fees, the closing costs charged for the loan; and a refund of any amounts paid.

This court will hold a hearing where all parties shall present any evidence as to actual damages and any other evidence not otherwise mentioned herein that may mitigate the findings of this court pertaining to the alleged intentional behavior of the Lender who violated several sections of the New York Banking Law § 6-L. The finding of intentional violation renders the home loan

---

a. This footnote is in 10-point type. By contrast, the text of this book is in 12-point type, as is this sentence.

agreement (mortgage) void, and strips the lender from having a right to collect, receive or retain any principal, interest, or other charges whatsoever with respect to the loan, as well as giving the borrower the ability to recover any payments made under the agreement.[19] The hearing shall also be used to determine the amount of damages.

Additionally, the defendant is entitled to receive reasonable attorneys fees in conjunction with the defense of this action.[20]

NOTES AND QUESTIONS

1. LaSalle Bank tried to argue that the Shearon home loan could not be a "high cost loan" because it did not violate the N.Y. usury prohibition. How did the court deal with that argument? What is the relationship, if any, between the predatory lending and usury prohibitions? Between predatory lending and the subprime mortgage market?

2. How would the court define "subprime loan"? If the Shearon home loan is a "high cost loan," does that alone make it a "subprime loan"?

3. What sort of "due diligence" inquiry is a lender supposed to make under the state law? Is it the lender's responsibility to determine whether or not the loan is appropriate for the borrower?

4. LaSalle Bank seems to be arguing that Shearon is estopped from arguing that he was a "low-income" borrower, and therefore he cannot trigger the "due diligence" provisions. Is that a relevant argument? How does the court respond to the argument?

5. *State Predatory Lending Statutes.* Many states have enacted laws to restrict the terms or provisions of predatory mortgage loans. According to the Congressional Research Service, as of November 2008 at least 30 states and the District of Columbia had enacted some version of a predatory lending law.[21] Many of these are similar to HOEPA, restricting the terms and characteristics of certain "high-cost" mortgages exceeding a specified interest rate or fee threshold. As with HOEPA, a state predatory loan statute will often restrict loan features that can be abusive – prepayment penalties, balloon payments, negative amortization, and "loan flipping." Some of these laws are more comprehensive than HOEPA.

6. State consumer protection statutes often provide very significant prohibitions and protections that would be applicable to the typical subprime

---

19. NY Banking Law § 6-L(10).
20. NY Banking Law § 6-L(8).
21. Congressional Research Service, *A Predatory Lending Primer: The Homeownership and Equity Protection Act (HOEPA)*, RL34259 (Washington, D.C.: Nov. 2008).

loan situation – prohibitions on excessive financing, lender due diligence requirements, prohibitions on "intentional and improper placement," disclosure requirements, and prohibitions on "coercive and concerted tactics." In addition to actual damages, they also provide other rather significant remedies for victimized borrowers – statutory damages, forfeiture or cancellation provisions, and other equitable relief. What consumer protection prohibitions, requirements, and remedies are at issue in *LaSalle Bank*, and which of them seems most effective in controlling predatory subprime loan practices?

7. Preemption was not an issue in the *LaSalle Bank* decision. The following case presents a situation very similar to *LaSalle Bank*, but one in which preemption is put in play by the mortgage holder. How would the *LaSalle Bank* court have reacted to a preemption argument?

THOMAS V. US BANK NATIONAL ASSOCIATION ND

575 F.3d 794 (8th Cir. 2009)

BYE, Circuit Judge.

[Mortgagors who had obtained second mortgages from a federally insured, state-chartered bank brought an action in state court against lenders that had assumed the mortgages, alleging violations of the Missouri Second Mortgage Loans Act (MSMLA), Mo.Rev.Stat. §§ 408.231-.241. Following removal on the grounds that the state law claims were completely preempted by the Depository Institutions Deregulation and Monetary Control Act (DIDA), 12 U.S.C. § 1831d, the U.S. district court denied the mortgagors' motion to remand to state court and dismissed their claims. On appeal, the Eighth Circuit reversed with instructions to remand to state court, holding that (*i*) DIDA did not completely preempt the mortgagors' claims; and, (*ii*) claims against national banks were not preempted by the National Bank Act (NBA).]

I

Thomas and the other appellants are Missouri homeowners who obtained "high loan-to-value" second mortgages (reflecting a total debt of 125% of the appraised value) on their homes from FirstPlus Bank. FirstPlus Bank was a federally insured, state-chartered bank when the loans were made. FirstPlus Bank became defunct, and the loans were purchased or assumed by other banks as assignees, including some national banks.

In June 2004, Thomas brought suit in Missouri state court on behalf of himself and others similarly situated against thirty-three assignee banks of FirstPlus alleging the loans they had received violated the MSMLA, which places limits on the type and amount of closing costs and fees a lender can charge on residential second mortgage loans secured by Missouri real estate.[1]

Specifically, Thomas alleged the subject loans violated Missouri law because: 1) the borrowers were charged nonrefundable finder's fees or broker's fees which were not allowed by or in excess of the fees allowed by the MSMLA; and 2) FirstPlus charged certain closing costs and fees on behalf of third parties which were in excess of the costs actually charged by those third parties and then retained the difference. Thomas sought to recover the interest paid on the allegedly unlawful second mortgage loans and an order barring the collection of additional interest. Notably, none of the subject loans violated Missouri law with respect to the maximum interest rate chargeable on a second mortgage loan, which exceeded the rate allowed by federal law pursuant to DIDA.

In August 2004, the defendant banks removed the case to federal district court. The banks alleged removal was proper because FirstPlus, the originator of the loans, was a federally-insured, state-chartered bank and DIDA (which applies to federally-insured, state-chartered banks) completely preempted the state law claims brought under the MSMLA. The banks relied primarily upon the Supreme Court's decision in *Beneficial National Bank v. Anderson,* 539 U.S. 1 (2003), which held that the National Bank Act (NBA), 12 U.S.C. §§ 85-86, completely preempted state law usury claims against national banks. *Id.* at 10-11.The banks alleged the similarity in language between DIDA and the NBA compelled the conclusion that DIDA, like the NBA, created the exclusive federal remedy for usury claims against federally-insured, state-chartered banks.

Thomas . . . argued the language of DIDA differed in material respects from the language in the NBA, and DIDA only preempted state usury laws in limited circumstances, that is, when the state laws set a lower allowable interest rate than that allowed by federal law. Because Missouri law allowed a higher allowable interest rate than the rate set forth in DIDA, preemption was not triggered. . . .

II

A

The general rule is when a claim filed in state court alleges only state law

---

1. Missouri law allows lenders to charge a higher interest rate for second mortgage loans than the general usury rate applicable to most loans. *Compare* Mo.Rev.Stat. § 408.030.1 (generally allowing a rate of 10% or the market rate, whichever is higher) *with* Mo. Rev. Stat. § 408.232.1 (prior to 1998, setting a maximum rate of 20.04% on second mortgage loans, and setting *no* limit on second mortgage interest rates after 1998). The limits on closing costs and fees provided for in the MSMLA act as a trade-off for allowing lenders to charge a higher interest rate on second mortgage loans.

claims, the existence of a federal defense, e.g., preemption, is not enough to support the removal of the case to federal court. *Rivet v. Regions Bank of La.,* 522 U.S. 470, 475 (1998). An exception to this rule is when the preemptive force of a federal statute completely displaces state law and it is clear Congress meant the federal statute to be the exclusive cause of action for the type of claim asserted. *Beneficial Nat'l Bank,* 539 U.S. at 8. Complete preemption, as opposed to ordinary or conflict preemption, is rare, however, and only applies if the "federal statutes at issue provide[ ] the exclusive cause of action for the claim asserted and also set forth procedures and remedies governing that cause of action."*Id.*

Complete preemption does not exist here because the language of DIDA, unlike the NBA, does not reflect Congress' intent to provide the exclusive cause of action for a usury claim against a federally-insured state-chartered bank. To the contrary, a close examination of the statutory language indicates Congress very clearly intended the preemptive scope of DIDA to be limited to particular circumstances.

Two provisions of DIDA are at issue – the subsection discussing the circumstances under which a federally-insured state-chartered bank may charge the interest rate allowed by federal law notwithstanding state law to the contrary, 12 U.S.C. § 1831d(a) (the substantive provision), and the subsection setting forth a consumer's remedy when a bank charges interest in excess of that allowed by DIDA, 12 U.S.C. § 1831d(b) (the remedy provision). The substantive provision is set forth as follows:

> In order to prevent discrimination against State-chartered insured depository institutions, including insured savings banks, or insured branches of foreign banks with respect to interest rates, if the applicable rate prescribed in this subsection exceeds the rate such State bank or insured branch of a foreign bank would be permitted to charge in the absence of this subsection, such State bank or such insured branch of a foreign bank may, notwithstanding any State constitution or statute which is hereby preempted for the purposes of this section, take, receive, reserve, and charge on any loan or discount made, or upon any note, bill of exchange, or other evidence of debt, interest at a rate of not more than 1 per centum in excess of the discount rate on ninety-day commercial paper in effect at the Federal Reserve bank in the Federal Reserve district where such State bank or such insured branch of a foreign bank is located or at the rate allowed by the laws of the State, territory, or district where the bank is located, whichever may be greater.

12 U.S.C. § 1831d(a).

The plain language of the statute clearly indicates the interest rate allowed by federal law only comes into play "*if* the applicable rate prescribed in this subsection exceeds the rate such State bank or insured branch of a foreign bank would be permitted to charge in the absence of this subsection." *Id.* (emphasis added). In other words, when the interest rate allowed by state law exceeds the interest rate set forth in DIDA, the federal statute does not apply. The limited nature of the preemptive effect the federal statute has on state law is emphasized by the qualifying phrase added to the statute's preemption language: "notwithstanding any State constitution or statute which is hereby preempted *for the purposes of this section.*"*Id.* (emphasis added). In other words, conflicting state constitutions or statutes are not preempted for every and all purposes, but only for purposes of "this section."

The remedy provision is set forth as follows:

> If the rate prescribed in subsection (a) of this section exceeds the rate such State bank or such insured branch of a foreign bank would be permitted to charge in the absence of this section, and such State fixed rate is thereby preempted by the rate described in subsection (a) of this section, the taking, receiving, reserving, or charging a greater rate of interest than is allowed by subsection (a) of this section, when knowingly done, shall be deemed a forfeiture of the entire interest which the note, bill, or other evidence of debt carries with it, or which has been agreed to be paid thereon. If such greater rate of interest has been paid, the person who paid it may recover in a civil action commenced in a court of appropriate jurisdiction not later than two years after the date of such payment, an amount equal to twice the amount of the interest paid from such State bank or such insured branch of a foreign bank taking, receiving, reserving, or charging such interest.

12 U.S.C. § 1831d(b).

This remedy provision, as does the substantive provision, clearly indicates the limited nature of the federal statute's preemption of state law, by stating the federal remedy only applies "*[i]f* the rate prescribed in subsection (a) of this section exceeds the rate such State bank or such insured branch of a foreign bank would be permitted to charge in the absence of this section."*Id.* The limited scope of preemption is emphasized by the subsection's phrase stating "and such State fixed rate is thereby preempted by the rate described in subsection (a) of this section" which follows the conditional circumstances under which the statute applies, i.e., *if* the federal rate exceeds the rate allowed by state law. In other words, the plain language of the statute ties the preemptive effect it has on state law to the condition being met. By stating "and such state fixed rate is thereby preempted," the statute plainly indicates the state rate is only preempted "if" exceeded by the rate prescribed in the federal statute.

A similar statute was interpreted by this court in *Firstsouth, F.A. v. Lawson Square, Inc. (In re Lawson Square, Inc.),* 816 F.2d 1236 (8th Cir.1987), involving section 1730g(a) of DIDA, which applies to federally insured savings and loan associations rather than federally insured, state-chartered banks. The language of the two statutes is, however, identical. The holding in *Lawson Square* makes clear that when the federal preemption language does not "fit," state law applies. *See id.* at 1239. . . .

In this case, the interest rate allowed by Missouri law for second mortgages was either as high as 20.4% or *unlimited* at all applicable times, well in excess of the rate allowed by DIDA. *See* Mo.Rev.Stat. § 408.232.1 (setting a maximum rate of 20.04% on second mortgage loans prior to 1998, and setting *no* limit on second mortgage interest rates after 1998). As a result, the federal statute does not apply. And, more significantly, for complete preemption purposes, the remedy set forth in the federal statute does not apply. Complete preemption only applies when it is clear Congress meant for the federal statute to "provide[ ] the *exclusive* cause of action." *Beneficial Nat'l Bank,* 539 U.S. at 8 (emphasis added). By its plain and unambiguous language, the remedy set forth in § 1831d(b) only applies in limited circumstances, and those circumstances are when the federal rate exceeds the rate allowed by state law. Because such a circumstance was not present in this case, just as it was not present in *Lawson Square,* the federal remedy does not apply and therefore is not the exclusive remedy. Accordingly the district court erred when it denied Thomas's motion to remand this case to state court.

We note other federal courts have interpreted the language in § 1831d differently. In *Discover Bank v. Vaden,* 489 F.3d 594 (4th Cir.2007), *rev'd on other grounds* — S.Ct. — (March 9, 2009) (2009 WL578636), the Fourth Circuit held DIDA, like the NBA, completely preempts state usury claims against federally-insured, state-chartered banks. *Id.* at 605.In so holding, the Fourth Circuit quoted the relevant provisions of § 1831d(a) in the following manner:

> In order to prevent discrimination against State-chartered insured depository institutions . . . with respect to interest rates . . . such State bank[s] . . . may, notwithstanding any State constitution or statute which is hereby preempted for the purposes of this section, take, receive, reserve, and charge on any loan or discount made, or upon any note, bill of exchange, or other evidence of debt, interest . . . at the rate allowed by the laws of the State . . . where the bank is located.

Id. at 604.

Comparing this redacted version of the statute with the full version of the statute does reveal the language eliminated by the Fourth Circuit's second set of ellipsis ["*if the applicable rate prescribed in this subsection exceeds the rate such State bank or insured branch of a foreign bank would be permitted to charge in the absence of this subsection,*" (emphasis added)] is critical to the substantive meaning of the statute. . . .

We will not alter the statutory language in such manner to support a conclusion as to DIDA completely preempting state law while providing the exclusive federal remedy for state usury claims against federally-insured, state-chartered banks. Rather, the unabridged language of the statute, which is both the starting and ending point of our analysis, . . . clearly establishes the limited effect DIDA has on such claims.

B

Alternatively, the national banks argue the claims against them are completely preempted under sections 85 and 86 of the NBA. We disagree. The national banks did not originate the loans at issue, but rather are assignee banks who subsequently purchased the loans. As assignees, they are subject to all the claims which could have been brought against the originator of the loan. *See* 15 U.S.C. § 1641(d) ("Any person who purchases or is otherwise assigned a [tainted[mortgage ... shall be subject to all claims and defenses with respect to that mortgage that the consumer could assert against the [original lender]."). To hold otherwise would allow an originating bank to cleanse an otherwise illegal loan merely by assigning it to a national bank. . . .

NOTES AND QUESTIONS

1. Is the way in which the *Thomas* court handles the preemption issues compatible with *Watters* and its progeny?

2. *Identifying a Viable Theory of Liability.* In retrospect, a home owner facing foreclosure when a subprime mortgage goes horribly wrong understandably feels victimized by the lender. But can this feeling be conceptualized into a viable theory of liability against the lender? Without specific factual support, claims of common law fraud are difficult to plead successfully. Contract-based claims of violation of good faith and fair dealing are often frustrated by the basic common law premise that parties negotiating at arm's length do not generally owe each other any affirmative duties. Statutory claims may therefore recommend themselves – if pertinent statutory provisions exist and support a claim on the particular facts of the case. The following case illustrates some of the difficulties that mortgagors may encounter in pursuing statutory theories of liability.

BIGGINS V. WELLS FARGO & COMPANY

— F.R.D. —, 2009 WL 2246199 (N.D.Cal. 2009)

JEFFREY S. WHITE, District Judge.

[Home mortgagors brought a class action against lenders, loan servicers, and other defendants, alleging they were sold exotic, high-cost adjustable rate mortgages (ARMs) without consideration of their ability to pay the hidden maximum interest rates of the loans, which far exceeded the low initial rates (sometimes referred to as a "teaser rate." The defendants moved to strike and to dismiss, and the district court granted the motions in part and denied them in part, holding that: (*i*) the fraud claims were not pled with particularity; (*ii*) the mortgagors failed to state a claim under California law for tortious breach of the implied covenant of good faith and fair dealing; (*iii*) the mortgagors failed to state a claim under the Home Ownership Equity Protection Act (HOEPA); and, (*iv*) the unfair competition claim under a California statute, specifically referring to loan modifications and the duties servicers owe loan pool participants, was preempted. The following excerpts deal with the court's disposition of the statutory claims.]

BACKGROUND

Plaintiffs are homeowners who, on behalf of themselves and a putative class, claim that they "discovered that [they] were sold an exotic high cost adjustable rate mortgage (ARM) by [a defendant] and/or its agent, subsidiary, parent, joint venturer or predecessor without consideration of [their] ability to pay the loan's hidden maximum interest rate, which far exceeded the initial teaser rate and made the loan unaffordable." . . . Plaintiffs allege that they "were not told that [they] would necessarily lose [their homes] when the teaser rate inevitably increased beyond [their] ability to pay barring some unforeseeable and unlikely windfall increase in income." . . .

Plaintiffs further allege that, during the Class Period (March 10, 2005 through the present), the Defendants "routinely and uniformly engaged in a pattern and practice of knowingly offering substantially inferior and unafford-able subprime IO and Option ARM (*i.e.* Negative Amortization Pick-A-Payment) mortgage products to elderly, minority and financially distressed consumers with the intent of artificially inflating their earnings and without regard to whether borrowers could repay the loans." . . . Plaintiffs also allege that Defendants "knowingly and affirmatively *misrepresented* the most important measurement of the affordability of a mortgage product: *the total amount of each monthly installment on the loan relative to the borrowers existing debt to income ratio*." ([E]mphasis in original.)

Plaintiffs contend that they have been damaged "by being evicted from their homes and in other ways (some of which are not readily apparent at this time), including, but not limited to, excessive fees, interest and other penalties and charges," and "by consenting to purchase loan [*sic*] that only defendants knew were ultimately affordable [*sic*] under plaintiffs' existing debt to income profile."[3]

---

3. In light of Plaintiffs' allegations, the Court presumes Plaintiffs intended to say Defendants knew the loans "were ultimately unaffordable."

ANALYSIS. . .

C. Individual Claims for Relief . . .

2. The Claim for Violations of the [HOEPA] Is
   Dismissed, With Leave to Amend, In Part.

HOEPA was enacted to supplement the Truth in Lending Act ("TILA"), and it requires specific disclosure obligations and substantive requirements on certain categories of high-cost mortgages. 15 U.S.C. §§ 1602(aa), 1639. Defendants move to dismiss this claim on the basis that Plaintiffs have not alleged facts to show that their loans are "covered loans," which are defined as:

> a consumer credit transaction that is secured by the consumer's principal dwelling, other than a residential mortgage transaction, a reverse mortgage transaction, or a transaction under an open end credit plan, if –
>   (A) the annual percentage rate at consummation of the transaction will exceed by more than 10 percentage points the yield on Treasury securities having comparable periods of maturity on the fifteenth day of the month immediately preceding the month in which the application for the extension of credit is received by the creditor; or
>   (B) the total points and fees payable by the consumer at or before closing will exceed the greater of –
>   (i) 8 percent of the total loan amount; or
>   (ii) $ 400.

15 U.S.C. § 1602(aa).

Plaintiffs allege that they "were required to pay excessive fees, expenses, and costs which exceeded more than 10% of the amount financed." . . . This allegation is not sufficient to establish that Plaintiffs' loans are covered under HOEPA. See *Marks* [*v. Chicoine*, 2007 WL 1056779 at *7 (N.D.Cal. April 6, 2007)]. Plaintiffs argue that they have stated a claim based on the allegation that Defendants failed to include the maximum monthly payment based on the maximum interest rate allowed. . . . However, because Plaintiffs have not alleged facts demonstrating that HOEPA applies to their loans, these allegations are insufficient to state a claim. Accordingly, the Joint Motion is granted in part on this basis. . . .

3. The Claims for Violations of Financial Code § 22302(b)
   and Civil Code § 1670.5 Are Dismissed, With Leave to
   Amend Within the Section 17200 Claim.

Civil Code § 1670.5 "applies to the provisions of a loan contract that is subject to" the California Finance Lenders Law. Cal. Fin.Code § 22302(a). Section 22302(b) further provides that "[a] loan found to be unconscionable pursuant to Section 1670.5 of the Civil Code shall be deemed to be in violation of this division and subject to the remedies specified in this division." Civil Code § 1670.5, in turn, provides that if a court finds, as a matter of law, that a contract, or any provision thereof, is unconscionable, it may "refuse to enforce the contract, or it may enforce the remainder of the contract without the unconscionable clause, or it may so limit the application of any unconscionable clause as to avoid any unconscionable result."

Plaintiffs allege that "the hidden terms specifying that the loans would reset multiple times are onerous to the point of being unconscionable," and allege that they rely on Financial Code § 22302(b) solely as a basis to support their allegation that Defendants' conduct is unlawful under [Cal. Bus. & Prof. Code] Section 17200[, defining unfair competition]. . . . Defendants argue that the former allegation is insufficient to state a claim because "nothing about a loan's adjustable rate being reset monthly" shocks the conscience. . . . However, a determination of whether specified provisions of the loan documents shock the conscience requires an examination of facts that are not amenable to resolution on a motion to dismiss. Nonetheless, the claim must be dismissed, because the allegation that "the hidden terms specifying that the loans would reset multiple times are onerous to the point of being unconscionable" is a bare legal conclusion unsupported by facts. *Twombly,* 550 U.S. at 555. Accordingly, the Joint Motion is granted in part on this basis.

Because the Court cannot say there are no facts that would support Plaintiffs' allegations that the loan provisions are unconscionable, Plaintiffs shall have leave to amend. However, if Plaintiffs choose to amend, they should not allege this claim as a stand-alone claim for relief and should include it only within their Section 17200 Claim.

4. The Claim for Violations of Civil Code § 2923.6 Is Dismissed, With Leave to Amend Within the Section 17200 Claim.

Civil Code § 2923.6 provides:

> (a) The Legislature finds and declares that any duty servicers may have to maximize net present value under their pooling and servicing agreement is owed to all parties in a loan pool, not to any particular parties, and that a servicer acts in the best interests of all parties if it agrees to or implements a loan modification or workout plan for which both of the following apply:
> (1) The loan is in payment default, or payment default is reasonably foreseeable.
> (2) Anticipated recovery under the loan modification or workout plan exceeds the anticipated recovery through foreclosure on a net present value basis.
> (b) It is the intent of the Legislature that the mortgagee, beneficiary, or authorized agent offer the borrower a loan modification or workout plan if such a modification is consistent with its contractual or other authority.

Defendants move to dismiss this claim on the basis that it does not provide a private right of action. Plaintiffs concede that they do not assert a separate claim for violations of this statute and assert it only as a basis on which to allege violations of Section 17200. . . . Defendants respond that Plaintiffs cannot premise their Section 17200 claim on violations of Section 2923.6, because the statute does not create such a duty between lenders or servicers and borrowers.

Defendants rely on *Pittman v. Barclays Capital Real Estate, Inc. .*, 2009 WL 1108889 (S.D.Cal. April 24, 2009) and *Farner v. Countrywide Home Loans,* 2009 WL 189025 (S.D.Cal. Jan.26, 2009) in support of their argument. *Pittman,* 2009 WL 1108889 at *3 (dismissing stand-alone claim and Section 17200 claim premised upon alleged violations of Section 2923.6); *Farner,* 2009 WL 189025 at *2; *see also Paek v. Plaza Home Mortg., Inc.,* 2009 WL 1668576 at *3 (C.D.Cal. June 15, 2009). None of those cases discuss the import of subsection (b) of Section 2923.6. In addition, it is not clear from the Legislative history whether subsection (b) applies only if a modification or workout plan was consistent with a lender's pooling and servicing agreement or whether it was intended to refer to other contractual relationships. *See* 2008 Cal. Legis. Serv. Ch. 69 (S.B.1137) (West). The Court, therefore, declines to follow the reasoning in *Pittman, Farner,* and *Paek.* As such, at this stage and on this record, the Court cannot say as a matter of law that Plaintiffs could not allege a Section 17200 claim premised on [alleged] violations of Civil Code § 2923.6(b). However, if Plaintiffs choose to amend, they should not allege this claim as a stand-alone claim for relief and should include it only within their Section 17200 Claim. The Joint Motion is denied in part on this basis.

5. The Section 17200 Claim Is Dismissed, With Leave to Amend.

Plaintiffs' Section 17200 claim relies upon the facts supporting their first through fifth and seventh claims for relief [the fraud claims]. The Court concluded that Plaintiffs have either failed to allege these claims with the requisite specificity or have failed to allege facts sufficient to state a claim. [T]o the extent Plaintiffs have relied on Civil Code § 2923.6 to support this claim, the Court shall dismiss it with leave to amend on terms consistent with the Court's rulings set forth above. The Joint Motion is granted in part and denied in part on this basis. . . .

The Individual Motions to Dismiss

Having resolved those issues that are common to all Defendants, the Court turns to the remaining separately filed motions to dismiss. . . .

B. Plaintiffs' Claims Against JPMorgan Chase Bank, N.A.
    Are Dismissed, Without Leave to Amend.

Plaintiffs Leblanc, Mendez and Nguyen assert claims against Chase on the basis that they obtained loans from Chase/Washington Mutual Bank ("WaMu") "and/or its agent, subsidary, parent, joint venturer or predecessor. . . ." . . . Plaintiffs also generally allege that "Chase is the parent company or is otherwise affiliated with WaMu in a manner that makes it the successor in interest to the ill-gotten gains from WaMu's wrongful conduct." . . . Chase moves to dismiss all claims on the basis that it did not acquire any of WaMu's liabilities with respect to borrower claims when it acquired certain of WaMu's assets and liabilities.

In support of this argument, Chase submits the Purchase and Assumption Agreement dated September 25, 2008. (Meinertzhagen Decl., Ex. A.) Section 2.5 of that agreement states:

> Notwithstanding anything to the contrary in this Agreement, any liability associated with borrower claims for payment of or liability to any borrower for monetary relief, or that provide for any other form of relief to any borrower, whether or not such liability is reduced to judgment, liquidated or unliquidated, fixed or contingent, matured or unmatured, disputed or undisputed, legal or equitable, judicial or extra-judicial, secured or unsecured, whether asserted affirmatively or defensively, related in any way to any loan or commitment to lend made by the Failed Bank [WaMu] prior to failure, or to any loan made by a third party in connection with a loan which is or was held by the Failed Bank, or otherwise arising in connection with the Failed Bank's lending or loan purchase activities are specifically *not assumed* by the Assuming Bank [Chase].

(Emphasis added.)

Chase argues that, based on the plain language of the Purchase and Assumption Agreement, any liabilities relating to these three Plaintiffs' loans were not assumed by Chase. Plaintiffs do not dispute that Chase did not originate their loans. Plaintiffs oppose Chase's motion on the basis that "if these contracts were induced by fraud, Chase has nothing upon which it can enforce a right to collect payment." . . . That argument does not, however, address the effect of Section 2.5 of Purchase and Assumption Agreement. Plaintiffs also rely on *Provident Bank v. Community Home Mortgage Corp.,* 498 F.Supp.2d 558 (E.D.N.Y.2007). However, the issue in that case was a dispute over which of two entities owned certain mortgage loans, when the entity that originated the mortgages made two copies of each mortgage and note and subsequently assigned the loan to both entities. The court resolved the issue of who owned the loans in question, in part by relying on principles relating to holders in due course. The facts in the *Provident Bank* case are inapplicable here. The claims asserted by Plaintiffs Leblanc, Mendez and Nguyen fall within Section 2.5 of the Purchase and Assumption Agreement and, thus, any liabilities associated with those were not assumed by Chase. All claims against Chase are dismissed on this basis. To the extent the Court has granted Plaintiffs leave to amend, Plaintiffs Leblanc, Nguyen and Mendez shall have leave to amend to assert their claims against the FDIC [as receiver of WaMu]. . . .

C. Plaintiffs' Claims Against Aurora Are Dismissed, With Leave to Amend.

Aurora also moves to dismiss Plaintiffs' claims on the basis that the claims are preempted and moves to dismiss the HOEPA claim on the basis that it is barred by the statute of limitations.

1. Preemption.

Aurora, as the subsidiary of a federal savings association, moves to dismiss Plaintiffs' first, second, third, fifth, sixth, seventh and eighth claims for relief on the basis that each of these claims are preempted by the Home Owners Loan Act of 1933 ("HOLA"). "Through HOLA, Congress gave the Office of Thrift Supervision ('OTS') broad authority to issue regulations governing thrifts. . . . As the principal regulator for federal savings associations, OTS promulgated a preemption regulation in 12 C.F.R. § 560.2." *Silvas v. E*Trade Mortgage Corp.,* 514 F.3d 1001, 1005 (9th Cir.2008). Section 560.2 reads, *inter alia:*

> OTS hereby occupies the entire field of lending regulation for federal savings associations. OTS intends to give federal savings associations maximum flexibility to exercise their lending powers in accordance with a uniform federal scheme of regulation. Accordingly, federal savings associations may extend credit as authorized under federal law, including this part, without regard to state laws purporting to regulate or otherwise affect their credit activities, except to the extent provided in paragraph (c) of this section. . . .

12 C.F.R. § 560.2(a).[15] Section 560.2(b) lists specific types of state laws that are preempted, including state laws that purport to impose requirements regarding:

> (3) Loan-to value ratios;
> (4) The terms of credit, including amortization of loans and the deferral and capitalization of interest and adjustments to the interest rate, balance, payments due, or term to maturity of the loan, including the circumstances under which a loan may be called due and payable on the passage of time or a specified event external to the loan;
> (5) Loan-related fees, including without limitation, initial charges, late charges, prepayment penalties, servicing fees, and overlimit fees; . . .
> (9) Disclosure and advertising, including laws requiring specific statements, information, or other content to be included in credit application forms, credit solicitations, billing statements, credit contracts, or other credit-related documents and laws requiring creditors to supply copies of credit reports to borrowers or applications; [and]
> (10) Processing, origination, servicing, sale or purchase of, or investment or participation in mortgages[.]

---

15. "Federal regulations have no less preemptive effect than federal statutes." *Fid. Fed. Sav. & Loan Ass'n v. de la Cuesta,* 458 U.S. 141, 153, (1982).

12 C.F.R. § 560.2(b). Section 560.2(c) sets forth certain types of state laws that are not preempted "to the extent that they only incidentally affect the lending operations of Federal savings associations or are otherwise consistent with the purposes of" Section 560.2(a), including contract, commercial law and tort law. *Id.* § 560.2(c).

In *Silvas,* the Ninth Circuit set forth the analysis to follow in order to determine whether a state law is preempted. First, a court should determine whether the law is the type of law listed in Section 560.2(b). If it is, the analysis ends, and the law is preempted. *See Silvas,* 514 F.3d at 1005 (quoting OTS Final Rule, 61 Fed.Reg. 50951, 50966-67 (Sept. 30, 1996)). If the law in question is not listed in Section 560.2(b), a court should determine whether the law affects lending. If the answer is yes, then, pursuant to Section 560.2(a), a presumption arises that the law is preempted. *Id.* "This presumption can be reversed if the law can clearly be shown to fit within the confines of paragraph (c)," which is to be interpreted narrowly and doubts should be resolved in favor of preemption. *Id.*

Although Plaintiffs' first, second, third, seventh and eighth claims for relief are premised upon state laws of general applicability, "that is [they do] not purport to directly regulate the conduct of mortgage lenders," those claims still "may be preempted by HOLA if, 'as applied,' [they are] a type of state law that falls within § 560.2." *Munoz v. Financial Freedom Senior Funding Corp.,* 573 F.Supp.2d 1275, 1280 (C.D.Cal.2008) (citing, *inter alia, Silvas,* 514 F.3d at 1006).

The remaining named Plaintiffs with links to Aurora are Remy Mendez and Karen Fomby. Aurora did not originate either of the loans associated with these Plaintiffs' property. . . . The Court has determined Plaintiff has not alleged facts sufficient to hold Aurora liable for origination based claims on an aiding and abetting theory. As currently drafted, the [complaint] is not sufficiently detailed to determine whether the first, second, third, fifth, seventh and eighth claims for relief would be preempted as to Aurora, and the Court denies in part the motion on this basis. However, the Court notes that many of Plaintiffs' allegations relating to the breach of implied covenant, fraud and Section 17200, and unjust enrichment claims are premised upon allegations that the Defendants did not adequately disclose certain information to them. . . . Courts within this District and other Districts within California have concluded that state law claims based on such allegations are preempted. *See, e.g., Spears v. Washington Mutual, Inc.,* 2009 WL 605835 at *5-*6 (N.D.Cal. March 9, 2009); *Andrade v. Wachovia Mortgage, FSB,* 2009 WL 1111182 at *2-*3 (S.D.Cal. Apr.21, 2009); *Cosio v. Simental,* 2009 WL 201827 at *5 (C.D.Cal. Jan.27, 2009); *Nava v. Virtualbank,* 2008 WL 2873406 at *5-6 (E.D.Cal. July 16, 2008).

In contrast, if the factual basis for Plaintiffs general allegations that

Defendants misrepresented material terms or benefits of the loans is, for example, that a Defendant represented to a Plaintiff that the interest rate on a loan would be 5%, when in fact the interest rate was actually 7%, such an allegation might "fall[ ] more on . . . the common law side of the ledger," and would not be preempted. *Ayala v. World Savings Bank, FSB,* 2009 WL 1364363 at * 5 (C.D.Cal. May 4, 2009) (concluding that slander of title claim was not preempted but that claims for quiet title and fraud were preempted). Plaintiffs should pay careful attention to these and other authorities as they amend any of these claims against Aurora.

The only claim for relief in the [complaint] that directly implicates servicer activities is Count VI, in which Plaintiffs allege that "Defendants have routinely refused to discuss good faith modifications of" their loans in violation of California Civil Code § 2923.6. That law specifically refers to loan modifications and references that duties servicers may owe to parties in a loan pool. To the extent this Plaintiffs' premise their Section 17200 claim against Aurora on a violation of this law, it directly implicates § 560(b)(10), which preempts state laws relating to "processing, origination, servicing, sale or purchase of, or investment or participation in mortgages." Accordingly, the Court concludes that this aspect of Plaintiffs' Section 17200 claim against Aurora is preempted. If they choose to amend, Plaintiffs shall not proceed against Aurora on this theory.

Accordingly, Aurora's motion is granted in part and denied in part. . . .

NOTES AND QUESTIONS

1. The HOEPA[22] amended the Truth in Lending Act (TILA),[23] and added new disclosure and consumer protection restrictions on certain home mortgage loans and credit sales with credit terms in excess of terms typically available from creditors. HOEPA was particularly aimed at "reverse red-lining," a practice where creditors impose unfair credit terms on customers who live in areas not serviced by "traditional lending institutions."[24] The Board of Governors of the Federal Reserve System was required to amend its TILA rules – Regulation Z, 12 C.F.R. pt. 226 – to implement HOEPA.[25] Is HOEPA

22. Pub. L. No. 103-325, §§ 151-158, 108 Stat. 2160, 2190-2198 (Sept. 23, 1994) (codified at 15 U.S.C. §§ 1601 note, 1602 note, 1602, 1604, 1610, 1639-1641, 1647-1648).

23. 15 U.S.C. §§1601 *et seq.*

24. *See* Conference Report on H.R. 3474, Cong. Rec. H. 6682 (Aug. 2, 1994) (discussing legislative objectives).

25. *See, e.g.,* 60 Fed. Reg. 15,463 (1995) (codified at 12 C.F.R. pt. 226) (implementing HOEPA); 65 Fed. Reg. 70,465 (2000) (codified at 12 C.F.R. pt. 226, Supp. I) (amending staff commentary); 66 Fed. Reg. 57,849 (2001) (making annual adjustment to dollar amount that

a useful and effective tool for addressing the problem of subprime mortgage lending? While the act itself focuses on home equity lines of credit and red-lining practices, it apparently left more complicated issues to regulatory policy making, which failed to address subprime mortgage practices. *See* 15 U.S.C. § 1639(l)(1), (2) (authorizing Fed to exempt or prohibit mortgage lending products and practices by rule or order).

2. Could common law concepts arising out of torts and contract theory be more responsive to the abuses of subprime mortgage lending? In dismissing the plaintiff's claim for breach of "implied covenants" of good faith and fair dealing, the *Biggins* court had this to say:

> Defendants move to dismiss this claim on the basis that a lender has no special duty to its borrower. It is unclear to the Court whether Plaintiffs intend to assert a claim for tortious breach of the implied covenant of good faith and fair dealing. If that was Plaintiffs' intent, the claim fails. "[A]s a general rule, a financial institution owes no duty of care to a borrower when the institution's involvement in the loan transaction does not exceed the scope of its conventional rule as a mere lender of money." *Nymark v. Heart Fed. Savings & Loan Ass'n,* 231 Cal.App.3d 1089, 1096, 283 Cal.Rptr. 53 (1991); *cf. Marks v. Ocwen Loan Servicing, LLC,* 2008 WL 344210 at *6 (N.D.Cal. Feb.6, 2008) (dismissing negligence based claims for failing to allege facts establishing that defendant owed plaintiff a duty). In this case, Plaintiffs do not allege facts demonstrating that any Defendants' involvement in the loan transaction exceeded the scope of its conventional role as a mere lender of money or that they otherwise owed a duty to Plaintiffs.
>
> If Plaintiffs premise this claim on a contract theory, it also fails. Plaintiffs' allegations suggest that any alleged breach occurred when they were negotiating their loans, *i.e.* before any particular Plaintiff entered into a contract with a particular Defendant. "[T]he implied covenant is a supplement to an existing contract, and thus it does not require parties to negotiate in good faith prior to any agreement." *McClain v. Octagon Plaza, LLC,* 159 Cal.App.4th 784, 789, 71 Cal.Rptr.3d 885 (2008) (citing *Racine & Laramie, Ltd. v. Dep't of Parks & Rec.,* 11 Cal.App.4th 1026, 1031-35, 14 Cal.Rptr.2d 335 (1992)). Because Plaintiffs' allegations pertain to conduct that occurred during the negotiation of the loans, they fail to state a claim. *McClain,* 159 Cal.App.4th at 789, 71 Cal.Rptr.3d 885; *see also Alicea,* 2009 WL 1766703 at *4 (dismissing breach of the implied covenant of good faith and fair dealing claim, with leave to amend, on the basis that allegations related to pre-contractual negotiations); *Marks v. Chicoine,* 2007 WL 1056779 at *4-*5 (N.D.Cal. April 6, 2007) (dismissing, with leave to amend, claims for breach of the implied covenant of good faith and fair dealing based on alleged oral contract).

Biggins, 2009 WL 2246199 at *7-*8.

3. State statutes may be more specific in targeting the predatory lending

---

triggers requirements for certain mortgages bearing fees above specified amount); 66 Fed. Reg. 65,604 (2001) (codified at 12 C.F.R. §§226.1(b), (d)(5), 226.32(a)(1)(i), (b)(1), (c)(3), (c)(5), (d)(8), 226.34, App. H; removing 226.32(e)).

practices that apparently typified subprime mortgage lending. Does *Biggins* suggest whether such statutes would be effective in protecting home buyers and owners from predatory lenders? The following case excerpt considers the application of one such state statute, specifically intended to protect the "homestead" – a principal family residence – from questionable practices.

KARNITZ V. WELLS FARGO BANK, N.A.

572 F.3d 572 (8th Cir. 2009)

HANSEN, Circuit Judge.

[The former owners of a foreclosed property, husband and wife, brought an action in state court seeking a declaration that the mortgage on the property was invalid under Minnesota law. The action was removed to federal court, where district court granted summary judgment in favor of the plaintiffs. On appeal, the Eighth Circuit reversed and remanded, holding that the plaintiffs were equitably estopped from claiming that the mortgage was void because it was signed only by the husband.]

I.

In 2001, the Karnitzes built their home on land they purchased in LaPorte, Minnesota. They financed construction of the house through a short-term construction loan from Centennial National Bank. Both Joel and Tanya signed the loan documents and a mortgage in favor of Centennial. Upon completion of the house, the Karnitzes sought to pay off the construction loan with a traditional 30-year mortgage loan, which Centennial arranged through Wells Fargo. Joel signed a note for $136,800 payable to Wells Fargo and executed a mortgage on the property in favor of Wells Fargo. The Karnitzes used the Wells Fargo loan proceeds to pay off the construction loan, thereby securing a release of the Centennial mortgage.

Tanya did not sign the Wells Fargo loan documents or the new mortgage because Wells Fargo never asked her to sign any of the documents. Tanya testified in her deposition that she knew Joel was seeking a loan and mortgage from Wells Fargo to pay off the Centennial construction loan; that she knew the loan would result in a mortgage in favor of Wells Fargo; that she approved of Joel obtaining the loan and granting the mortgage to Wells Fargo; and that she wanted to obtain the loan in exchange for the mortgage.

On April 17, 2005, the Karnitzes filed for bankruptcy protection under Chapter 7 of the United States Bankruptcy Code. They listed their house as secured by a first mortgage in favor of Wells Fargo and listed the Wells Fargo loan as a joint obligation. The Karnitzes received a discharge in bankruptcy on

August 8, 2005. Shortly thereafter, they fell behind on their mortgage payments to Wells Fargo. Wells Fargo initiated foreclosure proceedings and foreclosed on the house on January 17, 2007.

In the meantime, Joel learned that Minnesota law requires a mortgage on a married couple's homestead to be signed by both spouses under Minnesota Statute § 507.02. The Karnitzes took the position during the foreclosure proceedings that the mortgage in favor of Wells Fargo was invalid because Tanya had not signed it. They brought this action in Minnesota state court seeking a declaration to that effect, and Wells Fargo removed the case to federal court based on diversity jurisdiction. The district court concluded that the unambiguous language of § 507.02 required Tanya's signature on the mortgage, and without her signature, the mortgage was void *ab initio*. The district court rejected Wells Fargo's estoppel arguments and granted summary judgment in favor of the Karnitzes.

II. . . .

With exceptions not here relevant, § 507.02 of the Minnesota Statutes provides: "If the owner is married, no conveyance of the homestead . . . shall be valid without the signatures of both spouses." A conveyance under § 507.02 includes a mortgage. *See* Minn.Stat. § 507.01. A conveyance that fails to meet these statutory requirements is void and cannot be ratified. *See Dvorak v. Maring,* 285 N.W.2d 675, 677 (Minn.1979) (explaining that "there cannot be a ratification of a contract for the sale of a homestead that is void due to the lack of a spouse's signature" because of the interplay with Minn.Stat. § 519.06 concerning when a spouse can and cannot act as the other spouse's agent).

Despite the plain and unequivocal language of the statute, the Minnesota Supreme Court has "recognized that, even though great importance is attached to the homestead right, under certain circumstances a party may be estopped from denying a sale of the homestead even if the statutory requirements are not met." *Id.* The purpose behind the statute is to " 'ensur[e] a secure homestead for families,' " *Wells Fargo Home Mortg., Inc. v. Newton,* 646 N.W.2d 888, 895 (Minn. Ct. App. 2002) (quoting *Dvorak,* 285 N.W.2d at 677), and to protect against "the alienation of the homestead without the willing signature of both spouses," *Dvorak,* 285 N.W.2d at 678. In certain circumstances when the purpose of the statute is not at risk, the Minnesota courts have applied estoppel to prevent a party from challenging the validity of a conveyance of a homestead. In its most recent discussion of the equitable estoppel doctrine in this specific context, the Minnesota Supreme Court stated, in addressing whether a nonsigning spouse should be estopped from asserting the protections of § 507.02 to void a conveyance by her spouse, that estoppel applies where (1) the nonsigning spouse consents to and has prior knowledge of the transaction, (2) the nonsigning spouse retains the benefits of the transaction, and (3) the party seeking to invoke estoppel has sufficiently changed its position to invoke the equities of estoppel. *See Dvorak,* 285 N.W.2d at 677-78 (discussing *Seitz v. Sitze,* 215 Minn. 452, 10 N.W.2d 426 (1943); *Fuller v. Johnson,* 139 Minn. 110, 165 N.W. 874 (1917)). All three factors must be present, cf. *Anderson v. First Nat'l Bank of Pine City,* 303 Minn. 408, 228 N.W.2d 257, 260 (1975) (estoppel not appropriate where husband did not learn that wife forged his signature until after the transaction was complete (such that the first factor was not met), even though he did retain the benefits of the mortgage), and the third factor is critical, *Dvorak,* 285 N.W.2d at 678 ("[D]etrimental reliance by the party seeking relief is critical to a finding of estoppel."). . . .

Applying the equitable estoppel factors articulated in *Dvorak,* it is undisputed that Tanya knew of and intended to mortgage the homestead to Wells Fargo prior to its execution; she retained the benefit of that mortgage by using the proceeds to pay off the construction loan (which she had signed and was obligated to repay) and to obtain a release of the construction loan's accompanying mortgage; and Wells Fargo significantly changed its position in reliance on the validity of its mortgage by lending over $130,000 in exchange for a lien on the property. The Karnitzes do not dispute the existence of these facts. Further, they did not dispute the validity of the mortgage until four years after it was executed and they were facing foreclosure because they could not keep up with the obligations of the accompanying note. Under these facts, the Karnitzes should be estopped from now claiming that the mortgage is void in order to keep their home, on which they both intended to grant Wells Fargo a valid mortgage, without paying for it.[1] Strict compliance with the statute in these circumstances does not further the policy behind the statute; rather, it flaunts it by converting what the Legislature intended as a shield into a sword. *See Dvorak,* 285 N.W.2d at 677 n. 3 (" 'The doctrine [of equitable estoppel] is not invoked to render valid a contract which is void under . . . statutes for the benefit and protection of the homestead claimants, but it is invoked to prevent the successful perpetration of fraud by preventing wrongdoers from urging the provisions of such statutes to shield them in their tortious conduct.' ") (quoting *Engholm v. Ekrem,* 18 N.D. 185, 119 N.W. 35, 38 (1908)).

The district court in this case recognized that a party may be estopped from asserting the invalidity of the conveyance based on the lack of a spouse's signature, but rejected the estoppel defense based on a line of Minnesota cases

---

1. According to the parties, if the mortgage is invalid, the resulting unsecured note to Wells Fargo for the balance owed on the house would be discharged as part of a reopened bankruptcy estate.

holding that "an oral promise to give a mortgage on a couple's homestead by one spouse does not give rise to estoppel." . . . citing *Kingery v. Kingery,* 185 Minn. 467, 241 N.W. 583, 584-85 (1932); *Butler Bros. Co. v. Levin,* 166 Minn. 158, 207 N.W. 315, 316 (1926). The district court's reliance on this line of cases is misplaced. The point of the holding in *Butler Bros.* was that estoppel could not be based on a promise of future conduct[, *i.e.*, the wife's promise to make sure the husband's debt would be paid, and, if it was not, to sign the mortgage]. . . . The case at bar does not involve a promise at all, oral or otherwise. Further, there is no indication in *Butler Bros.* that the wife had prior knowledge or had otherwise acquiesced in the contested mortgage that lacked her signature. In fact, the court noted that estoppel may be held against a nonsigning spouse in the case of a homestead. . . . The district court here erred in focusing on the effect of a nonexistent oral promise without considering the factors described in *Dvorak.*

We recognize that the doctrine of equitable estoppel generally involves some type of misrepresentation or at least negligent culpability on the part of the person against whom it is claimed. *See, e.g., Birch Publ'ns, Inc. v. RMZ of St. Cloud, Inc.,* 683 N.W.2d 869, 873-74 (Minn.Ct.App. 2004) (describing equitable estoppel as arising "when 'one by his acts or representations, or by his silence when he ought to speak, intentionally or through culpable negligence, induces another to believe certain facts to exist, and such other rightfully acts on the belief so induced' " such that he is prejudiced (quoting *Transam. Ins. Group v. Paul,* 267 N.W.2d 180, 183 (Minn.1978))). Despite this general statement of the equitable estoppel doctrine, the Minnesota cases that apply estoppel in the specific context of the homestead signature requirement of § 507.02 have found such a "culpability" requirement satisfied by the nonsigning spouse's prior knowledge and agreement of the conveyance coupled with the retention of the benefits of the conveyance. For example, in Seitz, a son took care of his mother for several years in exchange for his father's promise that he would receive their homestead upon their deaths. When the father's other heirs challenged the conveyance to the son for failure to comply with the homestead signature requirement, the Minnesota Supreme Court used the doctrine of equitable estoppel to hold that § 507.02 "cannot now be invoked after full performance of the contract by [the son] and after acceptance of the benefits of such performance by his parents with full knowledge of the agreement." *Seitz,* 10 N.W.2d at 429. In *Bullock* [v. *Miley,* 133 Minn. 261, 158 N.W. 244, 245 (1916)], a husband was estopped from claiming title to the homestead he had sold where the original conveyance lacked his wife's signature. The Minnesota Supreme Court applied estoppel because "both plaintiff and his wife intended to convey the homestead . . . and believed that they had done so; [ ] no offer to return the consideration received for the homestead or any part thereof has ever been made; and [ ] plaintiff is seeking to recover the homestead without returning any part of such consideration." *Bullock,* 158 N.W. at 245. The Minnesota Supreme Court applied estoppel in these cases despite the absence of any type of misrepresentation or inducement.

The facts of *Bullock* are strikingly similar to the facts here. Both of the Karnitzes intended to convey a mortgage to Wells Fargo; they have made no offer to return the consideration received; and they now seek – several years later – to retain their homestead without paying for it. Fulfilling our duty to apply state law as we believe the highest court of the state would apply it, *see Leonard v. Dorsey & Whitney LLP,* 553 F.3d 609, 612 (8th Cir.2009), we are bound to follow the Minnesota Supreme Court cases most directly on point, particularly *Seitz, Bullock,* and *Dvorak.* Equitable estoppel is appropriate under the facts of this case, and the district court erred in concluding otherwise. . . .

BYE, Circuit Judge, dissenting.

Because the majority fails to explain how Wells Fargo relied to its detriment on Tanya Karnitz' misconduct or silence, I dissent.

The majority correctly notes that "detrimental reliance by the party seeking relief is critical to a finding of estoppel." *Dvorak v. Maring,* 285 N.W.2d 675, 678 (1979). . . . The majority fails, however, to explain how Wells Fargo relied to its detriment on anything said or done *by the Karnitzes.* Instead, the majority simply states that Wells Fargo relied "on the validity of its mortgage by lending over $130,000 in exchange for a lien on the property." . . . The problem with such an analysis is that Minnesota case law requires reliance on the conduct of the party seeking to disavow the transaction, not merely reliance on the validity of the transaction itself. *See Ridgewood Dev. Co. v. State,* 294 N.W.2d 288, 292 (1980) ("As a general rule, for equitable estoppel to lie, the plaintiff must demonstrate that the defendant, through his language or conduct, induced the plaintiff to rely, in good faith, *on this language or conduct* to his injury, detriment or prejudice.") (emphasis added). Here, Wells Fargo admits it had no contact with Tanya Karnitz prior to closing, and that nothing the Karnitzes did, said, or did not say caused Wells Fargo to lend the money or forego obtaining her signature on the necessary documents. Thus, Wells Fargo did not rely to its detriment on conduct by either of the Karnitzes in choosing to lend $135,000.

Tanya Karnitz did remain silent after the money was lent, which positioned Wells Fargo to operate for four years under the mistaken assumption its lien on the property was valid. While this conduct could form the basis for equitable estoppel, Wells Fargo did not rely to its detriment on Tanya Karnitz's continued silence. Thus, this case is materially different from the cases upon which the majority relies. In *Bullock v. Miley,* a case which the majority asserts is "strikingly similar" to the present case, the non-signing spouse allowed the purchaser to take possession of the property for several years without objection, and the purchaser relied to his detriment on the seller's silence *by making improvements to the property.* 133 Minn. 261, 263, 158 N.W. 244 (1916). Notably, the purchaser had "paid all the taxes thereon, and ha[d] placed improvements of the value of more than $1,000 upon the [property], and ha[d] also placed improvements of the value of more than $1,000 upon the remainder of the farm which he would not have placed thereon had he not believed that he was the owner of [the property]." *Id.* at 263-64, 158 N.W. 244. Moreover, the Minnesota Supreme Court was persuaded because the seller "knew that [the purchaser] was making improvements upon the homestead in the belief that he was the owner thereof, but made no claim thereto." *Id.* at 264, 158 N.W. 244. Thus, detrimental reliance on the spouse's alleged consent to the transaction was met not, as the majority contends, because the spouse knew of the transaction beforehand and accepted its benefits, but because the spouse "without objection permitted [the buyer] to occupy it for four years and expend large sums for improvements and taxes." *Id.*

Bullock demonstrates that the defense of equitable estoppel in cases involving Minnesota Statute § 507.02 requires more than the non-signing spouse's silence and apparent consent prior to the transaction; in addition, the buyer must continue to rely to his detriment on the non-singing spouse's post-transaction consent. This requirement was further elucidated in *Seitz v. Sitze,* 215 Minn. 452, 10 N.W.2d 426 (1943). In *Seitz,* a man entered into an agreement to care for his mother and father for the remainder of their lives and, in return, his parents agreed to transfer the property to him upon their deaths. *Id.* at 427. After they passed, other family members challenged the agreement because the son's mother was not a party to the contract. In applying equitable estoppel, the Minnesota Supreme Court focused on more than the mother's knowledge and apparent consent to the transaction. Critically, the court focused on the mother's post-contract silence *during which time the son continued to perform his part of the contract.* The son relied on his mother's after-the-fact silence and apparent consent to the contract by continuing to perform his obligations under the contract. *See id.* at 428 ("During all this time plaintiff purchased all food and clothing for his mother, paid all her medical expenses, paid all fuel bills, paid all taxes, and furnished repairs and improvements to the premises of the reasonable value of $804."). As in *Bullock,* the critical reason for applying equitable estoppel was not, as the majority asserts, that a non-singing spouse was aware of a transaction and would have consented to the transaction, but that the other party took some post-contract action in reliance upon the non-signing spouse's continued silence and consent.

This requirement is not met in the present case. Unlike the purchaser in *Bullock* – who relied on the non-signing spouse's post-contract silence and consent to possess the property for four years while making significant improvements – or the son in *Sietz* – who relied on his mother's post-contract silence and consent in continuing to perform his contractual obligations – Wells Fargo did not do anything after the transaction was completed which worsened its position, either in terms of money expended or legal rights forfeited. Wells Fargo tendered the full amount of the loan in 2002, and, though Tanya Karnitz remained silent for four years, Wells Fargo took no further action during such time frame. Thus, Wells Fargo is unable to identify any action it took to its detriment in the four years during which the Karnitzes did not object to the validity of the mortgage. Because Minnesota cases require a party seeking to invoke estoppel in this context to demonstrate detrimental reliance on a transferor's post-contract conduct, Wells Fargo's estoppel claim necessarily fails. The majority adulterates this principle by holding that equitable estoppel is met whenever a non-signing spouse *would have* consented to the transaction and a buyer, even one who never met the non-signing spouse, believed the transaction to be valid. Because Minnesota cases require more, I disagree with the majority's analysis.

While I am not unmindful of the inequities of allowing the Karnitzes to foreswear a security interest in their home they voluntarily gave to Wells Fargo, it is important to note that the fault in this case lies with Wells Fargo, not the Karnitzes. Wells Fargo failed to obtain Tanya Karnitz's signature because of its own negligence, not, most importantly, in reliance on anything said or done by the Karnitzes. While we can fault the Kartnitzes for accepting the benefit of the mortgage and remaining silent for four years, the die was solidly cast; Wells Fargo had already tendered an unsecured loan because of its own negligence, and the Karnitzes' actions or inactions for four years did not cause them to lend additional money or take any other action to its detriment. Therefore, I would affirm the district court and hold Wells Fargo's equitable estoppel claim fails. Because the court concludes otherwise, I respectfully dissent.

NOTES AND QUESTIONS

1. In *Karnitz*, the majority refused to apply the Minnesota statute, despite plain and unequivocal language that required the signatures of both spouses to make the mortgage valid and enforceable. As a matter of statutory interpretation this seems unusual, but what may make the decision even more unusual is the fact that "mortgage lenders normally face dismal chances in court when unsigned loan documents are involved." R. Christian Bruce, *Divided Appeals*

Court Upholds Mortgage Even Though Documents Lacked Signature, BNA BANKING DAILY (July 20, 2009), *available at* http://pubs.bna.com. Does the majority opinion explain the result convincingly?

2. Do you agree that "[s]trict compliance with the statute in these circumstances does not further the policy behind the statute; rather, it flaunts it by converting what the Legislature intended as a shield into a sword"? What is the policy behind the statute – a legislative preference for passive "shields"? Or does the homestead statute reflect a legislative decision to protect owners from the extreme dislocation that follows from foreclosure of a family home?

3. *Straining the System.* The dimensions of the Lehman collapse and the financial crisis related to it are so large, that they sometimes appear to distort available statutory remedies, like a black hole bending light. In March 2009, the New Jersey Department of Treasury, Division of Investment, filed suit in the Superior Court of New Jersey against former Lehman Brothers Chief Executive Officer Richard Fuld Jr. and other top executives, alleging three counts of violations of the Securities Act of 1933 (1933 Act) and four counts of violations of state laws. The Division claimed that the Lehman executives knew at the time the state invested more than $180 million in Lehman securities that Lehman's overvalued residential and commercial real estate portfolio was threatening its financial stability. As a result, their actions caused state pension funds to lose more than $100 million. Section 22(a) of the 1933 Act, 15 U.S.C. § 77v(a), bars removal from a state court hearing a case arising under the 1933 Act. Nevertheless, the defendants filed a motion for removal to the federal district court for the District of New Jersey, arguing that the Bankruptcy Code, 28 U.S.C. § 1452(a), allows removal of a cause of action to a competent district court if the cause of action is related to a case under the code. The defendants argued that their individual indemnification and contribution claims against Lehman were sufficiently related to the Lehman bankruptcy proceedings that the claims should be removed to in federal court, pursuant to 28 U.S.C. §§ 1334(b), 1452(a), despite the no-removal rule of the 1933 Act § 22(a). The court granted the Lehman motion, and the Division then moved for remand to the state court. In response, the defendants requested a stay while the Multi-District Litigation Panel considered hearing the matter in the Southern District of New York. The MDL Panel issued an order conditionally transferring the action to the Southern District, and the Division filed an objection to the conditional transfer. Shortly after the district court denied the Division's remand request, the MDL Panel vacated its transfer order! Is New Jersey's case against the former Lehman executives the kind of case that should be resolved in a commonplace state court action? In federal district court? Or is it only a small piece of a much larger puzzle that must be assimilated into the larger bankruptcy action involving the company itself? The district court confronted these concerns in considering the plaintiff's

motion for certification for interlocutory appeal of the court's order to the Third Circuit pursuant to 28 U.S.C. § 1292(b).

NEW JERSEY, DEPARTMENT OF TREASURY, DIVISION OF INVESTMENT V. FULD

— F.Supp.2d —, 2009 WL 2905432 (D.N.J. 2009)

THOMPSON, District Judge.

On July 10, 2009, Plaintiff filed the instant motion, pursuant to 28 U.S.C. § 1292(b), seeking certification for interlocutory appeal. Plaintiff presents two questions for potential certification: how to resolve the statutory conflict between 28 U.S.C. § 1452(a) and Section 22(a) of the Securities Act of 1933, 15 U.S.C. § 77v(a); and, whether indemnification and contribution claims form the basis of "related-to" jurisdiction under the provisions of 28 U.S.C. §§ 1334(b) and 1452(a). On August 10, 2009, the MDL Panel issued an Order vacating the CTO. For the reasons stated below, Plaintiff's motion is granted in part and denied in part.

DISCUSSION

A. Standard of Review

A district court may certify an order for interlocutory appeal when the party seeking certification shows that the order "involves a controlling question of law as to which there is substantial ground for a difference of opinion and that an immediate appeal from the order may materially advance the ultimate termination of the litigation." 28 U.S.C. § 1292(b); *Katz v. Carte Blanche Corp.,* 496 F.2d 747, 755 (3d Cir.1974). "The district court should certify an order for immediate appeal only if all three requirements identified in Section 1292(b) are met. Moreover, the burden is on the movant to demonstrate that all three requirements have been satisfied." *In re G-I Holdings,* 2005 U.S. Dist. LEXIS 31887, at *6 (D.N.J. Dec. 9, 2005). "Even if Section 1292(b) criteria are present, permission to appeal is wholly within the discretion of the district courts." *Id.* Additionally, certification "should be sparingly applied and used only in exceptional circumstances." *Id.* Certification was not "intended merely to provide review of difficult rulings in hard cases." *United States ex rel. Hollander v. Clay,* 420 F.Supp. 853, 859 (D.D.C.1976).

1. Controlling question of law.

When deciding if a question of law is a "controlling question of law," the Court finds guidance from the Third Circuit's opinion in *Katz,* 496 F.2d at 755.

Though it is true that "a controlling question of law must encompass, at the very least, every order which, if erroneous, would be reversible error on final appeal," the Court is not bound by such a strict framework. *Id.* In fact, in *Katz,* the Third Circuit explained that a question can be controlling if it "is serious to the conduct of the litigation, either practically or legally." *Id.*

2. Substantial ground for difference of opinion.

Section 1292(b)'s second factor, that there be substantial ground for a difference of opinion, must arise out of a genuine doubt or conflicting precedent as to the correct legal standard. *Royal Ins. Co. of America v. K.S.I. Trading Corp.,* 2006 WL 1722358, at *3 (D.N.J. June 19, 2006). "Conflicting and contradictory opinions can provide substantial grounds for a difference of opinion" as can "the absence of controlling law on a particular issue." *Knipe v. Smithkline Beecham,* 583 F.Supp.2d 553, 600 (E.D.Pa.2008) (citations omitted). However, when there are not conflicting precedents that control, substantial grounds for a difference of opinion may exist when the court is faced with issues of statutory interpretation that are somewhat novel and complex." *Zenith Radio Corp. v. Matsushita Elec. Indus. Co., Ltd.,* 494 F.Supp. 1190, 1243 (E.D.Pa.1980).

3. Whether certification materially advances the ultimate termination of litigation.

To determine whether certification will materially advance the ultimate termination of litigation, a district court should examine whether an immediate appeal would: "(1) eliminate the need for trial; (2) eliminate complex issues so as to simplify the trial; or (3) eliminate issues to make discovery easier and less costly." *Orson, Inc. v. Miramax Film Corp.,* 867 F.Supp. 319, 322 (E.D.Pa.1994).

B. Plaintiff's Motion for Certification

1. The statutory tension between Section 1452(a) and Section 22(a).

Section 22(a) of the Securities Act states "no case arising under this Act and brought in any State court of competent jurisdiction shall be removed to any court of the United States." 15 U.S.C. § 77v(a). Section 1452(a) explains that a "party may remove any claim or cause of action . . . to the district court for the district where such civil action is pending, if such district court has jurisdiction of such claim or cause of action under Section 1334." 28 U.S.C. § 1452(a). Section 1334 explains that "the district courts shall have original but not exclusive jurisdiction of all civil proceedings arising under title 11 [of the Bankruptcy Code], or arising in or related to cases under title 11." 28 U.S.C. § 1334(b).

The Court notes that, in this case, the tension between Section 1452(a) and

Section 22(a) implicates the Court's subject matter jurisdiction. *Carlisle v. United States,* 517 U.S. 416, 434-35 (1996). Furthermore, as prior courts have noted, jurisdiction issues are classic examples of controlling questions of law. *New Jersey Protection & Advocacy, Inc. v. New Jersey Dep't of Educ.,* 2008 WL 4692345, at *4 (D.N.J. October 8, 2008). Nonetheless, the Court is aware of the statutory tension between Section 1452(a)'s bankruptcy removal provision and Section 22(a)'s apparent bar on removal, and concludes that this question meets the three-factor framework, codified in Section 1292(b), to form the basis of certification for an interlocutory appeal.

First, it is clear that the question presented by the conflict between these two statutes is a controlling question of law. *Katz,* 496 F.2d at 755. Were the Court to have decided this question of first impression within the Third Circuit in a different way, it is clear that that ruling would be serious to the conduct of the litigation, both practically and legally. Thus, the Court concludes that Plaintiff's statutory conflict question is a controlling question of law.

Furthermore, the statutory question presented by Plaintiff's certification request yields substantial ground for a difference of opinion. As indicated previously, the Third Circuit has not addressed the question of how to resolve the statutory conflict between Section 1452(a) and Section 22(a). In fact, only one other Circuit has opined on the issue. The absence of precedent in the Third Circuit, and the fact that this question is one of statutory interpretation involving complex issues, about which there is substantial ground for a difference of opinion, qualify it for Section 1292(b) certification.

Lastly, the Court is persuaded that Section 1292(b) certification of the statutory conflict question would materially advance the ultimate termination of the litigation. Were the Third Circuit to affirm this Court's June 25, 2009 Order, this matter could join many others arising out of similar facts, filed throughout the country, currently pending before the MDL panel in the S.D.N.Y. for discovery and other pretrial proceedings. If, however, the Third Circuit were to conclude that remand was appropriate, the matter could proceed in the Superior Court of New Jersey, Mercer County, perhaps streamlined separate and apart from matters pending before the MDL, for a more prompt resolution in that court. Therefore, the Court concludes that the third prong of the Section 1292(b) analysis is satisfied and that the statutory conflict question warrants Section 1292(b) certification.

2. "Related-to" jurisdiction under 28 U.S.C. §§ 1334(b) and 1452(a).

Plaintiff also seeks Section 1292(b) certification of the question of "related-to" jurisdiction under 28 U.S.C. §§ 1334(b) and 1452(a). . . . Plaintiff objects to the Court's conclusion that indemnification and contribution claims are of sufficient relation to Lehman's bankruptcy proceedings, such that they confer "related-to" jurisdiction, as outlined in Section 1334(b). . . . The Court is not persuaded that Plaintiff has justified Section 1292(b) certification on this second question.

As an initial matter, it does appear to the Court that the second question is a controlling question of law because it is serious to the litigation both legally and practically. Therefore, it meets the first prong of the *Katz* framework. The second prong of the *Katz* framework, however, requires substantial ground for a difference of opinion. *Katz,* 496 F.2d at 755. The Court, in its June 25, 2009 Order, examined and rejected Plaintiff's argument that the individually-named Defendants' indemnification and contribution claims are not of sufficient relation to Lehman's bankruptcy. The Court found jurisdiction based on Section 1334(b) and Section 1452(a) proper, and cited consistent support for its conclusion from Third Circuit precedent.

It appears that Plaintiff's arguments in support of certifying the "related-to" question flow from a difference of opinion with the Court, and not from a genuine doubt as to the correct legal standard. As courts have previously held, "mere disagreement with the district court's ruling does not constitute a substantial ground for difference of opinion within the meaning of [Section] 1292(b)." *Kapossy v. McGraw-Hill, Inc.,* 942 F.Supp. 996, 1001 (D.N.J.1996). Therefore, because the "the court should not certify questions of relatively clear law merely because the losing party disagrees with the court's analysis," *In re chocolate Confectionary Antitrust Litig.,* 607 F.Supp.2d. 701, 705 (M.D.Pa. 2009) (citations omitted), the Court concludes there is not genuine doubt as to the correct legal standard applicable to this question. Therefore, the Court concludes Section 1292(b) certification is improper on Plaintiff's "related-to" argument.

NOTES AND QUESTIONS

1. *Six of One, Half of Another.* The district court confronted two questions for certification – (*i*) the apparent inconsistency between the permissive removal provision of 28 U.S.C. § 1452(a) and the no-removal provision of 1933 Act § 22(a); and, (*ii*) the "related-to" basis for jurisdiction of the indemnification and contribution claims under the provisions of 28 U.S.C. §§ 1334(b) and 1452(a). Can they really be separated as the court's decision suggests? If the 1933 Act provision trumps the permissive removal provision, then what becomes of the court's decision – which it did *not* certify to the Third Circuit – that the indemnification and contribution claims are "related to" the Lehman bankruptcy case?

2. *A Difference of Opinion.* The court refuses to certify the "related-to" question on the ground that there is no "substantial ground for a difference of opinion" as required by *Katz,* only "a difference of opinion with the Court."

Does that argument seem persuasive? Since presumably it is always the case that a litigant seeking appellate review disagreed with the lower court's ruling, is disagreement with the ruling pertinent to the question of whether there is a substantial ground for a difference of opinion? The "related-to" question is, by the court's admission, "a controlling question of law." It is one "which, if erroneous, would be reversible error on final appeal," according to *Katz*, so would not interlocutory appeal in this case promote efficiency in resolution of the dispute?

3. *Related to What?* Is it possible that the defendant's indemnification and contribution claims – claims *against Lehman*, not the plaintiff – may be related to the bankruptcy proceedings, but that the plaintiff's securities law claims – *against the executives* – are not?

4. *Unresolved Debt Resolution.* One niche industry that seemed to benefit from the financial fallout was the "debt settlement" business, service firms that offered to negotiate on behalf of highly debt-burdened consumers with the consumers' creditors in an effort to wipe out a portion of each consumer's total unsecured debt. This development led to a wide range of predatory schemes, taking advantage of the desperation of these consumers. How did these schemes operate? What sort of remedies are available to recoup consumer losses or to protect vulnerable consumers? Consider the following case.

PEOPLE EX REL. CUOMO V. NATIONWIDE ASSET SERVICES, INC.

— N.Y.S.2d —, 2009 WL 3277307 (N.Y.Sup. 2009)

PATRICK H. NEMOYER, J.

[The state brought a petition against out-of-state debt settlement companies seeking restitution, damages, injunctive relief, and other relief for alleged fraud, deceptive business practices, false advertising, and other illegal acts in the conduct of their business. The court granted the petition, holding that the state's claims were not time-barred, and that the companies had engaged in various deceptive business practices and false advertising. While the companies had disclosed setup and bank fees and were not shown to harbor an intent to defraud New York consumers, the companies' repeated and persistent illegal practices gave rise to liability for statutory fraud. Issuance of an injunction, enforcement of the companies' guarantee, a performance bond, and a civil penalty were warranted, but the state was not entitled to full restitution for all consumers. In the following excerpt the court describes the defendants' deceptive practices, which are typical of questionable debt settlement schemes.]

Respondents Nationwide Asset Services, Inc., Servicestar, LLC, and

Universal Debt Reduction, LLC (collectively, Nationwide) are interrelated entities created and headquartered in Arizona. Respondent FGL Clearwater, Inc., d/b/a American Debt Arbitration (ADA), is an entity incorporated and headquartered in Florida. Nationwide and ADA are in the business of "debt settlement" which is to say the business of negotiating on behalf of highly debt-burdened consumers with those consumers' creditors in an effort to wipe out a portion of each consumer's total unsecured debt. Respondent ADA markets Nationwide's debt reduction program through telephone sales presentations initially made during "cold calls" to credit-distressed consumers, and it is established on this record that Nationwide and ADA split the fees paid by the consumers according to a schedule, ADA for enrolling the consumers, and Nationwide for negotiating on those consumers' behalf with creditors (thus, the Court will refer to *respondents'* program, words, and actions).

Basically, respondents represent to consumers that they can eliminate their unsecured debt over a period of time, typically, two to three years, and moreover can do so in a way that will save the consumers a large portion, typically 25% to 40%, of the "Original Amount Due" or "Amount Originally Due" (AOD), a sum referring at once to the consumer's contemporaneous indebtedness on each account, and his/her aggregate indebtedness on all accounts, that the consumer opts to enroll in or designate to respondents' program. Respondents' promise of such significant savings assertedly takes into account the payment of all of the substantial fees charged by respondents. ... The consumers are promised that they can achieve such substantial savings by: 1) ceasing all payments to their creditors for the duration of the program; 2) making monthly payments (of amounts typically less than the sums that the consumers already are paying to their creditors each month) directly to respondents; 3) not negotiating personally with their creditors, or with attorneys or collection agencies who might contact the consumers on those creditors' behalf, for the duration of the program; and 4) instead authorizing respondents to negotiate favorable debt settlements with the creditors – albeit not immediately, but rather only after the lapse of some period, usually many months. Those four steps essentially constitute respondents' program. With regard to steps 1), 3), and 4), consumers are told that their default in paying the debt over some period of time contributes to a higher likelihood and probable more favorable terms of eventual settlement because creditors are more willing and likely to compromise debts that are more seriously delinquent. Consumers are told, however, that their enrollment in respondents' program is no guarantee against their creditors' continuing to dun them, placing the debt in collection, or taking legal action on account of such default. Consumers also are instructed or advised to disclose all of their unsecured debt to respondents, enroll or designate all such debt into the program, not withdraw any accounts/debts from the program, and not contract any new debt. With respect to step 2) of the program, after eliciting information regarding each consumer's monthly income and expenses and thereby determining that consumer's available monthly cash flow, respondents require a monthly payment intended to enable that consumer to pay the debt settlement(s) "target[ed]" for negotiation by respondents, as well as respondents' fees, over the anticipated duration of that consumer's participation in the program. Thus, the monthly payments (aside from any amounts earmarked to pay respondents' fees) are accumulated and used to pay any debts settlements. The amount of the monthly payment is typically set at a minimum of $300 but could be set much higher depending on the consumer's available income and expenses and the number of credit accounts and the amount of debt that the consumer opts to designate to be settled through respondents' program.

In exchange for providing such services, respondents charge various fees, including a setup fee, an enrollment fee, a monthly administrative fee (in conjunction with monthly bank fees), and an ultimate settlement fee. The setup fee is a one-time up-front charge of $399. The enrollment fee is equal in amount to three of the monthly payments set for the consumer (thus a minimum of $900 but sometimes a larger amount for those consumers who dedicate a large number and amount of debts to the program). The first three to five monthly payments by the consumer are applied first towards those two initial fees (as indicated, a minimum of $1299). Only after such payment is any portion of the consumer's monthly payment deposited into a special bank account set up to fund any debt settlement(s) negotiated by respondents. Of course, it is over the period of payment of such fees and the additional months spent waiting for significant sums to accumulate in the special bank account for payment of creditors that the consumer usually becomes seriously delinquent in paying his or her creditors. Once the special bank account is set up for receipt of the consumer's continued monthly payments, the consumer begins paying respondents an additional monthly administrative fee of $49, plus additional monthly fees (a minimum of around $7 per month) to the bank, Rocky Mountain Bank and Trust, chosen by respondents as the repository of those funds earmarked for settlement. The final fee is denominated the settlement fee and is earned at the time respondents settle each designated account. The settlement fee is invariably set at 29% of the difference between the AOD on each account at the time the consumer embarked upon the program and the amount of the settlement ultimately negotiated by respondents on that account. All of those fees likewise are deducted from the consumers' monthly payments and/or the special bank account funded thereby. Where the special bank account does not hold enough funds to pay the ultimately negotiated debt settlement and respondents' fees, the consumer must remit the shortfall in addition to his or her next scheduled monthly payment.

NOTES AND QUESTIONS

1. *What's Deceptive About Debt Reduction Schemes?* The state alleged that Nationwide and its affiliates were engaging in fraudulent and deceptive practices, including false advertising. If the service offered by the defendants were exactly as described by the court, would there be anything deceptive about it? Perhaps not, but the state alleged that Nationwide rarely achieved the represented savings of 25 percent or more on behalf of their New York customers. Of the 1,981 customers signed up from January 1, 2005 through May 5, 2008, only 64, or fewer than 3 percent, had successfully completed respondents' program by September 25, 2008, while 537 customers had canceled their participation. Of those 64, only 6 – approximately 0.3 percent of the original 1,981 participants – realized savings of 25 percent or more after taking into account their payment of fees. Furthermore, the state alleged that Nationwide systematically misrepresented the savings realized through the settlements, because it did not account for the enrollment and setup fees or the monthly administrative and bank fees in calculating the total percentage saved. Finally, Nationwide and its affiliates failed to honor their guarantee to customers that the total paid would not exceed the original debt owed. In fact, 27 of the 64 customers "successfully" completing the program paid more than their AOD when their various program fees were taken into account.

2. *Appropriate Relief.* The state asked for various types of relief, including: (*i*) an order prohibiting Nationwide and its affiliates from doing business in New York until they obtained authorization to do so (because they were "foreign corporations" not registered pursuant to N.Y. law); (*ii*) an order permanently enjoining them from engaging in fraudulent, deceptive, and illegal acts and practices (a fairly standard remedy in civil actions brought by state or federal agencies against fraud); (*iii*) a full accounting of all N.Y. customers since January 2005; (*iv*) full restitution and damages to all N.Y. customers injured by the defendants; (*v*) a performance bond of $1 million, to guarantee that the defendants complied with the injunctive relief and to provide a fund for additional restitution to customers defrauded or damaged by the defendants; (*vi*) civil penalties of up to $5,000 for each deceptive act committed by respondents; and, (*vii*) special costs of $2,000 against each defendant. Does the requested relief seem reasonable under the circumstances, or is the broad request just a tactical maneuver on the part of the Attorney General?

3. *The Court's Disposition of the Fraud Claims.* Wading through a large quantity of statistical and documentary evidence, the court had little trouble determining that Nationwide and its affiliates "have and are engaged in

deceptive business practices . . . and false advertising. . . ."[26] While the proof must show that the conduct was or is "likely to mislead a reasonable consumer acting reasonably under the circumstances," unlike common law fraud the statutory claims "need 'not necessarily rise to the level of fraud.'"[27] The defendants were not saved by their use of "weasel words" such as "typical" and "typically" in their promotional materials (*e.g.*, claiming that their services "typically save 25% to 40% off" a customer's total indebtedness). The problem was not simply with their use of those words. Rather, by joining use of the word "typically" with a predicted range of savings – rather than simply an average amount or percentage of savings – the materials misleadingly suggested "a great likelihood that enrollees in the program will achieve savings in that range and that the risk of deviation from the range is small."[28] However, statistical information submitted by the parties demonstrated that what the defendants represented to be the "typical" or "average" experience of their program participants was in fact atypical.

4. For a contrasting view of debt settlement regulation, see *U.S. Organizations for Bankruptcy Alternatives, Inc. v. Dep't of Banking,* — A.2d —, 2010 WL 653756 (Pa. Cmwlth 2009) (holding state Debt Management Services Act provisions requiring debt service providers to comply with Banking Department regulations and requiring providers to limit fees to those described in Act unconstitutional under state constitution).

5. *Private Litigation.* The preceding case involved a civil action by the state against a debt settlement business. The following case involves private litigation between a credit card issuer and a card holder who is also operating a debt settlement scheme. Which seems the more effective response to such schemes?

ISENBERG v. CHASE BANK USA, N.A.

— F.Supp.2d —, 2009 WL 2030431 (N.D.Tex. July 14, 2009)

TERRY R. MEANS, District Judge.

[Isenberg, a Chase card holder, brought suit to challenge an arbitration award in favor of the card-issuer. Chase sought to confirm its arbitration award against Isenberg for the unpaid balance of her credit card account. It also filed

---

26. *Cuomo*, 2009 WL 3277307 at *9.

27. *Id., quoting Gaidon v. Guardian Life Ins. Co. of America,* 94 N.Y.2d 330, 343, 704 N.Y.S.2d 177, 725 N.E.2d 598 (1999). On the differences between strict common law fraud and the "liberally defined" statutory fraud, see *Cuomo*, 2009 WL 3277307 at *12-*14.

28. *Cuomo*, 2009 WL 3277307 at *9.

a counterclaim for damages against Isenberg for tortiously interfering with its contracts with its card-holders by promoting a debt elimination scam created by North American Educational Services (NAES). Isenberg not only purchased the debt elimination scam herself, she also sold it to other persons with Chase credit card accounts. She maintained at least two web sites – primedebtfree123.com and intergritydebtoptions/suzy.com – through which she obtained potential customers, received payment for the sale of the debt elimination scam, and transmitted payments to NAES, through PayPal and Google. She assured her customers that her scheme was based on contract law and various federal statutes, and that banking and credit institutions were violating the law by lending money, charging interest, and making inadequate disclosures. Her customers were encouraged to withhold payments on their credit card balances while paying her fees, to the detriment of the card-issuer and ultimately the customers, since they still owed the card balances. The court found that Isenberg had defrauded the bank, and the bank was ordered to submit evidence in support of its damages claim. After reviewing the evidence, the court held that the bank had properly supported its damages claims, which were capable of mathematical calculation, and that punitive damages were warranted.]

The only objection levied by Isenberg that goes to the merits of Chase's damages calculations is her objection to Chase's inclusion of certain accounts in its damages calculations. But Isenberg's argument is based on the fact that Chase has not produced evidence that these account holders submitted a "dispute letter" – a letter used in Isenberg's scheme to challenge account balances and justify cessation of payments. Chase need not submit this specific piece of evidence in order to be entitled to recover damages. Regardless, Isenberg does not specify which of the account holders listed by Chase are objectionable.

Isenberg does not otherwise object to the merits of Chase's damages calculations. And after a review of the evidence provided by Chase, the Court concludes that Chase has properly supported its damages claims and that such damages are capable of mathematical calculation. *See James v. Frame,* 6 F.3d 307, 310 (5th Cir.1993) (affirming district court's decision not to conduct a hearing on damages but, instead, to base damages on evidence in the record, where the litigation had proceeded for some time and district court had become familiar with the defendant's conduct). Chase has provided the declaration of Anthony S. Demczak, a Chase operations manager. Demcsak used documents from the entities Chase subpoenaed, along with Chase's own business records, to determine the damage done to Chase by Isenberg's debt-elimination scheme.

Chase customers who participated in Isenberg's scheme stopped paying on their credit-card accounts as part of the scheme. Demczak multiplied the outstanding balance on these accounts by 2%, the minimum monthly payment required by Chase. Demczak then multiplied this figure by six to represent a six-month stream of minimum monthly payments to arrive at $116,990.91, which Chase refers to as its "minimum damages." Six months represents the typical amount of time between the point when an account holder stops making payments and the point at which the account is written off as uncollectible or sold as a receivable to another institution.

Demczak performed the same basic calculation, replacing 2% with 7% – which approximates Chase's actual historical monthly recovery on similar accounts. This calculation resulted in an actual damages figure of $409,468.19. Demczak explains his calculations in his declaration, and provides a detailed spreadsheet in support.

Based on the evidence, Chase is hereby awarded actual damages in the amount of $409,468.19.

Chase was awarded punitive damages in the Court's original order granting default judgment. . . . This was based on the Court's finding that, as part of her debt-elimination scheme, Isenberg engaged in fraudulent and malicious conduct. Because of this finding, Chase may be awarded punitive damages under Texas Civil Practice and Remedies Code § 41.003.

. . . [A]n award of punitive damages is justified. The nature of the wrong and the character of the conduct involved support an award of punitive damages. *See* Tex. Civ. Prac. & Rem. Code Ann. 41.003 (listing factors to consider in awarding punitive damages). Isenberg's actions worked to defraud both credit-card holders and credit institutions. The result was Isenberg's receipt of hundreds of thousands of dollars, while both credit-card holders and credit institutions suffered equivalent losses. *Philip Morris USA v. Williams,* 549 U.S. 346, 355 (2007) (court may consider harm to plaintiff as well as third parties in assessing the reprehensibility of defendant's conduct and resulting propriety of punitive damages). And Isenberg was highly culpable, actively marketing and distributing her scheme. A non-lawyer, Isenberg provided her customers legal advice along with the scheme, assuring them that her scheme was based on contract law and various federal statutes and that banking and credit institutions were violating the law by lending money, charging interest, and making inadequate disclosures.

And an award of punitive damages will vindicate the public sense of justice and propriety and deter similar schemes. *Alamo Nat'l Bank v. Kraus,* 616 S.W.2d 908, 910 (1981) (noting that a court is to consider the extent to which the defendant's conduct offends a public sense of justice in awarding punitive damages). The scope of Isenberg's scheme warrants an award of punitive damages.

Accordingly, Chase is awarded $116, 990. 91 in punitive damages. This sum is a reasonable amount of punitive damages as it is far less than the actual damages suffered by Chase as a result of Isenberg's scheme. *See Farm Mut. Automobile Ins. Co. v. Campbell,* 538 U.S. 408, 425 (2003) (discussing the relation between compensatory and punitive damages).

Finally, Chase seeks to have an arbitration award and an award of related attorneys' fees confirmed. The Court has previously confirmed the August 7, 2006, arbitration award of $24,609.18 in favor of Chase. Chase is entitled to recover this amount. [The court also awarded Chase attorneys' fees, court costs, and post-judgment interest at a rate of 0.48% from the date of the judgment until paid.]

B. REINVENTING TWO INDUSTRIES – OR ONE

After the Fall – One Year Out. What steps have the Congress and the regulators taken to address the crisis? How effective are these steps in resolving the current crisis? In making the next crisis less likely, or at least less likely to be so severe? Consider the following excerpt in answering these questions.

3 MICHAEL P. MALLOY, BANKING LAW AND REGULATION

§§ 11.4-11.4.3 (Aspen 2004 & Cum. Supps.)[a]

§ 11.4 National Responses to the Subprime Crisis

The failure of the subprime mortgage market in 2008 continued to deepen and spread in 2009. In May 2009, the FDIC announced that during Q1 2009 the Deposit Insurance Fund (DIF) balance had decreased from $17.3 billion to $13.0 billion.[2] Net income for Q1 2009 at FDIC-insured depository institutions decreased 60.8 percent from Q1 2008 ($19.3 billion 2008, $7.6 billion 2009). The FDIC added 53 banks to the problem bank list, from 252 as of Q4 2008. Furthermore, 21 FDIC-insured depository institutions failed in Q1 2009. . . .

A recent OECD report[5] has identified gaps in the U.S. regulatory structure as at least partly responsible for the crisis – in particular, the fragmented structure of regulation, with specialized regulatory agencies operating across artificially segregated lines of services, such as banking, insurance, securities

---

a. Some footnotes have been renumbered for the convenience of the reader.

2. Thecla Fabian, *DIF Dips Sharply; Bank Profit Falls 61% Comparing '08, '09 1st Quarters, FDIC Says*, BNA BANKING DAILY (May 28, 2009), *available at* http://www.bna.com. The FDIC Quarterly Banking Profile and related statistical information are available at http://www2. fdic.gov/qbp/index.asp.

5. For a summary of the OECD economic survey of the United States, *see* http://www.oecd.org/document/32/0,3343,en_2649_33733_41803296_1_1_1_1,00.html.

and futures. Thus, responses that focus on the supervisory and regulatory structure are likely to be critical components if policy makers wish to avoid future replications of the current crisis. However, to date little if anything concrete has been done to address any structural problems in the regulatory system that failed adequately to supervise the financial services sector and the risks it was generating. . . .

§ 11.4.1 Transactional Responses

Much of the national response so far has been a series of fatalistic attempts to spend our way out of the crisis. For example, on September 7, 2008, the Treasury Department entered into senior preferred stock purchase agreements with the Federal National Mortgage Association (Fannie Mae) and the Federal Home Loan Mortgage Corporation (Freddie Mac), providing in effect protection to the holders of senior debt, subordinated debt, and mortgage-backed securities (MBS) issued or guaranteed by Fannie and Freddie. In light of these agreements, in October 2008 the federal banking agencies and the OTS proposed a 10-percent risk weight for claims on, and the portion of claims guaranteed by, Fannie Mae or Freddie Mac, to remain in effect as long as an agreement remains in effect with the respective entity.[2]

On October 3, 3008, Title I of the Emergency Economic Stabilization Act of 2008 (EESA)[4] created the Troubled Assets Relief Program (TARP) for the purchase of troubled assets of financial institutions. From the onset of the TARP, Treasury appeared to be improvising, unsure of even basic issues such as how to price the targeted assets.[5] By mid-October 2008, Treasury shifted direction and began using TARP funds to purchase equity in troubled financial institutions (primarily nine large institutions) rather than purchasing troubled assets.[6] Treasury adopted this approach arguably on the basis of its EESA

---

2. 73 Fed. Reg. 63,656 (2008) (to be codified at 12 C.F.R. pts. 3, app. A, §3, (OCC proposed rule), 208, app. A, §III.C. 225, app. A, §III.C, (Fed proposed rules), 325, app. A, §II.A.1, (FDIC proposed rule); *id.* §567.6(a)(1) (OTS proposed rule). Under the generally applicable risk-based capital adequacy requirements, claims on, and the portion of claims guaranteed by, U.S. government-sponsored agencies receive a 20 percent risk weight. *See* 12 C.F.R. pts. 3, app. A, §3(a)(2) (OCC capital adequacy rule governing such claims), 208, app. A, §III.C.2.b., 225, app. A, §III.C.2.b. (Fed rules), 325, app. A, §II.C. (FDIC rules), 567.6(a)(ii) (OTS rule).

4. Pub. L. No. 110-343, tit. I, §§101-136, 122 Stat. 3765, 3767-3800 (2008) (codified at 5 U.S.C. § 5315, 12 U.S.C. §§ 461 note, 1715z-23, 1823(c)(11), 1828(a), (c), 5211-5241, 15 U.S.C. §1638 note, 1638(b)(2), 31 U.S.C. §§301, 3101).

5. See, e.g., Stephen Joyce, *Treasury Official Discusses Implementation of $700 Billion Program to Buy Bad Assets*, BNA Banking Daily (Oct. 7, 2008), available at http://news.bna.com (reporting on efforts of Treasury to implement TARP).

6. Thus, in October 2008, the Fed issued an interim final rule allowing BHCs that issued senior perpetual preferred stock to Treasury under a Capital Purchase Program to include such securities in Tier 1 capital for purposes of risk-based and leverage capital guidelines for bank holding companies. 73 Fed. Reg. 62,851 (2008) (codified at 12 C.F.R. pt. 225, App. A),

authority.[7] The new approach prompted criticism that Treasury has failed to require beneficiaries of its funding to use the capital infusions to strengthen the weak credit market.[8] Cluelessly, Treasury officials insisted that the Capital Purchase Program (CPP), under which Treasury was buying shares of preferred stock in selected financial institutions, taking, in most cases, a 5 percent dividend for the first few years, with an increase to 9 percent, would be profitable in the long run.[9] More recently, congressional concern has grown over the excessive levels of executive compensation at institutions benefitting from the CPP.[10] Whether as a result of the intense criticism of its use of the TARP or because of its own meandering approach to responding to the financial crisis, by mid-November 2008, Treasury was publicly moving away from its plan to buy mortgage-related assets; instead, it was reportedly considering other uses for what remained of the original $700 billion in TARP

---

corrected, 73 Fed. Reg. 63,624 (2008). In June 2009, the Fed adopted the rule as a final rule without any substantive changes. 74 Fed. Reg. 26,081 (2009).

7. *Cf.* R. Christian Bruce & Aaron Lorenzo, *Banks Receiving Treasury Investments See New Opportunities for Acquisitions,* BNA Banking Daily (October 28, 2008), *available at* http://news.bna.com (discussing allocation of $250 billion of EESA funding for capital injections under Treasury Capital Purchase Program (CPP)). For discussion of the CPP, see Stephen Joyce & Nora Macaluso, *Government Officials Say TARP Eligibility May Expand to Additional Types of Firms*, BNA Banking Daily (Oct. 29, 2008), *available at* http://news.bna.com.

8. For contrary studies, arguing that bank lending had increased during the credit crisis, see V. Chari, L. Christiano, & P. Kehoe, *Facts and Myths About the Credit Crisis* (Federal Reserve Bank of Minneapolis Working Paper 666, Oct. 2008), *available at* http://www.minneapolisfed.org/publications_papers/pub_display.cfm?id=4062; Octavio Marenzi et al., *Flawed Assumptions About the Credit Crisis: A Critical Examination of US Policymakers* (Celent, Dec. 2009) (arguing that U.S. government responses to credit crisis based on assumptions contradicted by government's own data), *available at* http://www.celent.com/PressReleases/20081210/CreditCrisis20081212DRAFT.pdf. *But see* Ethan Cohen-Cole, Burcu Duygan-Bump, Jose Fillat, & Judit Montoriol-Gerriga, *Minneapolis: Looking Behind the Aggregates: A Reply to* "Facts and Myths About the Financial Crisis of 2008" (Federal Reserve Bank of Boston Working Paper No. QAU08-5, Nov. 2008) (disputing Minneapolis Fed paper), *available at* http://www.bos.frb.org/ bankinfo/qau/wp/2008/qau0805.htm.

9. The text of prepared remarks on the CPP by Interim Assistant Secretary for Financial Stability Neel Kashkari is available at http://www.treas.gov/press/releases/hp1314.htm. *See also Capital Purchases Will Turn a Profit For Taxpayers, Treasury's Kashkari Says,* BNA BANKING DAILY (Dec. 8, 2008), *available at* http://news.bna.com (reporting on Assistant Secretary Kashkari's remarks).

10. . . . . Criticism was exacerbated by the apparent failure of CPP-assisted banks to increase lending. Treasury's Bank Lending Survey indicated that overall lending by financial institutions that received the largest amount of government investment under CPP declined in February 2009. Mike Ferullo, *Survey Shows Slight Decline in Lending Among Banks Receiving Government Capital,* BNA BANKING DAILY (Apr. 16, 2009), *available at* http://www.bna.com. The February lending survey is available at http://www.financialstability.gov/latest/tg_041509.html.

funds. Coincidentally, on November 14, 2008, the Administration reached agreement with congressional leaders to establish a TARP inspector general, and congressional leaders appointed three experts to the Congressional Oversight Panel, another EESA-mandated watchdog.[13] . . .

[T]he FDIC initiated the Temporary Liquidity Guarantee Program (TLG Program) in October 2008.[15] The program has two components: (i) the debt guarantee program, which guaranteed newly issued senior unsecured debt[16] of insured depository institutions and most U.S. holding companies of such institutions; and, (ii) the transaction account guarantee program, which guaranteed certain non-interest-bearing transaction accounts at insured depository institutions. . . .

In mid-November, the Fed provided nearly $50 billion in options for loans through the Term Securities Lending Facility (TSLF), under which options are offered to primary government securities dealers – banks and securities broker-dealers that trade with the Federal Reserve Bank of New York to draw upon short-term, fixed-rate loans in exchange for program-eligible collateral.[20]

By late November 2008, Treasury had completed a $40 billion purchase of American International Group (AIG) preferred stock and warrants through

---

13. R. Christian Bruce, *Oversight of TARP Comes into Focus with Action by White House, Pelosi, Reid*, BNA BANKING DAILY (Nov. 17, 2008), *available at* http://news.bna.com. The members of the five-member TARP Congressional Oversight Panel are appointed by Speaker of the House (who appointed Richard H. Neiman, the N.Y. Superintendent of Banks), the House Republican Leader (appointing Rep. Jeb Hensarling (R-Texas)), the Senate Majority Leader (appointing Harvard Law Professor Elizabeth Warren, who serves as chair) and the Senate Republican Leader (appointing former Sen. John Sununu) each selecting one member. The fifth member is jointly selected by the Speaker and the Majority Leader (who jointly appointed Damon Silvers, AFL-CIO associate general counsel). *See* R. Christian Bruce, *McConnell Names Sununu to TARP Panel; Thacher, Proffitt Tapped to Advise Treasury*, BNA BANKING DAILY (Dec. 18, 2008) (reporting on TARP panel).

15. 73 Fed. Reg. 64,179 (Oct. 29, 2008), amended, 73 Fed. Reg. 66,160 (2008). For background on the TLG Program, see 73 Fed. Reg. at 66,160-66,162.

16. For these purposes, the term "newly issued senior unsecured debt" was defined to mean senior unsecured debt issued by a participating entity on or after October 14, 2008, and on or before: (i) the earlier of November 12, 2008 or the date an eligible entity opts out, for an eligible entity that opts out of the debt guarantee program; or, (ii) June 30, 2009, for an eligible entity that does not opt out of the debt guarantee program. 12 C.F.R. §370.2(f). Based on the public comments received, the FDIC revised the definition in the final version of the rule to exclude debt with a stated maturity of thirty days or less. 73 Fed. Reg. 72,244, 72,267 (Nov. 26, 2008) (codified at 12 C.F.R. §370.2(f)).

20. For results of the TSLF program, see http://www.newyorkfed.org/markets/top/ topsec-lending.cfm. *See also* Aaron Lorenzo, *Fed Extends Almost $50 Billion in Options for Loans Through TSLF Options Program*, BNA BANKING DAILY (Nov. 12, 2008), *available at* http://news.bna.com (discussing TSLF program).

the TARP.[21] That transaction was part of a restructured rescue of AIG, in which the Fed reworked loans to the insurance company, relaxing some terms and offered two new lending facilities. In effect, AIG would use the proceeds from the Treasury transaction to reduce the credit extended by the Fed in September 2008.

In addition, the Fed initiated two programs to boost lending and limit damage from the weakening economy – (*i*) the Term Asset-Backed Securities Loan Facility (TALF), a $200 billion lending facility to facilitate purchases of loan-backed securities, with a Treasury pledge of $20 billion to assist the Fed in hedging the credit risk of possible defaults on the underlying credit exposure;[22] and, (ii) a program to purchase up to $600 billion in mortgage-related assets, involving a commitment to buy up to $100 billion in direct debt issued by Fannie Mae, Freddie Mac, and the FHLBanks, and a commitment to purchase up to $500 billion in MBS guaranteed by Fannie Mae, Freddie Mac, and the Government National Mortgage Association (Ginnie Mae).[23] . . .

Also in November 2008, an economic assistance package for ailing Citigroup was finalized. It involved an agreement by the government to purchase approximately $27 billion in Citigroup stock, and the issuance of over $300 billion in guarantees with respect to mortgage-back securities. Combining features of the Capital Purchase Program (CPP), financial assistance such as AIG received, and troubled asset purchases under the TARP, the transaction requires Citigroup to assume up to $29 billion in portfolio losses, and 10 percent of all losses thereafter, with Treasury, the FDIC, and the Fed each successively responsible for all remaining losses.[26] The arrangement bans dividend payments on common stock for three years without the consent of the regulators, establishes new regulatory approval requirements for executive compensation, and requires Citigroup to adopt

---

21. Aaron Lorenzo, *Treasury Completes $40 Billion Equity Buy in AIG; Transaction Proceeds to Repay Fed*, BNA BANKING DAILY (Nov. 28, 2008), *available at* http://news.bna.com (reporting on AIG rescue).

22. The TALF program since has been expanded to cover a wider class of collateral and extended maturities. Five-year loans for commercial mortgage-backed securities (CMBS) will be eligible, in addition to securities backed by insurance premium finance loans. Aaron Lorenzo, *Fed to Use TALF to Aid CMBS Markets, Aaron Lorenzo Allowing Five-Year Loans in the Process,* BNA BANKING DAILY (May 4, 2009), *available at* http://www.bna.com. For the terms and conditions of CMBS TALF, *see* http://www.newyorkfed.org/markets/talf_cmbs_terms.html.

23. *See* R. Christian Bruce & Aaron Lorenzo, *Fed, Treasury Announce New Actions*, BNA BANKING DAILY (Nov. 26, 2008), *available at* http://news.bna.com (reporting on TALF and MBS facility). For background information on Ginnie Mae, *see* www.ginniemae.gov.

26. For an interagency statement on the Citigroup assistance, *see* http://www.federalreserve.gov/newsevents/press/bcreg/20081123a.htm.

FDIC mortgage modification procedures.

On February 17, 2009, the President signed the American Recovery and Reinvestment Act (ARRA) into law.[27] The ARRA is primarily a $787 billion economic stimulus package intended to create or preserve approximately 3.5 million jobs and to jump start the failing economy, but it does not address the serious problems affecting regulatory and supervisory applicable to the financial services industry. Even Title V of the ARRA,[29] specifically dealing with financial services and general government, has no intended effect on the regulatory structure itself.

§ 11.4.2 Regulatory Responses

In some instances, the regulatory responses have adjusted regulatory requirements to create incentives for private firms to invest in troubled financial assets. For example, in September 2008, the Fed established a special lending facility that enabled depository institutions and BHCs to borrow from the Federal Reserve Bank of Boston on a nonrecourse basis if they use the proceeds of the loan to purchase certain types of asset-backed commercial paper (ABCP) from money market mutual funds.[1] To support this program, the Fed adopted, on an interim final basis, an exemption from its leverage and risk-based capital rules for ABCP held by a state member bank or BHC as a result of participation in the program.[2] Effective January 30, 2009, the exemption was made permanent.[3] To facilitate national bank participation in the program, the OCC adopted on an interim final basis an exemption from its risk-based capital guidelines for ABCP held by any national bank as a result of its participation in the program.[4] In March 2009, the OCC finalized the risk-based capital exemption and extended it to ABCP purchased beyond the original January 30, 2009, date.[5] The OCC final rule applies to any ABCP purchased as a result of a national bank's participation in the facility. The risk-

---

27. Pub. L. No. 111-5, 111th Cong., 1st. Sess., 123 Stat. 115 (2009) (codified at scattered sections of 1, 6, 7, 12, 15, 16, 19, 20, 26, 28, 29, 31, 33, 38, 42, 47 U.S.C.) (ARRA).

29. ARRA, tit. V, 123 Stat. at 148-161 (2009) (codified at scattered sections of 15 U.S.C.).

1. *See* 73 Fed. Reg. 55,706 (2008) (discussing ABCP lending facility). *See also* 73 Fed. Reg. 55,708 (2008) (codified at 12 C.F.R. §§ 223.42(o), 223.56) (exempting on interim basis member banks from certain provisions of FRA §§23A, 23B to increase authority of member bank to purchase ABCP from affiliated money market mutual funds in connection with ABCP Lending Facility).

2. 73 Fed. Reg. at 55,707 (codified at 12 C.F.R. pt. 208, app. A, § III.C.1, app. B, § II; *id.* pt. 225, app. A, § III.C.1, app. D, § II (implementing ABCP purchase policy for member banks and BHCs, respectively).

3. 74 Fed. Reg. 6226 (2009) (codified at 12 C.F.R. §§ 223.42(o), 223.56).

4. 73 Fed. Reg. 55,704 (2008) (codified at 12 C.F.R. pt. 3, app. A, § 3(a)(1)(ix)).

5. 74 Fed. Reg. 13,336 (2009) (codified at 12 C.F.R. pt. 3, App. A, §3(a)(1)(ix)).

based capital exemption will continue to apply as long as the lending facility remains in effect. . . .

Similarly, in October 2008 the Fed issued an interim final rule allowing BHCs that issued senior perpetual preferred stock to Treasury under the Capital Purchase Program (CPP) to include such capital instruments in tier 1 capital for purposes of risk-based and leverage capital guidelines for bank holding companies.[6] . . .

At the same time, the Fed published an interim final rule to support full implementation of the CPP by permitting BHCs that had made a valid election to be taxed as S Corps and BHCs organized in mutual form to include the full amount of any new subordinated debt securities issued to Treasury under the CPP in tier 1 capital for purposes of the risk-based and leverage capital guidelines, provided that the subordinated securities count toward the limit on the amount of other restricted core capital elements includable in tier 1 capital.[7] . . .

In light of the continuing unusual and exigent circumstances in the financial markets, the Fed also adopted a regulatory exemption for member banks permitting them to enter into securities financing transactions with affiliates, such as an SEC-registered broker-dealer, that the affiliate ordinarily would have financed through the U.S. tri-party repurchase agreement market.[8] The exemption is subject to the following conditions: (i) the member bank may use the exemption only to finance asset types that the affiliate financed in the U.S. tri-party repurchase agreement market during the week of September 8–12, 2008;[9] (ii) the transactions must be marked to market daily and subject to daily margin maintenance requirements;[10] (iii) the aggregate risk profile of the exempt securities financing transactions must be no greater than the aggregate risk profile of the affiliate's U.S. tri-party repurchase agreement transactions on September 12, 2008;[11] (iv) the member bank's top-tier holding company must guarantee the obligations of the affiliate under the securities

---

6. 73 Fed. Reg. 62,851 (2008) (codified at 12 C.F.R. pt. 225, App. A), corrected, 73 Fed. Reg. 63,624 (2008).

7. 74 Fed. Reg. 26,077 (2009) (codified at 12 C.F.R. pt. 225, App. A).

8. 74 Fed. Reg. 6225 (2009) (codified at 12 C.F.R. § 223.42(n)). The term "U.S. tri-party repurchase agreement market" means "the U.S. market for securities financing transactions in which the counterparties use custodial arrangements provided by JPMorgan Chase Bank or Bank of New York or another financial institution approved by the [Fed]." 12 C.F.R. § 223.42(n)(2)(ii).

9. 12 C.F.R. §223.42(n)(1)(i).

10. *Id.* § 223.42(n)(1)(ii). The member bank must be at least as over-collateralized in its securities financing transactions with the affiliate as the affiliate's clearing bank was in its U.S. tri-party repurchase agreement transactions with the affiliate on September 12, 2008. *Id.*

11. *Id.* § 223.42(n)(1)(iii).

financing transactions (or provide other security to the bank that is acceptable to the Fed);[12] and (v) a member bank may use the exemption only if the bank has not been specifically informed by the Fed, after consultation with the bank's appropriate federal banking agency, that the bank may not use this exemption.[13]

Finally, the Fed also adopted an exemption from its leverage and risk-based capital rules for ABCP held by any state member bank or BHC as a result of its participation in the program.[14] . . .

§ 11.4.3 Supervisory Responses

While much of the attention of U.S. policymakers has naturally been focused on short-term steps to address the immediate nature of the financial crisis, the crisis serves to demonstrate that the current U.S. financial regulatory system is in need of substantial reform. Indeed, as a January 2009 GAO study cogently argues, the current U.S. financial services regulatory system requires a significant restructuring.[1] The system involves a fragmented and complex set of federal and state regulations, rooted in a situation arising over 150 years ago, that has not kept pace with major developments in the financial services sector in recent decades.[2] While the government has apparently been reluctant to take pervasive supervisory responses to the crisis, an apparent result of the "too-big-to-fail" rationale transformed into a "too-big-to-touch" excuse,[3] certain supervisory actions have been undertaken. For example, in early September 2008, the government placed the Federal National Mortgage Association (Fannie Mae), and the Federal Home Loan Mortgage Corporation (Freddie Mac) in conservatorship and replaced their management.[4] As in a bank conservatorship or receivership, the end result of the process could be the

---

12. *Id.* § 223.42(n)(1)(iv).

13. *Id.* § 223.42(n)(1)(v).

14. 74 Fed. Reg. 6223 (2009) (codified at 12 C.F.R. pts. 208, app. A, §III.C.1, app. B, §II; 225, app. A, §III.C.1, app. D, §II).

1. U.S. Government Accountability Office, *Financial Regulation: A Framework for Crafting and Assessing Proposals to Modernize the Outdated U.S. Financial Regulatory System* (GAO-09-216, Jan. 8, 2009), *available at* 2009 WL 52168.

2. *Id.* At 2.

3. In March 2009 testimony before a Senate Banking Committee hearing and in a speech before the national convention of the Independent Community Bankers of America, FDIC Chairman Sheila Bair criticized the "too big to fail" concept and argued that it should be eliminated. *See* http://www.fdic.gov/news/news/speeches/chairman/spmar2009_2.html (posting Bair's prepared remarks). *See also* Thecla Fabian, *Bair Seeks New Playbook to Resolve Plight of 'Too Big to Fail' Financial Institutions*, BNA Banking Daily (Mar. 23, 2009) (reporting on Chairman Bair's remarks).

4. Stephen Labaton & Edmund L. Andrews, *In Rescue to Stabilize Lending, U.S. Takes Over Mortgage Finance Titans*, N.Y. Times, Sept. 8, 2008, at A1.

elimination of the value of private investment in the each of the two enterprises.

On September 22, 2008, the Fed announced that Morgan Stanley and Goldman Sachs Group would convert immediately from investment banks to BHCs.[6] The move would, on the one hand, subject the firms to Fed supervision, but it would also give them access to Fed credit facilities, and the extensive liquidity and funding resource of deposit-taking. There is no indication so far that the Fed has utilized its extensive supervisory authority over BHCs to shape the behavior of these investment banks. American Express followed the same path to BHC status in November 2008, again with no specific constraints on its behavior.[7]

The first major congressional response to the crisis, the Housing and Economic Recovery Act of 2008 (HERA)[8] evidences a concern with the supervisory implications of the crisis. The principal supervisory response of the

---

6. Malini Manickavasagam & Joe Tinkelman, *Changing Face of Wall Street, Goldman, Morgan Become Banks, BNA Banking Daily* (Sept. 23, 2008), *available at* http://pubs.bna.com/ip/bna/bbd.nsf/eh/A0B7C3F1Y3.

7. *See* Eric Dash, *American Express to Become a Bank to Access the Bailout*, N.Y. Times, Nov. 11, 2008, at B2 (reporting on American Express reorganization as BHC, in order to gain eligibility to Fed financial assistance).

8. Pub. L. No. 110-289, div. A (Federal Housing Finance Regulatory Reform Act of 2008), §§1001-1605, 122 Stat. 2654, 2659-2830 (July 30, 2008) (codified at 5 U.S.C. §§ 3132 note, 3132(a)(1)(B), (D)-(F), 5313, app. 3 § 11, 11 U.S.C. § 783, 12 U.S.C. §§ 250, 1422(11)-(12), 1423-1424, 1426(a)(3)(A), (B), (b)(1), (c)(4)(B), (d)(2), 1426a, 1427(a)-(d), (f), (i)(1), (l), 1428, 1430(a)-(b), (j)(2)(A), (B)-(C), (12)(C)-(D), (k), 1430c, 1431(b)-(c), (f), (l), 1432, 1435, 1436, 1440, 1440a, 1441(b)(5), 1441a-1441b, 1442-1446, 1452 note, 1452(a)(2)(A)-(C), (b)(2), (d)(4), (h)(2), (4), 1454 note, 1454(a)(2), 1455(c)(2), (i), (j)(2), (l), 1456(e)-(f), 1701 note, 1701x note, 1708(e)(5), 1715z-23, 1717 note, 1717(b)(2), 1718(c)(2), 1719(g), 1723 note, 1723(b), 1723a(d) (3)(B), (k)(1), (m)-(n), 1787(c)(10(C)(i), 1813(I), 1820(d)(5)(B), 1821(d)(2)(F), (G), (e)(10)(C)(i), (m)(1), (6), (9), (15)-(16), (18), (n)(1)(A)-(B)(i), (E), (2)(A), (4)(C)-(D), (H), (5)(D), (8)(A)-(B), (11)-(13), (t)(2)(A)(vii), 1822, 1831o(j)(2), 1833(a)(3), (b)-(c), 3413(o), 4501 note, 4502(2), (8)-(11), (13), (19)-(20), (24)-(31), 4511 note, 4511-4513, 4513a, 4513b, 4514, 4514a, 4515(a), (c)-(f), 4516-4521, 4523-4526, 4541-4548, 4561-4569, 4581-4588, 4588(c), 4611, 4612(a)-(f), 4613 note, 4613(a)-(b), 4614 note, 4614(a)-(f), 4615(b)(1)-(2), (c), 4616(a)(2), (b)(5), (7), (c), 4617, 4618, 4619(a)(3), 4622-4623(a)(1), 4624 note, 4624, 4631(a)-(e), 4632(a)-(e), 4633, 4634(a), 4635(a)-(b), 4636(a)-(d), (g), 4636a, 4636b, 4637-4642, 4715(a)(1), (4)-(5), 4716, 5101 note, 5101-5116, 15 U.S.C. §§ 78oo, 1639a, 7215(b)(5)(B)(ii)(II), 18 U.S.C. §§ 212, 657, 1006, 1014, 1905, 26 U.S.C. § 414(l)(2)(G), 42 U.S.C. §§1437f note, 4012a(f)(3)(A), 44 U.S.C. § 3502(5); *redesignating* 12 U.S.C. § 1422(2)-(9), (12)-(13) as § 1422(1)-(10); *redesignating* 12 U.S.C. § 4502(2)-(7), (8)-(12), (16)-(19) as § 4502(5)-(7), (12), (14)-(18), (21)-(23); *redesignating* 12 U.S.C. § 4614(c)-(d) as § 4614(d), (f); *redesignating* 12 U.S.C. § 4616(b)(5) as § 4616(b)(6); *redesignating* 12 U.S.C. § 4715(a)(1)-(2) as § 4715(a)(2)-(3); *repealing* 12 U.S.C. §§ 1422(1), (9)-(10), 1422a-1422b, 1427(f)(2), 1438(b), 1451 note, 4502(13)-(15), 4520(b), 4541, 4542, 4547-4548, 4562 note, 4589, 4616(b)(6), 4619-4621, 42 U.S.C. § 3534(d)). . . .

HERA was the transfer of the supervisory and oversight responsibilities of the Office of Federal Housing Enterprise Oversight (OFHEO) over Fannie Mae and Freddie Mac[9] and the oversight responsibilities of the FHFB over the FHLBanks and the Office of Finance (which acts as the FHLBanks' fiscal agent) to a new independent executive branch agency, the Federal Housing Finance Agency (FHFA).[10]

In November 2008, the OCC created a new procedure for chartering – a "shelf charter" – that allows a well-capitalized investor group to prequalify for a national bank charter, so that the group may actively compete in FDIC auctions of troubled institutions, secure in the knowledge that the group already has preliminary approval for a national charter into which it would fold the acquired entity.[11] If the FDIC accepts an investor group bid, the OCC would almost invariably grant a final charter, and if the bid is not accepted, the preliminary approval of the charter remains "on the shelf" to be used for other bids for up to 18 months.[12]

In February 2009, the interested regulators – Treasury, the OCC, the Fed, the FDIC, and the OTS, but not the NCUA – unveiled the details of Treasury's Capital Assistance Plan (CAP),[13] which required "stress testing"[14] of, primarily, the 19 largest U.S. banking enterprises that hold more than $100 billion in assets. The release of the results of the stress tests on May 7, 2009, indicated that 10 of the largest U.S. banking enterprises would need more capital to withstand worse-than-expected economic conditions (*see infra*

---

9. *See, e.g.*, 74 Fed. Reg. 2347 (Jan 15, 2009) (codified at 12 C.F.R. pt. 1250) (codifying FHFA authority and responsibility to oversee and enforce statutory requirements affecting flood insurance operations of Federal National Mortgage Association and Federal Home Loan Mortgage Corporation under the Flood Disaster Protection Act of 1973 (FDPA); implementing congressionally mandated adjustments to the civil money penalties applicable to violations of FDPA; replacing prior HUD regulations, 12 C.F.R. pt. 1773).

10. *See* Federal Housing Finance Agency, *Establishment of a New Independent Agency*, 73 Fed. Reg. 52,356 (2008) (announcing establishment). . . .

11. Mike Ferullo, *OCC Move to Create 'Shelf Charter' for Investors Welcomed by Banking Industry,* BNA BANKING DAILY (Nov. 26, 2008), *available at* http://www.bna.com.

12. *Id.*

13. For background information on the CAP, *see* http://www.treas.gov/press/releases/tg40. htm. *See also* R. Christian Bruce, *Capital Plan Gives Bank Firms Six Months to Raise Private Funds Following New Tests*, BNA BANKING DAILY (Feb. 26, 2009), *available at* http://news.bna.com (discussing CAP).

14. *I.e.*, submission to "forward-looking economic assessments" that will test the ability of a subject enterprise to function and lend under two different macroeconomic scenarios: (i) a "consensus estimate" that forecasts an economic upturn in 2010; and (ii) a further significant economic downturn, factoring in an environment with unemployment as high as 10.3 percent. For the methodology used in the stress tests, *see* http://www.federalreserve.gov/newsevents/ press/bcreg/bcreg20090424a1.pdf.

Figure 11.14), assuming a requirement of a tier 1 risk-based ratio of at least 6 percent, of which at least 4 percent must be common equity by the end of 2010.[15] The banks have 30 days to develop capital plans and six months to complete recapitalization. Stressed banking enterprises that fail to raise enough private capital would then be eligible for a federal capital injection if the pertinent supervisor approved. Enterprises that have already received funds under the CPP, which involved Treasury purchases of nonvoting preferred bank shares with a 5 percent dividend, will be permitted to exchange those shares for the new CAP instruments – convertible 9 percent preferred shares, convertible, at the issuer's option, to common stock equity.

Overall, it is clear that the financial services system is under critical stress. Recent failures of large and small insured institutions have increased significantly the Deposit Insurance Fund's loss provisions, with a resulting decline in the DIF reserve ratio. As of the end of Q2 2008, the reserve ratio was 1.01 percent, 18 basis points below the reserve ratio as of the end of Q1 2008.[16] This is the lowest reserve ratio for a combined bank and thrift insurance fund since March 31, 1995. In light of current expectations that insured institution failures will continue at a significant rate in the next few years, one may anticipate that the reserve ratio will continue to decline. Accordingly, the FDIC has established a restoration plan for the reserve ratio, to 1.15 percent within five years.

Figure 11.14 2009 Stress Test Results – 10 Most Critical

Enterprise	Capital Needs under Stress (in $billions)
Bank of America Corp.	$33.9
Wells Fargo & Co.	$13.7
GMAC LLC	$11.5
Citigroup Inc.	$5.5
Regions Financial Corp.	$2.5
SunTrust Banks Inc.	$2.2
Morgan Stanley & Co. Inc.	$1.8
KeyCorp	$1.8
FifthThird Bancorp	$1.1
PNC Financial Services Group Inc.	$0.6

In light of current financial crisis, the NCUA has been evaluating the role

---

15. For stress test results, *see* http://www.federalreserve.gov/newsevents/press/bcreg/bcreg 20090507a1.pdf.

16. *Federal Deposit Insurance Corporation Restoration Plan*, 73 Fed. Reg. 61,598, 61,598 (October 16, 2008).

that corporate credit unions play in the credit union system.[17] . . . The Federal Credit Union Act (FCUA) authorizes natural person federal credit unions (FCUs) to invest in the shares or deposits of central, or "corporate," credit unions.[19] A "corporate credit union" is an organization, chartered under the FCUA or under applicable state law as a credit union that receives shares from and provides loan and other services primarily to other credit unions.[20] Historically, corporate credit unions (currently 28 institutions) have provided approximately 7,900 credit unions with payment and clearing services, including access to wire transfer facilities and automated clearinghouse transactions, investment services, short- and medium-term credit facilities, and service as agents on behalf of NCUA Central Liquidity Facility (CLF) in connection with loans funded by the CLF. Corporate credit unions also have provided other operational services, such as coin and currency services and safekeeping of investments.[21] Since 2008, many corporate credit unions have seen dramatic reductions in the value of their investment portfolios, and that situation is undermining the stability of the corporate credit union system.[22] In addition to the evaluation of the system, the NCUA Board also has taken more immediate, remedial steps designed to stabilize the corporate system, including a $1 billion infusion of capital into U.S. Central Federal Credit Union, the corporate system's wholesale credit union, by the National Credit Union Share Insurance Fund (NCUSIF), and a temporary NCUSIF guarantee of all member shares, for any corporate credit union that decides to participate in a voluntary guarantee program offered by NCUA.[23]

NOTES AND QUESTIONS

1. *Evaluating the Government's Responses.* Of the various governmental responses to the crisis to date – transactional, regulatory, supervisory – which seem most effective in relieving the crisis conditions? Does the answer to this question depend upon the perceived objectives – easing the credit crunch at the wholesale or retail level? Saving the too-big-to-fail institutions? Preventing

---

17. 74 Fed. Reg. 6004 (2009) (to be codified at 12 C.F.R. pt. 704).

19. 12 U.S.C. §1757(7)(G).

20. 12 C.F.R. §704.2.

21. 74 Fed. Reg. at 6004.

22. *Id.* at 6005.

23. *Id. See also* 74 Fed. Reg. 25,777 (2009) (revising and extending NCUA Temporary Corporate Credit Union Liquidity Guarantee Program, to allow participating corporate credit unions to issue program-guaranteed debt from July 1, 2009 through June 30, 2010 that matures on or before June 30, 2017, and modifying prices for NCUSIF guarantee, regardless whether debt was issued before or after June 30, 2009).

future crises of this sort?

2. *TARP Operations.* On January 8, 2009, Treasury released the latest in a series of reports required under EESA concerning TARP expenditures.[29] Recent transactions have raised total TARP transactions to $266.9 billion, including $177.54 billion under CPP. According to a Financial Services Roundtable Lending Report, 9 of the 20 recipients of the largest amount of CPP financing increased lending in February 2009 as compared to January.[30] Mortgage originations for the period increased 30 percent overall (from $78 billion to $102 billion) among those 20 recipients. All other lending decreased during the period, from $243 billion to $231 billion. However, efforts to oversee the use of TARP aid delivered to financial institutions has been impeded by Treasury, according to Prof. Warren, chair of the Congressional Oversight Panel, and others charged with overseeing TARP.[31]

3. *Impact of EESA.* Aside from pouring government investment into the troubled financial institutions, what effect has EESA actually had on the crisis? In the following case excerpt, to what extent does the act have a significant impact on the outcome?

WACHOVIA CORP. v. CITIGROUP, INC.

---

634 F.Supp.2d 445 (S.D.N.Y. 2009)

SHIRA A. SCHEINDLIN, District Judge.

[Wachovia, a bank holding company with a troubled bank subsidiary was involved in FDIC-facilitated negotiations for its acquisition by one bidder, Citigroup, when it announced a merger with a subsequent bidder, Wells Fargo. Wachovia initiated suit for a declaratory judgment that the merger was valid and did not violate an exclusivity agreement with Citigroup. Citgroup moved for partial judgment on the pleadings. The district court denied the motion, holding that: (*i*) under EESA, the exclusivity agreement could not prevent the merger; (*ii*) the exclusivity agreement was unenforceable against Wachovia, not just against Wells Fargo; and, (*iii*) EESA was applicable to the exclusivity agreement even though the agreement existed prior to its enactment.]

---

29. http://www.treas.gov/initiatives/eesa/docs/Fourth-Tranche-Report.pdf.

30. http://www.fsround.org/askew/pdfs/LendingSurveyforFebruary2009.doc.pdf. *See also* Thecla Fabian, *Almost Half of Top 20 CPP Recipients Increased Lending; Mainly in Mort-gages,* BNA BANKING DAILY (Apr. 21, 2009), *available at* http://www.bna.com (discussing Financial Services Roundtable survey).

31. Brett Ferguson, *Auditors Blast Treasury as Uncooperative in Efforts to Improve TARP Accountability,* BNA BANKING DAILY (Apr. 1, 2009), *available at* http://www.bna.com.

II. BACKGROUND

A. The Citigroup Transaction and Wells Fargo Proposal . . .

On September 29, 2008, upon finding that "the liquidation of the insured depository institution subsidiaries of Wachovia Corporation [ ], as well as the likely consequent failure of Wachovia Corporation, would have serious adverse effects on economic conditions or financial stability and would create systemic risk to the credit markets," the board of the Federal Deposit Insurance Corporation ("FDIC") voted to authorize financial assistance to facilitate Citigroup's acquisition of Wachovia pursuant to section 13(c)(2) of the Federal Deposit Insurance Act ("FDIA")[, 12 U.S.C. § 1823(c)(4)(G)(i)]. To ensure the success of this transaction, the board also voted to recommend that the Secretary of the Treasury invoke the "systemic risk" provision of section 13 of the FDIA, which authorized the FDIC to "take other action or provide assistance [ ] as necessary to avoid or mitigate [serious adverse effects on economic conditions or financial stability]."

That same day, Wachovia and Citigroup entered into a non-binding agreement-in-principle whereby Citigroup would acquire the operations of Wachovia for approximately $2.1 billion, or $1 per Wachovia share ("Citigroup Transaction"). The FDIC informed the parties that if a transaction was not completed by October 6, Wachovia would be forced into receivership.

Citigroup and Wachovia also entered into an agreement that, *inter alia,* prohibited Wachovia from soliciting any acquisition proposals from third parties or entering into negotiations with any third party for the purpose of securing an acquisition proposal ("Exclusivity Agreement"). The agreement was set to expire on 12:00 a.m. on October 6, 2008.

In the evening of October 2, 2008, as Wachovia continued negotiations with Citigroup, Wells Fargo made an unsolicited offer to acquire Wachovia. The proposal provided that Wells Fargo would acquire all of Wachovia for $15 billion, or approximately $7 per Wachovia share ("Wells Fargo Transaction"). Also, under the terms of the proposal, FDIC assistance would not be necessary. Sometime during the night of October 2, 2008, the Wachovia board approved the proposal by Wells Fargo. A definitive merger agreement was signed in the morning of October 3, 2008, and the merger was announced to the public prior to the opening of the markets that day.

B. Section 126(c) of the Emergency Economic Stabilization Act

The Emergency Economic Stabilization Act ("EESA" or "the Act") was signed into law on the same day that the Wells Fargo Transaction was announced – October 3, 2008. One of the purposes of the Act is "to immediately provide authority and facilities that the Secretary of the Treasury can use to restore liquidity and stability to the financial system of the United States ."

[EESA § 2.] Section 126(c) of the Act[, 12 U.S.C. § 1823(c)(11),] provides [for the unenforceability, as "contrary to public policy," of any provision in any existing or future standstill, confidentiality, or other agreement that, directly or indirectly, "affects, restricts, or limits," or prohibits, any person from offering or acquiring, or from using any previously disclosed information in connection with such offering or acquiring, all or part of any insured depository institution, in connection with any transaction in which the FDIC exercises authority.]

C. Litigation Among Citigroup, Wells Fargo, and Wachovia

After the Wells Fargo Transaction was announced, Citigroup publicly denounced the transaction, arguing that Wells Fargo interfered with the Exclusivity Agreement and asserting that the transaction was "improper, unenforceable and prohibited by the agreement." On October 4, 2008, Citigroup filed an action against Wachovia and Wells Fargo in New York state court, alleging claims of breach of contract against Wachovia and tortious interference with contract against Wells Fargo.[20]

That same day, Wachovia filed the instant action against Citigroup, seeking a declaratory judgment that the Wells Fargo Transaction is "valid, proper and not prohibited by the [Exclusivity] Agreement." Among other grounds, Wachovia contends that section 126(c) of the EESA renders the Exclusivity Agreement unenforceable.[22] Citigroup now moves for partial judgment on the pleadings under Rule 12(c), contending that section 126(c) of the EESA does not interfere with the enforceability of the Exclusivity Agreement.

III. LEGAL STANDARD . . .

C. Retroactivity

When a case implicates a federal statute enacted after the events in suit, the court's first task is to determine whether Congress has expressly prescribed the statute's proper reach. If Congress has done so, [ ] there is no need to resort to judicial default rules. When, however, the statute contains no such express command, the court must determine whether the new statute would have retroactive effect, *i.e.,*

---

20. . . . Although Wells Fargo and Wachovia removed the action to this Court, the case has since been remanded to state court for lack of federal jurisdiction. *See Citigroup, Inc. v. Wachovia Corp.*, 613 F.Supp.2d 485, 2009 WL 749864 (S.D.N.Y. Mar.20, 2009).

22. . . . Wachovia also contends that the Exclusivity Agreement interferes with the fiduciary obligations of Wachovia's directors to consider, negotiate, and approve other acquisition proposals that might be superior to the Citigroup Transaction and is therefore unenforceable under state law. . . .

whether it would impair rights a party possessed when [it] acted, increase a party's liability for past conduct, or impose new duties with respect to transactions already completed. If the statute would operate retroactively, our traditional presumption teaches that it does not govern absent clear congressional intent favoring such a result.[23]

IV. DISCUSSION

A. Statutory Language

Both parties argue that the language of section 126(c) supports their respective positions. Citigroup contends that Congress' use of certain terms and phrases in section 126(c) of the EESA makes clear that the provision only applies to render unenforceable agreements that hinder third parties from making offers to acquire a bank when the transaction of such parties is assisted by the FDIC pursuant to section 13 of the FDIA. In other words, Citigroup asserts that the "offer to acquire" must be "in connection with" a "transaction in which the FDIC exercises its authority." Because the Wells Fargo Transaction was not assisted by the FDIC, section 126(c) does not apply.

Citigroup further contends that although the Citigroup Transaction was assisted by the FDIC, section 126(c), by its terms, does not apply to the Exclusivity Agreement that was entered into for the benefit of the Citigroup Transaction. Citigroup asserts that the use of the present tense in "exercises" indicates that section 126(c) "protects only those bank acquisitions that are in connection with a contemporaneous exercise of § 11 or § 13 authority by the FDIC." Because the FDIC had already *exercised* its authority under section 13 by offering to give assistance to the proposed Citigroup Transaction, Citigroup argues that the "transaction" in section 126(c) cannot refer to the Citigroup Transaction.

Moreover, Citigroup contends that Wells Fargo's offer to acquire or acquisition cannot be "in connection with" a transaction in which the FDIC exercises section 13 authority because the phrase "in connection with" in section 126(c) should be read consistently with use of the same phrase in securities law, where it indicates a causal relationship. Citigroup therefore contends that the inclusion of "in connection with" in section 126(c) indicates that "the offer to acquire or acquisition must be an integral part of the process leading to the transaction in which the FDIC exercises its § 11 or § 13 authority." Because the Wells Fargo Transaction had no FDIC assistance, but rather followed a commitment of FDIC assistance to a different entity, the "transaction" referred to in that provision cannot be the Wells Fargo Transaction.

---

23. *Landgraf v. USI Film Prods.*, 511 U.S. 244, 280 (1994).

Finally, Citigroup argues that the term "transaction" cannot refer generally to the sale of Wachovia and must instead refer to a "specific deal" because the "FDIC cannot perform its duties under this section except in the context of a specific deal." As a result, if section 126(c) is referring to *any* transaction between Wachovia and either of the two acquirer banks, Citigroup maintains, it must be referring to the Citigroup Transaction.

Wachovia does not dispute that the Citigroup Transaction was the only transaction that received approval of FDIC assistance pursuant to section 13 of the FDIA. Nevertheless, Wachovia contends that the FDIC exercised its authority pursuant to section 13 not only when the FDIC offered assistance to the Citigroup Transaction, but also throughout the process as it facilitated the competitive bidding of Wells Fargo and Citigroup over Wachovia. Thus, Wachovia contends, the "transaction" referred to in section 126(c) is not merely the Citigroup Transaction, but is "extended to the entire FDIC-supervised 'transaction' in which the Wachovia crisis was resolved by a sale to Wells [Fargo]." Consistent with this interpretation, Wells Fargo's offer to acquire or acquisition is undoubtedly "in connection with" a sale of Wachovia, and therefore section 126(c) applies.

Wachovia argues alternatively that even if this Court takes a narrow view of "transaction," concluding that this term applies only to the Citigroup Transaction, the Court should nevertheless interpret the phrase "in connection with" broadly. Wachovia argues that an interpretation of "in connection with" to mean "some relationship or association" would be consistent with case law and dictionary definitions.[57] Because "the Exclusivity Agreement unquestionably had the effect of limiting other offers 'in connection with' [the Citigroup Transaction]," it "falls squarely within § 126(c)'s reach."[58]

As a preliminary observation, Wachovia does not dispute that the "transaction" referred to in section 126(c) is one in which the FDIC *exercises* section 13 authority. The difference in interpretations stems from the divergent meanings the parties ascribe to two key terms – "transaction" and "in connection with." I must therefore resolve this disagreement in order to rule on this

---

57. [*See*] *United States v. Loney,* 219 F.3d 281, 284 (3d Cir.2000) ("[T]he phrase 'in connection with' expresses some relationship or association . . . that can be satisfied in a number of ways such as a causal or logical relation or other type of relationship."); American Heritage Dictionary 390 (4th ed.2000) (defining "connection" as "an association or relationship")).

58. . . . Wachovia also notes that section 126(c) can be read another way – instead of the phrase "in connection with" modifying the "offer to acquire," the phrase "in connection with" may also modify "provision" or "agreement." . . . If section 126(c) is read this way, any provision or agreement in connection with a transaction in which the FDIC exercises its authority would be unenforceable. Wachovia argues that this reading would also support its position because section 126(c) would prevent the Exclusivity Agreement entered into for the purpose of the Citigroup Transaction from being enforced. . . .

motion.

Citigroup observes that the term "transaction" exists elsewhere in section 13 of the FDIA, and that an examination of its uses indicates that "transaction" must refer to a specific deal. For instance, Citigroup notes that under the least-cost provision of section 13, "the FDIC must assess '[f]ederal tax revenues that the Government would forego as the result of a proposed *transaction*. . . .'"[59] Citigroup argues that the FDIC cannot determine tax revenues without an "identifiable" transaction. Citigroup also points to the use of the term "transactions" in "Purchase and assumption *transactions,*" the heading of section 1823(c)(4)(E) (iii).

Citigroup also argues that in a section 1823 note, Congress had provided that "'the *transaction* [in which the FDIC rescues a troubled bank] should involve substantial private investment'"[63] and that "'the [same] *transaction* should give the [FDIC] an opportunity to participate in the success of the resulting institution.'"[64] Finally, Citigroup notes that Congress also provided that "'[t]he *transaction* should be *negotiated competitively'*" and argues therefore that the "transaction results from the competitive negotiation; it is not negotiation itself."[65]

While Citigroup is correct that terms should be presumed to share a meaning when they appear in the same section of a statute, Citigroup fails to explain why the term "transaction" cannot refer generally to the competitive sale of Wachovia. As Wachovia explains, section 1823(c)(4)(B)(ii) – which refers to foregone tax revenues – does not require an identifiable purchaser, but only directs the FDIC to assess tax revenues foregone as the result of the accrual of tax-deductible losses to the entity that ultimately purchases Wachovia. In addition, the heading of section 1823(c)(4)(E)(iii) says nothing about the meaning of "transaction." The same could be said of the use of "transaction" in the section 1823 note. Congress was merely providing that the sale of a failing bank should include "substantial private investment," should "give the [FDIC] an opportunity to participate in the success of the resulting institution," and should be competitively negotiated.

At most, the use of the word "transaction" in these provisions suggests the unremarkable proposition that the word "transaction" is qualified by the words surrounding it.[66] Applying this statutory rule to section 126(c), the word "transaction" refers to a transaction "in which the FDIC exercises its authority

---

59. . . . quoting 12 U.S.C. § 1823(c)(4)(E)(iii) [(emphasis added)].

63. . . . quoting 12 U.S.C. § 1823 Note, *Early Resolution of Troubled Insured Depository Institutions* ("Section 1823 Note"), § 143(b)(3) (1991) [(emphasis added)].

64. . . . quoting Section 1823 Note, § 143(b)(6)) [(emphasis added)].

65. . . . quoting Section 1823 Note, § 143(b)(1)) [(emphasis added)].

66. For example, *"proposed* transaction" and *"purchase and assumption* transactions."

under section [ ] 13."[67] Thus, in order to define "transaction," I must determine when the FDIC exercises its authority.

At oral argument, Citigroup argued that section 1823(c)(2)(A)(iii) was the authority that the FDIC had exercised with respect to the Citigroup Transaction. That section states:

> In order to facilitate a merger or consolidation of an insured depository institution [which is in danger of default or which threatens the stability of a significant number of institutions] with another insured depository institution [ ], the Corporation is authorized, in its sole discretion and upon such terms and conditions as the Board of Directors may prescribe to guarantee such other insured depository institution or the company which controls or will acquire control of such other insured depository institution against loss by reason of such insured institution's merging or consolidating with or assuming the liabilities and purchasing the assets of such insured depository institution or by reason of such company acquiring control of such insured depository institution.

Thus, Citigroup contends, the FDIC exercised its authority pursuant to section 13 of the FDIA when it voted to provide assistance in the form of a guarantee to the Citigroup Transaction.

However, read strictly, the provision appears to indicate that the FDIC exercises its authority when it *actually* provides assistance – in this case, when it guarantees the acquirer's losses. Although the FDIC had *approved* such assistance on September 29, 2008, the guarantee would not have been put in place until after Citigroup and Wachovia had consummated the transaction in a binding agreement. Such agreement had not been signed by the time Wells Fargo made its offer. Citigroup's position therefore finds no support in this provision.

In addition, although Citigroup discusses the FDIC's exercise of authority to provide financial assistance to the Citigroup Transaction, it fails to mention that the FDIC may also exercise authority pursuant to the "systemic risk" provision of section 13, which was invoked by the Secretary of the Treasury upon the recommendation of the FDIC. The "systemic risk" provision allows the FDIC to act contrary to its "least-cost" obligations under section 13, which require the FDIC to provide financial assistance only when it has determined that the assistance is the least costly of all possible methods for protecting a bank against the possibility of default.[71] Invocation of the "systemic risk" provision by the Secretary of the Treasury permits the FDIC to "take other action or provide assistance [ ] as necessary to avoid or mitigate [adverse

---

67. 12 U.S.C. § 1823(c)(11).
71. *See* 12 U.S.C. § 1823(c)(4)(A)(ii).

effects on economic conditions or financial stability]."[72]

Citigroup contends that the declaration of systemic risk was made specifically in connection with the Citigroup Transaction. Indeed, the board of the FDIC recommended the invocation of this provision during the same meeting that it approved the provision of financial assistance to the Citigroup Transaction. However, when the systemic risk provision is read together with the least-cost resolution requirement, it becomes plain that the FDIC's priority was not the sale of Wachovia to Citigroup but the rescue of Wachovia using any necessary means. Interpreted in this way, the FDIC's exercise of authority pursuant to section 13 encompasses not only its guarantee of the Citigroup Transaction but also its participation in a broad range of actions necessary to rescuing Wachovia, including conducting a competitive sale of Wachovia.

Once it is established that the competitive sale of Wachovia was a "transaction in which the FDIC exercises its authority," then there is no need to define the breadth of the phrase "in connection with." There is no doubt that Wells Fargo's offer to acquire or acquisition was "in connection with" a sale of Wachovia, and therefore section 126(c) applies to render the Exclusivity Agreement unenforceable.

B. Purpose of Section 126(c)

The application of section 126(c) to this case is also consistent with its purpose. Consistent with the name of the statute, one of the purposes of the EESA is to "immediately" provide the "authority and facilities that the Secretary of the Treasury can use to restore the liquidity and stability to the financial system of the United States."[75] Section 126(c) was likely incorporated into section 13 of the FDIA in order to accord the FDIC the authority to aid the Secretary of the Treasury in achieving such liquidity and stability by removing obstacles to bank consolidation.

The provision's purpose may also be gleaned from an examination of the historical context surrounding the enactment of the EESA. In the weeks leading to the enactment of the EESA, Lehman Brothers had been forced into bankruptcy, Merrill Lynch was sold to Bank of America, Fannie Mae and Freddie Mac were seized and subsequently controlled by the Treasury Department, and AIG received a bailout from the federal government. At the end of September 2008, Washington Mutual's bank subsidiary was put into FDIC receivership and involuntarily sold to J.P. Morgan Chase.

There is no dispute that the nation was confronted by an alarming banking crisis. The EESA was enacted on October 3 in this economic climate. Read

---

72. *Id.* § 1823(c)(4)(G)(i).
75. EESA § 2.

with this historical context in mind, section 126(c)'s purpose was to give the FDIC the full flexibility to rescue troubled banks.

Citigroup agrees that the purpose of section 126(c) was to afford the FDIC significant discretion, but argues that the provision applies only to the benefit of those bidders participating in an FDIC-assisted bank rescue. Citigroup asserts that Congress did not intend to permit "a virtually endless form of open bidding to displace an FDIC-engineered rescue." In other words, Citigroup argues that allowing a non-FDIC supervised transaction to interfere with the progress of an FDIC-supervised transaction would conflict with the purpose of section 126(c).

It would be unreasonable indeed to interpret section 126(c) in a way that would allow a non-FDIC-supervised transaction to interfere with one that is engineered by the FDIC. Nonetheless, when the term "transaction" in section 126(c) is interpreted to refer to the sale of Wachovia, Citigroup's reasoning loses much of its power. Read in this way, the Wells Fargo Transaction was part of an FDIC-supervised rescue and therefore was permitted to benefit from section 126(c).

Citigroup proffers a number of arguments in support of its belief that Congress wished to preserve deal protections in FDIC-assisted transactions. *First,* Citigroup notes that "[t]he government did not need § 126(c) to keep deal protection mechanisms out of FDIC-assisted transactions. The FDIC could simply decline to support a transaction involving such provisions, or condition approval on their deletion, if they would disserve the public interest." However, the fact that the FDIC supported the Citigroup Transaction notwithstanding the Exclusivity Agreement and that it failed to condition approval of the Citigroup Transaction on its deletion says nothing about its approval of the Exclusivity Agreement itself. In addition, section 126(c) is necessary because in its absence, bidders who participate in an FDIC-supervised transaction would be subject to liability pursuant to an Exclusivity Agreement arising out of a non-FDIC-supervised transaction.

Second, Citigroup contends that Congress did not intend for section 126(c) to render unenforceable exclusivity agreements in FDIC-assisted transactions because doing so "would make it more difficult for the FDIC to arrange successful rescues of failing banks." This argument is also unpersuasive. Citigroup overlooks that this interpretation would prevent the FDIC from agreeing to a subsequent, more attractive proposal. Citigroup's reading would make it more difficult for the FDIC to arrange a successful rescue.

Third, Citigroup asserts that reading section 126(c) to bar deal protections in FDIC-assisted transactions would discourage future bidders from making proposals to rescue failing banks. However – as Citigroup itself suggested – the FDIC has the power to prevent a future bidder from interfering with a transaction that it prefers. Other regulatory bodies – whose approval is required for the merger or acquisition of banking institutions – could also refuse to approve a less favorable transaction.[83]

C. Application of Section 126(c) to Wachovia

Having decided that section 126(c) applies to render the Exclusivity Agreement unenforceable, I turn to the next question: Is the Exclusivity Agreement unenforceable with respect to Wachovia?

Neither party disputes that the text of section 126(c) supports its application to protect subsequent bidders from liability. Subdivision (A) speaks of "the ability of any person to offer to acquire or acquire," and subdivision (B) discusses any person who is "offering to acquire or acquiring."[84] Later, the provision provides that no limiting agreement "shall be enforceable against or impose any liability on *such person.*" When read as a whole, "such person" must refer back to subdivision (A) and (B) to implicate parties that offer to acquire or are acquiring – in other words, bidders and acquirers.[86]

However, Congress also included a phrase at the end of the provision, explaining that enforcement of agreements such as standstill, confidentiality, and exclusivity agreements against subsequent bidders and the imposition of liability on those parties would be "contrary to public policy."[87] Congress clearly meant to exempt subsequent bidders or acquirers from penalties for interfering with a transaction that is protected by an agreement such as the Exclusivity Agreement at issue here.

Because Wells Fargo acquired all of Wachovia, imposing liability on Wachovia would be equivalent to penalizing Wells Fargo. For instance, a remedy of specific performance would invalidate the Wells Fargo Transaction, thereby injuring not only Wachovia, but also Wells Fargo. A judgment invalidating the Wells Fargo Transaction would have the same effect. Any imposition of contract damages on Wachovia would effectively be an imposition of damages on Wells Fargo. Interpreting the provision in this way

---

83. This would eliminate the unattractive scenarios that Citigroup projects – for instance, when a subsequent bidder is less financially sound than a bidder that the FDIC supports; when the subsequent bidder's proposal requires more taxpayer money; and when a subsequent bidder must rely on monetary assistance from the federal government to effect a merger transaction. . . .

84. 12 U.S.C. § 1823(c)(11).

86. Subdivision (C) is more ambiguous and discusses a person that is "using any previously disclosed information in connection with any such offer to acquire." 12 U.S.C. § 1823(c)(11) (C). The "person" referred to here could theoretically include an acquiree. However, when subdivision (C) is read in conjunction with the other subdivisions, it is most plausible to interpret that subdivision to also refer to acquirers.

87. 12 U.S.C. § 1823(c)(11).

would defeat the purpose of section 126(c) and produce an absurd result.[88] I therefore find that section 126(c) renders the Exclusivity Agreement unenforceable with respect not only to Wells Fargo, but also Wachovia.

D. Retroactivity

Finally, Citigroup contends that the EESA "should not be read to retroactively immunize conduct that preceded EESA's enactment." As noted, the EESA was enacted on October 3, 2008 – after the Exclusivity Agreement was signed and after Wells Fargo submitted its bid.

Citigroup concedes that "Congress does appear to have prescribed one retroactive effect in saying that some provisions in 'existing' contracts shall not be enforceable." Nevertheless, Citigroup asserts that at the time of the EESA's enactment, a cause of action for breach of contract and tortious interference with contract had already accrued. It argues that Wachovia's construction of section 126(c) would have the retroactive effect of extinguishing causes of action that accrued prior to the EESA's enactment.

However, Citigroup cannot escape the conclusion that Congress intended for the provision to apply retroactively because the provision expressly applies to "existing" contracts. In addition, section 126(c) impairs the *enforceability* of the Exclusivity Agreement. Even if it is true that Citigroup's cause of action accrued prior to the EESA's enactment, there is no dispute that Citigroup brought its *enforcement* action on October 4 *after* the enactment of the statute. Section 126(c) therefore properly applies to bar enforcement of the Exclusivity Agreement.[93]

NOTES AND QUESTIONS

1. *Constitutional Concerns.* Does EESA impermissibly interfere with – or "take" – Citigroup's contract rights? *See Lingle v. Chevron U.S.A. Inc.*, 544 U.S. 528, 538-545 (2005) (discussing alternative tests for "regulatory taking" of contract rights). Of course, the Supreme Court has frequently stressed that

---

88. . . . I do note that even in a partial acquisition, although a remedy of specific performance would still injure a subsequent bidder by invalidating its acquisition of a target, the imposition of contract damages on the target would not penalize the acquirer. I leave this question for another court on another day.

93. There may be constitutional concerns with respect to applying section 126(c) to render the Exclusivity Agreement unenforceable. However, the parties have agreed that those constitutional issues will be the subject of a subsequent motion. I therefore do not address them here.

almost any contract is susceptible to government regulation,[32] and as a result any contracting party should be aware that future government regulation could affect the value of contractual rights.[33]

2. *Contract Concerns.* The FDIC agreed to provide financial assistance to facilitate Citigroup's acquisition of Wachovia pursuant to 12 U.S.C. § 1823(c)(4)(G)(I). Did this create compensable rights in Citigroup that the government triggered when it enacted EESA? *Cf. United States v. Winstar Corporation,*[34] in which the Court upheld the enforceability of agreements between the Federal Home Loan Bank Board (through the Federal Savings and Loan Insurance Corporation) and each of three acquirers of failing savings associations, notwithstanding the subsequent enactment of more restrictive accounting rules mandated by the Financial Institutions Reform, Recovery, and Enforcement Act of 1989 (FIRREA).[35]

3. *Systemic Risks in the Credit Swap Market.* The OTC market for credit default swaps (CDS)[36] – operating without meaningful regulation, with little

---

32. *See, e.g., Lucas v. S.C. Coastal Council*, 505 U.S. 1003, 1027-1028 (1992); *Connolly v. Pension Benefit Guar. Corp.*, 475 U.S. 211, 223-224 (1986) (quoting *Norman v. Balt. & Ohio R.R. Co.*, 294 U.S. 240, 307-308 (1935)); *see also* Christopher Mayer, Edward Morrison & Tomasz Piskorski, *A New Proposal for Loan Modifications*, 26 YALE J. ON REG. 417, 424-425 (2009) (applying regulatory taking jurisprudence to proposal for resolving aspects of mortgage crisis).

33. *See, e.g., Lucas*, 505 U.S. at 1027-1028 (1992); *Connolly*, 475 U.S. at 223-224 (1986).

34. 518 U.S. 839 (1996).

35. Pub. L. No. 101-73, 103 Stat. 183 (1989). *See Winstar*, 518 U.S. at 856-858 (plurality) (discussing FIRREA). *See generally* Michael P. Malloy, *When You Wish Upon Winstar: Contract Analysis and the Future of Regulatory Action*, 42 ST. LOUIS U. L.J. 409 (1998) (discussing implication of *Winstar* for future regulatory action).

36. A CDS is a bilateral financial contract between two parties, known as counterparties. For the basic structure of the CDS, see Figure 1, *infra*. CDS were initially created to meet the demand of banking institutions looking to hedge and diversify the credit risk related to with their lending activities. More recently, financial institutions such as insurance companies, pension funds, securities firms and hedge funds have entered the CDS market. *See* Bank for International Settlements, *Semiannual OTC derivatives statistics at year-end 2007, available at* http://www.bis.org/statistics/otcder/dt1920a.pdf (noting recent rapid increase in CDS market volumes). The value of the contract is based on underlying obligations ("reference obligations") of a single entity (a "reference entity") or on a particular security or other debt obligation ("reference security"), or an index of several such entities, securities, or obligations. The obligation of the seller to make payments under a CDS contract is triggered by a default or other credit event as to such entity or entities or such security or securities. Investors may use CDS for a variety of reasons, for example to offset or insure against risk in their fixed-income portfolios, to take synthetic positions in bonds or in segments of the debt market as represented by an index, or to capitalize on the volatility in credit spreads during times of economic uncertainty.

According to a May 2009 report from the BIS, the total notional amount of OTC derivatives contracts outstanding at year-end 2008 was $592 trillion, representing a 13.6 percent decrease

Figure 1 Overview of CDS Contract

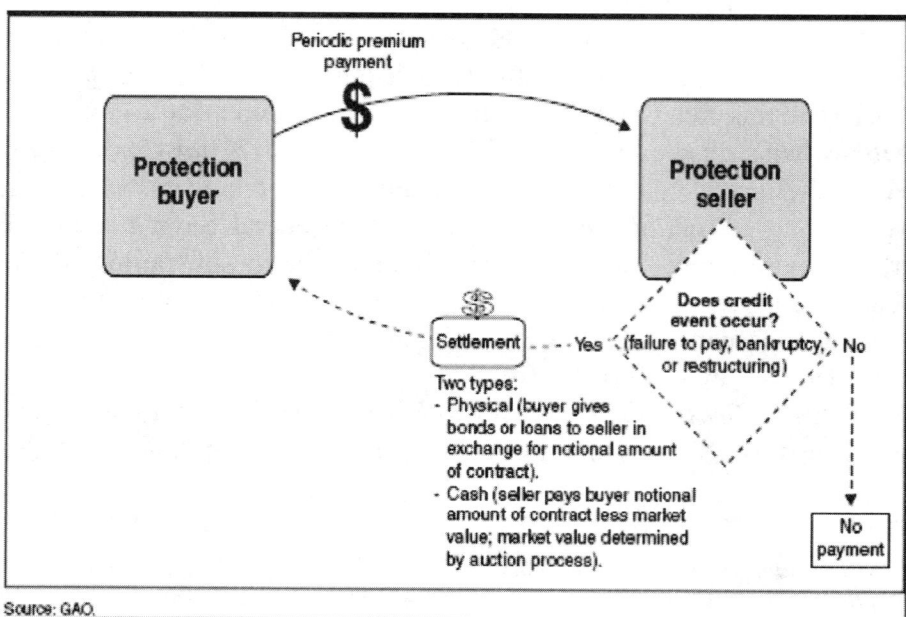

Source: GAO.

or no transparency,[37] and without central counterparties (CCPs) – has been a source of interrelated concerns for the SEC and the other financial regulators, including the systemic risk posed by CDS, the possible inability of counterparties to meet their obligations, the potential adverse effects on other markets and the financial system as a whole, in addition to operational risks, risks relating to manipulation and fraud,[38] and regulatory arbitrage risks.[39] Recent

---

from the Q2 2008 figures ($683.7 trillion). Daniel Pruzin, *BIS Cites Sharp Drop in Global OTC Trading of Financial Instruments in Second Half '08*, BNA INT'L BUS. & FIN. DAILY (May 19, 2009), *available at* http://www.bna.com. Disaggregated, the decline consisted of a 27 percent decrease in outstanding credit default swaps (CDS), an 8.6 percent decrease in OTC derivatives contracts outstanding in the interest rate market, and a 21 percent decrease in the foreign exchange market. *Id.* Most dramatically, commodity derivatives experienced a 66.5 percent drop in notional amounts outstanding in the same period, while outstanding contracts for equity derivatives decreased 36 percent. *Id.*

37. *Cf.* President's Working Group on Financial Markets, Policy Objectives for the OTC Derivatives Market (Nov. 14, 2008), *available at* http://www.ustreas.gov/press/releases/reports/policyobjectives.pdf (calling for "[p]ublic reporting of prices, trading volumes and aggregate open interest ... to increase market transparency for participants and the public") (hereinafter "Policy Objectives").

38. In May 2009, the SEC filed its first insider trading case involving CDS, alleging that a hedge fund portfolio manager and an employee at Deutsche Bank Securities Inc. (DBS) had illegally traded on information about bonds issued by VNU N.V., holding company of Nielsen Media and other media businesses. *SEC v. Negrin*, S.D.N.Y., No. 09-CV-4329 (May 5, 2009),

credit market events emphasized the need for CCPs to help mitigate systemic impacts.[40] In pursuit of this objective, the SEC, the Fed and the CFTC signed a Memorandum of Understanding[41] establishing a framework for consultation and information-sharing on issues related to CCPs for CDS. The interim final temporary rules are intended to facilitate the ability of one or more CCPs for CDS to operate, by providing exemptions from regulatory provisions that might otherwise prevent them from engaging in such activities. The operation of a well-regulated CCP could significantly reduce counterparty risks by preventing the failure of a single market participant from having a disproportionate effect on the overall market. A CCP would novate[42] bilateral trades, resulting in separate contractual arrangements undertaken by the CCP with each of the counterparties becoming buyer to one and seller to the other. In contrast, contemporary CDS agreements usually are negotiated and entered into bilaterally, though both parties may agree that one party may novate the agreement and substitute another party to take responsibility for performance, by acting as the counterparty under the agreement.

4. *Other Regulatory Action: The Securities and Exchange Commission.* The SEC has taken multiple actions to protect investors and ensure the integrity of U.S. securities markets in response to the turmoil in the financial

---

available at http://www.sec.gov/litigation/complaints/2009/comp21023.pdf. The SEC alleges that the employee tipped the manager about a change to a proposed VNU bond offering being underwritten by DBS that would increase the value of CDS on VNU bonds. The manager purchased CDS on VNU for a Millennium hedge fund and closed the position after news of the restructured offering became public, realizing $1.2 million profit.

39. *See The Role of Credit Derivatives in the U.S. Economy Before the House Agriculture Comm.,* 110th Cong. (2008) (Statement of Erik Sirri, Director, SEC Division of Trading and Markets) (discussing seriousness of risks in CDS market).

40. *See* Policy Objectives, *supra* (identifying implementation of CCP for CDS as top priority). *See also* President's Working Group on Financial Markets, Policy Statement on Financial Market Developments (Mar. 13, 2008), *available at* http://www.treas.gov/press/releases/reports/pwgpolicystatemktturmoil—03122008.pdf; President's Working Group on Financial Markets, Progress Update on March Policy Statement on Financial Market Developments (October 2008), *available at* http://www.treas.gov/press/releases/reports/q4progressüpdate.pdf.1.

41. Memorandum of Understanding Between the Board of Governors of the Federal Reserve System, the U.S. Commodity Futures Trading Commission and the U.S. Securities and Exchange Commission Regarding Central Counterparties for Credit Default Swaps (Nov. 14, 2008), *available at* http://www.treas.gov/press/releases/reports/finalmou.pdf (hereinafter MOU).

42. "Novation" is a "process through which the original obligation between a buyer and seller is discharged through the substitution of the CCP as seller to buyer and buyer to seller, creating two new contracts." Committee on Payment and Settlement Systems, Technical Committee of the International Organization of Securities Commissioners, Recommendations for Central Counterparties 66 (Nov. 2004).

markets.[43] Most recently, the SEC adopted interim final temporary rules providing exemptions under the Securities Act of 1933, the Securities Exchange Act of 1934, and the Trust Indenture Act of 1939 for certain CDS, to facilitate the operation of one or more CCPs for these instruments.[44] The rules define such credit default swaps as "eligible credit default swaps"[45] and exempt them from all provisions of the Securities Act[46] – other than the anti-fraud provisions of §17(a) – as well as from Exchange Act registration requirements[47] and the provisions of the Trust Indenture Act,[48] provided certain conditions are met. In March 2009, the SEC published an order granting temporary exemptions to ICE U.S. Trust LLC, relating to central clearing of CDS.[49] Initially, ICE Trust's business will be limited to the provision of

---

43. For a selective list of major SEC actions taken in an effort to stabilize financial markets during the credit crisis, see Securities & Exchange Commission, *Temporary Exemptions for Eligible Credit Default Swaps to Facilitate Operation of Central Counterparties to Clear and Settle Credit Default Swaps*, 74 Fed. Reg. 3967, 3968 n.4 (2009).

44. 74 Fed. Reg. 3967 (2009) (codified at 17 C.F.R. pts. 230, 240, 260). For recent specific orders of exemption in this regard, see *Order Pursuant to Section 36 of the Securities Exchange Act of 1934 Granting Temporary Exemptions from Sections 5 and 6 of the Exchange Act for Broker-Dealers and Exchanges Effecting Transactions in Credit Default Swaps*, Release No. 34-59165 (Dec. 24, 2008) 74 Fed. Reg. 133 (Jan. 2, 2009); *Order Granting Temporary Exemptions Under the Securities Exchange Act of 1934 in Connection with Request of Liffe Administration and Management and LCH.Clearnet Ltd. Related to Central Clearing of Credit Default Swaps*, Release No. 34-59164 (Dec. 24, 2008), 74 Fed. Reg. 139 (Jan. 2, 2009).

45. However, for those CDS that are "swap agreements" as defined in GLBA §206A, 15 U.S.C. §§77b(b)-1, 78c-1, SEC authority is limited, since those swap agreements are excluded from the definition of "security," and the interim final temporary rules do not apply to them. GLBA §206A defines a "swap agreement" as "any agreement, contract, or transaction between eligible contract participants (as defined in section 1a(12) of the Commodity Exchange Act...) ... the material terms of which (other than price and quantity) are subject to individual negotiation...." 15 U.S.C. §78c note.

46. 17 C.F.R. §§230.146(c)T, 230.239T (providing temporary exemption for eligible credit default swaps).

47. *Id.* §§ 240.12a-10T, 240.12h-1(h)T (providing temporary exemption of eligible credit default swaps from Exchange Act registration requirements).

48. *Id.* § 260.4d-11T (providing temporary exemption for eligible credit default swaps offered and sold in reliance on Rule 239T).

49. 74 Fed. Reg. 10,791 (Mar. 12, 2009). *See also* 74 Fed. Reg. 10,647 (2009) (publishing order granting temporary exemptions from certain provisions of the Government Securities Act and Treasury's Government Securities Act Regulations in connection with request on behalf of ICE US Trust LLC related to central clearing of CDS). In contrast, well into Q1 2009, the derivatives and swaps market in Europe had still made no progress toward the establishment of a clearinghouse to mitigate counterparty risk as well as to interject transparency into CDS transactions. Stephen Joyce, *Citing Industry Inaction, McCreevy Asks EU Parliament to Support CDS Regulation,* BNA INT'L BUS. & FIN. DAILY (Feb. 4, 2009), *available at* http://www.bna. com/corp/index.html. In early February 2009, EU Internal Market and Services Commissioner Charlie McCreevy called for regulation of credit default swaps, in light

clearing services for the OTC CDS market.[50] ICE Trust will act as a central counterparty for ICE Trust participants by assuming through novation the obligations of all eligible CDS transactions accepted by it for clearing and collecting margin and other credit support from ICE Trust participants to collateralize their obligations to ICE Trust. ICE Trust's trade submission process is designed to ensure that it maintains a matched book of offsetting CDS contracts.[51] A similar order was issued a week later to Chicago Mercantile Exchange Inc. and Citadel Investment Group, L.L.C.[52]

5. *Other Regulatory Action: The Federal Trade Commission.* Section 626 of the 2009 Omnibus Appropriations Act,[53] signed by the President on March 11, 2009, introduced a new regulatory approach to the crisis. The provision directed the FTC to initiate, within 90 days of the date of enactment, a rulemaking proceeding with respect to mortgage loans. Accordingly, in June 2009, the FTC commenced a two-part rulemaking. The Mortgage Acts and Practices Rulemaking (MAP)[54] targets activities that occur throughout the life cycle of a mortgage loan (i.e., practices with regard to mortgage loan advertising and marketing, origination, appraisals, and servicing). A separate rulemaking proceeding, the Mortgage Assistance Relief Services Rulemaking (MARS),[55] focuses on the practices of entities (other than mortgage servicers) that offer assistance to consumers in dealing with owners or servicers of their loans to modify them or avoid foreclosure. The FTC is seeking comment with regard to unfair and deceptive acts and practices that should be prohibited or restricted pursuant to any rules adopted in either of these proceedings. Rules adopted in these proceedings would apply to entities other than banks, thrifts, federal credit unions, and non-profits that are engaged in such acts and practices.[56] Although section 626 does not specify the types of conduct or entities the proposed rules should address, the FTC has used its organic statute, the FTC Act, to establish the parameters for the rulemakings.[57] Thus, the types of conduct that the FTC proposes to cover would include acts and practices

---

of the private sector's failure to act. *Id.*

50. 74 Fed. Reg. at 10,793.

51. For a fuller explanation of the operation of the clearing services and the conditions imposed by the SEC, see 74 Fed. Reg. at 10,796-10,799.

52. 74 Fed. Reg. 11,781 (Mar. 19, 2009).

53. Omnibus Appropriations Act of 2009, Pub. L. No. 111-8, § 626, 123 Stat. 524 (Mar. 11, 2009).

54. 74 Fed. Reg. 26,118 (2009) (to be codified at 16 C.F.R. pts. 321–322).

55. 74 Fed. Reg. 26,130 (2009) (to be codified at 16 C.F.R. pts. 321–322).

56. 74 Fed. Reg. at 26,118.

57. This approach is consistent with the available legislative history. *See* 155 Cong. Rec. S2816-S2817 (2009).

that meet FTC standards for unfairness or deception under FTC Act § 5,[58] and the entities that the FTC intends to cover are those over which the FTC has jurisdiction under the FTC Act, specifically, entities other than banks, thrifts, federal credit unions,[59] and non-profits.[60] Pursuant to section 626, any violation of a rule adopted under that section will be treated as a violation of a rule promulgated pursuant to section 18 of the FTC Act.[61] Hence, pursuant to section 5(m)(1)(A) of the FTC Act,[62] the FTC may seek civil penalties as a remedy for these violations. In addition, pursuant to section 626(b), a state may bring a civil action in state or federal court to enforce the FTC mortgage loan rules and obtain civil penalties and other relief for violations.[63]

6. *Transnational Reach of the Financial Crisis.* The crisis has had a significant impact far beyond U.S. borders. One reason for this is the fact that some of the troubled entities – like Lehman – themselves had operations in other jurisdictions. When the headquarters fell, it pulled offshore affiliates down along with it. So, for example, in Japan the Financial Services Agency issued an administrative order to Lehman Brothers Japan Inc. late on September 15, 2008 (and posted on its official website early on September 16) effectively freezing Lehman-Japan's assets.[64] The FSA explained that "[i]t is necessary to make assurance doubly sure concerning the finances of [Lehman-Japan] to not damage the position of creditors and investors through the outflow of money from Lehman-Japan's] assets to overseas affiliated companies triggered by the [bankruptcy] announcement of Lehman Brothers Holdings Inc." At the time of the bankruptcy filing, Lehman-Japan was the largest underwriter of Japanese government securities and ranked fourth among certified government securities underwriters. The FSA ordered Lehman-Japan to retain assets within the jurisdiction, except those related to overseas liabilities, to contact investors and examine assets deposited from investors, to take measures for the maintenance of deposited assets for investors and not to use them for purposes other than as agreed with investors, to protect fully investors and to treat them fairly, and keep investors informed about retention of deposited assets.

7. *After the Fall – One Year Out (Part Two).* Another reason why the

---

58. 15 U.S.C. §45(a)(1).

59. *Id.* § 45(a)(2).

60. *Id.* § 44.

61. *Id.* § 57a.

62. *Id.* § 45(m)(1)(A).

63. Before initiating an enforcement action, the state must notify the FTC, at least 60 days in advance, and the Commission may intervene in the action. 74 Fed. Reg. at 26,119.

64. *See* Toshio Aritake, *Japan Orders Lehman Japan to Keep Assets in Country, Respect Investors*, BNA BANKING DAILY (Sept. 16, 2009), *available at* http://pubs.bna.com (reporting on FSA order).

financial crisis has been international in its dimensions is that *securitization* of mortgage obligations spread the risks of the subprime mortgage market into the portfolios of institutional investors – many of them banks and securities firm themselves. When the subprime mortgage market collapsed, it destroyed portfolio values and threatened the financial viability of national economies and markets around the world. Hence, no assessment of the situation would be complete without consideration of the transnational responses to the crisis. What steps have other jurisdictions taken to address the crisis? How effective are these steps likely top be in resolving the current crisis? Consider the following excerpt in answering these questions.

3 MICHAEL P. MALLOY, BANKING LAW AND REGULATION

§ 12.5.1 (Aspen 2004 & Cum. Supps.)

The subprime mortgage crisis that has been ravaging the United States since 2008 has also had devastating effects internationally. By late October 2008, the Bank of England sounded the alarm in its semi-annual Financial Stability Report, estimating that total losses to banks, insurance companies, and pension funds in Europe and the United States as a result of the financial crisis could reach $2.8 trillion.[2] The Bank acknowledged "the need for a fundamental rethink internationally of appropriate safeguards against systemic risk, including through the development of macroprudential policies to dampen the financial cycle."[3] Increasing capital and liquidity requirements for individual institutions was not a sufficient response to a systemic problem, and the Bank has argued for "a fundamental overhaul of the regulatory safeguards used to mitigate systemic risk within the financial system."[4] Enhanced safeguards were needed to address "problems within the banking system [that] were deep seated, rooted in structural weaknesses in banks' balance sheets that had developed during the boom years."[5] These weaknesses included:

---

2. *See* Bank of England Financial Stability Report 11 (Oct. 2008), *available* http://www. bankofengland.co.uk/publications/fsr/2008/fsrfull0810.pdf. *See also* Ali Qassim, New Counter-cyclical Tools Needed Against Systemic Risk, Bank of England Says, BNA INT'L BUS. & FIN. DAILY (Oct. 29, 2008), *available at* http://news.bna.com (discussing Bank of England report).

3. Financial Stability Report at 4. Fed Chairman Bernanke has also endorsed, if in somewhat vaguer terms, "macroprudential oversight" to maintain lending practices across the financial services system, as opposed to prudential supervision of specific troubled institutions. For the text of Chairman Bernanke's speech, see http://www.federalreserve.gov/newsevents/speech/bernanke20080822a.htm.

4. Financial Stability Report at 51.

5. *Id.* at 8.

- Inflated aggregate balance sheets, whose expansion had in many cases far outpaced growth in the real economy.
- Expansion into certain assets whose underlying value, credit quality and liquidity were uncertain whether lending to higher-risk households and corporates or the holding of complex securities.
- Liability structures which were overly reliant on the sustained availability of wholesale funding and whose maturity was often short.
- Capital levels which, given these asset and liability structures, became in some cases low relative to underlying balance sheet risks.
- Underappreciated, but potent, interconnections between firms in the global financial system.[6]

In October 2008, EU finance ministers agreed to raise the minimum standard for bank account guarantees to €50,000 (about $67,500).[7] In addition, in an effort to create a more coordinated response to the financial crisis among EU member states, in October 2008 EU finance ministers adopted a range of principles dealing with liquidity, accounting, and recapitalization issues. These principles include: (i) a commitment that regulatory intervention should be timely and support temporary; (ii) an intervening government should be watchful of taxpayers interests, and existing shareholders should bear the due consequences of the intervention; (iii) an intervening government should be empowered to bring about a change of management; (iv) management should not retain undue benefits and governments should have the power to intervene when it comes to remuneration; (v) the legitimate interest of competitors should be protected, especially with regard to state aid rules; and, (vi) negative indirect or "spill-over" effects with respect to other EU member states should be avoided. There is a peculiar oscillation in the responses emanating from the EU. At the EU level, there is a determined push towards increased global supervision in financial services markets, while at the member-state level, the individual member states are repudiating legislative proposals to establish enhanced regional supervision in the insurance[9] and banking sectors.[10] The

---

6. *Id.*

7. Joe Kirwin, *EU Ministers Raise Bank Guarantee Threshold, Adopt Guide to Crisis Response*, BNA INT'L BUS. & FIN. DAILY (Oct. 8, 2008), *available at* http://pubs.bna.com/ip/bna/ibd.nsf/eh/A0B7E7J6H0. Current EU law requires member states to guarantee bank accounts to a maximum of €20,000 ($27,000). *Id.*

9. Joe Kirwin, *EU Finance Ministers Reject Enhanced Supervision in Insurance, Banking Sectors* BNA INT'L BUS. & FIN. DAILY (Dec. 3, 2008) (reporting that EU member state agreement to new insurance regulatory regime conditioned on omission of EU-wide insurance supervision), *available at* http://news. bna.com.

10. Joe Kirwin, *Despite G-20 Stance, EU Members Resist EU-Wide Supervision of Insurance, Banking*, BNA Banking Daily (Nov. 24, 2008), *available at* http://news.bna.com. *But see* Joe Kirwin, *EU, U.S. Should Work to Forge Joint Economic Recovery Package, Barroso Says*, BNA Int'l Bus. & Fin. Daily (Dec. 10, 2008), *available at* http://news.bna.com (reporting that

result was a "shared approach" in which the 27 EU member states agreed in mid-December 2008 to a $256 billion economic stimulus response that set parameters for individual member states to increase domestic spending and reduce taxes, with EU-wide measures covering the automotive industry, broadband Internet penetration, and road and rail infrastructure.[11]

By the end of October 2008, the European Commission had already approved bank rescue plans to stabilize financial markets in Denmark, France, Germany, Ireland, the Netherlands, Portugal, Sweden, and the United Kingdom.[12] By mid-November, approval was extended to Finland and Italy.[13]

France and United Kingdom had embraced commission plan for EU-wide stimulus package, with Germany still dissenting).

11. Joe Kirwin, *EU Leaders Back $256 Billion Package of Economic Stimulus*, BNA Int'l Bus. & Fin. Daily (Dec. 15, 2008), available at http://news.bna.com.

12. *Sweden, Portugal Latest Nations to Receive EC Approval of Financial Rescue Plans*, BNA INT'L BUS. & FIN. DAILY (Oct. 31, 2008), *available at* http://news.bna.com; Bengt Ljung, *Rescue Plans for French, Dutch Banks Approved by EC, Spain, Italy Plans Up Next*, BNA BANKING DAILY (Nov. 3, 2008), *available at* http://news.bna.com. In light of relaxed state aid guidelines put forward in early December, the European Commission approved on December 23, 2008, changes submitted by the U.K. government to alter its bank guarantee and recapitalization plan, in order to stimulate more lending by financially sound banks. Joe Kirwin, *European Commission Gives Green Light to Amended British Bank Bailout Program*, BNA INT'L BUS. & FIN. DAILY (Dec. 24, 2008), *available at* http://news.bna.com.

Commission review is necessary because of treaty restrictions on state aid limiting member state ability to grant aid or other incentives or supports under certain specified circumstances. *See* Consolidated Version of the Treaty Establishing the European Community art. 87, Mar. 25, 1997, 2002 O.J. (C 325) 33 ("[A]id granted by a Member State…in any form whatsoever which distorts or threatens to distort competition…shall, in so far as it affects trade between Member States, be incompatible with the common market…."). *See also* art. 88, formerly Article 93 (providing for review of state aids provided by member states to determine compatibility with single market). However, responding to pressure from EU member states, in early December 2008 the European Commission agreed to issue more flexible, expeditious rules for review of member state bank bailout plans. Joe Kirwin, *European Commission Bends to EU States, Will Ease Controls on Bank Bailout Proposals*, BNA BANKING DAILY (Dec. 3, 2008), *available at* http://news.bna.com. The new state aid guidelines for banks, published on December 8, 2008, differentiated between "distressed" financial institutions compared to "sound" ones and imposed "safeguards" ensuring that a bank receiving state funds would use the resources to make loans rather than simply improving its capital position or acquiring other financial institutions. Joe Kirwin, *EC Outlines New Guidelines for Aid by States to Banks in Need of Bailout*, BNA INT'L BUS. & FIN. DAILY (Dec. 9, 2008), *available at* http://news.bna.com. This is in striking contrast with the disingenuous approach of the U.S. Treasury Department, which has essentially allowed large firms to dictate their own terms of use, to the detriment of the retail market. . . .

13. Joe Kirwin, *EC Quickly Gives Green Light to Plans to Rescue Italian, Finnish, Dutch Banks*, BNA INT'L BUS. & FIN. DAILY (Nov. 17, 2008), *available at* http://news.bna.com; Joe Kirwin, *Italian Bank Recapitalization Plan Approved by European Commission*, BNA INT'L BUS. & FIN. DAILY (Dec. 29, 2008), *available at* http://news.bna.com.

In late December, approval of a financial aid plan for Spanish commercial banks was also approved.[14] It is expected that most if not all of the 27 EU member states would seek approval of bank rescue plans, although some of these may only be pursued as a precaution.[15]

Three leading Asian economies, Japan,[16] China, and Korea, reached an agreement in October 2008 to monitor financial institutions and to strengthen financial disclosures and risk management.[17] The three states are planning a macro economy and financial stability workshop, which might ultimately lead to the establishment of an "Asian Financial Stability Forum," a regional version of an International Monetary Fund facility. The forum is intended to analyze current economy conditions, regional capital and financial markets and financial services systems, and related concerns.

Despite these efforts, transactional efforts and traditional government intervention have so far remained the typical response to the crisis. For example, in mid-September 2008, the European Central Bank made an extra €30 billion in overnight funds available to Euro Zone banks, in an effort to calm money markets and reassure lenders.[20] However, this total amount was only about one-third of the aggregate amount being requested by banks in the zone. In late October 2008, European Commission proposed to double the EU crisis fund for troubled member states, to €25 billion, to assist them in providing economic recovery supports.[22]

Also in late October 2008, the Bank of Japan announced that it would begin lending unlimited amounts of U.S. dollars for one month to Japanese financial institutions within the value of collateral that they tender to the

---

14. Joe Kirwin, *European Regulator Approves Spain's Plan to Provide Guarantees to Commercial Banks*, BNA INT'L BUS. & FIN. DAILY (Dec. 29, 2008), *available at* http://news.bna.com.

15. *Sweden, Portugal, supra.*

16. According to the Japanese Financial Services Agency, as of second quarter 2008, Japanese depository institutions had experienced losses of ¥895 billion from securities tied to subprime loans, an increase of 5 percent over first quarter 2008. Toshio Aritake, *Japanese Banks' Subprime Securities Losses Rise 5 Percent to $8 Billion in Latest Quarter*, BNA BANKING DAILY (Sept. 8, 2008), *available at* http://news.bna.com.

17. Toshio Aritake, *Japan, China, Korea Reach Agreement for Meeting to Monitor Financial Institutions*, BNA BANKING DAILY (Oct. 23, 2008), *available at* http://news.bna.com (reporting on financial stability agreement).

20. *ECB Pumps 30 Billion Euros in Cash into Banks in Wake of Lehman Failure*, BNA BANKING DAILY (Sept. 16, 2008), *available at* http://news.bna.com.

22. Bengt Ljung, *EC Moves to Double EU Crisis Fund; Almunia Urges Rate Cuts, Stimulus Spending*, BNA INT'L BUS. & FIN. DAILY (Oct. 30, 2008), *available at* http://news.bna.com. *See also* Joe Kirwin, *EC to Announce Major Economic Stimulus Plan to Include Infrastructure, Green Tech*, BNA INT'L BUS. & FIN. DAILY (Nov. 26, 2008), *available at* http://news.bna.com (reporting on EU proposal for major economic stimulus package).

central bank, at a fixed rate of 2.11 percent, in an effort to spur lending.[23] This was followed by the Bank of Japan's injection of significant amounts into the Japanese banking system in an ultimately unsuccessful effort to ameliorate the wave of selling of U.S. dollars.[24] Within the week a second economic stimulus package followed, totaling ¥26.9 trillion yen in tax cuts, spending, regulatory relief, monetary policy measures, and public-private cooperation.[25] Likewise, in November 2008, the Chinese Government initiated a 4 trillion yuan (approximately $587 billion), two-year economic stimulus package to keep the Chinese economy on a positive growth track.[26] Indeed, the World Bank is predicting a 7.5 percent GNP growth for China in 2009, with over half of projected growth linked to government spending.[27]

C. LESSONS

School is not out for the Congress on measures to reform U.S. financial services regulation. More than two years after the meltdown began, the nation is still without any federal protection against the next one – and the new Administration can take half the blame for this situation. Had it made financial services reform its top legislative priority at the outset and provided the Congress with a concrete, vigorous proposal – as the first Bush Administration did in 1989 in the wake of the S&L crisis[28] – we would already have a safe and sound regulatory system in place.[29] With financial services policy in the new Administration coopted mostly by tired old faces – Obama Administration

---

23. *Japanese Central Bank to Lend Unlimited Amount of U.S. Dollars to Banks*, BNA INT'L BUS. & FIN. DAILY (Oct. 22, 2008), *available at* http://news.bna.com.

24. Toshio Aritake, *BOJ Injects Liquidity; ASEAN Plus 3 Agree to Expand Chanmai Initiative*, BNA INT'L BUS. & FIN. DAILY (Oct. 27, 2008), *available at* http://news.bna.com.

25. Toshio Aritake, *Japan's 26.9 Trillion Yen Stimulus Package for Global Crisis Much Larger than Planned*, BNA INT'L BUS. & FIN. DAILY (Oct. 31, 2008), *available at* http://news.bna.com.

26. Kathleen E. McLaughlin, *China Unveils Substantial Stimulus Plan; Will Spend $586 Billion over Two Years*, BNA INT'L BUS. & FIN. DAILY (November 12, 2008), *available at* http://news.bna.com.

27. Kathleen E. McLaughlin, *World Bank Labels China's Stimulus Plan Critical to Sustain Economy's Growth Track*, BNA INT'L BUS. & FIN. DAILY (Nov. 26, 2008), *available at* http://news.bna.com.

28. On the swift enactment of the Financial Institutions Reform, Recovery, and Enforcement Act of 1989 by the Bush I Administration, see 1 MICHAEL P. MALLOY, BANKING LAW AND REGULATION § 1.4.3 (1994 & Cu. Supp.).

29. FIRREA was proposed and submitted to the Congress within the first 100 days of the incoming Administration. It was enacted into law within the first seven months of the new Administration. Pub. L. No. 101-73, 103 Stat. 183 (1989) (codified at scattered sections of 2, 5, 12, 15, 18, 26, 28, 31, 40, 42 & 44 U.S.C.).

Treasury Secretary Timothy Geithner, for example, was the president of the New York Federal Reserve who let the big institutions roll him for financial support, with no commitment from them to offer mortgage renegotiation or foreclosure relief – it should not be surprising that it is still quite conceivable that no significant reform of financial services regulation may occur.

So far, supervisory responses to the meltdown have been merely hanging fire, waiting for a significant statutory initiative with respect to regulatory reform. Most observers stopped holding their breath in expectation of substantial reform long since the Administration announced in mid-June 2009 the broad outline of proposed comprehensive reform legislation.[30] By late June 2009 the Administration announced that it would soon send to Congress legislative language for a proposed Consumer Financial Protection Agency (CFPA),[31] as part of "a broad, still-evolving overhaul of the regulatory system."[32] Unfortunately, this overhaul effort was about six months too late in starting, and as of January 2010 had still not reached fruition.

On June 30, 2009, the Administration released its legislative proposal for the CFPA.[33] As proposed, the CFPA would consolidate all consumer financial protection functions currently spread among the various federal banking agencies and the Federal Trade Commission. CFPA functions would include research, rulemaking, supervision, and examination. The agency would also have enforcement authority with respect to consumer financial products and services, including the authority to assess and collect fees. Unlike the preemptive situation under the *Watters* case, under the Administration proposal state regulators could have a role of some significance, with authority to enact oversight measures that go beyond CFPA powers. The CFPA proposal triggered a broad chorus of criticism and questions about the feasibility and desirability of this approach to consumer protection,[34] and it is still at the center of the sniping that continues to delay any legislative action on financial

---

30. For the text of the Administration proposal for the overhaul of financial system regulation, see http://www.treasury.gov/news/index1.html. *See also* Aaron Lorenzo, *Administration Outlines Regulatory Overhaul in Plan Concentrating Many New Powers at Fed*, BNA Banking Daily, June 18, 2009, available at http://www.bna.com (reporting on proposal).

31. Aaron Lorenzo, *Treasury to Forward Legislative Language for Consumer Financial Protection Agency*, BNA Banking Daily, June 26, 2009, available at http://www.bna.com.

32. *Id.*

33. For the text of the administration draft bill, see http://www.financialstability.gov/docs/CFPA-Act.pdf. *See also* Aaron Lorenzo, *Obama Administration Floats Draft Bill for Financial Consumer Protection Agency*, BNA Banking Daily, July 1, 2009, available at http://www.bna.com (reporting on CFPA proposal).

34. Aaron Lorenzo, *Financial Consumer Protection Draft Plan Proposed by Obama Receives Mixed Reviews*, BNA Banking Daily, July 2, 2009, available at http://www.bna.com.

services regulatory reform.

After months of hard slogging, the House version of the regulatory reform legislation pulled ahead of the Senate version, and by mid-October 2009 parts of it were nearing floor consideration. On October 17, 2009, the House Financial Services Committee approved by voice vote an amendment to the proposed legislation that would explicitly roll back *Watters* and subject national banks and federal savings associations to state financial services and consumer protection law.[35] On October 23, the House Financial Services Committee approved, largely along party lines, H.R. 3126, a bill to consolidate federal financial consumer protection in a new CFPA, an federal agency to regulate mortgages, credit cards, and other financial products and activities.[36] A battle over the details would await the bill as it headed to the floor.[37]

On December 11, 2009, by a vote of 223-202, the House approved the Wall Street Reform and Consumer Protection Act of 2009,[38] legislation to overhaul financial services regulation, with almost all Republicans opposed. The major features of H.R. 4173 re as follows:

- Establishment of the Financial Services Oversight Council, charged with identifying and regulating systemic risk and consisting of the Treasury Secretary as chair, the Comptroller of the Currency, the FDIC, the FHFA, the Securities and Exchange Commission, the Commodity Futures Trading Commission, and two non-voting state-level representatives;

- Creation of the CFPA that would, among other things, prevent predatory mortgage lending, and would not preempt more stringent state consumer protection rules (unless the Comptroller of the Currency intervened under limited circumstances);

- Limits on executive compensation of financial services firms;

- Enhancement of SEC enforcement powers;

---

35. R. Christian Bruce, *House Panel Clears Watt-Moore Amendment Limiting Preemption of State Financial Laws*, BNA Banking Daily, Oct. 18, 2009, available at http://www.bna.com.

36. R. Christian Bruce, *Frank Cheers Passage of CFPA Measure, Vows More Changes Ahead of Floor Action*, BNA Banking Daily, Oct. 23, 2009, available at http://www.bna.com.

37. *Id. See, e.g.*, Jewel Edwards, *Energy and Commerce Passes CFPA Bill; Splits with Financial Services Panel's Version*, BNA Banking Daily, Oct. 30, 2009, available at http://www.bna.com (reporting on competing proposals).

38. H.R. 4173, Cong., 1st Sess. (2009).

- Supervision of derivatives markets, with clearance of derivative risk-management products through an appropriate clearinghouse that would have authority to decide whether to accept any such contract;[39]

- Supervision of the credit rating agencies (CRAs);

- Creation of a private right of action against rating agencies that are "grossly negligent," a lower liability standard than that applicable to other market participants;

- Authority for investors to sue market participants that "knowingly or recklessly" aid and abet securities fraud, repudiating *Central Bank of Denver, N.A. v. First Interstate Bank of Denver, N.A.,*[40] and *Stoneridge Inv. Partners, LLC v. Scientific-Atlanta;*[41]

- Authority, if the SEC acts, for investors to litigate instead of being forced to arbitrate disputes with their brokers, ameliorating the harsh mandatory arbitration rule of *Shearson/American Express, Inc. v. McMahon;*[42]

- Authority for the Government Accounting Office to monitor activities and policymaking at the Fed.

With this development, attention once again turned to the Senate Banking Committee, which seemed to be embroiled in a fundamental dispute over the direction of regulatory reform, mainly along party lines. The regulatory reform proposal put forward by Senator Chris Dodd, the Committee chair, gave a significantly smaller role to the Fed. Under the Senate Banking Committee proposal, the Fed would be relatively more confined to its role as central bank,

---

39. The ownership stake in a clearinghouse of a swap dealer or major swap participant would be limited to 20 percent. The Commodity Futures Trading Commission or the SEC (for security-based swaps) would have authority to initiate a review as to whether a particular contract should be cleared, but this would not require a clearinghouse to accept an instrument for clearance. A joint paper issued by the UK Treasury and the Financial Services Authority – Reforming OTC Derivative Markets, a UK Perspective – criticized these provisions of H.R. 4173 as "potentially damaging impacts on financial markets," and argued that it was "unclear what benefits forcing trade flow through organized trading platforms will deliver." For the text of the joint paper, see http://www.hm-treasury.gov.uk/d/hmt_fsa_otcderivativemarkets.pdf.
40. 511 U.S. 164 (1994).
41. 552 U.S. 148 (2008).
42. 482 U.S. 220 (1987).

with authority over monetary policy and supervision of the payment system. However, there appears to be little support for the Dodd proposal at full strength, and by early February 2010, Senator Dodd announced that committee members were at an impasse on the creation of the CFPA and several other issues concerning financial regulatory reform.[43]

A somewhat watered-down version of the Dodd proposal eventually made it through the Senate Banking Committee, on a strictly party-line vote. There is considerable convergence between the Senate and House versions, but enough difference to raise some serious issues if the Dodd proposal ever makes its way out of the Senate. For example, the House has endorsed the establishment of a CFPA, while the Dodd proposal opts for a consumer protection bureau within the Federal Reserve – the same agency that made too-big-to-fail "too big to touch" (TBTT) throughout much of the build-up to the current crisis. Both the House bill and the Dodd proposal endorse a systemic risk regime to supervise system-wide risk concerns, but the House bill adds to that a consolidated Federal Banking Agency, while the Dodd proposal allows the Federal Reserve to continue to play a significant role as a bank supervisor – at least of the largest TBTT banks – and would revise the governance structure of the Federal Reserve System. Both provide for a Financial Rescue Fund for TBTT financial firms – prefunded at $50 billion in the Dodd proposal, and $150 billion in the House bill.

The Dodd proposal includes restrictions on proprietary trading in hedge funds and private equity funds. In addition, both bills mandate SEC regulation of hedge funds larger than $100 million (in the Dodd proposal) or $150 million (in the House bill). In addition, both would require issuers of securitized financial products to retain five percent of the issue, and material disclosures concerning the underlying securities would be mandated. Both bills would mandate significant derivatives regulation by the SEC and the Commodities Futures Trading Commission.

Both would authorize a private right of action against credit rating agencies (CRAs) for flawed evaluations of financial products, but the Dodd proposal would also mandate supervision of CRAs by the SEC. Both also contain various approaches to regulating executive compensation.

What lessons should we draw from our examination of the anatomy of the current financial crisis? As the Congress enters what may be the final stages

---

43. Mike Ferullo, *State Attorneys General Make Push for Consumer Financial Protection Agency*, BNA Banking Daily, Feb. 10, 2010, available at http://www.bna.com.

in fashioning a response to the meltdown, here are some basic concepts that it should keep in sharp focus.

---

① **Broad structural reform of U.S. financial services regulation is essential.**

The inordinately complicated structure of U.S. financial services regulation made supervision of safe and sound practices harder to accomplish, and eventually allowed a "race to the bottom" in terms of consumer protection. A simpler structure makes the regulators more accountable, because they cannot as easily hide amidst a thicket of regulators.

② **This is not just a "subprime mortgage" problem, like the S&L crisis of the 1980s was just an "S&L" problem – it is about unaccountable market participants pursuing the next big thing at any cost.**

Solutions that try to respond to the meltdown by containing or eliminating the defects in the subprime mortgage market achieve nothing more than a false sense of security. That is how we got from the S&L crisis, to the dot.com crisis, to this one.

---

③ **These first two principles suggest that complicated "enhancements" to the regulatory structure are not only "fighting the last battle," they are actively interfering with any effort at improving safety and soundness in the markets.**

A new Financial Services Oversight Council – one more supervisor on top of the five or so we already have – is a waste of effort and counterproductive, if your desired outcome is a safer, sounder, more productive financial services market. Likewise, a new CFPA – just another duplicative federal supervisor waiting to be co-opted by the industries it regulates. Ditto, the proposal for the Government Accounting Office to monitor the Federal Reserve – instead, just put financial services supervision in the hands of a responsible and responsive agency and take the Fed out of it.

④ **If financial services supervision is to proceed effectively and efficiently, structural form should follow function.**

The complexity and redundancies of the current regulatory structure exacerbated the market vulnerabilities that precipitated the meltdown.[44] The concept of "functional regulation" has been in play for over twenty years,[45] and in the wake of the current crisis, the establishment of a consolidated Federal Banking Agency would promote efficiency and effectiveness – *if* this new agency were fully charged with the task of supervising *all* depository institutions, with the Federal Reserve returned and confined to central bank functions for the maintenance of fiscal and credit policy.

---

44. *See, e.g.*, OECD, ECONOMIC SURVEY OF THE UNITED STATES (2008) (identifying fragmented structure of regulation responsible in part for financial crisis).

45. *See* 1 MICHAEL P. MALLOY, BANKING LAW AND REGULATION § 1.4.1 (1994 & Cum. Supps.) (Discussing 1984 Task Group recommendations for regulation by function).

⑤ **Consumer protection works best at the micro- or local level, and progressively worse as you get further removed from the action – broad, systemic approaches to consumer protection are to that extent ineffective.**

Engaging in a battle over whether there is a CFPA, and whether it should be an independent agency or an adjunct of some bigger supervisory agency, is not an efficient use of legislative fire power. But it is a neat distraction from the real issues, and so both sides will bang the drum on this one.

⑥ **Nothing is as effective at protecting consumers from fraud as unleashing state and local consumer protection agencies on the perpetrators – whether they are banks, or brokers, or other back alley thugs.**

Why else would the OTS and the OCC have fought so hard, for so long, to preempt the stuffing out of state consumer protection legislation? The preemption initiative meant good business for the agencies' beneficiaries – the national banks, federal savings associations, and their affiliates. Legislatively reversing *Watters* would be the optimal use of legislative fire power.

⑦ **The Securities and Exchange Commission needs to be given the resources and the staffing to pursue fraud cases – blatant ones, subtle ones, quotidian ones, marquee ones – because, ultimately, that is what the "protection of investors" is all about.**

When it comes to ensuring the integrity of markets and protection of investors, one case against an arrogant TBTT player[46] is worth more than all the "enhanced enforcement authority," and new authority against CRAs and brokers.

⑧ **Legislatively reversing the Supreme Court's rejection of aiding-and-abetting theories of liability for securities fraud would decisively discourage CRAs, brokers, and appraisers from playing dodgy games with institutional and retail securities markets.**

Cases like *Central Bank of Denver* and *Stoneridge Inv. Partners* have created ideal conditions for intermediaries and minor gatekeepers to advance and exacerbate fraud perpetrated by the primary participants in issuing and marketing unusual securities. Legislatively reversing such cases would create conditions for a safer, more responsible market.

---

46. *See, e.g.*, Louise Story & Gretchen Morgenson, *S.E.C. Accuses Goldman of Fraud in Housing Deal*, N.Y. TIMES, Apr. 17, 2010, at A1, *available at* 2010 WLNR 7964392 (reporting on SEC enforcement action alleging investment bank's marketing of mortgage-backed securities that it apparently intended to bet against in its trading).

⑨ **Creating authority to supervise the derivatives markets is an admirable goal and would materially contribute to the safety and stability of the markets – but it's not worth vetoing any credible piece of regulatory reform legislation.**

There seems no doubt at this stage that derivatives trading strategies – particularly instruments like CDS – exacerbated the size and scope of the market meltdown. Should the president veto a bill that doesn't include authority to supervise derivatives?[47] There is too much else to gain – like, perhaps, getting clear legislative language confirming that derivatives are securities subject to U.S. securities fraud prohibitions.

⑩ **Limits on executive compensation are a laughable distraction from the real issues concerning fraud and manipulation in the financial services markets.**

That people can be grossly overreaching and insatiable – and that investors are saps enough to tolerate such behavior in the executive suite – are facts not worth wrangling over, at least not without *first* securing ample resources to fight fraud and manipulation in the markets. Discouraging predatory and conflicted behaviors on the part of executive management is better addressed by attacking fraud and manipulation, rather than "tsk-tsking" over levels of compensation.

Would attention to these ten concepts have allowed us to avoid the financial meltdown, or to prevent the next crisis? Probably not decisively – but the next big meltdown certainly cannot be avoided without them.

---

47. *See, e.g.*, Edward Wyatt, *Veto Threat Raised over Derivatives* , N.Y. TIMES, Apr. 17, 2010, at B1, *available at* 2010 WLNR 7964505 (reporting threat from White House).

SELECTED BIBLIOGRAPHY

Once you have read this book, you may want to continue your reading with the following articles, a very selective assortment of the scholarly literature on the meltdown.

Ramyn Atri, Comment, *Cuomo v. Clearing House Association: The Latest Chapter in the OCC's Pursuit of Chevron Deference*, 14 N.C. BANKING INST. 467 (2010).

Daniel J. Boyle, *Greenspan's Lament: Incentive Mechanisms and the Contamination of the Safety and Soundness of Depository Institutions from Risky Derivative Securities*, 10 TRANSACTIONS: TENN. J. BUS. L. 199 (2009).

Lawrence A. Cunningham & David Zaring, *The Three or Four Approaches to Financial Regulation: A Cautionary Analysis Against Exuberance in Crisis Response*, 78 GEO. WASH. L. REV. 39 (2009).

Keith Fisher, *Toward a Basal Tenth Amendment: A Riposte to National Bank Preemption of State Consumer Protection Laws*, 29 HARV. J.L. & PUB. POL'Y 981 (2006).

José Gabilondo, *So Now Who Is Special?: Business Model Shifts Among Firms That Borrow to Lend*, 4 J. BUS. & TECH. L. 261 (2009).

Anna Gelpern, *Financial Crisis Containment*, 41 CONN. L. REV. 1051 (2009).

Paul L. Lee, *Risk Management and the Role of the Board of Directors: Regulatory Expectations and Shareholder Actions*, 125 BANKING L.J. 679 (2008).

Adam J. Levitin, *The Crisis Without a Face: Emerging Narratives of the Financial Crisis*, 63 U. MIAMI L. REV. 999 (2009).

Michael P. Malloy, *The Subprime Mortgage Crisis and Bank Regulation*, 3 BANKING & FIN. SERV. POL'Y REP. 1 (2008).

Christopher Mayer, Edward Morrison & Tomasz Piskorski, *A New Proposal for Loan Modifications*, 26 YALE J. ON REG. 417 (2009).

Daniel J. Morrissey, *The Road Not Taken: Rethinking Securities Regulation and the Case for Federal Merit*, 44 U. RICH. L. REV. 647 (2010).

Saule Omarova, *The Quiet Metamorphosis: How Derivatives Changed the "Business of Banking"*, 63 U. MIAMI L. REV. 1041 (2009).

Saule Omarova & Adam Feibelman, *Risks, Rules, and Institutions: A Process for Reforming Financial Regulation*, 39 U. MEM. L. REV. 881 (2009).

John L. Ropiequet, *Cuomo v. Clearing House Association, L.L.C.: The Supreme Court Redefines the Federal-State Regulatory Balance for National Banks*, 28 BANKING & FIN. SERVICES POL'Y REP. 14 (2009).

Arthur Wilmarth, *The OCC's Preemption Rules Exceed the Agency's Authority and Present a Serious Threat to the Dual Banking System and Consumer Protection*, 23 ANN. REV. BANKING & FIN. L. 225 (2004).

Wook Bai Kim, *Challenging the Roots of the Subprime Mortgage Crisis: The OCC's Operating Subsidiaries Regulations and Watters v. Wachovia Bank*, 21 LOY. CONSUMER L. REV. 278 (2009).

Timothy R. Zinnecker, *When a Hundred Grand Just Isn't Enough: Fifty Hypotheticals that Explore the Contours of FDIC Deposit Insurance Coverage*, 72 TENN. L. REV. 1005 (2005).

TABLE OF CASES

Italics indicate principal cases.

INDEX